**W9-CDS-886**

Turning
Operations

Turning
Operations
Feminism, Arendt, and Politics

Mary G. Dietz

Routledge
New York & London

Published in 2002 by
Routledge
29 West 35th Street
New York, NY 10001

Published in Great Britain by
Routledge
11 New Fetter Lane
London EC4P 4EE

Routledge is an imprint of the Taylor & Francis Group.

10 9 8 7 6 5 4 3 2 1

Library of Congress Cataloging-in-Publication Data

Dietz, Mary G.
    Turning Operations : feminism, Arendt, politics / Mary G. Dietz
        p. cm.
    Includes bibliographical references.
    ISBN 0-415-93244-0 — ISBN 0-415-93245-9 (pbk.)
    1. Arendt, Hannah—Contributions in political science. 2. Political science—Philosphy. 3. Feminist theory. 4. Democracy. I. Title.

JC251 .A74 D53 20002
320.5—dc21
                                                                    2001058884

Contents

for Jim

"Decide if you want to share the work, the deed."

—Sophocles, *Antigone*

Acknowledgments

In this book I undertake a variety of "turning operations" upon certain elements of feminist theory, upon Hannah Arendt's concept of political action, and upon politics itself, especially as it has been understood in some recent works of contemporary political thought. Like many works in political theory, this book makes extensive use of primary texts, secondary sources, and quoted material from a wide array of scholarly literatures. In other words, this book is intended as an academic work although I hope it can be read both within and beyond the domain of political theory. In many respects, however, this is also very personal book, almost an intellectual autobiography, because it reveals my own development as a political theorist over approximately the last fifteen years. Within these pages, the political thinkers and texts that have most engaged my attention in separate projects now turn around each other and come into light together. In so doing, they have at times surprised and puzzled me; at times they have exerted a kind of necessity that was well beyond my immediate control and, at still other times, these thinkers and texts have provided me with a strange sort of reassurance: all will be well.

In his famous letter to his friend Francesco Vettori, Machiavelli acknowledges the relief he finds within "the ancient courts of men of old," where he is "welcomed kindly," and "fed on that fare" which he takes to be his alone. Reading, thinking, and conversing among these companions, Machiavelli allows that, "for two hours I forget all my cares, I know no more trouble, death loses its terrors: I am utterly translated in their company" (1950, xxix). Did Machiavelli realize that someday, he too, would provide a "court" of companionship, as he has done for me? The companions whose courts I seek here are ancient thinkers, but also modern and contemporary political theorists; they span the centuries of Western political thought, from Thucydides, Aristotle, and Machiavelli to Nietzsche, Weber, Weil, and Arendt. I turn to and around these thinkers and I am forever indebted to them, as this book will reveal. I thank them for feeding me on that fare which is spectacularly their own. In return I can only hope that I have done them a little justice.

I am also truly fortunate to have many other, living and breathing, companions in whose company I have been utterly "translated" and with whom I inhabit a world of conversation, argument, serious play and deep learning. Over the years, these uniquely distinct human beings have woven with me a rich and complex tapestry of friendship that is my most valuable treasure. Many of them have read and commented upon some (or all of these essays); others have offered the gift of inspired interlocution; and many have provided insights into political theory and written great books that I wish had been my own. First and foremost, I give thanks to and for my friend Joan Tronto, who transcends all categories and remains my model of all things decent, honest, and noble in life. Without her, my own life would be a lot less worth living.

I am grateful also to my friends and colleagues in the domain of political theory, for helping me to forget all my cares, in ways large and small, through their various intellectual offerings: Terence Ball, master carpenter, will always be my very best "theory bud," and Edwin Fogelman remains my most magnificent friend. The intellectual and personal debts that I owe to my teachers, Penny Gill and Stephen Ellenburg and especially Hanna Pitkin, and to my friends Michael MacDonald and Jennifer Ring are truly incalculable. I also thank Don Herzog, Harry Boyte, Norman Jacobson, Peter Euben, John Dunn, George Kateb, Sheldon Wolin, Stephen White, Michael Rogin, Booth Fowler, Patrick Riley, Chantal Mouffe, Tracy Strong, Tom Dumm, Ian Shapiro, Don Moon, Steve Leonard, Kathy Ferguson, Russ Hanson, Rich Dagger, Terrell Carver, John Dryzek, John F. Burke, Doug Long, Joan Landes, Joan Cocks, Sonia Kruks, Jeff Isaac, Annmarie Levins, Kirstie McClure, Wendy Brown, the philosophers Lawrence Blum and Naomi Scheman, and, most recently, Lucy Knight, Glyn Morgan, Bill Scheuerman and Jeff Lomonaco. Amy Gutmann and William Connolly gave me my start in the journal *Political Theory*; it is time I thanked them for that. My Berkeley compatriots of various generations have been welcome sources of solidarity; for that I thank Linda Zerilli, George Shulman, Dan Hallin, Pat Boling, John Seery, Jackie Stevens, and Dean Mathiowetz. I must also thank the following colleagues who, by inviting me to speak or write on various occasions, encouraged me to chart new territory and take leaps in the dark: Carole Pateman and Molly Shanley;

Edward Portis, Bonnie Honig, Dana Villa, Marion Smiley, Bernie Yack, Arlene Saxonhouse, Jim Gibson, Steven Rosenstone, and Seyla Benhabib. Thanks also, in the domain of political science, to my friends Steven Van Evera, Robert Arseneau, Don Baumer, Bruce Berkowitz, and my colleagues at University of Minnesota, especially Martin Sampson, August Nimtz, and John Freeman, among others. There's not an opponent of theory or theorists among this group; but they have, I am sure, sometimes had their doubts about my plans and purposes.

For providing me with respite *from* political theory (if not politics) and also, in a variety of wonderful ways, care, cuisine, and shelter from the storm, I thank my dear friends Judith Ball and Sara Mushlitz, my beloved "prof" Gene Borgida, my "dearest darling" Chad Breckinridge, my painter Sally Brown, my playwrights and producers Kent Stevens and Patty Lynch, my poet Eva Hooker, the beautiful Margarita Estevez-Abe, the brave and cheerful Cece Moore, and my extraordinary friends from Mount Holyoke College, Class of '72: Zan Blendell and Mary Ferol DiFilippo, and also Robert Meyers, Sandy Shinner, Steve MacIntyre, Susan Mayes, Kathy Crittenberger, Bobbie Dughi, and Nancy Carter. I am grateful as well to Ana Oakes, Brian Ahlberg, George Merritt, Anthony Tamburri, David and Autumn Tysk, Elaine and Lary May, Pete and Bebe Magee, Sara Evans, Riv-Ellen Prell, Cheryl Rackner Olsen, Milda Hedblom, Joel and Joyce Weinsheimer, Susan Wolf, Eileen Briddell, Tom and Fran Wolf, Janet Spector, and the late Susan Geiger. I cannot overlook my stalwart high-school comrades, 40 years on, from York, Pennsylvania: Phil (Bird) Briddell, Dave (Gart) Garten, John Root, Steve (Beef) Sherrick, Norm (Boat) Grim, and Larry (Rug) Cartwright. More than once, they made me laugh and early on they rescued me from a deep grief.

One of my great good fortunes as a teacher of political theory in the Department of Political Science at the University of Minnesota has been the gift of exemplary graduate students. For the past fifteen years, their unflagging interest in my scholarly preoccupations and their acute and sympathetic critical sensibilities in seminars have made me a far better teacher and thinker than I otherwise would have been. They are the reason that I finally became convinced (after teaching at Bowdoin College and Smith College) that the rewards of teaching graduate students are equal to the joys of teaching undergraduates. These students, now Ph.D.s, and teachers and scholars themselves, have become special friends. I am constantly grateful for their presence in the world; they always help me, in their various miraculous ways, "to know no more trouble." I thank especially: Simona Goi, Laura Janara, Susan Bickford, Steven Gerencser, Maria Wyant Cuzzo, Catherine Guisan-Dickinson, John Zumbrunnen, Barbara Cruikshank, Paul Soper, Mark Mattern, Andrew Seligsohn, Rob Geroux, Dana Chabot, Larry Biskowski, Andy Davison, and the philosophers Denis Arnold and Ida Baltikauskas. Dan Hope deserves my special thanks, including for his excellent and tireless work as my research assistant some years ago.

My remarkably talented sister, the jazz pianist Katharine Rudolph, has been the constant of my entire life (with the exception of about 11 months at the very beginning). For better or worse, in sickness and in health, Kay and I are tied at the wrists and ankles forever. I thank her, and love her, for helping me through some very difficult years, with combinations of her usual idiosyncratic wisdom, searing intelligence, formidable memory, sharp wit, beautiful music, and seemingly endless repertoire of quotes, ideas, and books.

I would surely be remiss if I did not thank the shrewd and inventive Eric Nelson, political theory editor at Routledge, for his enthusiastic support and early encouragement of this project. I could not have hoped for a more sympathetic editor, or a more reliable source of common sense and good advice. Particular thanks go also to Nicole Ellis, who set a pace of production that left me breathless with admiration, to Joseph Murphy for his attentive copyediting, and to Stefanie Forster for responding to my many questions and requests.

Finally, a word of thanks fortuna, that impetuous goddess who surely smiled upon me in 1983, when I met James Farr in Chicago, Illinois. We had a fierce but friendly argument at the APSA about the merits of Hannah Arendt. I still haven't convinced him. Jim, you are my dearest companion in life, my compensation, my consolation, and my own true joy. To you I owe the deepest debt of gratitude, for your everlasting love, for my happiness in it, and for your word processing and editing capabilities, without which this project could not have come to fruition. Without you (and the dear ones, Willie and Tycho) I am quite sure that my life would not be worth living. I thank you for everything —and for helping me care for this book. It is to you that I dedicate it.

I am grateful to editors and publishers for permission to use material previously published under their auspices:

Chapter 1 is a revised and extended version of "Context Is All: Feminism and Theories of Citizenship," *Daedalus* 116 (1987), 1–24.

Chapter 2 is a revised and extended version of "Citizenship with a Feminist Face: The Problem with Maternal Thinking," *Political Theory* 13 (1985), 19–37.

Chapter 3 first appeared as "Merely Combating the Phrases of This World: Recent Democratic Theory," *Political Theory* 26 (1998), 112–139.

Chapter 4 is a revised version of "Introduction: Debating Simone de Beauvoir," *Signs: Journal of Women in Culture and Society* 18 (1992), 74–88.

Chapter 5 is a revised and extended version of "Hannah Arendt and Feminist Politics," in *Feminist Interpretations and Political Theory*, edited by Mary Lyndon Shanley and Carole Pateman (Polity Press, 1991), 232–252.

Chapter 6 first appeared as "Feminist Receptions of Hannah Arendt," in *Feminist Interpretations of Hannah Arendt*, edited by Bonnie Honig (Pennsylvania State University Press, 1994), 17–50.

Chapter 7 is a revised version of "Working in Half-Truth: Some

Premodern Reflections on Discourse Ethics in Politics," in *Political Theory and Partisan Politics*, edited by Edward Portis, Adolf G. Gundersen, and Ruth Lessl Shively (State University of New York Press, 2000), 117–145.

Chapter 8 first appeared as "The Slow Boring of Hard Boards: Methodical Thinking and the Work of Politics," *American Political Science Review* 88 (1994), 873–886.

Chapter 9 is a revised version of "Arendt and the Holocaust," in *The Cambridge Companion to Hannah Arendt*, edited by Dana Villa (Cambridge University Press, 2000), 81–103.

Introduction

In her essay "Tradition and the Modern Age," Hannah Arendt (1969, 25) introduces the metaphor of "turning operations" to help us visualize how
Kierkegaard, Marx, and Nietzsche brought the tradition of political thought to
an end in the nineteenth century, trying "desperately" to think against it while
using its own conceptual tools. "In complete independence of one another,"
Arendt (1969, 35) writes, these three great figures "arrive at the conclusion
that this enterprise in terms of the tradition can be achieved only through a
mental operation best described in the images and similes of leaps, inversions,
and turning concepts upside down: Kierkegaard speaks of his leap from doubt
into belief; Marx turns Hegel, or rather 'Plato and the whole Platonic tradition'...'right side up again,' leaping 'from the realm of necessity into the realm
of freedom'; and Nietzsche understands his philosophy as 'inverted Platonism'
and 'transformation of all values.'"[1]

For Arendt (1969, 25) this tale of desperation, concealed by the "seemingly
playful, challenging and paradoxical mood" of the great authors of the late
nineteenth century, is the denouement of a grand narrative concerning the
philosophical experience in relation to politics. This narrative began with Plato
and reached its apotheosis with him, too, in the unforgettable parable of the
cave. Arendt (36) calls Plato's masterful invention the "first great turning operation on which all others ultimately are based," it was "the turning-about of

1

the whole human being" that takes the singular and solitary figure, the "lover of truth and light," away from the shadows to the artificial fire, then toward "that light that illuminates the ideas" and then, in the third and final turning, back into the dimness of the cave, where the philosopher endeavors to impose his standards upon human affairs. This beginning with Plato, Arendt (18) writes, "sounds in its endless modulations through the whole history of Western thought" until its modulations end with Marx. Yet, despite their fundamentally different features, the beginning and the end of the tradition have this in common: "that the elementary problems of politics never come as clearly to light in their immediate and simple urgency as when they are first formulated" (in Plato) "and when they receive their final challenge" (in Marx).

These three turnings, each of which Arendt (1969, 36) says is "accomplished by a loss of sense and orientation," thus set in motion within Western political thought yet another turn. What disappears in the philosophical tradition is "the common world of human affairs"; all that remains of it is the opposition of thinking to acting, which, Arendt writes, "depriving thought of reality and action of sense, makes both meaningless" (25). The exertions of Marx, Kierkegaard, and Nietzsche—brilliant, rebellious, outstanding—were ultimately, in Arendt's view, also self-defeating, partly because they remained unavoidably caught up in oppositions that were predetermined "by the conceptual structure" initiated by the incomparable Plato and in which the tradition (until its ultimate breakdown) was forever fated to move. The "three challenges" posed by Marx, Kierkegaard, and Nietzsche were also doomed, however, because they seemed, as Arendt (35) contends, "to be concentrated on the same ever-repeated subject," namely, "the alleged abstractions of philosophy and its concept of man as an *animal rationale.*" Vexed by the Platonic project, the three challenges reconfigured but did not escape the problem of "what the specifically human quality of man is" (39). Ultimately they returned to the philosophical conundrums of "oppositions" (practice against theory; the relative against the absolute; the universal against the particular; faith against intellect; appearance against reality), occluding once again a thinking of the possibilities of action, politics, and the common world of human affairs. In the face of these developments, as Hanna Pitkin (1998, 243) asserts, Arendt "undertook to join Marx, Kierkegaard, Nietzsche, and Heidegger, but in a way that would not end in 'self-defeat' and would serve rather than deny action and politics."[2]

Although Arendtian political theory itself offers us some powerful conceptual and theoretical tools with which to proceed "in search of politics" (Bauman 1999), it seems as though political theory has been regularly distracted by its own version of the "same ever-repeated (philosophical) subject." Today, the intellectual constructions of a considerable amount of political theory seem to constitute, in Max Weber's (1946, 141) telling words, "an unreal realm of artificial abstractions [whose] bony hands seek to grasp the blood-

and-the-sap of true life without ever catching up with it." The activity in this unreal realm is often bolstered by indiscriminate assaults upon various narratives of modernity (especially liberal discourses) that are matched by equally intemperate attacks upon the disparate field of "postmodern theory" (especially Foucaultian discourses). Caught up in this new (but yet another) opposition of modernity against postmodernity, political theory remains distracted by the philosophical question of what the specific human quality of "man" is, although this question now proceeds under the terms "identity," "difference," and "diversity." To put this otherwise, many contemporary political theorists want (for good reasons) to reject any sort of universalized quality attached to the entity known as "man," but they seem unable to resist talking about it from various ontological and epistemological levels that assiduously avoid the political. Abstract (and often pseudo) philosophical concepts thus prevail over historical and political ones. The "same ever-repeated subject" takes form (quite literally) in discourses that proceed by way of "the problem of the subject" or through contestations that situate "the sovereign subject" and the "rights-bearing individual" against "the postmodern subject," "the objectified subject," "the disciplinary subject," or the "situated subject." All such notions, in short, circulate around "subjectification" (Rabinow 1984, 11).[3] To be sure, there are efforts from time to time to call political theorists out of this dazzling realm of "heavenly abstractions" (Pitkin 1998, 248) and back toward the cave, where philosophy's pretenses are put to the test and, as Weber (1946, 141) writes, "genuine reality is pulsating." But these summonses back to existing earthly arrangements tend to collapse under their own compulsory weight or remain ensnared by questions about what political theory "is" rather than actually engaging in the theorizing of politics, action, and the common world of human affairs.

So what does it mean to reassert politics, action, and the common world of human affairs in political theory? This is the main question behind the interlocking chapters in this book, within which Arendt's political thought, especially *The Human Condition*, commands the central but by no means uninterrogated position. It is not within the compass of these chapters (even if I wished it were so) to posit some vast unified theory or a totalizing worldview of politics. Nor do these chapters aim to advance some definite ideological project (or "ism") in the vein of contemporary liberalism, communitarianism, civic republicanism, social pluralism, multiculturalism, and so on, that in turn advocates position taking or formulates a political doctrine or carries recommendations for policy. Thus, I am not out to "build *Weltanschauungen* on this or that premise," as Arendt (1969, 39) puts the point in her discussion of those turning operations of Nietzsche, Marx, and Kierkegaard whom, she notes, were not themselves moved toward this sort of strategy. Rather, the approach throughout these chapters is inclined toward critique, as well as the contingent, the particular, the tactical, the immanent, and the revelatory. My inclination is to turn toward the surprising and revealing aspect of specific texts and theorists. Moreover, in the spirit of Foucault (1984c, 375), I especially want "to question politics" or, more exactly, to question what Ulrich Beck (in Mueller 2000, 220) calls "a politics of politics." In this questioning, I will challenge specific and contemporary modes of theorizing politics (for example, in feminist theory, deliberative democratic theory, Habermasian discourse ethics, public realm theory, and in the text of *The Human Condition* itself) while at the same time appropriating some of political theory's own conceptual tools (especially the concepts of citizenship, work, political action, strategic action, democracy, and political space) and some of its most striking figures (especially Thucydides, Aristotle, Machiavelli, Nietzsche, Weber, Weil, Beauvoir, Habermas, and Arendt) in order to foment some leaps, inversions, reversals, and turns on politics along the way.

If, then, there is any sort of methodological orientation—or perhaps just an *attitude*—behind this enterprise, it takes its inspiration precisely from Arendt's notion of "turning operations."[4] This attitude aims neither to subvert nor recover any sort of tradition, but rather more modestly to bring various concepts and vocabularies to bear on (and turn upon, turn against, turn about) each other in the course of thinking critically about three specific yet related "problemizations." The (rather unwieldy) term "problemization" addresses a way of approaching political questions and comes from Foucault (1984b, 384). Foucault explains it as an "attitude" when he says, "my attitude isn't a result of the form of critique that claims to be a methodical examination in order to reject all possible solutions except for the one valid one. It is more on the order of 'problemization'—which is to say, the development of a domain of acts, practices, and thoughts that seem to me to pose problems for politics. . . . It is a question, then, of thinking about the relations of these different experiences to politics, which doesn't mean that one will seek in politics the main constituent of these experiences or the solution that will definitively settle their fate." I am appropriating this Foucaultian "attitude" by identifying three domains that I wish to pose to politics—feminism, Arendt (especially *The Human Condition*), and politics. This means, in relation to the third problemization, that I will be thinking about politics as a problem to be posed to politics, or at least to the ways in which "the politics of politics" is theorized in some domains of contemporary political thought. As Foucault also observes, however, "the problems that [acts, practices, and thoughts] like these pose to politics have to be elaborated. But it is also necessary to determine 'what posing a problem' to politics really means." With this reminder in mind, I will offer a very brief sketch of how the turning operations will work on and within the problemizations (feminism, Arendt, politics) that structure this text, as well as what the activity of posing problems to politics might mean.

Posing Problems to Politics

Each of the problemizations that structure this text are situated against the background of an immense capitalist world order that has successfully reduced most citizens to a condition where watching things (from the most banal and routinized to the most horrible and catastrophic), on television, in movies, on videotape, within the Internet, is the primary mode of what passes for political engagement. And perhaps this is truest, right now, in the so-called advanced democracies of the West, perhaps more true in the United States of America than anywhere else. In this world of streaming images and facile interconnections the problem for politics is to provide what Pitkin (1998, 280, 281) calls "the existential impetus that might carry us across the conceptual gap between the spectator's outlook and that of the engaged citizen." "A political approach," Pitkin elaborates, "must include not just thinking *about* action but thinking *as* an actor . . . as one free citizen among others, whose joint commitment and effort will be required for accomplishing the right sort of changes." What is important within political theory, then—rudimentary as it may sound—is the theorizing and articulating of concepts and meanings that foster in human beings the capacity for thinking and doing as actors in the world. One of the ironies of the new *imperium* is that as it steadily envelopes vast numbers of people around the globe, forging transnational connections of telecommunication and opening up new dimensions of social, cultural, and cyber space, it diminishes those realms of action that might manifest themselves against ever more formidable, poisonous, and insidious forces of destruction or control. Thus we are rightly warned of "invasions" of the agora (Bauman 1999, 86, 65) that have rendered the public "emptied of its own separate contents [and] left with no agenda of its own" except for "an agglomeration of private troubles, worries and problems." And we are correctly informed that "political spaces are scarcer and thinner today than even in the most immediately prior epochs of Western history" (Brown 1995, 50).

In times like these, we (whoever actually "we" are now) need to theorize, particularize, specify, and work upon a politics of action and free citizenship that can change or challenge, or at least act within the interstices of, an increasingly domineering capitalist world order that relentlessly exacts itself upon everything, under the politically perilous dictum familiar to the arrogance of empire: "the strong do what they can and the weak suffer what they must" (Thucydides 1982, 351). Through this sort of theorizing can we find resources for the invigoration of the work of politics and the action of citizens that so many of us now fear are lost? This, it seems to me, is one place where a solution might present itself, but it probably involves the hardest work of all.

Problemization 1
With this condition in mind, perhaps we can consider what posing a problem of politics to feminism might mean. In a number of ways contemporary femi-

nist theorizing both reflects and perpetuates the situation of the shrinking public space. In recent years, the effective theorizing of political action and democratic politics has been substantially lacking at the academic end of the feminist movement that, in reality, began as a historically constituted, local and global, social and political struggle against the (still existing) two-sex system. As a historical movement, feminism was and remains (at least in some of its provinces) geared toward action and social transformation, the mobilization and organization of participants, and opposition to ruling elites in the name of justice, equality, and freedom. But at the same time it has failed to produce any compellingly articulated emancipatory commitment to politics at the theoretical level, despite (or perhaps because of) its credo "the personal is political," which essentially displaces politics in favor of politicizing the personal, a move that has proved to be as substantial and enlightening as it is problematic and confining.

This problem is particularly evident within so-called difference feminism, which is conceptually rooted in a dichotomy that morally privileges the female sphere of the "private" over the masculine sphere of the "public." Exacting its own turn against the dichotomy of public:private that (it alleges) distinguishes the tradition of Western political thought and inscribes the subordination of women, difference feminism privileges and valorizes politically the heretofore maligned private realm of woman. Thus it attempts to reverse the normative relation that it identifies in patriarchal Western thought, even as it leaves the terms of two of its primary dichotomies—man:woman, and public:private—theoretically intact. The result is a feminism that not only reconfirms a traditional concept of "woman" but also forwards a kind of privatization of the public realm through the exercise of maternal virtues and (metaphorical) mothering. Paradoxically, this simple reversal (a mere turning upside down) that difference feminism exacts upon the tradition of Western political thought renders its positively valued elements (for example, biology, nature, labor, nurturance, mothering, and the maternal) exceptionally agreeable to the purposes of traditional "family values" conservatism with its ingrained hostility toward the aspirations of women and its commitment to the sovereign patriarchal family. Equally significant, since difference feminism confines itself to theorizing politics at the level of normatively loaded and specified "realms" that turn upon an unproblematic reassertion of the concepts of public and private, it confines the task of "thinking *as* an actor" to a dualistic choice between the terms articulated by a fixed gender binary: masculine and feminine, male and female, man and woman. In so doing, difference feminism reduces the actor to "man" or "woman," thereby making it difficult to find within it the vision of an alternative politics that resolutely resists the simple reformulation of the existing gendered status quo.

My own first turn consists of bringing an action concept of politics indebted to Arendt and a concept of citizenship specifically informed by Aristotle up against the rigidified conceptual dichotomies that difference fem-

inism either explicitly articulates or implicitly underwrites. This is an impertinent turn to be sure, since difference feminism (in some of its guises) has been
hostile to both Aristotelian and Arendtian political theories, which it regards
as simply reinforcing the domain of "public man" over "private woman." Of
course there are some legitimate criticisms attached to these hostilities, and
they go well beyond "scoring points over a dead society" (Finley 1983, 86) in
Aristotle's case or accusations concerning "masculinist thinking" in Arendt's. In
both Aristotle and Arendt, the theorization of public and private is indeed
problematic, although not for the reasons divined in difference feminism.
Nevertheless, in turning to these two theorists, I do not wish to fall into the
trap of difference feminism by deploying an action concept of politics and citizenship that simply reconfirms (and thereby just turns around again) the public side of the public:private dichotomy. Rather I want to leap beyond this
confinement and see what happens when a dynamic concept of politics as citizenship is inserted into the staid and stabilized discourses of "public," "private," "man," and "woman" that control so much of feminist political theory.
From this perspective we might consider whether these discourses and their
attendant dichotomies, once scrutinized and challenged, can (or should) be
dismantled or overturned.

Problemization 2

The very concept of a "public realm"—with its "space of appearance" where
citizens gather and engage together as actors—is the freeing formulation of
Hannah Arendt's political thought. Yet it was Aristotle (1962, 98) who decisively reoriented the relationship between the polis as a physically secured and
organized space on the one hand and its citizenry as political actors on the
other, when he wrote, "The identity of a *polis* is not constituted by its walls. It
would be possible to surround the whole of the Peloponnese by a single wall:
[but would that make it a single *polis*?]." Aristotle proceeds to observe that
Babylon had been captured for three whole days "before some of its inhabitants knew of the fact" (98). In Babylon, the concept of the polis was lost, swal-
lowed up by the sheer number of inhabitants. The question that Aristotle asks
of the Peloponnese not only involves the matter of the size or population of
the state but also carries with it a notion of the polis as an association of citizens, acting and speaking together and seeking "a life of true felicity and goodness" (120), no matter where they happen to be.[5] Although Arendt differs from
Aristotle in many respects (not least in the abandonment of "goodness" as the
telos of political association), she follows him in thinking that "the *polis*, properly speaking, is not the city-state in its physical location; it is the organization
of the people as it arises out of acting and speaking together, and its true space
lies between people living together for this purpose" (1958, 198).

The abandonment of a concept of politics that relies upon something
"physically secured" and "physiognomically guaranteed" (Arendt 1958, 198)

does not, however, render the notion of a public realm or "space" inoperative in Arendt's thinking. Arendtian politics may privilege action in concert over the "walls of the *polis*," but whatever its *dynamis*, it still requires (and delivers) a conceptual "space" within which politics can be located, generated, and acted out. It is this concept of a political realm, or a public "space of appearance," that gives Arendt's political thought its distinctive quality. It also offers to late modernity a concept of politics as "spaces for political action as freedom" that have actually mobilized something new, as we have seen in those nations and among those peoples who are still riding the heady waves of the "annum mirabilis" (Weschler 1999, xi), or "the great caesura of 1989" (Mueller 2000, 224).[6]

If Arendt's concepts of politics and political space do not exactly bestride this book like an "intellectual colossus" (a term once applied to Aristotle), they surely form the conceptual posting points around which turn the problems of politics that are under consideration here. Or, to shift the metaphor, Arendt is the theorizing figure and the point of reference that dominates this project. Even more exactly (for this is not a book about Arendt the person, or even about her political writings as a whole), it is *The Human Condition* (1958) that sets the terms of engagement, not only against some elements of feminism but also in relation to theorizing "the politics of politics" more generally. To appreciate how this is so, it is necessary to recognize that as a work of political theory saturated by "the concept," *The Human Condition* persistently rejects one of the features of the Western philosophical tradition that Plato so brilliantly set in motion: the positing of weighted dichotomies. Arendt's text (despite much criticism to the contrary) does not deal in dichotomizing constructs; it offers instead ever-proliferating (but not dialectical) tripartite conceptual schemas (especially, labor:work:action; public:private:social; natality:mortality:plurality) that can, in turn, be exacted upon simplistic oppositions (for example, in the positing of an action concept of politics against the familiar public:private binary of difference feminism). Arendt's concepts are themselves situated within a narrated historicity of being (or *vita activa*) that reveals their own various turning operations upon each other over the course of history and philosophy in the West. The grand narrative that Arendt produces of these operations in *The Human Condition* and situates in relation to the earth and the world centers upon the relations among labor, work, and action; it ends (if only temporarily) with the victory of labor in the modern age. These conceptual turnings capture a long and winding process, full of leaps and reversals that began with the triumph of the Greek city-state, where action reigned existentially supreme, continued with the gradual displacement of action by work (*homo faber*), the hallmark of modernity, and ended (up to now) in the age of automatism, with the displacement of work by labor (*animal laborans*).

Arendtian politics, with its complementary concepts of the public realm and the space of appearance, is a theoretical effort to cut through the triumph of *animal laborans* by glorifying action (and that which is public and political) over labor and work (and that which is private and social). The result is a powerful political reassertion of the generative capacities of people acting and speaking together in the face of giant state entities, impenetrable organizational structures, and the homogenizing formations of mass society and economy. Yet despite its considerable power as a theory of political action, the Arendtian concept of politics must also be problemized and questioned about the positions it takes and the formulations that it poses to politics. In this regard, *The Human Condition* can be a posting point for this project, but not a stopping point. There are at least two problems that immediately come to mind, and they initiate my own turn on Arendt. Both involve the Arendtian public space. One exerts itself at the level of history, the other at the level where, to recall Weber, genuine reality is pulsating.

The first problem calls up Aristotle's question about the determination of a *polis,* but by way of a decisively feminist perspective on Arendt. There is a very real sense in which contemporary feminist theory (including difference feminism), with its heightened state of alert to matters of exclusion and marginalization, domination and oppression, turns up the heat on the Arendtian public realm. Whatever its limitations, feminist identity politics has put forth and pressed the question "who are 'we'?" Those Arendtian "speakers of words and doers of deeds," who populate the space of appearances, can, in the domain of this imaginary, seem peculiarly untouched by the displacements, the segregations, the mortifications, the perversions, and the calamities that were (and are still) required of others so that the Arendtian *drontes* (or "acting people"), wherever they are or whomever they constitute, can disclose themselves in the public realm. If we wish to make any headway in "thinking as actors" and theorizing the terms that are necessary in order to make "the future formulation of a 'we' possible" (Foucault 1984b, 385), then an Arendtian politics will have to become more historically self-reflexive and concrete, especially about the transgressions that have always accompanied the emergence (and the dispersal) of public realms, even when they are at their most admirable and evanescent. To put this point more simply, an Arendtian politics cannot afford to presume that there is always at the ready a preexisting, receptive, and waiting "we," anticipating the call to action. But even more important, the appeal to a public realm or for spaces of political action as freedom has to begin by recognizing that the realm that potentially constitutes this "we" has itself been historically and politically problematic. Thus, the caution to the Arendtian theorist must be that this "we" cannot be a previously fixed designation, because it can be forged only within the activity and tumult that constitutes politics itself.

The second problem to be posed to Arendtian politics concerns the displacement and the shrinkage of the public realm through the effects of a centralized but dispersed *imperium* that now constitutes a part of contemporary worldly reality. In its full significance, of course, the discontinuities of empire and the widening of contexts of power and control that threaten radically to transform political life were discovered by Aristotle, the one great thinker who lived in a period that, in crucial respects, resembles our own. In the face of the organization of Hellenic empires, the transformation, if not disappearance, of the city-state raised huge problems for Aristotelian politics, especially concerning the nature and composition of political life. "What is true of a chorus," Aristotle (1962, 99) writes, "is also true of every other form of association, and of all other compounds generally. If the scheme of composition is different, the compound becomes a different compound. A harmony composed of the same notes will be a different harmony according as the 'mode' is Dorian or Phrygian." The "scheme of composition" that now confronts the contemporary world is often called "globalization," but perhaps it can be better understood in the more pointed political vocabulary of empire(s), sovereignty, order, and organizational control. This new imperial scheme, wherein the *dynamis* of politics has surrendered to the dynamo of advanced consumer capitalism, poses the problem of gigantic forms to the *drontes*. A political theory of the *drontes* must therefore consider the implications that these forms of governance and control carry for conceptions of politics that rely upon the notion of citizen association within an identifiable public realm.

Problemization 3

When Aristotle and Arendt produced their different but equally transforming visions of a polis beyond walls, the concept of politics itself was drastically and importantly reoriented toward the human capabilities of language and, especially, toward speech. "The mere making of sounds belongs to animals in general," Aristotle (1962, 6) states. But "man alone," he continues, "is furnished with the faculty of language . . . [which] serves to declare . . . what is just and unjust." Arendt writes often of the "revelatory quality" of action and speech. In truth, however, it is speech (or speech-acts) that takes precedence in Arendtian politics. For its "full appearance," Arendt (1958, 180, 181) observes, action needs "the shining brightness" of glory. Yet glory relies upon the disclosure of the agent in the act, and that disclosure is accomplished only within the "flux" of speech. The privileging of speech in the theorization of political action from Aristotle to Arendt appears, at first glance, to be the theorist's most effective riposte to the threat of the gigantic and the shrinkage of public space. The famous words "Wherever you go, you will be a *polis*," Arendt (1958, 198) writes, "became not merely the watchword of Greek colonization, they expressed the conviction that action and speech create a space between participants which can find its proper location almost anytime and anywhere." Can one speak, then, of the stifling of public space by the establishment and strengthening of the overarching structures of empire, but still hold out for the persistence of politics through the collective, malleable, and fluid activity of speech? Does it still make sense, in other words, to understand the "politics" of politics in terms of linguistic interaction, communicatively generated power, and democratic political discourse?

I think that the answer to these questions can only and must be "yes"; but it is a qualified and tempered "yes." Whatever its manifold merits, the concept of politics that a model of speech-action carries must still be questioned and problemized, and "politics must answer these questions" (Foucault 1984b, 384). Thus the final turn on politics that I wish to take involves questioning some of the assumptions that underlie contemporary political theories of action that valorize speech (notably Arendt) or communication (notably Habermas) at the expense of other political action concepts, including (and perhaps primarily) the concepts of work and strategic action. Almost invariably, theories that rely upon linguistic interaction for the expression of politics differentiate themselves by way of conceptual exclusions that eschew all forms of instrumental or strategic action. As a result, speech interaction and discursive intersubjectivity (if not consensus) become ends in and of themselves, and politics gets defined in terms of a matrix of speech-acts that constitute their own meaning. I do not want to contest the notion that speech concepts of politics may indeed at a given moment serve as a liberating force (as we have seen in Europe in 1989) and also serve as a warning about action processes that rely exclusively upon the model of "ends and means" and the strategic manipulation of goals and purposes. Nevertheless, I think that we can and must question the adequacy with which these theories address two problems of politics. The first problem (already articulated) is the gigantism of the capitalist world order and the concomitant disappearance of the public realm; the second involves the question "what is to be done?"

The near obliteration of the public realm by increasingly complex gigantic formations is indeed a threat to political theory's efforts to provide the "existential impetus" that will bridge the conceptual gap between the spectator who watches and the citizen who acts. In the face of this reality, any political theory that relies exclusively upon a public realm concept of politics must ask itself whether this spatial formulation is any longer adequate for imagining the field of action within which the "joint commitment and effort" of one free citizen among others is possible (Pitkin 1998, 281). The dangers of continuing to rely upon the concept of the public realm as a site or location for politics (whether a politics of speech or anything else) are not merely matters concerning anachronism, nostalgia, or therapeutics (insofar as visions of such realms attempt to ease apprehension within a world turned upside down and denied the security of constituent communities). The dangers also go to matters of assigning politics to limiting conceptual confines such as the notion of "civic space" or "civil society," or to fictive formulations of political "community" and "consensus." Posed with the dilemma of how to provide an adequate impetus to bridge a gap between realms (that is, the private world of the spectator, the public world of the citizen) that have invaded each other or no longer exist, political theory might begin the task of reconceptualizing politics

in ways that offer possibilities for political action (both continuous and intermittent) without taming it.

At the very least, an untamed concept of politics must turn the powers of
political action against the domination of gigantic forces and "objective relations" (Mueller 2000, 229) that threaten to overwhelm us (whoever "us" is
now). The problems that these forces and relations pose have to be elaborated;
but these dilemmas are ultimately, as Arendt (1958, 5) writes, "matters of practical politics, subject to the agreement of many; they can never lie in theoretical considerations or the opinion of one person." Nevertheless, it is precisely
at this juncture, between the elaboration of "the problem" and the undertaking of "what is to be done," that speech-act theories of politics meet their limitations. For they cannot, as currently constituted, allow for a distribution of
concern that extends equally to strategic as well as communicative mentalities,
and to work as well as to action. To put this more definitively, the only speech-
action concept of politics that stands a chance of providing the "existential
impetus" necessary for thinking *as* an actor in the contemporary world is the
one that admits to its practice the human capacities for purposeful work and
strategic action. Thus political theory must work to establish an elective affinity between modes of speaking on the one hand and modes of doing that
value the notion of continued exertion (that is, work) directed toward a clearly articulated purpose and activated by a strategic mentality.

In physics, "work" is understood as a concept that captures the transfer of
energy from one body to another resulting in the motion or displacement of the
body acted upon. This phenomenon is summarized as the product of the force
and the amount of displacement in the line of its action. This formulation of
work, with its emphasis on the displacement of a body and the exertion of
"force," is, of course, anathema to speech-action concepts of politics, where the
dignity of the individualized human being and the "web of togetherness" (or at
least model of consensus) are at stake in the disclosure of the self among others.
As a metaphor for politics, the concept of work in physics raises within the
domain of speech-action the specter of inhuman forces of terror and totalizing
instruments of "displacement" whose purpose is to annihilate. If we turn this
meaning in another direction, however, we might be able to see there an alternative way of understanding. Instead of viewing work as unavoidably bound up
with the displacement of human bodies or the exertion of "means" in the objectification of human beings, would it make a difference to think of this transfer
of energy (from the Greek *energeia* < *energes*, active < *en*, in + *ergon*, work) as the
shared capacity of human beings to "act upon" and thereby (possibly) displace
(or at least discomfit) dehumanizing structures of domination and control? What
would it mean, then, under the concept of "work" to transform force into action
and to secure within the human capacity for continued exertion (or endurance)
a decisively political effort that is directed toward freedom and exercised against
all forces of annihilation, destruction, dehumanization?

The *Handbook of Engineering Fundamentals* defines work as follows: "[W]ork is a transient form of mechanical energy by means of which certain transformations of other forms of energy are brought about through the agency of a force acting through a distance. . . . Work done by lifting a body stores mechanical potential energy in the system consisting of the body and the earth" (in Fairchild 1998, 41). Again, from the viewpoint of speech-action concepts of politics, these words presage something ominous and foreboding. The "agency of a force acting through a distance" suggests again, as in physics, a dehumanized construct that exerts itself against both the earth and the world and from a field that seems far away, unable to be located or designated in any particular space. I suspect that the *Handbook's* reference to work's "lifting a body" would not fare well once transliterated into the humanistic domain of the public realm of speech-action, where (at least for Arendt and Habermas) the memory of totalitarianism and its horrors lingers still. But what if we stop for a moment and try to turn this metaphor for work around. Can we also recognize within it the possibility of a "lifting up" of bodies that restores to human beings that untapped potential energy manifested in motion? With the help of Arendt, can we think of this energy as the politics of acting in concert and appreciate its transformations as the agentic and active exercise of power in plurality? If this seems at all possible, then we may have found a way to begin the creation of an embodied elective affinity between speaking and working as politics. This is, however, an affinity that requires from speech-action theories of politics a decisive change in perspective, if not a complete turning about. It also requires a tempering, perhaps, of some of the lightness and joy that accompany Arendt's finest reflections upon speaking within the space of appearance. We should also listen to the poetry of work from B. H. Fairchild (1998, 41):

> Outside, the man approaches the iron block,
> a rotary table, judging its weight,
> the jerk and pull on the hoist chain.
> A bad sun heaves the shadow of his house
> outward. He bends down. A day begins.

The reconciliation of working and speaking as politics requires a new beginning with regard to our understanding of political action in the world and on earth.

To be forced to abandon the ideal (even a pragmatic ideal) in favor of the actual—whether that ideal is embodied in a Hellenic conception of the glory of the public realm, or in a reconstructive analysis that offers a regulatory principle for speech interaction, or in carefully articulated norms to guide democratic political discourse—is never an easy or pleasant process. But if our most democratic and praxis-oriented theories cannot deliver an action concept of

politics that appreciates the significance of working (not just speaking) together and the centrality of strategic (not just communicative) purposes, then we
should hardly be surprised to find political freedom undermined (if not
defeated) by the nullity that is the new and globally encompassing world
order. The chapters in this book are all, in various ways, directed toward the
problem of thinking *as* an actor. With this problem in mind, we might consider whether politics can be rendered more possible and citizens made more
powerful in this world.

A Preview

It is now time to turn specific, or at least descriptive, regarding the structure
of this book. The nine chapters that constitute it are divided into three parts.
Part One addresses various issues of "Feminism, Citizenship, Democracy." In
chapter 1, "Context Is All: Reconsidering Feminism and Citizenship," I address
some contemporary feminist critiques of liberalism's conception of citizenship
and assess two current feminist challenges to it, the "Marxist" and the
"Maternalist." Finding the latter inadequate as both programmatic and critical
approaches to feminist politics, I forward a democratic alternative that feminist
political theorists might consider with a view toward an emancipatory politics. The most immediate implication of this chapter is the analytical and political importance of calling feminist theory to more expansive and detailed
accounts of democratic participatory citizenship as a collective identity, and
citizen politics as a democratic public activity.

Chapter 2, "Citizenship with a Feminist Face: More Problems with
Maternal Thinking," returns to the problem of maternalist (or "social") feminism and extends the critique by addressing the work of Jean Bethke Elshtain.
Elshtain's feminism argues for a mode of citizenship and public life that is rooted in the "special knowledge" of women as mothers and the distinctive virtues
of private, familial life. Elshtain's insistence that good citizenship requires the
politicization of virtues that are expressly female and even maternal—a powerful trend in some feminist theorizing—prompts a number of epistemological, ontological, and political issues that remain quite central to debates in
feminist theory. Foremost among them is the claim that particular practices
(like mothering) and domains (like the "private") give rise to special ways of
knowing (like "maternal thinking") that are worthy of emulation across a variety of fields of human interaction (like politics and the "public"). This chapter
challenges such assumptions by questioning the coherence of constituting the
practical and complex realities of politics in terms of such a gendered ideal of
the private realm and a fictive community of virtuous mothers. It also emphasizes the theoretical and practical costs of abandoning a more labyrinthine
understanding of politics than this formulation affords in favor of an ethics that
reinforces rather than resists the binary configuration "male:female" and the
conventional gender relations this hierarchical dualism underwrites.

Chapter 3, "Merely Combating the Phrases of This World: Liberalism, Communitarianism, and Recent Democratic Theory," identifies a problem of imaginative incapacity in some recent works on citizenship and democracy: their tendency to rely repetitiously upon an empty formulaic conceptual construct and the abstracted vocabulary of liberalism:communitarianism, in order to frame and contain the meaning of democratic politics. The chapter considers the unfortunate implications of theorizing politics in terms of the reconciliation or "synthesis" of this artificially constructed opposition, wherein the desire for theoretical simplicity ultimately overrides the difficult task of grasping the complexities and power dynamics of the real political universe. Under this strategy, I argue, the multifaceted phenomena of democratic politics are reduced to a singular analytical matter of conceptual resolution, thus voiding them of any material embodiment in the actually existing, perpetually discordant political world. The question is whether democratic theorizing can proceed without this simplistic apparatus and thereby allow theorists of citizenship and democracy to give up deploying the formula of "Liberty + Community" as a placeholder for politics and instead develop richer, deeper, more polychromatic (and less tractable) conceptual pictures of the political world.

Part Two, "The Second Sex and The Human Condition," analyzes the current state of feminist interpretive affairs in relation to two of the most influential theorists of the twentieth century who happen to be (coded as) female: Simone de Beauvoir and Hannah Arendt. The effort here is to review the state of the literature, but also to consider how Beauvoir's and Arendt's respective primary texts, *The Second Sex* and *The Human Condition*, serve as locales upon which contemporary academic feminists play out their own discursive political struggles. Chapter 4, "Debating de Beauvoir," was written on the occasion of the fortieth anniversary of the publication of *The Second Sex*. It conducts a quick survey of the fortunes of Beauvoir's totemic manifesto in the feminist second wave in the United States and then considers the transformations in Beauvoir studies in academic feminism in the 1980s, along with the rise of "difference," "diversity," and "deconstructive" approaches within feminist theory. Albeit briefly, the essay shows that the overall terrain of Beauvoir studies remains a highly contested field, not unlike feminist political theory itself.

The next two chapters explore by way of textual and political interpretation the uneasy relationship between feminism and the political thought of Arendt. Chapter 5, "The Woman Question in Arendt," addresses the theorist's seeming failure to explore adequately the subordination of women in the *The Human Condition* and to theorize the relation between public, private, and social realms with a view toward the historically enforced exclusion of women from politics. These are inadequacies that substantially undermine the effectiveness of Arendt's text as a phenomenal commentary on gender relations within the classical and the contemporary worlds. At the same time, however, the overall picture is more complicated than a first reading of "Arendt as antifeminist" permits. For *The Human Condition* also provides (usually between its lines) feminist political theory with a powerful critique of gender in modernity, one that questions (through the concepts of labor, work, and action) the coherence of a feminist politics grounded in biology, reproduction, nature, and female subjectivity to which much contemporary feminist theory remains susceptible.

Chapter 6 amplifies and extends the analysis begun in chapter 5 but also turns in a different direction. "The Arendt Question in Feminism" argues that Arendt's political thought, again as illuminated in *The Human Condition*, is far more nuanced and complex than most recent feminist critical commentary allows. The simple, gendered binary configuration of "public (man):private (woman)" a conceptual staple in 1980s feminist critiques of Arendt's thinking is, I argue, a distorted lens through which to read her political thought. It is also a conceptual imprisonment for critical interpretation in feminism. In Arendt's case, not only does the "private:public" formula miss the truly provocative gender subtext of *The Human Condition* (particularly the relation between *animal laborans* and *homo faber*); it also fails to see how Arendt displaces that very relation (and hence the gender binary itself) in her forwarding of an existential speech-action concept of politics. The essay concludes by attending to some very recent Arendt commentaries in feminism that are not as fixated upon the private:public binary but are problematic nonetheless in their respective efforts to interpret and appropriate Arendtian politics under the names of "difference" or "diversity" or "deconstruction." My critique of these approaches does not seek to salvage an Arendtian politics of my own making so much as to discern—by way of critical interpretation—the current state of affairs in feminist political theorizing within which Arendt has been both a visible and invisible figure of considerable importance.

Part Three, "The Politics of Politics," takes a closer look at the presuppositions that respectively inform the public realm theories of Jürgen Habermas and Hannah Arendt, with an aim toward conceptual innovation in the theorizing of politics as a human activity. Chapter 7, "Working in Half-Truth: Habermas, Machiavelli, and the Milieu Proper to Politics," conjures a "Machiavellian" alternative to Habermas's theory of practical discourse. Exacting a turn on Habermas's reconstructive understanding of politics as a communicative ethics of discursive truth and intersubjective regard, the chapter forwards speech in politics as an activity irredeemably suffused with power, strategy, calculation, and rhetorical manipulation, not just at the level of the professional politician or the elites but in the realm of ordinary, everyday citizen politics as well. Thus it challenges the Habermasian bifurcation of "communicative" and "strategic" action, and calls for more "Machiavellian" orientations than contemporary discourse ethics is currently inclined to support.

Chapter 8, "The Slow Boring of Hard Boards: Weil, Arendt, and the Work of Politics," continues the exploration of politics by moving from the plane of political speech to political action more generally, in order to identify some inadequacies in Arendt's concept of work that also bear upon her concept of politics. To rethink an action concept of politics, I turn upon Arendt the French political and social theorist Simone Weil, who in many respects is Arendt's equal as a diagnostician of modernity. Unlike Arendt, however, Weil develops a concept of work that draws a distinction between technological determinism and objectification on the one hand and instrumental action as "methodical thinking" and purposefulness on the other. As a result, Weil's theory of action embraces something that Arendt's theatrical speech-action politics rejects: a concept of purposeful, methodical performance that is grounded in working as well as speaking.

Chapter 9 is titled "A Transfiguring Evening Glow: Arendt and the Holocaust." The chapter returns, for one last time, to *The Human Condition*. It rests rather uneasily alongside the rest of these chapters, as it should. Here I want to pay tribute to the exemplary nature of Arendt's magnum opus by proposing that we read it within the context of the most fiercely inhuman and horrific event of the twentieth century and as a direct existential response to the ruination that this event brought upon humanity. It is also a reminder of what is at stake when political life is totally sucked into the totalitarian processes of automatism (*animal laborans*) and instrumentalism (*homo faber*), both of which facilitate the utter objectification and destruction of living human beings. The title takes its first part from Nietzsche's commentary on Thucydides's rendering of Pericles's Funeral Oration, which Nietzsche reads as a "transfiguring evening glow" in whose light the Athenians might be guided away from the darkness of plague and war. As Nietzsche suggests of Thucydides's text, so I suggest of Arendt's: *The Human Condition* undertakes an existential act of political theorizing in response to a trauma that even now continues to exhibit itself in terms of guilt, complicity, and hatred. This is the "empty space" left after Auschwitz. With its powerful countersymbol of the "space of appearance," *The Human Condition* confronts the burden of this shared and terrible history and calls forth the capacity in all humans to act politically and therefore to endure.

Part One

Feminism,
Citizenship,
Democracy

Chapter 1

Context Is All

Reconsidering Feminism and Citizenship

In Margaret Atwood's powerful novel *The Handmaid's Tale* (1986) the heroine Offred, a member of a new class of "two-legged wombs" in a tyrannous dystopian society, often reminds herself that "Context is all." Offred's reminder, born out of her own immediate situation, encapsulates a significant existential insight: each moment of our lives, from the most mundane to the most lofty, is constituted out of a complex of existing institutions and relations that are themselves shaped by particular political, social, and historical arrangements. These arrangements and the realities they construct must be recognized, differentiated, and scrutinized if our lives and our fortunes are to resist domination by seemingly alien forces beyond our control. But context, as Offred understands, is also about the peculiar, concrete, and contingent elements that structure and condition individual lives, events, and situations. In her reduced and all-encompassing circumstances, Offred comes to see that matters beyond one's immediate purview and personal experience, perhaps most significantly relations of political power, make a great deal of difference with respect to living a more or less free and fully human life. But her realization comes too late, as the possibilities for liberation and collective resistance are dimmed, if not entirely extinguished, under the relentless pressures of a repressive, sexist, authoritarian state.

Unlike Offred, feminist theorists, academics, and activists have long recognized as imperative the task of seeking out, defining, and criticizing the complex historical, material, and political realities that shape and situate relations of gender and sexuality, divisions of labor, the intersection of family, society, and state, and particularly the lives of those human beings persistently grouped together and constructed as "women." Indeed, one of the first and most powerful insights of theoretical feminism was a point about context: Beauvoir's claim in *The Second Sex* ([1949] 1974) that "one is not born a woman, but, rather, becomes one." Since then, feminist theorists have understood this insight about becoming as also a question about context and circumstances; hence feminism in its various guises has been committed to scrutinizing the material, ideational, discursive, and political worlds in order to reveal the power relations that condition how we become "women" (and "men"), and the women (and men) that we become. "The personal is political" is the credo of this critical investigative practice.

Speaking of context, the discursive and ideational world that most persistently conditions political experience in the United States is liberalism and its attendant set of values, beliefs, and practices. Without question, the liberal tradition can count many among its adherents; but it has not escaped the scrutiny of feminism's discerning eye. Over the past two decades in the United States, few critics of liberal political theory have been as persistent and relentless as academic feminists (although we could add to this list contemporary communitarians, post-Marxists, a variety of postmodernists, critical race theorists, some democratic theorists [see chapter 3], multiculturalists, and, of course, conservatives of various stripes). Certainly no critics have been as committed to articulating alternatives to liberal views of gender, the family, the sexual division of labor, and the relationship between the public and the private realms as feminist theorists, historians, and sociologists.[1]

In this chapter I shall focus on the liberal view of politics and citizenship and some recent feminist theoretic responses to it. First I will outline (in a necessarily schematic way) the dominant features of liberalism's conception of citizenship, and then I will examine two current feminist challenges to that conception and those features. What I ultimately want to argue, however, is that although both of these feminist challenges offer important correctives to the liberal view, neither of them leads to a suitable liberatory alternative of the sort that might invigorate (resuscitate?) a compelling feminist politics and reassert what appears to be feminism's fading identity as a political movement. In the third section, then, I offer a preliminary sketch of what a better feminist theory of citizenship would entail were it to embrace the specificities of the political and commit itself more expressly and concretely to democratic action.

The terrain of liberalism is vast. Its historical, political, moral, and philosophical dimensions have been extensively articulated, surveyed, and assessed in social, political, and moral theory. All I shall present here are the barest of bones of a particular element of liberalism—its conception of citizenship—but this skeletal reconstruction may at least establish a theoretical context in order to situate the feminist alternatives that follow. With this in mind and with the caveat that all concepts and conceptualizations change through time, let us begin by considering the political principles that have more or less consistently distinguished liberal political theory. The exclusion of women (as well as ethnic and racial minorities) from some of these principles is a historical and contingent if not a contemporary or necessary feature of liberalism and has by now been widely interrogated and analyzed by feminist scholars and political theorists across a variety of fields of inquiry. A discussion of whether liberal theory has (or can) adequately correct some of its earlier exclusions and inequalities I leave for another day. For now I will simply outline five basic and overlapping elements of liberalism's view of citizenship.

Liberalism's Conception of Citizenship

The first and perhaps most basic element of liberalism's conception of citizenship is the notion that humans are free and rational beings whose existence and interests are ontologically prior to society's. From a liberal perspective one might say that context is not "all," for at a normative and philosophical level, liberalism conceptualizes the needs, capacities, and rights of individuals—and the individual him- or herself—as being universal and independent of (if not unaffected by) any immediate social or political context or condition. As Teresa Brennan and Carole Pateman (1979) observe, the contemporary liberal idea that the individual is by nature a free and autonomous being, ontologically prior to the bonds of society, the context of history, and the lineaments of tradition, was an originary element of theories of social contract (perhaps most powerfully formulated by Thomas Hobbes and John Locke). In *De Cive*, Hobbes ([1839] 1966, 102) set the stage for this idea when he wrote, "[L]et us . . . consider men as if but even now sprung out of the earth, and suddenly, like mushrooms come to full maturity, without all kinds of engagement to each other." The emergence of this notion of the autonomous individual or "the unencumbered self" (Sandel 1984) not only marked "a decisive break with the traditional view that people were 'naturally' bound together in a hierarchy of inequality and subordination" (Brennan and Pateman 1979), but also established a conception of "natural" individual freedom as the condition of individual isolation and independence prior to the (artificial) creation of civil society. What counts is that the human being is a rational individual who, as such a persona, bears intrinsic worth.

A second feature of liberal political thought is that society should ensure the liberty of all its members to realize their capabilities as diverse, differentiated individuals. This "self-development" principle is one of the basic elements of the Western liberal tradition. Perhaps the classic formulation can be found in John Stuart Mill's *On Liberty* ([1854] 1961, 266) and in his observation that "the only freedom which deserves the name, is that of pursuing our own good in our own way, so long as we do not attempt to deprive others of theirs, or impede their efforts to obtain it." One of the prevailing difficulties of liberalism is that it has tried to combine the idea of individual freedom as heterogeneous self-development with the entrepreneurial notion of liberalism as, in C. B. Macpherson's (1977, 2) terms, "the right of the stronger to do down the weaker by following market rules." Macpherson argues that the two freedoms are profoundly inconsistent, but he also asserts that the liberal position "need not be taken to depend forever on an acceptance of capitalist assumptions although historically it has been so taken."

Closely associated with the principle of individual liberty is a third feature: an emphasis on human equality. Liberal theorists may differ in their formulations of this principle but not on its primacy. Locke, for example, held that "reason is the common rule and measure that God has given to mankind"; therefore all men must be considered created equal and worthy of the same dignity and respect. Jeremy Bentham famously argued (not always consistently) that the case for equality rests on the fact that all individuals have the same capacity for pleasure and hence that the happiness of society is maximized in "the greatest good of the greatest number." In "Liberal Legislation and Freedom of Contract," T. H. Green ([1880] 1964) proclaimed that everyone has an interest in securing to everyone else the free use, enjoyment and disposal of his possessions, so long as that freedom on the part of one does not interfere with a like freedom on the part of others, because such freedom contributes to that equal development of the faculties of all, which is the highest good of all. Since liberal theories historically begin with some version of the presumption of equality among individuals, it is a relatively small step from this to the related argument that modern democracy requires equal suffrage, in which every single person should count for as much as any other single individual in the polity. As Allison Jaggar (1983, 33) writes, "Liberalism's belief in the ultimate worth of the individual is expressed in political egalitarianism." As we know, of course, this liberal belief was more readily secured in theory than in the actual lived experiences of gender, race, and class in the United States, where political egalitarianism was and remains a not fully unrealized ideal.

This egalitarianism takes the form of what some theorists call "negative liberty," which Sir Isaiah Berlin (1969, 122) in his classic essay on freedom characterizes as "the area within which a man can act unobstructed by others." In this view, freedom is the absence of obstacles to possible choices and activities. What is at stake in this liberal conception is neither the good life nor the virtuous community but simply the freedom of the individual to choose his or her own values or ends without interference from others and consistent with a similar or equal liberty for others. At the core of negative liberty, then, is a fourth feature of liberalism that speaks to the individual in his political guise as citizen: the conception of the individual as the "bearer of formal rights" designed to protect him (and, later, her) from the infringement or interference of others and to guarantee him (and, later, her) the same opportunities or "equal access" to the protection of the law and to public institutions as are granted to others.

The concept of rights is of fundamental importance to the liberal political vision. In *A Theory of Justice*, John Rawls (1971) offers this classic formulation of the liberal view: "Each person possesses an inviolability founded on justice that even the welfare of society as a whole cannot override. . . . The rights secured by justice are not subject to political bargaining or the calculus of social interests." Not only does the concept of rights reinforce the underlying liberal principles of individual freedom and formal equality; it also sets up the distinction between "private" and "public" that informs so much of the liberal perspective on family and social institutions. Individual rights correspond to the notion of a private realm of freedom—separate, distinct, and protected from that of the public and the state. Although liberal theorists disagree about the nature and degree of state intervention in the public realm—and even about what counts as "public"—they nevertheless accept the idea that certain rights are inviolable and exist in a private realm where the state cannot legitimately interfere. For much of liberalism's ideological history this private realm has subsumed marriage, family, housework, and child care. Historically the liberal notion of "the private" was (often explicitly) identified as "woman's sphere," albeit a sphere ultimately controlled and organized through the terms of "male property" and patriarchal power. These terms effectively excluded women from the public sphere reserved for citizens even as they valorized women's place and purpose in the private domains of the household and the family, as wives, mothers, sisters, daughters, and the caretakers of children.

The fifth feature of liberalism, to which I alluded above, is the idea of the liberal individual as competitor. To understand it, we might recall liberalism's own context—its distinctive history and origin. In its earliest incarnation in Europe (long before the term "liberalism" was a part of Western political discourse), the elements that came to constitute liberal political thought—most important the proclamation of individual rights and social equality—were acts of high rebellion against king and court. The Levellers, the True Whigs, the Commonwealthmen, and revolutionary "patriots" appealed to political freedom and against hierarchy and the patriarchal defense of the divine right of kings (most notably articulated by Robert Filmer and brilliantly challenged by Locke). Meanwhile *economic* appeals of the character that Macpherson (1962) famously termed "possessive individualism" began to develop in a separate but related set of practices in the seventeenth century, amid the final disintegration of, in Karl Marx's felicitous description, those "motley feudal ties" that marked the decline of aristocracy and the rise of a new order of merchants and entrepreneurs with a "natural propensity," as Adam Smith wrote, "to trade, truck,

and barter." The life of economic liberalism, in other words, began in capitalist market societies, and as Marx argued, it can only be fully comprehended in
terms of the social and economic institutions that shaped it. In turn, however,
liberalism as a political ideology lent support to the active and competitive
pursuit of things beneficial to an economic system based on production and
investment for the sake of profit.

Among these "things beneficial" is the notion of the rational man as a
competitive individual who tends naturally to pursue his own interest and
maximize his own gain. Although it would be mistaken to suggest that all liberal theorists conceive of human nature or conduct as fundamentally egoistic,
most do argue that people tend naturally in this direction and must work to
develop moral capacities to counter their basic selfish, acquisitive inclinations.
Thus, we can at least generally conclude that for many liberals, the motive
force of human action is not to be found in any noble desires to achieve the
good life or the morally virtuous society but rather in the inclination toward
self-interest, individual advancement, or (in capitalist terms) the pursuit of
profit according to the rules of the so-called free market.[2] Taken in this light,
then, the liberal individual might be understood as the competitive entrepre-
neur, his civil society as an economic marketplace, and his ideal as the equal
opportunity to engage, to paraphrase Smith, in "the race for wealth, and honors, and preferments."

What liberty comes to mean in this economic context is a set of formal
guarantees to the individual that he (and, later, she) may enjoy a fair start in
"race." What citizenship comes to mean in this liberal economic guise is something like equal membership in various competitive social spheres, more or less
regulated by government and more or less dedicated to the assumption that the
"market maketh man." To put this otherwise, under economistic liberalism, citizenship is primarily construed as a competitive activity rooted in the right to
pursue one's interests without hindrance or interference in the marketplace of
goods and ideas. Not surprisingly, modern democracy under liberal individualism is more generally linked to representative government and the right to vote
than to the collective, participatory models of citizen action in the public realm.

This notion of the citizen as the bearer of rights, of liberty as the aim of
the discrete individual, and of politics as representative government is precisely what makes liberalism, despite its admirable and vital theoretical insistence
on the values of individual freedom and equality, seem so politically barren to
so many of its feminist critics, past and present, conservative and radical. As far
as feminism is concerned, perhaps the political theorist Mary Shanley (1983,
360) best sums up the problem that liberalism poses when she writes:

> While liberal ideals have been efficacious in overturning restric-
> tions on women as individuals, liberal theory does not provide the
> language or concepts to help us understand the various kinds of
> human interdependence which are part of the life of both fami-

lies and polities, nor to articulate a feminist vision of "the good life." Feminists are thus in the awkward position of having to use rhetoric in dealing with the state that does not adequately describe their goals and that may undercut their efforts at establishing new modes of life.

Two Feminist Responses to Liberal Citizenship: Marxists and Maternalists

For good and obvious reasons, one might expect that a feminist critique of liberalism would best begin by inspecting the rhetoric and the practical-normative value of the notions of equal access and equal opportunity, since that is where so much liberal feminism begins. Not only is equal opportunity a central tenet of liberal thought; it is also a driving part of our contemporary political discourse that is used both to attack and to defend special pleas for women's rights. But a complementary approach may be in order as well. There is merit, I think, to the argument that to begin with the question of equal access or equal opportunity as the centerpiece of a feminist politics is already to presume too much, to deal too many high cards to the liberal hand. Quite literally, "equal access is not enough," for once in the domain of equal access talk, we are tied into a whole network of liberal concepts—rights interests, contracts, individualism, representative government, negative liberty. These open up some avenues of discourse but at the same time block off others. As Shanley implies, for feminists to sign on to these concepts may be to obscure rather than to illuminate a vision of politics, citizenship, and "the good life" that is important for feminist values and concerns, although not necessarily hostile to some of liberalism's basic philosophical tenets.

By this I do not mean to suggest that feminists who proceed from the question of equal access or equal opportunity are doing something unhelpful or unimportant. On the contrary, by using gender as a unit of analysis, feminist scholars and analysts have uncovered the inegalitarianism behind the discourse of equal opportunity, making us aware of how such presumptions deny the social reality of unequal treatment, sexual discrimination, cultural stereotypes, and women's subordination both in the polity and the economy. To the extent to which this sort of gender analysis and critique help to advance liberal social and political programs and encourage liberal practices to live up to liberal principles—for example, the extension of parental and family leaves, government support of day care workers and child care facilities, salaries of comparable worth, reasonable sexual harassment policies and protections, health care benefits that extend to the working and nonworking poor, a decent living wage, workplace safety regulations, the protection of the civil rights and civil liberties of all citizens—liberal feminists give indispensable assistance to efforts to secure a more just and egalitarian society. However, we should not overlook the fact that this sort of analysis also carries limitations determined by the ruling concepts of liberalism and the worldview that they represent. In this sense a liberal vocabulary may inhibit the effective theorizing of what Shanley calls "new modes of life." For example, if power is conceptualized primarily in terms of equal opportunity or equal coverage under existing laws and institutions and in a way that seeks to adjust but basically supports the status quo, then it is difficult to conceive of power as the transformation or dismantling of certain laws or institutions through citizen action, protest, or resistance. If freedom is conceptualized primarily in terms of (negative) liberty and protection of rights, then it is difficult to conceive of it as collective action geared toward human emancipation and fundamental social and political change.

Of course, few feminist political theorists would find these remarks startling or new. As I have already indicated, a great deal of recent feminist thought (liberal feminism included) has been directed toward revealing the problems and limitations of liberalism and liberal political theory, not only by way of critique but also by offering alternative theoretical frameworks for conceptualizing women's liberation, gender justice, and female emancipation. Over the past two decades, critiques of liberalism have become a kind of cottage industry within feminist theory; indeed, few are the contemporary theorists who, whatever their predilections, do not find themselves obliged to situate their theorizations in some relation to liberalism or liberal thinking. In this critical aspect, liberal theories have presented to feminism a variety of claims and positions that have, in effect, encouraged innovative and oppositional conceptualizations and responses from feminist theorists themselves. Some of these responses have focused on the epistemological and ontological roots of liberalism, others on its implications for an ethical and moral theory, still others on the assumptions that underlie liberal political thought and inform its politics. On the latter front, and with specific attention to the role of the state, the relation between public and private, the nature of political community, and the meaning of citizenship, feminist political theorists who do not consider their views "liberal" seem to fall into two different camps (both of which distinguish themselves in various ways from liberalism). I will call these camps (with due recognition of the limitations of such labels) "Marxist" and "Maternalist."[3] A brief overview of each should suffice to bring us up to date on the two main feminist political alternatives to the liberal conception of citizenship that currently circulate in the theoretical domain. I shall go on to suggest that neither of these alternatives satisfactorily counters the liberal view despite providing some suggestive and thought-provoking contributions to the political debate.

Marxist Feminism
First, the Marxists. Feminists working within the Marxist tradition seek to reveal the capitalist and patriarchal foundations of the liberal state as well as the

oppression inherent in the sexual division of labor—or as one theorist puts it, "the consequences of women's dual contribution to subsistence in capitalism"(Hartsock 1983, 235).[4] At stake in this economic critique, as another theorist argues, is the notion of the "state's involvement in protecting patriarchy as a system of power, much in the same way it protects capitalism and racism" (Eisenstein 1981, 223). Insofar as they believe that the state participates in the oppression of women, Marxist feminists tend to consider the rights granted by the state as a sham, a convenient ideological fiction that serves to obscure the underlying reality of a dominant patriarchal ruling class. Accordingly, the liberation of women will be possible only once the liberal capitalist state is overthrown and its patriarchal structure dismantled. What will emerge is an end to the sexual division of labor and "a feminist politics that moves beyond liberalism" (Eisenstein 1981, 222). What most Marxist feminists seem to mean by these politics is the egalitarian reordering of productive and reproductive labor and the achievement of truly liberating human relations, a society of "propertyless producers of use values" (Hartsock 1983, 247).

The strengths of this critique should be obvious. Marxist feminists recognize that a system of economics and gender rooted in capitalist, male-dominant systems underlies much of liberal ideology, from the notion of independent, rational man to the conception of separate private and public realms, from the value of individual liberty to the capitalist equation of freedom with free trade. (This does not necessarily mean that they reject working with the liberal feminist movement on issues of strategy and unification.) As such, Marxist feminist analysis reveals numerous inadequacies in the liberal capitalist sphere, particularly the organization of women's work and the system's reliance on the law, the state, interest groups, and state-instituted reforms as the source of social justice, individual equality, and access. The advantage of the Marxist feminist approach lies not only in its critique of capitalism, which reveals the exploitative and socially constructed dimensions of women's work, but also in its political critique, which challenges the liberal position that the state and its organs of representative government (legislative, juridical, administrative) are the legitimate arbiters of social change. Nevertheless, even though the Marxist feminist critique has much to offer from the standpoint of historical materialism, it has little to say on the subject and significance of citizenship as an emancipatory category (that is, not simply as an oppressive relation in capitalism). This is not to say that Marxist feminists eschew the language of agency, collective action, transformation, and change; but rarely do they frame these things in terms of the vocabulary of citizens and citizenship, civic association and democracy, which (loosely following Marx in *On the Jewish Question*) they tend to associate with a stage of political emancipation within civil society and not with human emancipation in a more expansive and world-encompassing sense of freedom. As Sheldon Wolin (1982, 17–28) observes, "Most Marxists are interested in the 'masses' or the workers, but they dismiss citizenship as a bourgeois conceit, formal and empty"—and liberal. Marxist feminism appears to be no exception to this rule, where the agents of action are rarely identified as citizens. Marxist feminists have, in effect, ceded the vocabulary of citizens and citizenship to liberalism, thereby inhibiting the political, conceptual, and discursive regeneration of the subject-as-citizen within the action-coordinating domains of feminist theory.

To the extent to which Marxist feminists rejuvenate the concepts of citizen and citizenship at all, they usually incorporate them within an account of social change (from "capitalist patriarchy" to "socialist feminism") and the liberatory transformation of economic conditions. In this view, freedom is realized along with the collective ownership of the forces of production, the transformation of wage work prescribed for women by patriarchy, and the end of oppression in the relations of reproduction. These goals are, in turn, associated with revolutionary action and the disappearance of the patriarchal state. Thus in their approach to citizenship, Marxist feminists tend to thematize politics in terms of revolutionary struggle that emerges out of relations with the working class and is directed toward transformation in social relations. Under these terms, feminism becomes "a force for revolution" (Hartsock 1983, 66). What remains unclear in Marxist feminism is what feminism becomes *after* the revolution and what, if anything, constitutes its postrevolutionary politics other than, in Marx's own words, "the administration of things." In sum, the "economism" of Marxist feminism, with its tendency to focus on sociological and economic conditions of existence, wage labor under capitalism, and the class "system," tends to ignore the subject of politics or at least to assign to it the status of an epiphenomenon, secondary to matters of economy and society. To put this another way, the great strength of Marxist feminism as a mode of theoretical inquiry lies in its "analysis of women's subordination for the purpose of figuring out how to change it" (Gordon 1979, 107), that is, in its ruthless criticism of existing social and economic relations as interrogated through the lens of gender. But in most instances, the sociological critique overwhelms and suppresses any innovative or imaginative articulation of a democratic citizen politics.

Now no one would deny that economic equality and social justice are vital and important political principles. A society that values and strives for these principles with all of its members in mind deserves admiration and respect. What I am suggesting, however, is that because Marxist feminism tends to stop here, its programmatic vision is incomplete, for what emerges is a picture of economic freedom, a society of fulfilled social beings, but not so much a polity of self-governing, energetic, interacting citizens or freedom as politics. This is not ruled out so much as unattended. As a result, a whole complex of vital theoretical questions is sidestepped or ignored: What is political (as distinguished from economic or social) freedom? What does it mean to act (not merely "be") as a member of a polity as well as a society? What does an expressly political feminism require by way of an analysis of power, action, and responsibility? What does it mean to think about feminism in terms of the public sphere or the polity in ways that make it expressly political, not social? Or, to put the matter more bluntly, is there more to feminist politics than revolutionary struggle against capitalist patriarchy and, if so, what sorts of theoretical and conceptual frameworks might help us think about this?

Maternal Feminism

The second camp of feminist theorists, the Maternalists, answers this last question in the affirmative. They would have us reconsider both the liberal and the Marxist feminist views of citizenship[5] and become committed to a conception of female political consciousness that is grounded in the virtues of the private and domestic sphere, especially in the practice of mothering and the attitude of "maternal thinking." Unlike the Marxists, the Maternalists hold that as important as social justice is it is not a sufficient condition for a truly liberatory feminist politics. Women must be understood more fully as mothers (not simply as "reproducers") and as the protectors of family and community values, not just in terms of class identity. Like the Marxist feminists, however, the Maternalists eschew the liberal notion of the citizen as an individual holder of rights protected by the state. For the Maternalist, such a notion is at best morally empty and at worst morally subversive since it rests on an allegedly masculinist conception of the person as an independent, self-interested, economic being. When one translates this notion into a broader conception of politics, the maternal feminist argues, one is left with a vision of citizens as competitive marketeers and entrepreneurial jobholders for whom civic activity is, at most, membership in interest groups. Thus, the maternal feminist denies precisely what the liberal would defend: an individualist, rights-based, contractual conception of citizenship and a view of the public realm as one of contest and competition. As Jean Bethke Elshtain (1982c, 617) writes, for example:

> The problem—or one of the problems—with a politics that begins and ends with mobilizing resources, achieving maximum impacts, calculating prudentially, articulating interest group claims . . . and so on, is not only its utter lack of imagination but its inability to engage in the reflective allegiance and committed loyalty of citizens. Oversimply, no substantive sense of civic virtue, no vision of political community that might serve as the groundwork of a life in common, is possible within a political life dominated by a self-interested, predatory, individualism.

Maternal feminism is expressly designed to counter what it thinks are the arid and unimaginative qualities of the prevailing liberal view and, more emphatically, to present an alternative sense of civic virtue citizenship. As a first step, it wants to assert the moral primacy of the family. Although this may seem to some a strange start for a feminist politics, the Maternalists would have us rethink the overly simplified liberal separation of public and private and consider instead the "private" (or the family, or the domestic sphere of the household) as the locus for a possible public morality and a model for the activity of citizenship itself. Or, to put this another way, the Maternalists criticize "statist" politics and individualist persons, and offer in their place a politics informed by the virtues of the private realm, where women practice a set of values committed to relational capacities, love, compassion, care, and other-directedness.

What makes this view expressly feminist (rather than, say, traditionally conservative) is its "womanism," which is decisively expressed in the idea that women's special experience as mothers endows them with a capacity and a "moral imperative" for countering the male liberal individualist worldview and its masculinist notion of citizenship. Thus Elshtain (1981, 243), perhaps the best-known academic Maternalist, describes mothering as a "complicated, rich, ambivalent, vexing, joyous activity" that upholds the principle that "the reality of a single human child [must] be kept before the mind's eye." For Elshtain (1982a, 58), the implications that mothering holds for citizenship are clear: "Were maternal thinking to be taken as the base for feminist consciousness," she argues, "a wedge for examining an increasingly overcontrolled public world would open immediately." Not only does maternal thinking chasten what Elshtain calls the "arrogant" (male) public; it also provides the basis for a whole new conception of power, citizenship, and the public realm. The citizen who emerges is a loving being "devoted to the protection of vulnerable human life" and to making the virtues of mothering the "template" for a new, more humane public world.

Much of the Maternalist argument takes its inspiration from, or finds support in, two highly influential gender studies of the late 1970s and early 1980s: the object-relations theory of the sociologist Nancy Chodorow (1978) and the moral development theory of psychologist Carol Gilligan (1982). These social scientists argue that striking contrasts exist between men and women and can be understood in terms of certain experiential (not natural or biological) differences in the early stages of development. At the crux of Chodorow's and Gilligan's findings is the implication that women's morality is tied to a different (and possibly more humane) set of moral values than men's (although Gilligan seems to leave open whether the "different voice" is exclusive to women or open to men, or even a normatively superior perspective in all situations and contexts).[6] Gilligan identifies a female "ethic of care" that differs from the male "ethic of justice." The ethic of care revolves around responsibility and relationships rather than rights, and attends more to the needs that emanate from particular situations and contexts than to the universal application of general rules of conduct. Maternalism has adapted these psychological and sociological accounts, which rest conceptually upon an assumed "binary opposition" between women and men, and politicized them. In their work, "the male voice" is that of the liberal patriarchal individualist and competitor who stands in stark contrast to the female voice of the compassionate citizen as loving mother. For the Maternalists in political theory (if not for Chodorow or Gilligan), there is no doubt about which side of the gender binary is normatively superior and deserving of elevation, both as a basis for political consciousness and as an ethical way of being. The Maternalists might say that the female morality of responsibility "must extend its imperative to men," but they nevertheless grant a pride of place to women and to "women's sphere" of the family as the wellspring of this new "mode of public discourse" (Elshtain 1982c, 621). They also maintain that public discourse and citizenship should be informed by the virtues of mothering—love, attentiveness, compassion, care, and "engrossment"—in short, by all the virtues that the statist realm of patriarchy and paternalism allegedly disdain.

What are we to make of this vision of feminist citizenship? There is, I think, much to be gained from the Maternalist approach, especially if we consider it within the context of the liberal and Marxist feminist views. First, the Maternalists are almost alone among other feminisms in their concern with the moral attributes of citizenship (hence their affinity with some contemporary communitarians) and the content of feminist political consciousness. Although one might take considerable issue with their formulations, they deserve acknowledgment for making citizenship, and its attendant vocabulary of the relation between public and private, family and society, a matter of significance. Second, the Maternalists remind us of the inadequacy and limitations of a rights-based conception of the individual and a view of social justice informed primarily by the idea of equal access, equal opportunity, and equal rights formulations of the law. They understand the dimensions of political morality in ways that constitute politics (or at least the governance of the polity) itself as potentially virtuous and elevating. Third, in an era when politics has become a pejorative term, the maternal feminists direct us toward rehumanizing the way we think about belonging and membership and recognize how, as interrelated, "encumbered" selves, we can strive for more humane, relational, and shared communities than our current circumstances allow.

Despite these contributions, however, much is troubling about the Maternalists' conception of citizenship. It carries the same problem as do all theories that hold one side of an opposition to be superior to the other. For the Maternalists, women are more moral than men because they are, or can be, or are raised by, mothers and because mothering itself is necessarily and universally an affective, caring, loving activity. Leaving aside the psychological, cultural, and sociological difficulties behind these claims (see chapter 2 for an elaboration), suffice it to say that the Maternalists stand in danger of committing precisely the same sort of conceptual move they find problematic in the liberal view. When it comes to thematizing the citizen, that is, they erase the specificity of the human subjects with whom they are concerned through a set of categories that homogenize differences and reduce identity to a singular, abstract, and universalizing categorization. If liberalism performs this act under the category of the "rational individual," then Maternalism does it under the category of the "mother."

Equally serious is the guiding assumption of the Maternalists that feminists must choose between two worlds—the masculinist, competitive, statist public and the maternal, loving, virtuous private. To choose the public world as it now exists, they argue, is to endorse a politics and an ethics that recapitulate the dehumanizing features of the paternal liberal-capitalist state. To choose the private world, however, is to reassert the value of a "women's realm" and adopt a maternal model as the basis for citizenship, a mother:child relation that provides (so the Maternalists contend) a deeply moral alternative to the liberal account of citizens as rights-bearing individuals who are essentially strangers, unencumbered and autonomous. Here again the Maternalists simply reregister a liberal conceptualization—the dichotomy between public and private—rather than contesting it. As a political theory, Maternalism tends to accept the givenness of certain existing binaries (for example, male:female; public:private) and simply rearrange their normative content without challenging their fundamental conceptual coherence or their adequacy as frameworks for thinking politically. Perhaps the most striking example of this tendency not to think outside "the binary box" is the Maternalist inclination to equate politics in its most positive mode with the moral community and politics in its most negative mode with the state or the institutions of representative government. Thereby, politics itself is boxed in (if not utterly erased) by way of the relation between the community and the state, another dichotomy that carries decisively gendered, normative components (that is, in the Maternalist lexicon, the "community" is usually coded as virtuously female while the "state" is masculine, lacking in moral worth and in need of chastening and correction). The problem with this formulation is that by conceptually privileging the community on the one hand and the state on the other, it obliterates any notion of politics as a realm of action. Thus Maternalism, like liberalism and Marxist feminism, carries with it a diminished account of citizenship and, accordingly, a truncated understanding of freedom and politics.

What we need is an entirely different way of thinking about politics, freedom, and citizenship, something that might provide feminism with a theoretical alternative to the existing modes of liberal, Marxist, and Maternalist discourses, respectively.

A Third Alternative: Democratic Feminism and the Politics of Action

My basic point is simple and straightforward: for a concept of citizenship, feminists should turn to relations and practices that are expressly contextual, institutional, and political, informed by and situated within particular cultures and histories, and oriented toward action. What this requires, among other things, is a project that conceptualizes politics—and the politics of politics—differently than the liberal, the Marxist, or the Maternalist views. That conception I will loosely call "democratic" insofar as it takes politics to entail the collective and participatory engagement of historically situated and culturally constituted persons-as-citizens in the determination of the affairs of their polity. The polity is a public space, a locale or realm or arena; it may manifest itself at the level of the neighborhood (rural, urban, metropolitan, suburban), the town or city, the state, the region, the nation, or the globe, or even in "cyberspace." Its politics may form on the streets (in protests, parades, performances, demonstrations, or acts of civil disobedience and revolution); in voluntary associations; in social or economic institutions (for example, in churches, courts, prisons, hospitals, schools, universities, the military, community centers, business and financial corporations); in transnational environments. And of course these forms of citizen politics can and often do intersect with political parties, interest groups, and formal, representative structures of government. What counts normatively and politically, regardless of the particular site or form through which political action is initiated and sustained, is that all matters relating to politics are undertaken as "the people's affair."[7]

We might thus understand democracy as the form of politics and a "subordinate foundational good" (Shapiro 1994) that brings people together as citizens, or in struggle to assert themselves dynamically as citizens. Whereas liberalism (and liberal feminism) tends to privilege the legal-institutional structure of the nation-state, Marxist feminism to privilege class, economy, and the sphere of production, and Maternalism to privilege the family and society, democratic feminism's guiding principles emanate out of the very activity of popular engagement itself. To paraphrase John Dewey ([1939] 1993), "democratic ends need democratic methods for their realization." Democratic methods are what give rise to the articulation of democratic ends. Hence citizenship, as the people's power, is itself both the end and the means of democracy. Indeed, one of the many powers of democracy rests in its capacity to transform the individual as teacher, trader, corporate executive, child, sibling, worker, artist, friend, or mother into a political being (not a universalized entity), a citizen among other citizens, endowed with the capacity to speak, act, organize, and potentially change the world collectively. This is not a matter of uniformity or universality. Nevertheless, as Wolin (1996a, 44) writes, drawing upon a contemporary example of politics at its most powerful, "localism cannot surmount its limitations except by seeking out the evanescent homogeneity of a broader political. Recall the remarkable phenomenon of Polish Solidarity, a movement composed of highly disparate elements—socialists, artists, teachers, priests, believers, atheists, nationalists and so on." The "evanescent homogeneity" of citizen politics to which Wolin (1996a, 44) refers should not be taken as the theoretical equivalent of an abstract formalism of a universal "citizen ideal," but rather as a picture of solidarity—of the "perfect coincidence of (or between) interests"—as they are enacted in a concrete moment in a particular political world.[8] Thus democracy, as I am using the term here, offers an identity that neither liberalism, with its propensity to view the citizen as an (already constituted) individual bearer of rights, nor Marxism, with its tendency to view the citizen in terms of class struggle, nor Maternalism, with its attentiveness to mothering and community, provide. Democracy gives feminists a conception of citizens as, in Hannah Arendt's striking phrase, "speakers of words and doers of deeds" mutually participating in plurality in the public realm. To put this another way, the democratic vision does not center upon the individual's pursuit or protection of his or her discrete, individual interests; nor does it fixate upon the transformation of private into public virtues, or limit its concept of action to the revolutionary overturning of the state. Insofar as democracy as a politics derives its meaning from the collective homogeneity of "the people" acting together as diverse and heterogeneous equals, it introduces something different into the meaning of citizenship—a conception that moves beyond the rights-bearing individual, the comrade in struggle, or the maternal care-taker.

Under this view the exercise of democratic citizenship is a practice and activity unlike any other; it has a distinctive set of relations, virtues, and principles all its own, and they can be readily distinguished from other theoretical positions. Its relation is that of human beings as political equals and peers (therefore democratic practices do not give hierarchy or caste systems the benefit of the doubt); its guiding principle is freedom (which Arendt has called the raison d'être of politics); its primary orientation is the power of "positive liberty" of action that does not take the nation-state and its institutions as the primary unit of control. To assume, then, that the relations that accompany the capitalist marketplace or the virtues that emerge from the intimate experience of mothering are the models for the practice of citizenship is to conceptualize inadequately the characteristics of democratic political action and to misconstrue its unique and distinctive form and content.

The Maternalists might wish to believe that this democratic political condition would, in fact, flow from the "insertion" of women's virtues as mothers into the public world. However, there is no reason (as I shall argue at more length in chapter 2) to think that mothering or the maternal practices of loving, caring for, or intimacy necessarily induce commitment to, much less generate, democratic practices. Nor are there good grounds for arguing that a motto like "care for vulnerable human life" (or its current variant, "leave no child behind") by definition encompasses a commitment to democratic participatory citizenship. I do not wish to contest for a moment the political imperative of protection of the vulnerable that all polities must recognize and pursue if they wish to consider themselves decent and just. What should we make of the United States of America, for example, where at present one in four children live in poverty (the highest rate in the industrial West); eleven million children have no health insurance; hundreds of thousands are in foster care; five hundred thousand are homeless; and the infant mortality rate is higher than in some developing countries? But an enlightened despotism, a welfare state, a single-party bureaucracy, and a democratic republic may all respect mothers, protect children's lives, and show compassion for the vulnerable (or not). Even Atwood's authoritarian dystopia does this in its glorification of mothers-to-be and its reverence for the products of their wombs. Accordingly, the political issue for feminists must not just be whether children are protected but how and by whom these goals are determined, fought for, and enacted. In other words, the issue for feminists must also be about power. As long as feminists focus only on "issues"—about children, family, schools, work, wages, pornography, abortion, abuse—their politics will be problematic from the perspective of action-coordination. For feminism as a social and political movement, the focus needs also to be upon "what is to be done," upon who is doing it, and doing it. Only when feminism (in both its theoretical and its practical modes) recognizes that the pursuit of particular social and economic concerns must be undertaken through the active engagement and expression of democratic actors, of feminists as citizens of the public realm, will it become truly political. And only when feminist theorists declare citizen action a value will they be able to claim a truly liberatory politics as their own. To bring citizen democracy to feminist politics is to make feminist politics more democratic.

I hope it is clear that what I am also arguing for is feminism's democratization of the polity, not simply interest-group or single-issue politics of the sort that focus on instrumental ends defined by "women's issues," or, say, on electing more women to Congress. Assessing the sources and meaning of the "gender gap" in electoral and institutional politics, at the levels of both federal and state government, is an important thing to do; but these hardly exhaust the tasks of feminist political thought. In any case, a feminist commitment to democratic citizenship should not be confused with the notion that once victory has been achieved in some sector of electoral politics, or a problem is solved in law or public policy, the feminist citizen can have done with the political and move on (or return) to something else. That orientation instrumentalizes politics, reducing it to one more piece of equipment in the toolbox of everyday life. But as Lummis (1982, 9) notes:

> The radical democrat does not agree. . . . that after solving [a] problem it will be safe to abandon the democratic struggle and disband the organization . . . The radical democrat does not believe that any institutional or social arrangement can give an automatic and permanent solution to the main question of political virtue, or can repeal what may be the only scientific law political science has ever produced: power corrupts.

The key idea here is that the citizenship of democrats must be conceived of as a continuous activity requiring sustained work and vigilance. Politics in this key is not a momentary engagement (whether reformist or revolutionary) undertaken with an eye toward securing an end or goal or a new societal arrangement. This does not mean, of course, that democratic citizens do not pursue specific social and economic ends or fight for particular positions. Politics is about such things (as I shall argue in chapter 8), and the debates and activities of civic equals and peers will necessarily center on issues of social, political, and economic concern to the polity. But at the same time the democratic vision is, and feminist citizenship must itself be, more than this. Perhaps it is best to say that this is a vision and an understanding that is inspired by the principle of freedom and generated by a political activity—collective speech and action in the public realm. This activity never ends, for it is rooted in the continuous engagement of public expression and debate, the challenging of authorities, the organizing and coordination of action, and the sharing of responsibility for self-governance. What I am pressing for, in both theory and practice, is a feminist revitalization of these activities, as a part of feminism's own self-definition as a political movement. If this sort of revitalization were possible, feminism could infuse democracy with new purpose and meaning. Thus to bring feminist politics to democratic citizenship is to make democracy more feminist.

The Political Task of Feminist Theory

The reader who has followed me this far is perhaps now wondering whether I have not simply reduced feminist politics to democratic citizenship, leaving nothing in this vision (by way of either form or content) for feminism itself. A fair objection, but it requires a more far-reaching discussion of the relation between feminism and its political subjects, women, not to mention the task of theory and the nature and meaning of politics than I can pursue here (although these topics will be addressed in later chapters). Nevertheless, on the matter of position taking or substantive policy formulations (as opposed to critical thinking) as the task of feminist theory, suffice it to say now that my inclination is not to hold feminist theory "accountable" to existing political discourses or policy expectations (although this does not mean that feminist intellectual work should be indifferent to these things). Nor should the feminist theorist take upon herself the task of articulating principles, purposes, and policies "for" the movement in such a way that it becomes the programmatic and systematic guide and guru for its adherents. In a liberatory movement (especially one that defends democracy) such matters are best addressed, discussed, and debated in ordinary, everyday theoretic terms, within the context that feminist theory itself makes available through its articulation and defense of active citizenship and public spaces. In concluding these reflections, then, let me summarize why I think the revitalization of democratic action is an especially appropriate task for feminists to undertake as theorists and citizens.

Like Offred in *The Handmaid's Tale*, we contemporary citizens live in reduced circumstances, politically speaking. How we understand ourselves as citizens has little to do with the democratic norms and values of citizen action that I have just defended, and it is probably fair to say that most citizens of the United States do not think of citizenship in this way at all. We seem hypnotized by a liberal conception of citizenship as rights, an unremitting consumerism that we confuse with freedom, a capitalist ethic that we take as our collective identity, media that serve up emptiness in the name of entertainment, and money, to which we accord just about every value. Wolin (1981) has noted that in the American political tradition there exist two "bodies" within the historic "body of the people"—a collectivity informed by democratic practices on the one hand and a collectivity informed by an antidemocratic political economy on the other. The latter is the "liberal-capitalist citizenship" that has emerged triumphant today. Truly democratic practices are at best a rudimentary part of politics in the United States, at least in any sort of sustained fashion. They exist only on the margins and manifest themselves, it seems, only under the most extraordinary circumstances. (The contemporary environmental movement provides a counterexample to this claim, especially in its effective combination of scientists, experts in public policy, teachers, students, farmers, lawyers, union members, physicians, politicians, journalists, and "just" concerned citizens, who have created a citizen politics and citizen groups, united by a commitment to the earth and to the collective flourishing of humans, plants, and animals.) Even the historical memory of democratic citizen politics seems to elude our collective political imagination. As Arendt (1965, 223) writes, public freedom, public happiness, and public spirit are the "lost treasure" of American political life, "what remain[s] of them in this country . . . [are] civil liberties, the individual welfare of the greatest number, and public opinion as the greatest force ruling an egalitarian, democratic society."

What I want to argue is that we may yet recover the lost treasure. We may be able to breathe new life into the peoples' other "body," thus into our democratic selves-as-citizens. This prospect brings us back to feminism, which I think is one potential source for the political resuscitation of public freedom, public happiness, and public spirit. From its inception, feminism has been more than a social cause; it has been a political movement with distinctive attributes and decisively public features. From its inception at the turn of the previous century and throughout its second wave in the United States, the movement has been informed by democratic organization and practice—by spontaneous gatherings and marches, diverse and multitudinous action groups, face-to-face assemblies, consensus decision making, combinative organizing, nonhierarchical power structures, open speech and debate. That is, embodied within both the distant and immediate political past of feminism in the United States are "forms of freedom" (Mansbridge 1984) that are far more compatible with the democratic body of the American polity than with the ideals and purposes of liberal-capitalism. These particular feminist forms are, potentially at least, compatible with the idea of collective, democratic citizenship on a wider scale. One political task for feminist theory is to remember and appropriate these lost treasures for present purposes, to get action going.

Accordingly, I think that feminist theory must reorient itself toward a sustained commitment to citizenship and action—an expressly *democratic* theory—if it wishes to produce a viable alternative to the problematic political elements of liberal, Marxist feminist, and Maternalist theories that I have identified here. Despite its history of democratic and participatory practices as a political movement, feminism today has not generated, at either the level of theory or practice, the inspiration for a new and vigorous democratic citizenship. The reasons for this are many and complex; but one of them surely involves academic feminist theory's recent preoccupation with matters of epistemic justification (especially concerning the identity of the subject "woman") that privilege "knowing" over "doing," being over acting, and epistemology over politics.[9] As Linda Zerilli (2000, 175) contends, "the debate over foundations in feminism keeps us tied to explanatory hypotheses and empirical explanations insofar as it continues to pose the central problems of feminism in epistemic terms." To correct this limitation, feminist theory needs to become more reflexively political, directing its intellectual energies away from what Zerilli calls "the incessant debate over [epistemic] criteria and foundations" that persistently displaces the political, and toward theorizing democracy as its "subordinate foundational good." What this requires, among other tasks, is theorizing "political mobilization, which would open for women the possibility of a collective action of resistance," as Pierre Bourdieu (2001, viii) suggests. A newly politicized feminist theory also requires a reinstitution of the value of political freedom, or what Arendt (1965, 221) calls "the right 'to be a participator in government,'" in ways that lend citizenship both conceptual and practical power in feminism. To be sure, these theoretical tasks are neither easy nor shortterm. It is possible for feminists to undertake them in earnest, however, partly because models of mobilization and political freedom are already available within the context of the movement's own historical experiences, in its persistent attention to issues of power, structure, organization, coordination, and democracy, and in the long history of women, before and after the Nineteenth Amendment, acting as citizens, or demanding their rights and identities as citizens, or both, from within and outside of institutional structures in the United States.[10]

A warning is in order, however. What a feminist democratic theory must strive to avoid is the temptation of "womanism." To turn to historical or political examples of women's political lives for inspiration in articulating democratic values is one thing; it is quite another to insist that therein lies evidence of women's "superior moral nature" or of their more "mature" or "relational" or "democratic" political voice. A truly democratic defense of citizenship cannot afford to launch its appeal from a position of gender opposition or the normative posture of women's collective superiority as a group identity. Such a premise would posit as a starting point precisely what a democratic attitude must deny: that one group of citizens' voices (or one nation) is generally better, more deserving of attention, more inclusive, more worthy of emulation, more moral, than others. A feminist democrat cannot give way to this sort of theoretical temptation, lest democracy itself lose its meaning and citizenship its peculiar embedment in the principles of diversity and plurality, equality and difference. With this in mind, feminists would be well advised to secure their examples of democratic citizenship expansively, by drawing not only upon women's political history and activism (see Kerber 1980; Evans and Boyte 1986) but also upon other historical and contemporary movements, events, and practices that might infuse the notions of participatory citizenship and political freedom with generative power. We might include in this project of practical and historical theorizing the examples of townships and councils of revolutionary America; the populist National Farmers Alliance; the sit-down strikes and the labor movement generally in the 1930s in the United States; the 1960s civil rights movement in the United States; the antiwar movement against U.S. involvement in Vietnam; the organization of self-governing soviets after the Russian Revolution; the French political clubs of 1789; the anarchist affinity groups that fought fascism in interwar Spain; the KOR (Workers' Defense Committee) and, later, Solidarity in postwar Poland. But there are contemporary examples of concerned citizens acting democratically too: the International Monetary Fund-World Bank protests in Washington, D.C., in 2000; the protests against the World Trade Organization in Seattle in 1999 (a remarkable confluence of many progressive and often divided groups); the G-7 protests in Genoa in 2001, marking the increasingly international quality of the "antiglobalization" movements; the renewed street actions against corporations that utilize sweatshop labor or do business with nations that violate protocols of international human rights; and so on.

Of course, the point is not to distort or misrepresent these events by romanticizing them. Some of these examples of collective action were neither expressly democratic nor particularly pure forms of freedom (if such things are possible in politics); some of them were evanescent, others plagued by larger forces that eventually undermined them. (And many of them suffered from unfair and distorted media coverage.) But in almost all of these disparate events, one can identify "the people's affair"—a spirit of public happiness and popular participation and the commitment to collective, civic action in the name of political freedom and economic justice. At the very least, these instances should be recognized and remembered as real historical and material eruptions of mobilized people and emancipatory politics that can be drawn upon for action as well as inspiration. As Arendt (1965, 20) observes, "What saves the affairs of mortal men from their inherent futility, is nothing but the incessant talk about them, which in turn remains futile unless certain concepts, certain guideposts for future remembrance and even for sheer reference, arise out of it." If this sounds like a call for feminist theory to become more expressly historical, concrete, situated, and expansive in its articulation of a democratic politics, then the reader has rightly grasped my point.

I began these reflections by agreeing with Atwood's Offred: "context is all." Yes, we are indeed conditioned by the contexts in which we live, but we are also, within limits, the creators of our political and social relationships and institutions and we can change them if we are so determined. The recent history of democratic politics in this country (perhaps especially the debacle of the 2000 presidential election and the travesty of its outcome) has not been an altogether happy one, despite some considerable successes and advances of political freedom within the polity. The recent history of feminist political theory has also been less than elevating. Therefore I appreciate Wolin's (2000, 21) rather resigned remark that "It would be nice to end on an uplifting note and invoke political theory to come to the aid of democracy, but besides being fatuous that call may be too late in the day." Rather than occasion cynicism perhaps this warning can work to strengthen and renew our sense of urgency—and agency—regarding what is to be done and doing it. First, however, the urgency must be felt, and the public spirit necessary for revitalizing a participatory citizenship that resists "oppression in the name of management" to paraphrase Simone Weil, must be enlivened in the political realm. Democracy, in other words, again awaits and anticipates its "prime movers." Feminism in its intellectual, academic, and theoretic modes would do well to heed this call to action. In so doing feminism might also reaffirm its commitment to political freedom and public life.

Chapter 2

Citizenship with a Feminist Face
More Problems with Maternal Thinking

In the past twenty years, perhaps no other theoretical issue has created as much controversy within feminism as the role of women in the family. First-wave feminists as varied as Kate Millet (1969), Betty Friedan (1963), Juliet Mitchell (1971), and Shulamith Firestone (1970) all shared at least one common task: to desanctify the family and demystify motherhood. These first-wave thinkers considered the bureaucratic state, capitalism, and the patriarchal family to be three sides of an iron triangle of women's oppression. By the mid-1970s, later feminists were deepening first-wave criticism by further examining the relations between capitalism and patriarchy, the family and the capitalist mode of production, housework and surplus labor, motherhood and oppression.[1] Needless to say, the family did not fare well under this withering criticism. Far from being an idyllic haven in a heartless world, the family appeared to reproduce capitalism at home and to subordinate and oppress women on a daily basis.

But the family soon came to have its feminist defenders, and for some time now a battle has been raging between those feminists who stand by the earlier critiques of the family and those who argue that we must reconsider the value of the family and motherhood for feminist consciousness. The "pro-family" feminists' aim is both a practical and a theoretical one: practical insofar as they seek to wrest the defense of the family from the New Right (which they correctly perceive as having distorted and mystified the role of women as mothers and wives), and theoretical insofar as they intend to reclaim mothering as a dimension of women's experience and defend it as necessary for both gender identity and feminist political consciousness. Among these "pro-family" feminists, two are particularly important in feminist political thought: Sara Ruddick (1980, 1983a, 1983b, 1989) and Jean Bethke Elshtain (1979, 1981, 1982a, 1982b, 1982c, 1982d, 1983a, 1983b, 1986). Seizing upon the "social practice of mothering" and its attendant virtues and "metaphysical attitudes," Ruddick has sought to promote "maternal thinking" as an antidote to a male-dominated culture and as an alternative vision of a "way to be" in the world. Elshtain challenges what she takes to be the matriphobia of the feminist movement by bringing out the political implications of maternal thinking and attempting to restructure political consciousness on the basis of what she calls "social feminism," a term that continues to carry conceptual resonance in contemporary feminist political studies.

In this chapter, I want to pursue the case against "social feminism" that I began in chapter 1 under the label "Maternalism." As I indicated there, Maternalism poses some serious problems that feminists may wish to consider before embracing it as a politics. For example, its emphasis as a political theory on "family values," moral instruction, and the articulation of what constitutes "the good" for all position it in an awkward tension with the liberal principles of negative liberty and individual rights. Whatever else we might think of liberalism, at least it promises to secure the individual (as a rights-bearing fictional entity) against a maternalist "family state" that seeks to promote particular ethical or religious values in the name of uniformity and the good. Maternalism's identification of a "female" sphere where women are the purveyors of truth and virtue also accords (on the basis of a very shaky epistemology) special moral and political status to a gendered category (that is, women as mothers) that does more to reassert some fundamental patriarchal suppositions than challenge them. Finally, the Maternalists' commitment to mothering as a model for politics and political consciousness is based upon a hierarchical, inegalitarian ideal (that is, the mother-child relation) that is not evidently rooted in democratic principles (for example, political egalitarianism, collective self-governance, the activity of citizens as equals and peers, the pooling of sovereignty, reflexive cooperation and respect—not love—for others), or even particularly committed to them. In spite of its effort to find something unique in women's identity as (actual and potential) mothers, Maternalism distorts or defines too narrowly the meaning of women's lives (voices, feelings) by privileging domestic and caretaking activities as the source of a transformational politics. But women are not uniquely identified by maternal thinking, nor does maternal thinking necessarily promote the kind of democratic politics that social feminism purports to foster.

My critique proceeds as follows. In the first section, I briefly reconstruct Elshtain's argument with an eye to its political implications. In the second section, I counter Elshtain's view of the relationship between the public and private realms by way of considering her interpretations of Aristotle and *Antigone* (1982a). The implications of these interpretative excursions into Greek political thought are developed in the final section where I argue that maternal thinking and social feminism cannot deliver on the kind of politics or feminist political consciousness they claim to underwrite as a social ideal.

The Case for Social Feminism

The hallmark of Elshtain's "social feminism" is her attempt to "make a case for family ties" and the practice of mothering (1982b, 447). Her case proceeds both historically, by reconsidering episodes in the history of political thought from the standpoint of the treatment of women, and programmatically, by criticizing current feminist theories and by offering her own "reconstructive ideal of public and private" (1981, 337, 343). Elshtain wants to show that the family is neither the reactionary and repressive institution that its Marxist feminist and leftist critics expose nor the perfectly harmonious world of Filmerian patriarchs and the New Right. In the face of these critics and apologists, both left and right, she insists, "the family remains the locus of the deepest and most resonant human ties, the most enduring hopes, the most intractable conflicts, the most poignant tragedies and the sweetest triumphs human life affords" (1983a, 183).

Making short work of the radical right, Elshtain levels criticism mainly at recent, second-wave, feminist thought. In her view, previous feminism threatens to demean or destroy women's most powerful experiences, perhaps their very identities. What survives the demeaning or the destruction are some unacceptable alternatives: the distortion of identity for purposes of shock value (that is, the way some radical feminists appropriate the terms "hags" and "witches"); the juridical leveling of identity and the elevation of the "social" (that is, the way liberal feminists understand women and men merely as equal legal entities); or the reduction of female domestic practices into an instrumental, detached language (that is, the way some Marxist feminists categorize women as reproducers).

Social feminism is expressly designed to correct these liabilities and to supplant these other feminist alternatives. For the sake of new feminist politics, it seeks to foster the identity of women-as-mothers and establish the moral primacy of the family along with the private realm of human life. For Elshtain (1982a, 56) the family is existentially paramount because humans are, as she writes, "first and foremost not political or economic man, but family men and women." Moreover, because the family has a "trans-historical" existence, it "constitutes our common humanity" and so is the "universal basis for human culture" (1981, 327). These claims are both morally and existentially significant, for it is in the family that human beings experience the most ennobling dimensions of existence: long-term ties with specific others, the need for roots, obligation to kin, intimacy, love, reciprocity, and attentiveness.

Thus the family makes a morality of responsibility possible. So Elshtain (1982b, 447) hardly dissembles when she openly declares that "the feminism I seek is not reducible to a clever strategic move; it is, instead, the affirmation of moral imperatives and their insertion into the heart of feminist politics." The result of this angioplastic theoretical maneuver is, in Elshtain's telling, a life-saving event for feminism.

Thus for Elshtain, the family is the most elevated and primary realm of human life. It has existential priority and moral superiority over the realm of politics, as well as civil society and the state. To dramatize the radicalness of this position, Elshtain (1981, 327) contrasts social feminism with the 2,500-year-old tradition of Western political thought:

> Aristotle and all the other political theorists down through the centuries who asserted the primacy of politics and viewed man (the male, at any rate, if not generic humanity) as preeminently a political animal even as they downgraded or simply took for granted the private sphere, were guilty of a serious distortion.

To remedy this Aristotelian distortion, Elshtain suggests, social feminists not only must reject the patriarchalism (whether implicit or explicit) in centuries of Western thought but also reverse the normative priority of the (allegedly) male public realm over the (allegedly) female private realm.

At least in light of its attempted reversal of the tradition of political thought, social feminism has an affinity with traditional conservatism. Both emphasize the family, traditional bonds of kinship, the web of relationships that emerge from a respect for and remembrance of past generations, and a sense of rootedness. All of these values are "conservative" in their attempt to conserve and maintain the moral fabric of the family and its gendered practices. Nevertheless, social feminism does not purport to be a conservative case against liberalism, but rather a feminist one. What makes Elshtain's argument expressly feminist is her claim that women's experience in the private realm, as mothers, provides the only grounds, indeed the "moral imperative," for countering the prevailing liberal-individualist worldview. Elshtain (1981, 243) explicitly rejects the notion that mothering is simply one "role" among others in the social world. Rather, mothering is "a complicated, rich, ambivalent, vexing, joyous, activity" that "carries profoundly resonant emotional and sexual imperatives." Women as mothers, in Elshtain's account (1982a, 55), are the preservers of "vulnerable human life," and the attitude that distinguishes maternal thinking upholds the principle that "the reality of a single human child [must] be kept before the mind's eye." Accordingly, what counts as failure within the maternal perspective is "the death, injury or damage of a child through carelessness or neglect or the shunting or shaming of a child through over-control and domination" (1982d, 346).

With the reality of a single human child before its eye, maternal thinking entails some striking political implications. In contrast to the kind of bureaucratic-administrative abstractionism that is fathered by the liberal order, the social practice of mothering generates a mentality that emphasizes attentiveness toward others and is personal, empathic, and loving. The tragedy of the contemporary world is that concrete human lives are in jeopardy. A "technocratic public order," a "socially irresponsible corporate structure," an "unjust economic system that denies families a living," and "bureaucratic statism" Elshtain writes, undermine the "concrete specificity" of human beings and "the needs of children" (1982b, 448). Thus "seizure," "control," and the "judgment by impersonal standards"—the hallmarks of these administrative-bureaucratic entities—must be rejected. The political point, argues Elshtain (1982a, 49), is this: "Were maternal thinking to be taken as the base for feminist consciousness, a wedge for examining an increasingly overcontrolled public world would open immediately." In this way, maternal thinking can "chasten arrogant public power" while assisting in the creation of a new mode of public discourse centered on the entity commonly referred to today as "our children."

Social feminism, guided by maternal thinking, also chastens what Elshtain (1979, 497) calls the "article of faith" of the contemporary feminist movement: "the personal is political." She reads this credo as a theoretical justification to politicize, criticize, and manipulate the private world of the family and personal life. Social feminism would seek to protect the private sphere from this sort of desecration. By preserving and protecting its "moral imperatives," social feminism would purge feminism's soul of its antifamilial and matriphobic specter and restore an authentic and unique identity to women. From this identity emerges a vital public-moral consciousness and a renewed vision of citizenship. This is the more constructive—or rather, reconstructive—vision of social feminism. Drawing upon the "private virtues" and the "humanizing imperative" that emerge from the social practice of mothering, social feminism forwards a "politics of compassion" and seeks to create an "ethical polity." Although this reconstructive politics is not (yet) fully elaborated, it appears that the "ethical polity" that social feminism imagines embodies a kind of amalgamation of (potentially conflictual) liberal and communitarian principles. Thus Elshtain (1981, 349–353) endorses: (1) privacy and the protection of the private realm from politicization; (2) individual freedom ("from some all encompassing public imperative"); (3) equality (because all individuals are "irreplaceable beings and immortal souls"); (4) pluralism (of "diverse spheres and competing ideals"); (5) nonviolence; (6) civic virtue (based on a "devotion to public, moral responsibilities and ends"); and (7) an active citizenry (in which "men and women alike partake of the public sphere on an equal basis for participatory dignity and equality").

Social feminism promises a great deal, then, from the restoration of women's identities as (potential) mothers, to the creation of a free and ethical polity. Let us now assess the significance of these promises, especially as they apply to a feminist understanding of politics.

Some Questions for Social Feminism

The social feminism that Elshtain supports is open to a number of criticisms (see, for example, Ehrenreich 1983; Berman 1983; Pollitt 2001b). Many of these criticisms seize upon the sociological incompleteness of Elshtain's accounts of the family, the psychological ambiguities that attend the notion of "maternal thinking," and the ontological coherence of her account of women as mothers and practitioners of mothering. There are, for example, the definitional and conceptual problems of just what sorts of relationships and structures count as a "family" and who gets to decide which human relationships count as such and which do not. Elshtain runs against the grain of contemporary developments in law and society that have significantly recast or redefined family structures and practices. She wishes to maintain a coherent account, and not "throw the honorable mantle 'family' over every ad hoc collection of persons who happen to be under one roof at the same time" (1981, 448, 322 n. 30). But where legitimately to throw (or take away) the honorific mantle is not clear. Contemporary feminists and women generally may rightly wonder whether an extended nonnuclear family, a kibbutz, an ashram, a polygamous arrangement of husband and wives, a hippie commune, a single-parent household, a divorced couple who share child care responsibilities, an unmarried couple without children, or a gay or lesbian partnership qualify under what Elshtain (1981, 441) calls the right sort of "genuine commitment of family men and women who [retain] their commitments to and for one another." Elshtain's reference to "family men and women" seems to imply that her image of the family is framed by a heterosexual, two-parent, male:female arrangement (although she does not state this explicitly). How far she wishes to elasticize the normative concept of "family" (and whether children are a required part of the picture) remains a rather cloudy element of her argument.

Feminists with empirical and sociological sensibilities may also want to call attention to the lack of caring and love often displayed in actually existing modern families (however defined and for whatever reasons). This lack may range from professional or upper-class families in which children are not in fact "kept before the mind's eye," although they are otherwise well treated, to those terrible cases of families where battered wives or partners and abused children live in constant fear of mental and physical cruelty at the hands of husbands, boyfriends, partners, brothers, fathers, "uncles" and the like. Should not actual families be investigated before we place women's and feminists' political commitments on an idealized concept that bears only a tentative connection to reality or to real human experience? Of course, some critics contend (rightly, according to the last U.S. Census) that the family is still generally the scene of women's housework, unpaid labor, or of their second shift. As

Katha Pollitt (2001b, 10) notes, "Women are incredibly disadvantaged when they perform traditionally female work—childcare, housework, eldercare— unpaid within families."[2]

These socioeconomic features of the domestic sphere surely impinge upon social feminism's elevation of the family to the status of a normative maternal ideal.[3] Even if we can sort out these problems, however, the question of what constitutes the prerequisites for maternal thinking remains. Does maternal thinking arise biologically, as the consequence of female reproductive organs and the act of giving birth? If you are infertile or without children for whatever reason, can you still practice maternal thinking? Or is maternal thinking a sociological phenomenon, the consequence of practicing resolutely the raising of and caring for children? Does this practice give rise to a special sort of disposition or attitude?[4] Are women maternal thinkers only if they are actual, practicing, mothers, or is it sufficient to have been the daughter of a caring mother, or the child of a loving caretaker who was not your mother? Or are all women, by virtue of being women, somehow universally endowed with the capacity for maternal thinking? If this is so, why call these female capacities *maternal* (as opposed to, say, "female" or "womanly")? And under these circumstances, what constitutes being a female, or a "woman," or acting as a "mother"? Can a man who raises and cares for his children practice "maternal thinking," or is he a "paternal thinker," or by virtue of being a "man" not much of a parental thinker at all? Or is maternal thinking simply shorthand for a particular kind of ethic that is attentive to principles of reciprocity, obligation, caring for, sharing, and love? And, if so, who or what determines which virtues define maternal thinking and which do not? Because social feminism makes its claims and stakes its identity in the name of its unitary subject—women—it must provide adequate responses to these sorts of questions, lest its subject-centered, epistemologically driven foundations crumble into meaninglessness.[5]

These ontological and epistemological issues may or may not prove to be insuperable problems; but until they are addressed and overcome the case for social feminism is incomplete. Nevertheless there are also political problems with social feminism that even a sound foundational epistemology cannot solve. These problems raise questions about social feminism's adequacy as an emancipatory political theory (or at least as a complex of political ideas) bearing upon a new feminist political consciousness. I want to begin this political criticism of social feminism by considering Elshtain's appropriation of two emblematic figures: the philosopher Aristotle and Sophocles's (441 B.C.E.; 1991) tragic character Antigone. Elshtain considers Aristotle and Antigone to be important moments in a reconstructed history of feminist political thought. One of them (Aristotle) is a negative model whom Elshtain interprets as a kind of paradigm for centuries of patriarchal Western philosophical thought.[6] The other (Antigone) she wants to recommend as a source of feminist inspiration in the quest for an ethical polity: we are called forth as "Antigone's

Daughters" (1982a). Elshtain's interpretations are inventive, illustrative of the critical conceptual powers of her social feminism in the case of Aristotle and her programmatic, prescriptive sensibilities for feminists in the case of Antigone. Still, I think these social feminist hermeneutics are open to question and (at least as they are revealed here) illustrative of some of the weaknesses of social feminism as a political project.

Aristotle Meets Antigone

Elshtain's reading of Aristotle focuses upon his conceptualization (primarily in the *Politics*) of the relation between the public realm of the Greek *polis* and the private realm of the household. Aristotle leaves no doubt, Elshtain argues, as to who rightly occupies the private realm of necessity and "mere life," and who rightly occupies, as a citizen, the public realm of the *polis*, the highest form of human association. Preserving "mere life" and undertaking the tasks of household acquisition and economy are the purview of women, slaves, certain kinds of laborers, and "metics" or foreigners. Children also live in this realm, although young males are liberated from it when they come of age as citizens. The private realm Aristotle configures as mute, and its primary occupants are without voice. Here he (1962, 36) pays heed to Sophocles's line: "a modest silence is a woman's crown." The private realm is functional, serving mainly to satisfy primary needs. Here he (1962, 4) quotes Hesiod: "First house, and wife, and ox to draw the plough." The private realm is hierarchic and inegalitarian by nature, according to the rule of nature. Here Aristotle (1962, 32f) relies upon his own authority: "the male is naturally fitter to command than the female. . . . The relation of the male to the female is permanently that in which the statesman [temporarily] stands to his fellow-citizens." Aristotle allows that rule of this familial sort is of a higher nature than, say, rule over an animal, but the fact is that, in his view, women and slaves rank only slightly above oxen in their relation to male Greek citizens. Conversely, women and slaves cannot partake or participate in the good life of the *polis* where Greek males, "naturally fitter to command," bask in heroic admiration of themselves and each other and "aim at being equal" as public citizens (Aristotle 1962, 32; Elshtain 1981, 346).

Although she does not put it quite this way, Elshtain seems to read Aristotle as an objectionable elitist because, in his normative account of political life, the sociological status quo and the existing conventions of Greek culture and society are simply reinforced: women are confined to the private realm of the household, slavery is justified, and aliens are dealt with as barbarians who have only limited recourse to equal treatment within the state. Elshtain rightly calls attention to the oppressive institutions and "necessary" identities that Aristotle accepts and methodically justifies as naturally given. But Elshtain's criticisms go also to Aristotle's conceptual foundations, especially to the practical-normative content that he assigns to the public versus the private sphere, a distorted opposition that serves to glorify the ethical and political superiority of the public space while undermining the private realm of the household (*oikia*). "It is important to remember," Elshtain (1981, 346) argues in a realist mode, "that most of the debates in the 'public space' had little to do with great or noble ends, and much to do with jockeying for position and pelf, raising money by any means necessary." So Aristotle's ethical conception of the public, Elshtain suggests, is driven by a sociological deceit. Accordingly, the social feminist response to Aristotelian elitism is to rescue the *oikia* in the name of "family man and woman" while embracing the (Christian) virtues of love and humility, reverence and care, as touchstones of a public, feminized political consciousness.

In effect, social feminism turns Aristotle's account of public and private on its head. The private realm of women (and children, slaves, mechanics, and foreigners) is now privileged over the *polis* of the public man, and the domestic sphere of the maternal household is accorded normative priority over the male polis of citizens. Under this critique, the public realm is affiliated with "the state," and cast as the dark and ominous opposition to the virtuous private realm that is affiliated with the family. Indeed, in Elshtain's telling, the public is statist, cold, brutal, bureaucratic and imminently in need of maternal chastening. The political conclusion that feminism must draw from this Aristotelian somersault is that women should embrace "the perspective that flows from their experiences" and resist "the imperious demands and overweening claims of state power" and a public life "created by men" (Elshtain 1982a, 56; 1982b, 447). Nevertheless, it is important to notice that in effecting this rather creative act of normative-conceptual repositioning, social feminism does not really dismantle the framework of public:private, it simply reconfigures it. Elshtain (1989, 225; 1982a, 49 f.) herself claims that she wants to reinvest "the powers and dignities of women's private sphere" with meaning and counter the notion of the public world "as the only sphere within which individuals made real choices . . . or [have] efficacious control." In effect, then, as a conceptual program social feminism remains locked into the same basic framework of public and private spheres and the same gendered identification of those spheres that it identifies in Aristotelian political thought.[7] The virtues of private woman may now be lauded over the vices of public man and bureaucratic statism, yet social feminism remains conceptually indebted to an Aristotelian public:private dichotomy.[8]

Nowhere is the impact of Elshtain's commitment to this public:private model revealed more graphically than when she mobilizes a particular interpretation of Sophocles's (441 B.C.E.; 1991) tragedy *Antigone*. Antigone, Elshtain tells us, is the exemplar of the private realm in all its robust strength and familial attentiveness. There is no question as to which of her alternatives Elshtain thinks Antigone chooses. This is the drama of a woman pitted against "the arrogant insistencies of statecraft," a defender of the "domain of women" and "primordial family morality." Antigone defies the abstract obligations of the state as represented by Creon the king, and rejects public life. Not surprisingly, Elshtain (1982a, 55) offers Sophocles's heroine as an archetype for a "female identity" and a "feminist perspective."[9]

Now it may seem to some that using Antigone as an archetype for feminists in the late twentieth century is odd or anachronistic. But assuming that this strategy makes sense, it is not clear to me that Elshtain has interpreted the meaning of *Antigone* in a way that is particularly efficacious for feminism. To appreciate this, let us first consider a more generous interpretation of Aristotle's account of politics, and then return to Antigone.

Aristotle's Politics

On a generous reading of the *Politics,* Aristotle might be understood as arguing that politics (or the activity of political association) is not (as Elshtain implies) solely a spatial category that is locatable in a particular "realm." Rather, it is a special kind of human activity that is existentially primary to all other human activities (for example, weaving, cooking, farming, herding, shipping, building, acquiring, banking, sculpting, fighting, playing sports, making money, and the like) regardless of whether they are elements of the public or the private realms. Aristotle appears to think this for two reasons: First, human existence must be viewed as a complex of diverse practices and "associations" that have distinct natures and ends but are nonetheless integrally connected and aim toward some good. These practices include the provision of necessities of life, procreation, the care of children, the acquisition and exchange of goods, the production of artifacts and institutions, the making of culture—in short, all those things that distinguish human societies. But Aristotle goes on to illuminate one activity or association as existentially primary because it surveys all other particular activities, relationships, and structures from a general point of view and determines which will be "private" and which "public." This primary activity is politics (or citizenship) which Aristotle (1962, 1) calls "the most sovereign and inclusive" of all associations. By this, he means to suggest that politics is an integrative activity; hence the *politikos* bears an essential difference in relation to all other persons in all other associations.

To put this otherwise, in Aristotle's formulation, all human relations, arrangements, and occupations are examined in light of *politikos* and made its subject matter. Thus it was the case in Aristotle's world, just as it is in ours, that household life and its activities, as well as social practices and economic arrangements, are subject to political power and political decision making. Family practices, control over family property, the rights of children, the nature of schooling and child labor laws, benefits for single mothers, the regulation of birth control, subsistence insurance—all of these things are actually or potentially open to political control and determination. Even the decision to allow them to remain "private"—that is, untouched or unregulated by the institutions and organs of government—is ultimately a matter of politics. Now, the forms for reaching these decisions have varied from era to era, polity to polity, constitution to constitution—they have been made by kings, oligarchs, dictators, czars, presidents, sultanates, politburos, parliaments, clerics, revolutionary cadres, constitutional monarchies, faceless bureaucrats, and "the people" as self-governing citizens. Aristotle was interested in categorizing these constitutional forms according to who rules (the One, the Few, the Many) but also in terms of just and unjust. Thus justice is the norm in kingship, aristocracy, and polity (or "constitutional government"), while injustice prevails in democracy, oligarchy, and tyranny (1962, 114–115). But the driving point behind all of these various forms of constitutions is that politics, however organized, is the activity through which the parameters of society are delineated, relations of power are secured (or challenged), and the institutions of family or economy are sanctified (or dismantled). This is why, according to Aristotle (1962, 6), politics is existentially prior to all other human activities and practices.

There is another way in which Aristotle conceives of politics as existentially primary, and it involves the arrangement of "ruler and ruled." Aristotelian metaphysics and ontology are generally informed by the idea that all things in the world, from oak trees, bronze vases, calico cats, triremes, and harbor walls to Achilles's body, the House of Atreus, the constitution of Thebes, and the relations of the household are arranged according to the "natural" relation of form (the structural principle that rules) over matter (the "stuff" that is ruled over and ordered). "We may thus conclude," Aristotle (1962, 35) writes, "that it is a general law that there should be naturally ruling elements and elements naturally ruled." Within the political association alone, however, Aristotle thinks that human beings potentially break the hierarchical arrangement of ruler over ruled, collectively and inclusively relating to one another not as strong over weak, fast over slow, beautiful over ugly, master over apprentice, or parent over child—that is, not according to the principle of rule and subordination—but as equals who render judgments on matters of shared importance, deliberate over issues of common concern, and act together in concert. In other words, in the political association, the relation among equals is the relation of each to all, simultaneously ruling and being ruled. Or, as Aristotle (1962, 32) puts it, "the members of a political association aim by their very nature at being equal and differing in nothing," by which he means that in political activity alone, differences of wealth, strength, talent, or beauty are not the standards, nor is the relation among citizens characterized by superior over inferior. Aristotle's word for this activity of simultaneously ruling and being ruled is "citizenship"—which he also calls the good life (32, 4–5, 110–113). For when human beings realize their identities through the unique and shared activity of citizenship, as a *politai*, they exercise together the power to determine the conditions of their "mere" lives. Aristotle's point is not that citizens are the glorious warrior heroes of a male public realm, but rather that citizenship *as an activity* is the best form of public life; it possesses great value in itself and is thereby a public good. This endless activity of collective self-determination, of (rightly) deliberating and deciding on matters of significance to the polity, of sharing in the holding of office, is what it means to live virtuously day by day. This normative ideal that Aristotle forwards is rooted in a principle that favors equality over inequality, and a worldly orientation that argues for the diverse activity of the many over the static unity of the one.

Now, without question, Aristotle's political theory is, at one very evident level, exclusionary and elitist, as many commentators and critics have charged. Very few political theorists today (well, almost none) would find Aristotle's views on the "right relation" of women and slaves in the social order defensible in any way, although the interpretations that inform these judgments certainly vary in their adequacy and fair-mindedness.[10] But do Aristotle's arguments on the status of women and slaves form a *necessary* part of his account of politics and citizenship so that his conception of political association is rendered utterly irredeemable? Or can we rightly and justifiably read and extract from Aristotle's political thought an egalitarian dimension that is worth defending with a view toward a programmatic and ethical vision of citizenship? These questions raise difficult matters in text interpretation and the politics of hermeneutics that have long vexed feminists working in the history of political thought. And I cannot pursue them here. For the moment, however, all I want to recommend is a minimal hermeneutic position that finds in the text of the *Politics* a conceptualization that is worth pursuing, whatever other elements we may wish to abandon or dismiss. This conceptualization is Aristotle's picture of the good life as a context within which citizens relate to each other as equals, act politically, and collectively deliberate about the ends of the polity. I want to suggest that this Aristotelian idea warrants consideration, if not wholesale appropriation, as part of a feminist project. At the very least, it carries within it a normative principle that is also central to feminism: the principled refusal to accept hierarchical arrangements and solutions imposed from above as the best and most just way to organize political life. Thus my aim is not to make feminist theory into a mirror of Aristotelianism, but rather to recommend Aristotle's conceptualization of politics and citizenship to feminist theory.

Antigone Speaks

Related lessons follow if we deploy some of these Aristotelian insights by way of interpreting *Antigone*. Rather than viewing the tension in the drama, as Elshtain does, as about public (man) versus private (woman) that pits the vices of patriarchal public power against the virtues of private familial love, we might read *Antigone* as illustrative of two opposing *political* positions. In this reading, Creon represents the power of the state, and Antigone marks the *ethos* (traditions, habits, norms, and mores) of a particular privileged community

(Thebes) that Creon's mandate threatens in the form of arbitrary and authoritarian rule. If we interpret *Antigone* this way, the character emerges not simply as sister to Polyneices whose familial loyalties place her against the king (who is also her uncle), but as a citizen of Thebes whose defense of her brother is rooted in a devotion to the gods and to the ways and laws of her city. On the other side, Creon is not simply a manifestation of "the male public" in all of its overweening power but rather the exemplar of a certain kind of political relation (of ruler over ruled) to which Antigone, at least in this circumstance, stands in opposition.

Elshtain's reading of *Antigone* as a paragon of familial values is not so much mistaken as incomplete, for it tends to overlook the thing that makes Antigone more than a just another prototypic female who symbolizes the virtues of the private realm. The reason why Antigone is a heroine (or at least a most interesting Greek female figure) and Ismene, her sister, is not has nothing to do with female virtues or loyalty to the family as such, for both sisters loved their brother. Both of them vividly feel the sting of Creon's insult to the community's rituals of burial and the family's honor. The difference between Antigone and Ismene rather involves political action and performative speech, the things that cross (and thereby renegotiate) the boundary between the private (family) and the public (state). Thus Antigone treats Creon's refusal to allow Polyneices's burial not just as a singular personal insult but as a wholesale threat to the *sensus communis*, to the sense that founds a particular community called Thebes and gives it its direction. But Antigone is not simply reaffirming an existing cultural norm. As Judith Butler (2000, 82) contends, "in acting, as one who has no right to act, [Antigone] upsets the vocabulary of kinship that is a precondition of the human, implicitly raising the question for us of what those preconditions really must be." To get at the difference between Antigone and Ismene, then, we might say that Antigone quite consciously and readily performs a citizen's political speech act, an act that constitutes a courageous defiance of the king, a challenge to the political norm of "ruler over ruled." Ismene, obviously conflicted, nevertheless remains locked in the structure of the despotic household, accepting (if begrudgingly) the rulership of Creon's state, abjuring politics.[11] She begs her sister not to challenge Creon, to stay at home and remain silent. Ismene cannot get over the wall of the household, partly because she is afraid and partly because she simply does not carry within herself the will to challenge hierarchy and resist tyranny or the determination to speak truth to power. (Nor does Ismene share her sister's morbid fascination with corpses, decay, and death; but that is another matter worthy of a longer analysis of Sophocles's all too human tragedy.)

Elshtain wants to make Antigone a model for social feminism, so there are some interesting matters of politics at stake here. Because Elshtain's social feminism posits a world divided into dual realms and human beings as either virtuous private females or arrogant public males, it tends to present a picture of the world as a static relation between bounded and divided "realms," not to mention bounded and divided sexes. Part of the problem may be Elshtain's difficulty in distinguishing conceptually the male public realm from politics and action—she tends to collapse the two into one, leaving no conceptual room for that dynamic zone "in between" public and private, the phenomenological and conflictual zone of human speech and interaction. This is the zone that Antigone enters when she takes up the challenge to Creon and engages him in direct, intense, dialogic interaction, refusing to aid and abet his undermining of the *sensus communis*. But Antigone is a model for Elshtain not because she represents the dynamic force of political speech coming alive as performative action, but rather because she is a stand-in for the private realm and family piety (if not maternalism or sisterhood), which are also the objects of Elshtain's veneration. Hence the defining aim of social feminism is not political action but rather the norm that Elshtain extracts from the familial:female side of her binary spatial model: "the preservation of life."[12]

Do Maternal Values Promote Democratic Politics?

Without question, the protection of life is a necessary prerequisite for any ethical political order. Who would disagree that the growth and preservation of children are vital social imperatives, or that the protection of vulnerable human life is a vital concern? But surely a movement or a political consciousness committed simply to caring for "vulnerable human existence," as Elshtain's social feminism is, offers no standards—indeed it can only echo the silence of Ismene—when it comes to judging between political alternatives or establishing political values that are worthy of feminist support. An enlightened despotism, a socialist welfare state, a theocracy, and a democratic republic may all protect children's lives or show compassion for the poor. But what standards for judging further among these political orders can social feminism offer us? Its moral imperative—the preservation and growth of children—has been fulfilled. This should be a matter of considerable concern for social feminists because, as we have seen Elshtain (1981, 349–353) intimates that social feminism is committed to a particular kind of political order—namely, a democratic community (if not a democratic politics) in which "men and women alike partake of the public sphere on an equal basis for participatory dignity and equality." In a generous acknowledgment, she applauds "those aspects of Aristotelian thought that turn on the imperative that acting in common together with others to agreed upon ends is a worthy form of human life" (1981, 351). But Elshtain fails to provide a theoretical argument that links maternal thinking and the social practice of mothering *to* "acting in common together," much less to democratic values or a democratic "community." So there is a considerable amount of slippage between the normative account of women's maternal, familial practices that frames Elshtain's social feminism and the political theory of democracy that this account is presumed to support.

What would it take for social feminism to secure its connection to democracy in a way that moves it beyond merely calling for a more ethical polity? As a start, social feminism would need to be able to show, at the theoretical-conceptual level, that maternal virtues are conceptually connected to, or that the social practice of mothering causally brings about, specifically democratic values and practices: active citizenship, collective participation, the pooling of sovereignty in the interest of self-governance, a respect for deliberation, discussion, and debate, a commitment to political equality. But this social feminism (at least as Elshtain has constructed it so far) cannot do. Neither can maternal virtues be political in the required sense, nor can maternalism be the model for (a new politics of) democracy. This is because, on Elshtain's own account, mothering emerges out of an activity that is special, distinctive, unlike any other. We must conclude, then, that this activity is unlike the activity of democratic citizenship; the two cannot be viewed as parallel, encompassing the same attributes, abilities, and ways of knowing. Simply being a mother—no matter how perfect or imperfect, knowledgeable or ignorant, loving or withholding—is not in itself the embodiment of the requisite capacities for citizenship. (Good) mothers may also be (good) citizens (just as good citizens may be lousy mothers), but their being (good) mothers does not make them (good) citizens. These two kinds of human association are not interchangeable, nor are their respective modes of knowing or doing synonymous.

We might press this point further by considering also the structural relationship and the distribution of power between a mother and child. Mother:child is not analogous to the relationship among citizens even when (and that is, as yet, empirically undetermined) it displays the virtues that Elshtain praises. The mother:child relation is (if only temporarily) hierarchic and, in Aristotle's terms, marked by the arrangement of ruler over ruled. (Indeed, Aristotle [1962, 11, 33] himself identifies "the parental association" as one in which the principle of rule and subordination prevails; it is "like that of a king over his subjects.") Within this arrangement, mother and child occupy radically different positions in terms of power and control. The child is unavoidably dependent upon the mother, in a situation of subordination. What psychologists call "the need relations" in this arrangement are highly differentiated as well: the infant's is absolute; the mother's is relative.[13] In other words, regardless of whether it is benign, punishing, or loving, the special and distinctive aspects of mothering emerge out of a decidedly lopsided dyad, in which one person, the adult, has significant power and exercises a great deal of control over another, the child.[14] One might rightly contend that "the hand that rocks the cradle *rules* the world"; it does not share in ruling it. Thus, mothering is an intimate, exclusive, dualistic, and particularistic activity within which the mother is directed toward the preservation of the child, not toward the activity of mothering for its own sake. Following Elshtain, we might call this activity (at least in its ethically reconstructed dimension) the exercise of attentive love.

Democratic politics, on the other hand, is collective, inclusive, and generalized (I do not mean "universalized"). Because it is a condition in which the many aim at acting as peers and equals, it is decidedly nonhierarchic and nondualistic. If Aristotle is right and citizenship is an active condition in which many persons are simultaneously in a condition of ruling and being ruled, then nothing seems farther from this activity than the structural arrangement that distinguishes the ruler-over-ruled relation between mother and child. Furthermore, the relation among citizens is not like the attentive love that a mother invests in a child, for citizens are not intimately, but politically, involved with each other. (In the *Nicomachean Ethics* Aristotle theorizes the relation of citizens in political association in terms of friendship, not in terms of love. But in the face of the technicization of modern life and the disenchantment of the polis, even Aristotle's model is inadequate to the task of citizenship in modernity.) Indeed, social feminism may be dangerously close to committing a version of one of the metaphorical extravagances of the French Revolution, namely, the demand that citizens exemplify the "brotherhood of man" (only in social feminism we might readily substitute the "motherhood of women").

Literally, of course, citizens cannot relate to one another as sister to sister or mother to child; but even metaphorically the terminology depoliticizes by familizing. (It also leaves open the question of who determines which citizens are the "children" and which are the "mothers.") Consider Aristotle's (1962, 47) pertinent riposte to Plato's move to familize the polity: "Just as a little sweet wine, mixed with a great deal of water, produces a tasteless mixture, so family feeling is diluted and tasteless when family names have so little meaning as they have in a constitution of the Platonic order." The attempt to familize the vocabulary of politics was also anathema to Marx, which is why he refused to join The League of the Just (later the Communist League), until they agreed to eliminate their slogan "All Men Are Brothers." Marx is said to have observed that in any case there are some men whose brother he would not want to be.[15]

To argue, then, that the virtues that arise from the social practice of mothering give rise to the values that inform the political practice of citizenship is to misperceive the meaning of political life and, if Elshtain is right, misconstrue the "metaphysical attitudes" that mothers are said to experience. Intimacy, love, and the special attentiveness between mother and child are valuable things in part because they are exclusive; they cannot be experienced just anywhere or by just anyone with just any other. That is why, if they are to sustain women's identities in the way Elshtain wants, they must not be made the principles to guide a democratic politics, for intimacy can quickly lose its purchase, and love its "concrete specificity," when they are marshaled for public, political ends. This prohibition does not necessarily apply to caring, a quite different principle than love or intimacy, as Joan Tronto (1993) persuasively argues. Indeed, Arendt (1958, 57, 72) contends that the intimacy that marks "the realm of privacy" offers shelter and harbor—a place to remain hidden—from the harsh glare of the public realm. "Only the modern age . . ." she observes, "has discovered how rich and manifold the realm of the hidden can be under the conditions of intimacy."[16]

When Elshtain reminds us of the fragility and the resiliency of family life and the special capacities or attitudes of women-as-mothers, she seems to allow all of this. But when she urges us to make maternal thinking a "wedge" for examining the public world and to see it as a way of "diffusing" attentive love throughout society, she is undermining precisely what is most valuable about mothering and love—their deeply personal and intensely intimate natures.[17] Perhaps this is why Elshtain's language tends to strain when she attempts to make maternal virtues the basis for democratic action. The very impossibility of such a task reveals itself in a rhetoric of sharp-edged words like "wedge" or "insert" or "template" or terms like "diffused" that inadvertently reveal the difficulties of making maternal thinking an evenly distributed ethical-political norm. To spread it is to diffuse it; to diffuse it is to dilute it into something that is no longer recognizably maternal. To paraphrase Aristotle (1962, 47) again on a somewhat related matter regarding love and political association in Plato, the result would be "merely a watery sort of fraternity" (or in this case perhaps a maternity). Once it is extended and made the condition of political association, maternal thinking loses its meaning and politics loses its appearance.[18]

I want to reiterate that the object of my concern involves what Elshtain can vindicate conceptually for social feminism, given her claims that mothering and maternal thinking provide not simply an ethical model for political community but a framework for a democratic politics. Hence I am anxious to argue that the conceptual (and practical) affinity between social feminism and democratic citizenship that Elshtain thematizes carries difficulties not only at the level of ethics but also (and more important for my purposes) at the level of politics. This is because Elshtain recommends a hierarchical and exclusive model of human interaction (mother:child) as the basis for a presumably emancipatory and democratic politics. But, at the level of theory, the first move cannot conceptually vindicate the second if we presume (as we should) that at the very least democracy challenges hierarchy and exclusivity as bases for political life rather than seeking to recapitulate them.

Women, Mothers, Feminist Politics

A point of clarification: On the practical-normative level of actually existing political action, I do not wish to contest the efficacy or the relevance for democracy of what Patricia Boling (1996, 119) calls private "intimate-realm experiences."[19] As Boling reminds us, over the past decades some women have organized politically and taken effective action under a consciously appropriated vocabulary of "mothers" (whether as an interest group or more spontaneously within the public realm). Women may be motivated in the first instance to enter politics because of special interests they have as mothers or potential mothers, under the sign of "protectors of children" or "under a profound imperative to preserve human life" or family values (Elshtain 1982a), and they have done so. The examples we now have are plentiful and important: in the United States, Mothers Against Drunk Driving, Mothers of Love Canal, the "Million Mom March" in Washington, D.C., in support of gun control; in England, the mothers of Greenham Common who protest nuclear war and the proliferation of nuclear weaponry; the mothers and wives of victims of the Chernobyl nuclear reactor explosion who recently held demonstrations against nuclear power and state obstruction; and, perhaps most famously, the Mothers of the Plaza de Mayo in Buenos Aires, Argentina, who (often at great risk) continue to demand accountability from the military and the government about the fate of their disappeared sons, daughters, husbands, brothers, and friends (and about whom Elshtain herself writes instructively). My aim, therefore, is not to recommend that feminism in its theoretic mode reject or dismiss democratic movements or politics that issue out of the action-coordination of self-identified mothers, or in the name of a politicized motherhood, for these activities are not only practical guideposts in the political history of female citizenship, resistance, rebellion, protest, and power in the public world but also integral to the ground-level flourishing of democratic politics itself.

However, once feminism in its *theoretic* mode attempts to impose upon the subject of women a unifying category (as social feminism does with mothering and the maternal), then the politics of democratic action and the discursive modalities of its distribution are for all intents and purposes obliterated. The threat to a feminism that seeks to be expressly democratic lies precisely in theoretic frameworks like social feminism, where the theorist's urge to assign a valorizing and unitary group identity (like "mother") suppresses a concept of the political that recognizes the individual particularity of women as citizens in the political world. In this sort of move a static, ascriptive social-familial categorization is granted theoretic priority over a dynamic politics of action so that "the social" supersedes the political. (In this sense Elshtain's "social" feminism is aptly named.) At the level of feminist theory, the privileging of social identity poses at least two more threats to a democratic feminism. First, by assigning predominance to a carefully prescribed "whatness," social feminism abjures the open-ended boundlessness Arendt (1958, 187) calls "the living flux of acting and speaking" that discloses "who" somebody is. Thus when a theoretical perspective like social feminism succeeds in convincing its intended audience that emancipatory possibilities lie not in the articulations of each individual "who," but rather in the appropriation of a singular identity infused with a singular purpose (such as "the preservation of vulnerable human life"), feminist politics (in the Aristotelian, Antigonian, and Arendtian senses that I have been conceptualizing here) reaches a dead end. In other words, social feminism's shift from politics to identity brings with it the gradual displacement of the Aristotelian principle that "life is action and not production" (Aristotle 1962, 10) in favor of the production and deployment of a construct ("all women are mothers, or potential mothers") that severely restricts the content of political life. In a theory like social feminism, the identity of women as mothers is reproducible, thus called into the service of shaping the "stuff" of a degenerated public realm that awaits its correction. Under these circumstances, politics is objectified into a thing ("public realm") and political speech is made instrumental, a set of means geared toward a specific end ("chastening arrogant public power").

The other threat that attends the theoretical privileging of a social group identity over the action dynamic of politics involves the direction of what we might loosely call the "causal arrow" between the social and the political. Consider, for example, Boling's (1996, 118) claim that "Women's distinctive approach to political organizing in many cases has had . . . much to do with their role as mothers" (this is a formulation that often appears, in various articulations, within Maternalist and standpoint political theories). The causal arrow in this formulation points decisively from the social (taken as primary) toward the political (taken as secondary), so that it presents the politics of female citizens as a derivative of attitudes, practices, or orientations that develop out of the private sphere and then become "politicized." But what if we turned this arrow, so that feminism actually held a theoretic stance that privileged participatory citizenship and the plurality of action over social roles and attitudes? If feminism did this, then "political organizing" could be grasped in reverse, as an activity that potentially politicizes the family, opening its hierarchic structures to scrutiny, its modalities of domination to possible democratization, and its practices to debate. Could not the experience of acting and speaking together with others in the public realm even challenge the order of mothering? From this viewpoint, which follows Arendt in giving politics an existential priority over labor and work, is it possible to suppose that by acting and speaking in differentiated plurality, ruling and being ruled as citizens, women can also become better (or at least different kinds of) mothers? As Aristotle puts the matter (in the usual gendered language), "A good man, like a good citizen, will need knowledge from both points of view" (1962, 105). The causal arrow moves in both directions. Most important, however, in the thematizing of politics over social identity, feminist theory might escape the identitarian grip of the maternal (without undermining real, existing mothers) and restore to itself a political project that values citizen action and struggles for democracy.[20] When and if this happens, perhaps feminism's reconciliation of theory and *praxis* can begin.

Chapter 3

Merely Combating the Phrases of This World

Liberalism, Communitarianism, and Recent Democratic Theory

Some books are important not because they resolve a puzzle or pose a problem in a new way but because they are symptomatic of certain deeply rooted and collectively shared patterns of thinking or conceptualizing within a particular moment in time. Such books are potentially illuminating insofar as they point to issues, even crises, in thinking or theorizing that far outweigh the subject matter that is immediately to hand. The books in political theory at issue in this chapter address the subject matter of Western democracy and citizenship.[1] I am pleased to report that none of them exhibit the alleged "strange silence" (Isaac 1995) toward the European revolutions of 1989, the dissolution of communism, or the end of the cold war that, a few years ago, provoked a spirited group symposium about the political relevance of political theorizing (including William Connolly, Kirstie McClure, Elizabeth Kiss, Michael Gillespie, and Seyla Benhabib) in the pages of the international journal *Political Theory*.

Quite explicitly, these books locate themselves within the historical and political context of the "collapse of Communism" (Mouffe 1993, 3; Zolo 1992, vii); "the dissolution of the Soviet Union" (Phillips 1993, 2); and "the end of the Cold War" (Bridges 1994, 14). Each recognizes the perils for democracy that accompany the subsequent rise of "destructive nationalisms [in] Central Europe" (Phillips 1993, 2); or the "recrudescence of nationalism" (Botwinick 1993, 3); and the fragmentation of "previously united multinational political communities" (Beiner 1995, 3). If these introductory remarks do not exactly secure their authors' intentions to heed the symposium's call to open political theory "to the dramatic political experiences of our time," at least they encourage the reader to anticipate some sort of confluence between contemporary democratic theory on the one hand and what C. B. Macpherson once called "the real world of democracy" on the other, in the turbulent context of the third millenium (Isaac 1995, 650).

In the face of the post–cold war era, each of these authors also identifies particular political crises that face liberal democratic societies in the West and constitute what Ronald Beiner (1995, 3) terms "the problem of citizenship." Chantal Mouffe (1993, 4) and Anne Phillips (1993, 5), in their respective collections of previously published essays, link the defeat of communism to a "deep crisis of political identity" that confuses our understandings of friend and enemy and confounds our "yearnings for an undifferentiated unity" as the basis for democratic politics. Beiner (1995, 3) introduces his edited volume (of previously published articles by J. G. A. Pocock, Michael Ignatieff, George Armstrong Kelly, Richard Flathman, Michael Walzer, Iris Marion Young, Alasdair MacIntyre, Joseph Carens, Jürgen Habermas, and Will Kymlicka and Wayne Norman) by noting a series of "political dilemmas"—ethnic and sectarian conflicts, mass migration and unemployment, economic globalization— that exacerbate already "jeopardized identities" and raise "anew deep questions about what binds citizens together into a shared community." Thomas Bridges (1994, 16) addresses what he calls "the most significant cultural task facing North Atlantic liberal democracies"—the precise formulation of "civic moral ideals." Aryeh Botwinick (1993, 4, 12, 59, 14) considers "the true globalization of democracy" and the possibilities of "participatory praxis" in terms of the reality of limited economic growth, "homogenizing technology," and the erosion of "modernist culture."

As Beiner's excellent and wide-ranging collection of essays makes clear, the crisis of identity/difference (in national and international, as well as group and cultural terms), the creation of shared yet diverse communities, the articulation of civic moral ideals, the meaning of civil society, the challenges of multiculturalism, the problems facing participatory social movements, the procedures of deliberative democratic practices, and, above all, the phenomenon of *citizenship*—whether as an "ideal" (Pocock), a "myth" (Ignatieff), or a "theoretical problem" (Beiner)—are the themes that animate much democratic political theory today. Kymlicka and Norman's "Survey of Recent Work on Citizenship Theory" (in Beiner) also provides a very useful overview of the state of the current literature. Insofar as the other books here under review also take up these themes in various ways, they offer a composite sketch of just how diversified the subject matter of democratic theory has become since the era when, in Flathman's words, "notionally scientific theories of citizenship" predominated (in Beiner 1995, 106), and economic models of party competition, pluralist concepts of the democratic "market," and paradigms of "elites and masses" governed the field. The theorizing of citizenship, as Beiner's collection reveals, has come a long way since then.

Yet, at the same time, and despite the lively expansion and diversification of the problem of citizenship that they exhibit at the level of subject matter, I find in Bridges, Botwinick, Mouffe, Phillips, and Beiner's introduction (to his otherwise varied collection), a startling uniformity at the level of political theorizing. Upon close inspection, the uniformity appears to be built upon a shared conviction that is itself linked to a binary conceptual picture, which all of these theorists appropriate. The conviction and the conceptual binary so thoroughly pervade these texts that they constantly threaten to resolve the manifold problem of democratic citizenship into a shared formula that bears a single solution. To paraphrase Aristotle's shrewd criticism of Plato's *kallipolis*, it is as if you were to turn harmony into mere unison, or reduce a theme to a single beat. In this chapter, I want to examine more closely this shared pattern of thinking because I think it is symptomatic of a problem in theorizing democracy, and perhaps also indicative of certain political confusions of our time.

Polemics

Has anyone ever seen a new idea come out of a polemic?
—Michel Foucault

The conviction that unites Beiner, Bridges, Botwinick, Mouffe, Phillips, and Zolo (who is otherwise the exception in this group) holds fast to the idea that we must dismantle a modern Western juggernaut that is allegedly on its way to wreckage, but under whose wheels too many devotees continue to throw themselves. Zolo (1992, vii) calls this juggernaut "liberal-democratic theory *tout court* [as] established in the political culture of Europe." Mouffe (1993, 1) refers to it as "liberal thought" and "Western universalism." Phillips (1993, 15, 62) conceives of it as "liberal democracy" linked to the "abstract universals of the Enlightenment tradition." Beiner (1995, 16) calls it "liberalism" in contrast to an equally objectionable "nationalism." Botwinick (1993, 59) identifies the danger as "the historical era of liberalism," and Bridges (1994, x, ix, 8, xii) variously denounces it as "the world view of the Enlightenment," "modernist Western rationalism," "modernist liberal doctrine," and "a universalist world view that rejects the cognitive and moral validity of culturally particularistic beliefs and moral ideals." In short, whatever its various guises and manifestations, something called "liberalism" is the threat that must be controlled and contained.

Now, analyzing contemporary historical and political crises (such as the challenges of democratization) in terms of political, ideological, or theoretical perspectives (such as "liberalism") is the reliable stock-in-trade of much academic political theorizing and not, in and of itself, a *déformation professionelle*.

Botwinick's (1993, 2) observation that "history in the 1990s seems to be keeping pace with and embodying the latest insights of theory" captures at its surface the deeper assumption among political theorists that one not only can organize the processes of theory formation into a historical pattern but also understand history as variations in a theoretical pattern. Under this assumption, for example, the historical field of Western citizenship might be grasped as a kind of "unfinished dialogue" between "a duality of values" embodied in the Aristotelian *politikon zōon* and the Roman *legalis homo*, as Pocock does (in Beiner 1995, 34, 49), or as "two mutually contradictory interpretations" of the citizen's role that pit the Aristotelian communitarian against the Lockean individualist, with each vying for "pride of place," as Habermas does (in Beiner 1995, 261). The persuasiveness of such arguments depends, however, upon whether the theorist avoids polemics, or a polemical attitude, by conceptualizing and clarifying the perspectives or patterns at issue, putting them to the test, modifying them when necessary, and bringing them to bear exactingly upon the historical subject matter at hand. This sort of enterprise within "the order of theory," as Foucault (1984c, 374) puts it, requires "a demanding, prudent, 'experimental' attitude . . . at every moment, step by step, one must confront what one is thinking and saying with what one is doing."

The problem with much democratic political theory nowadays—to which Beiner, Bridges, Botwinick, Mouffe, and Phillips all succumb in varying degrees—is that polemics have taken over the task of determining the subject matter of citizenship, particularly in the confrontation with liberalism. "Polemics," Foucault (1984b, 382 f.) observes, "defines alliances, recruits partisans, unites interests or opinions, represents a party; it establishes the other as an enemy, an upholder of opposed interests, against which one must fight until the moment this enemy is defeated and either surrenders or disappears." Polemics "isn't dealing with an interlocutor, it is processing a suspect" (382). The polemics that afflicts so many current studies of democracy and citizenship is most evident at the level of discourse on liberalism, where this complex and multifaceted historical phenomenon has become little more than an ideational enemy, or a suspect to be processed and called forth for "rebuke" (Beiner 1995, 19). Given the power of polemical thinking, it is not surprising to find even a theorist as astute as Beiner (1995, 16) declaring that "theory typically involves radical simplification, in the interests of sharpening our sense of fundamental alternatives in the midst of complexity." Under the press of polemics, it is apparently more tempting to simplify the task of theory than to theorize the dangers of oversimplification.

The temptation to polemics in these works is aggravated by their shared recourse to a common conceptual binary that defines alliances, recruits partisans, and thereby undermines political theory's capacity to deal adequately with what Mouffe (1993, 35) terms "the legitimation crisis which affects the democratic system." The binary, which functions as a kind of principle of categorical analysis, positions the abstraction "liberalism" against an equally abstract adversary, namely, "communitarianism."[2] Over the past ten years the liberalism:communitarianism binary has come to reign supreme in the polemics of Anglo-American academic theory as the party identification "Democrat:Republican" and its "bipartisan" attendant "liberal:conservative" do in American politics (and with an equivalent and increasing amount of blurring within each of its two entities). Within academia at least, the representation of interests that operates under the respective "liberal" and "communitarian" banners still proceeds in a fashion that is somewhat more elevated than its ideological counterpart in American politics, but it is no less polemical for all that. At the level of the binary opposition, the opposing sides present themselves as follows: liberalism generally marks "the Enlightenment" which, in turn, encompasses the "universal" values of reason, impartiality, and objectivity, the ideal of universal citizenship, "rights," the "disembodied" or "unitary" or "autonomous" subject, and "abstract" individualism; communitarianism generally marks group identity and membership, the "embodied" or "encumbered" subject, the family, tradition, locale, virtue ethics, and situatedness in "community." The communitarian side of the binary often (but not always) gets the better of the liberalism side in this adversarial contest, if only as the friendly dupe that is exploited to expose all of the grand suspect's alleged crimes and misdemeanors.

Theorizing by Phraseology

> *Only because and insofar as man actually and essentially has become subject is it necessary for him, as a consequence, to confront the explicit question: Is it as an "I" confined to its own preferences and freed into its own arbitrary choosing or as the "we" of society; is it as an individual or as a community . . . that man will and ought to be the subject that in his modern essence he* already *is?*
>
> —Martin Heidegger

During the 1970s and 1980s, the Cartesian mode of thinking generated by the binary construct liberalism:communitarianism was more or less contained within the arena of Anglo-American analytical liberalism and specifically mobilized in philosophical responses to and critiques of the political philosophy of John Rawls (1971). After the world-transformative events of 1989, however, as the tendency to theorize democracy in terms of *liberal* democracy became more urgent and pronounced (perhaps in this case, theory in the 1990s was keeping pace with and embodying the latest developments in history), the conceptual apparatus of liberalism:communitarianism was simply transferred onto the terrain of democratic theory. There it resides today, threatening to subsume the latter into just one more subdivision of the by-now-vast and monotonously repetitive literature on liberalism, communitarianism, antiliberalism, and anticommunitarianism.

As democratic theorists, Phillips, Mouffe, Botwinick, Bridges, and Beiner (and some of Beiner's contributors) all allow the liberalism:communitarianism binary to frame their approaches to democratic theory and set off their discussions of alternative modes of approaching the politics of citizenship. Phillips (1993, 59), for example, posits the dilemma of democracy as a choice between "the kind of abstract theorizing that deduces principles of rights or justice from metaphysical assumptions" (that is, "liberalism"), on the one hand, and "a perspective that grounds our moral and political beliefs in the experience of specific communities" (that is, "communitarianism"), on the other. Beiner (1995, 13) introduces his book by noting the "competing perspectives" between the liberal, "emphasizing the individual, and the individual's capacity to transcend group or collective identity," and the communitarian, "emphasizing the cultural or ethnic group, solidarity among those sharing a history or tradition"—against which he offers a third "republican" alternative.

Mouffe, Bridges, and Botwinick each devote a chapter to the liberal:communitarian "debate" and presuppose the challenge to democracy in terms of the same tension that Phillips and Beiner respectively identify between the (atomized or deracinated) liberal individual and the constituted or culture-bound member of a (habituated) community. Thus, the "radical-liberal-democratic political philosophy" that Mouffe (1993, 112) ultimately defends is set off by the dominating opposition of "Kantian liberals and their communitarian critics," while Bridges (1994, 56 f.) situates his discussion of civic culture in terms of the "Lockean and Kantian varieties of modernist liberal political theory," on one side, and a "communitarian identity" that he links to Charles Taylor's ethics of authenticity, on the other. Although Botwinick (1993, 34) allows that certain features of the "worldwide postindustrial socioeconomic context" introduce an "element of artificiality" into the distinction, he also situates his discussion of democracy as a response to liberalism and communitarianism, the "two salient types of political theory of the 1990s," except that now Rawls (team L) and Sandel and MacIntyre (team C) substitute for Locke and Kant (team L) and Taylor (team C).[3]

In all of these works the formulaic binary liberalism:communitarianism has somehow managed to invade and structure the subject of citizen in democratic theory. The two amorphous posits of "the atomized liberal individual" and the "situated communitarian self" serve as categories into which diverse thinkers or texts, often from vastly different historical periods, can be pigeonholed or made ready stand-ins for one another (as in the mixing and matching within team L and team C, above). Through the use of this formulaic binary, then, the democratic theorists before us secure, organize, and articulate "democracy" by way of little more than a war of phrases (occasional bouts of hesitation and expressions of theoretical or conceptual concern notwithstanding).[4] As Marx ([1845] 1978, 149) once observed in the somewhat parallel case of the Young Hegelians, "They forget, however, that to these phrases they themselves are only opposing other phrases, and that they are in no way combating the real existing world when they are merely combating the phrases of this world."[5]

But we have yet to see an even more dubious consequence of this sort of theorizing by phraseology. In the texts before us, the problem is not just that the idea of democracy is resolved into the adversarial phraseology of liberalism:communitarianism. At least here the problem is still posed politically, insofar as the two categories mark, however elusively, the identity of the subject-as-citizen. The more dubious consequence involves a parasitical binary that feeds off the original but at the same time reduces the political entity "citizen" to the philosophical entity "subject" (Heidegger's *subiectum*) and leaches out the content of some basically political concepts (liberal, communitarian) so that they become, we might say, vacuously philosophical. The offending parasitical binary is universalism:particularism.

The introduction of the vacuous phraseology of universalism and particularism (which rarely rises to the level of any truly philosophical discourse) further depoliticizes democratic theory by beckoning a philosophical entity—the subject and its "identity"—to come hither. As such, it asserts a claim that Beiner (1995, 9) terms "post-modern": "the philosophical universalisms that we know from the canonical tradition of the West all involve what we might call a 'hegemonic function,' which is to suppress various particularistic identities." Botwinick (1993, 6) supports the same linkage between postmodernism and particularism (and against the "fixity of meaning," "foundationalism," or "ultimate positions"), and adds "in a certain sense, we might say that with postmodernism we are back in the world of tradition." Bridges (1994, 62 f.), too, appropriates the term "postmodern" in his call for a "postmodern civic culture" that "turn[s] away from the universalism of the modernist rhetoric of pure theory." In this arena, where democratic theorizing has now transmogrified into the subject matter of so-called postmodernist critiques of Western foundationalist metaphysics (or philosophy), the *subject's* identity is what is at stake: caught by the hegemon of Western (abstract) universalism, but open to the possibilities of a postmodern (concrete) particularism.

What are these suppressive Western philosophical, abstract "universalisms" that threaten the particular citizen-as-subject? The answer is not very clear, for like its originary binary, the universalism:particularism doublet serves in these formulations as a kind of portmanteau category into whose two compartments some very sweeping claims are thrown and then hurriedly transported from place to place. Bridges's book (1994, x), for example, is framed as a "civic" response to the "wreck" of the Enlightenment and contends that universalisms include an entire ominous "cultural vocabulary" whose claim "was to provide a purely universal language for a universal humanity, a language purged of all perspectives grounded in particularistic religious belief and the accidents of local history." Exactly which thinkers formulated this Enlightenment Esperanto, in what theories or context(s), and with what implications, Bridges neither specifies nor grounds in any particularistic critique. Mouffe (1993, 56, 71) refers to a "universalistic, individualistic and natural-right type of discourse" that she associates with the (early) Rawls (1971); and she also mentions a "universal point of view, made equivalent to Reason and reserved to men" that is affiliated with "the liberal conception of citizenship"—but neither the philosophizing creators of the universal view nor the particular characteristics of the universal "R" are systematically studied or addressed.

A chapter in Phillips's book is entitled "Universal Pretensions in Political Thought." Phillips (1993, 55, 56, 71) links its topic to "Enlightenment thinking" and the "transcendent" and "abstract" universals of morality, justice, and rationality, as well as to "pretensions towards a universal truth or universal humanity." "The tendency toward universality," she reports (58), "sometimes crops up as unthinking assumption, sometimes as grand aspiration, but in either case it should be firmly resisted." Exactly whose pretensions she has in mind (not to mention whose justice or which rationality), and how any particular theorist or theory in the tradition of Western thought articulates these pretensions as all-encompassing, is not further articulated, specified, or particularized. Given the impassioned claims in these pages that the "false abstractions of citizenship must indeed be challenged" on other fronts (14), this lack of specificity concerning "universals" is puzzling. (And is the phrase "concrete specificity" never itself an abstraction?)

The negative posit of "the Enlightenment," insofar as it is linked to the (equally negative) posit of "universalism" and opposed to particularism, is common to all of these works. In contemporary political theory, as Phillips (1993, 56) remarks in a phrase that reflects the level to which the matter has sunk, "the Enlightenment has been getting itself a pretty bad name." In Bridges's book (1994, 109, 147, 15, 116, 213), the Enlightenment (now a "wreck" in "demise") is repeatedly polemicized in phrases like "the defunct cultural vocabulary and world view of the Enlightenment," "the totalizing character of modernist Enlightenment culture in general," and "the rationalist world view of the Enlightenment." The "cultural vehicle" of Western global hegemony, Bridges (ix) writes, "was the universalist and secularist world view of the Enlightenment," wherein "the concepts of reason and knowledge spoke with the same authority as Western bombs and machines." Given the excess and hyperbole of such remarks, I fear it may be too late to reissue Foucault's (1984a, 45, 43) warning that "we must free ourselves from the intellectual blackmail of 'being for or against the Enlightenment,'" and remember that "we do not break free of this blackmail by introducing 'dialectical' nuances while seeking to determine what good and bad elements there may have been in the Enlightenment."

Whatever the term "Western universalism" and its accomplice "the Enlightenment" have come to mean, the verdict on them is more or less unanimous across these works: "Universalism is merely the cover for an imperialistic particularism" (Beiner 1995, 9), and itself "a form of Western cultural particularism" (Bridges 1994, xi), as well as "an obstacle in the path of understanding those new forms of politics" (Mouffe 1993, 11) that compel us to recognize that "multiple differences have become the focus of the day" (Phillips 1993, 145). Thus, a problem emerges that Beiner (1995, 12) identifies as follows: "So we are left with two competing visions—liberal universalism and antiliberal particularism—both of which tend to subvert, from opposing directions, the idea of a civic community. . . . Lying at the heart of this dilemma is what I would call the 'universalism/particularism conundrum.'" Mouffe (1993, 13) dons the same suit and calls for "a new kind of articulation between the universal and the particular"; Phillips (1993, 58, 51) seeks "a more middle route" between "abstract impartiality" and "concrete specificity"; and Bridges (1994, 6, 159, 34) wants to shift away from "the universalism and essentialism characteristic of the doctrinal claims of modernist liberalism" and toward a "rhetorical concept" that recognizes "particularistic cultural communities." Botwinick's (1993, 55) defense of a "postmodernist liberal communitarianism" is framed in terms of a skeptical, "generalized-agnostic" epistemological model that is itself an alternative to objectivist universals on the one hand, and relativist particulars on the other.

What is going on? If I understand them correctly, all of these theorists have resolved the contemporary crises of democracy and the problem of citizenship into two things: (1) a matter concerning the identity of the subject (as framed by the philosophical binary of universalism:particularism), and (2) a task requiring the mediation, reconciliation, synthesis, or transcendence of the tension between individualism, equality, and liberty, on the one hand, and collectivity, community, and group membership, on the other (as framed by the political binary of liberalism:communitarianism). The role of theory in this enterprise is to settle or renegotiate the (artificially created) tension between the two (conceptually constructed) "traditions," by way of an alternative epistemology (Botwinick), language (Mouffe), vision (Beiner), route (Phillips), or vocabulary (Bridges). Thus, the task, as Mouffe (1993, 62) puts it, "is not that of replacing one tradition with the other but rather of drawing on both and trying to combine their insights in a new conception of citizenship adequate to a project of radical and plural democracy."

Next, I want to consider the five particular positions (in Phillips, Mouffe, Botwinick, Bridges, and Beiner) that emanate out of the generic-collective exercise of theorizing democracy as the transformative reconciliation of the oppositional binaries liberalism:communitarianism and universalism: particularism.

Democracy as Synthesis

*Truth, in the great practical concerns of life, is so much a question of
the reconciling and combining of opposites, that very few have minds
sufficiently capacious and impartial to make the adjustment with an
approach to correctness, and it has to be made by the rough process
of a struggle between combatants fighting under hostile banners.*

—John Stuart Mill

Iris Marion Young was one of the first theorists to underscore the complexities that identity, expressions of identity, and "group differentiation" pose for
what she calls the "ideal of universal citizenship" (her influential essay "Polity
and Group Difference: A Critique of the Ideal of Universal Citizenship"
[1989] is reprinted in Beiner). Young (in Beiner 1995, 184) is interested in
specifying a citizen politics that moves beyond the abstraction of "citizenship"
as a universal ideal and toward certain principles that call for "a group differentiated citizenship and a heterogeneous public," within which the multiple
differences and diverse perspectives of previously excluded others might be
recognized, affirmed, and represented. She is, therefore, one of the first thinkers
to contribute the concepts of "heterogeneity, diversity, and group difference"—in Walzer's terms, "a new sensitivity for what is local, specific, contingent" (Beiner 1995, 174)—to contemporary democratic theory. These ideas
have now taken shape as part of a complex of elements that might be called
the democratic theorist's working answer to the question "what does it mean
to be on the left today?" (Mouffe 1993, 9). The working answer is: the new
pluralism.[6] In brief, the new pluralism issues from combining, reconciling, or
adding together the liberal's defense of equality and liberty and the communitarian's respect for particularities, cultures, and histories in a way that simultaneously circumvents both the laissez-faire detachment of the "atomized
individual" and the custodial attachment of the "moral community" in the
name of "individual difference" and "cultural heterogeneity."

  Phillips (1993, 5) and Mouffe (1993, 131) appeal to (the new) pluralism in
the wake of the disarray of European socialism, and as something that "actively celebrates heterogeneity and difference" and is (now) nothing less than "the
whole question of modern democracy." Their works are animated by a set of
sociological values captured in the term "difference": the multiplicity of individuals as social agents, the diversity of social relations, and the heterogeneity
of society. Both Phillips and Mouffe contend that the assertion of these values
is central to the project of escaping liberalism's universalizing tendencies.[7]
Indeed, Phillips's various essays (on socialism, liberalism, consociationalism, and
feminism) ultimately circulate around the same theme and the same phenomenon: "the recuperation of pluralism" as "the growing emphasis on the political significance of sub-groups that are defined through gender, ethnicity,

religion, disability, sexuality, language and so on" (Beiner 1995, 144). Phillips (77, 71) compliments feminism for "redefining the political" in ways that "warn against the fruitless pursuit of a genuinely degendered universal" and guide us toward "a greater emphasis on sexual and other kinds of difference." Mouffe (1993, 13, 12) also acknowledges feminism's "unmasking of the particularism hiding behind . . . universal ideals" and dismisses the modern "rationalist concept of the unitary subject" as a "homogeneous and unified" entity, in favor of a theory that demands 'that we acknowledge difference—the particular, the multiple, the heterogeneous—in effect, everything that had been excluded by the concept of Man in the abstract."

Yet, Phillips and Mouffe also point to inadequacies in Young's formulation of group differentiation that ultimately liberalize their respectively pluralistic concepts of democracy and thereby distance them from Young's. Hence, Phillips (1993, 117) notes that Young's concept of differentiated citizenship tends to dislodge if not obliterate "the older language of civic republicanism" and the idea of a broader polity that encompasses without erasing individual groups.[8] Mouffe (1993, 86, 12, 87) persuasively charges that despite its apparent radicalism, Young's view of politics is static and immobile, insofar as it begins "with already constituted interests and identities," and thereby precludes the true aim of a radical democratic citizenship: the "construction of a common political identity" at the intersection of a "multiplicity of subject positions" and "various struggles against oppression."[9]

Even as they advocate pluralism, then, and the proliferation of particularities, heterogeneity, and difference, Phillips and Mouffe are concerned to bring to democracy some political principle that will, as Mouffe (1993, 57) writes, "combine the defence of pluralism and the priority of right characteristic of modern democracy with a revalorization of the political understood as collective participation in a public sphere." The problem, as Phillips (1993, 160) sees it, is "how to generate *that more comprehensive understanding* that validates the worth of each group" (emphasis added). Universal is out, comprehensive is in. The comprehensive political principles that Phillips and Mouffe recommend are derived from the very doctrine whose universal "philosophy of man" (Mouffe 1993, 150) they otherwise seek so strenuously to suppress: the liberal principle of political equality (Phillips 1993, 160) and the principles of the "liberal democratic regime," namely, liberty and equality (Mouffe 1993, 150). Thus, the reconciliatory project that is "the new pluralism" issues, for both Phillips and Mouffe, in something like a defense of heterogeneity, difference, and diversity in the name of a liberalism that is political, not metaphysical. Under "the new pluralism" in academia, it appears that the liberal convict is being rehabilitated. By contrast, in the aftermath of Clintonite "new progressivism," the convict was not just apparently condemned to death but was actually, as Wolin (1996b, 23) observes, "volunteering its own epitaph."[10]

Amid all of this combining and reconciling of opposites, one may well ask: What has happened to democracy as a *politics*? Phillips's essays provide an instructive example of how the exercise of balancing binary oppositions, no matter how skillfully undertaken, can persistently impede the enterprise of theorizing politics, especially if the oppositions are taken as givens. For despite her repeated assertion that "the questions of democracy and difference are ones that lie at the heart of contemporary dilemmas in democracy," Phillips (1993, 117, 71) registers rather than resolves the difficulties of defending "a politics of greater generality and alliance" on one hand, and a politics of difference on the other. The reason for this, I think, has to do with her appreciation of some of the real dilemmas that face contemporary social movements rooted in the common yet divisive identifications of race, class, and gender that today preoccupy theorists of cultural pluralism. But Phillips's difficulties with resolution also involve her ambivalence about feminism (and feminist theory), which she positions in organized opposition to liberalism (and liberal theory) and about which she is equally ambivalent. In her account (66, 114), feminist particularism opposes liberal universalism, feminist difference opposes liberal equality, "female specificity" opposes "male abstraction," a feminist politics of participation opposes liberal democracy, and all of these oppositions presuppose a philosophy of subjectivity rooted in the terms of the by now familiar binary of women:men.

As we have seen, Phillips (1993, 71, 52) clearly wants to counter liberal universalism and abstraction with a politics of difference, but she wants to defend universality, abstraction, and liberal democracy, too. She also raises cautionary flags about the potential excesses of celebrating "femininity or female values" (160, 138) and radical forms of particularism. As a result, the chapters in her book keep getting caught between the very oppositions that they identify in contemporary political and feminist theory, and trapped in rhetorical cul-de-sacs that empty out in the form of mere exhortations to move beyond "either/or" (64) and search for a "middle ground" (67). It is not surprising, then, that Phillips's most decisive theoretical expressions are framed in the face of dual alternatives and alternate, ambivalently, between claims like "We need both the one and the other" (51) and we must "[recognize] difficult choices between what may be equally desirable but perhaps incompatible ends" (129).

Mouffe's new pluralism is more conceptually innovative and politically satisfying than Phillips's, partly because it refuses to begin where Phillips's feminism does—with fixed identities like "female specificity" and "male abstraction" that in turn give rise to "false dilemma[s]" (1993, 78) like "equality versus difference," that are difficult to escape. Whatever Mouffe's regard for "difference" as an aspect of collective identities, she wisely does not subscribe to the "difference" or "standpoint" feminism that appears to guide Phillips's thinking and assumes the given-ness of that other seemingly intractable sex-differentiated binary opposition: male and female. Mouffe (78) challenges the prior posit of "sexual difference" (and similar kinds of presupposed bifurcated signifiers) by posing instead the notion of a "multiplicity of social relations in which sexual difference is always constructed in very diverse ways and where the struggle against subordination has to be visualized in specific and differential forms." Her pluralism thereby begins with the reality of activity and struggle, or what she calls "the constitutive role of antagonism" (2) in political life. Social activity and political struggle construct identity (or "differentiated positions"); identity-as-such does not construct social activity. The advantage of this "agonistic pluralism" (4) is that it allows Mouffe to frame modern democracy as a context of antagonism, conflict, and struggle, and to ask a decisively political question about the sorts of institutions, practices, and structures that can channel democracy's "agonistic dynamic" (6), without evading, repressing, submerging, or obliterating "the ineluctability of antagonism" (7).

Mouffe's attunement to conflict, struggle, and politics as a world of combatants fighting under hostile banners thus appears to give her a way to theorize democracy and citizenship without constructing or presupposing the systematic support of the constant notational principle of liberalism:communitarianism. Yet, in political theorizing, as in political life, one should not underestimate the need for constants and the desire for reconciliation, even among thinkers who are otherwise not afraid to acknowledge the contingency of human affairs and the flux of politics. The desire for reconciliation in the face of flux might explain the tendency at the level of Mouffe's theorizing to oscillate between a (radical) account of democracy grounded in the rough process of struggle and antagonism and a (reformist) account of democracy attuned to the reassuring constant liberalism:communitarianism. The second point is where Mouffe (drawing upon both Quentin Skinner and Michael Oakeshott) seeks "a way of conceiving liberty which . . . includes political participation and civic virtue" (63), and therefore rejects the "false dichotomy between individual liberty and political community" (65). But it is at precisely this second point—where the binary conceptual picture reasserts itself—that Mouffe offers the illusion of a reconciled liberal communitarianism[11] as though it could be the real basis for the very politics that (at the other end of the oscillation) her agnostic pluralism declares resistant "to a final resolution of conflicts" (8) and the comforting presence of some underlying norm of reality. The theorist's need to reconcile oppositional givens thereby overcomes the theorist's recognition of the intractability of politics to any permanent solutions or final "adjustments."

In short, Mouffe's new pluralism is as vulnerable to the presence of presupposed opposites demanding reconciliation as is Phillips's, although in a different and more interesting way. For Mouffe's reconciliatory impulses are in struggle with her agonistic impulses; they constantly dilute her politics of antagonism (a volatile brew of Machiavelli and Carl Schmitt) with the pacifying additives of (an equally diluted) Rawlsian liberalism and Aristotelian republicanism.[12] To be sure, Mouffe's combinative theorizing goes somewhere;

there is a resolution to these efforts that is entirely lacking in Phillips. Yet, there is also a difference between a theory that is "sufficiently capacious" to absorb antipodes and one that is so accommodating that it loses its substance. The watery mixture that Mouffe (1993, 112) ultimately recommends comes closer to the latter and betrays itself by the very name that she is honest enough to give it: "a radical-liberal-democratic political philosophy."

Democracy as Solution

Once upon a time a valiant fellow had the idea that men were drowned in water only because they were possessed with the idea of gravity. If they were to knock this notion out of their heads, say by stating it to be a superstition, a religious concept, they would be sublimely proof against any danger from water. . . . This honest fellow was the type of the new revolutionary philosopher.

—Karl Marx

"What I am searching for under the title of citizenship," writes Ronald Beiner (1995, 8) "is an elusive middle term between opposing alternatives that I find unacceptable." Beiner's search ends with the promissory note of a mediatory republicanism of "civic bonds" (14) and "robust civic involvement" (19), but it begins with a visit to "post-modernism," which he summarizes as the theory that "*all* social reality is untranscendably local, plural, fragmentary, episodic, and infinitely rearrangeable" (9). Although Beiner's visit to postmodernism elicits the by-now-predictable, quasi-philosophical condemnation of universalism and Western rationalism (9), it is unproductive politically, since he maintains a healthy suspicion that "the more citizens become fixated on cultural differences within the political community, the more difficult it becomes to sustain an experience of common citizenship" (10). I doubt that it is coincidental that the Canadian Beiner, as well as the Canadians Ignatieff, Kymlicka, and Norman, all problemize rather than celebrate the prospects of "difference" and multicultural rights in a way that leaves them self-conscious about "the difficulty of conceptualizing the experience of citizenship" (Beiner 1995, 15) and uncertain about "what we can expect from a 'theory of citizenship'" (Kymlicka and Norman in Beiner 1995, 309) even if they have one to recommend.

No equivalent hesitations trouble the respective theoretical projects of the Americans Bridges and Botwinick. Unlike Beiner, both Bridges and Botwinick find in postmodernism a new, even revolutionary, philosophy that promises to help us assess the transformation of "modernist political society" into "postmodernist political society" (Botwinick 1993, 14) and the development of a "postmodernist civic culture" (Bridges 1994, 59, 114).[13] The question of whether postmodernism can live up to this promise notwithstanding, both Botwinick's and Bridges's rhetorical appropriation of it—as a unitary justificatory term and a solid legitimating category—is a sign of how even the most unruly and disparate theoretical positions are susceptible to homogenization-by-phraseology. Nowhere is postmodernism's incipient demotion signaled more decisively, however, than in the name of the general project both Botwinick and Bridges want to undertake. The general project reintroduces that by-now-familiar binary to which both Botwinick and Bridges grant lexical authority and into whose service they commend "postmodernism." For Botwinick (1993, 170, 57, 55), the project is directed toward "a coalescence (or merging) between liberalism and at least some forms of communitarianism," indeed toward a "postmodernist liberal communitarianism." For Bridges (1994, 57, 35), the project requires "lay[ing] the basis for a postmodern liberal democratic civic culture" that effects a "balancing act" between "two opposing standpoints," namely, the citizen's communitarian identity (shaped by "particularistic values") and his or her civic identity (as a free and equal individual).

The notion that Bridges (1994, 112, 103, 29) wants us to knock out of our heads, in the name of his postmodern liberal democratic civic culture—or simply a "postmodern civic culture"—is something he calls "modernist liberal political theory" and "modernist liberal doctrines." Following doggedly along the path already marked by Sandel (whom he never mentions),[14] Bridges (27, 101) argues that modernist liberal doctrine issued out of Lockean and Kantian liberal "types," "varieties," or "versions." It was shored up philosophically by (the early) Rawls (63) and relentlessly reinforced by "modernist liberal civic culture" (58). Modernist liberalism perpetuates an "essentialist interpretation" of citizenship that promulgates a myth of the free individual who is "unencumbered" by "membership in particularistic ethnic, class, or religious communities" (37). It mistakenly and modernistically grants priority to the right over the good and the universal over the particular (62, 51).

Bridges (1994, 141, 62) proposes to free us from the totalizing worldview of modernist liberal doctrine by summoning a "postmodern liberalism" that, in its "teleological" and "de-totalizing" modes, affirms "the ideal of citizenship as a particularistic moral ideal capable of giving life particularistic content and direction." This postmodern ideal is something that is augured, although not achieved, on the "new cognitive ground" of Rawls's *Political Liberalism* (1993), where "a concept of liberal morality [is] validated by a constructivist procedure" (Bridges 1994, 141). If Rawls is now "recommending his liberal theory to us on communitarian grounds," as Botwinick (1993, 48) succinctly puts it, then this is a move that Bridges wishes to endorse. Rawls's unfinished "rhetorical turn" is what Bridges (52, 125, 148) seeks to augment in the name of "a postmodern version of liberal doctrine" whose rhetorical aim is to "establish clearly the cultural limits of the public sphere."

Now, postmodernism may be a cat with nine lives, but when it is summoned in the name of Rawls (even a constructivist, rhetorical Rawls), one can be pretty sure that this dog won't hunt. Bridges's postmodern prospects are doomed to defeat on conceptual and methodological grounds. "The project of inventing a postmodern civic culture," he declares (114), "is the project of inventing [a] new vocabulary [of citizenship]." Bridges undertakes this project against a background that he identifies in terms of the oppositional dualism between a (nearly dead) "modernist liberal civic culture," on the one hand, and a (nascent) "postmodern civic culture," on the other. His search for "rhetorical resources" (99) then proceeds at the level of conceptualization by way of multiplying many more dualisms, including modernist metaphysical liberalism versus political or rhetorical liberalism (115); the civic ethics of authenticity versus the civic ethics of autonomy (88); civic moral ideals as "secondary" moral language versus communitarian moral ideals as "primary" moral language (89, 122); the rhetorical turn versus the teleological turn (88, 160); civic freedom versus civic good; and civic friendship versus communitarian solidarity (241).

Full cultural citizenship in liberal democratic civic culture, Bridges (1994, 94, 124 f.) argues, requires a person "to develop the capacity to make a distinction between *communitarian identity* and *civic identity*," between the "*accidental*" and the "*humanly essential*," while at the same time aiming to achieve "a balance of forces" between the "totalizing" drives of *communitarian* culture and the "detotalizing resources" of *civic* culture. Citizens must learn "to desire civic freedom . . . as a component of the civic good" (175), but the *communitarian good* is "comprehensive" while the *civic good* is merely "partial" (238). The citizen's civic duty "to cultivate equally both civility and communitarian solidarity can thus seem to be self-defeating," Bridges (250 f.) admits, and "to require the development and reconciliation of hopelessly contradictory and mutually undermining normative standpoints." Nevertheless, such reconciliation amounts to nothing less than a "civic obligation" (264). Bridges recommends "a Christian community" as a model for all other cultural communities who strive to cultivate "civic freedom and civic justice" through "life-narrational equalization" (264).

My purpose in recounting the veritable Noah's Ark of twosomes that populate Bridges's reconciliatory project and relentlessly organize his argument is to underscore an obvious but nonetheless telling characteristic of the mode of theorizing that completely defeats the so-called postmodern purpose of his book. To put the matter bluntly, Bridges's theorizing is fixated upon dualisms that proliferate out of the Ur-binary of liberalism (in the form of the concept of "civic identity") and communitarianism (in the form of the concept of "communitarian identity"). It is also seized, as the liberal:communitarian mentality almost always is, by the possibility of mastering these dualisms through the achievement of a harmonious synthesis of them. In the (oxymoronic) name of a "teleological postmodernism," Bridges (114) calls forth a "new vocabulary of citizenship" that "will be shaped by concepts of liberal moral ideals that emphasize their cultural particularism and their partial nature." But what lurks behind this supposedly "new vocabulary" is nothing new, much less anything "postmodern" at all. Here we find the same old dualistic vocabulary recirculating and reasserting itself, assuaging the theorist's urge for mastery-by-synthesis and producing yet another rendition of the persistent liberalism:communitarianism theme: A + B = C. Thus, even as Bridges (210) advises that "to attain full cultural citizenship, persons must learn to break open closed cultural worlds," his theorizing remains so utterly closed to breaking open the prison of his binary conceptual world that it seems indeed "sublimely proof," as Marx had it, against the danger of thinking politics at all.

Like Bridges, Botwinick is interested in plotting the transition between modern and postmodern society. But *Postmodernism and Democratic Theory* offers a far more copiously developed version of the new revolutionary philosophy under the claim of an "epistemological model" that reflects a "consistent pragmatism" or a "generalized agnosticism" (23). Construed "postmodernistically," as opposed to modernistically, Botwinick (1993, 32) asserts, "postmodernism in the sense of a generalized agnosticism enables us to withdraw instantaneously from our skeptical and relativist affirmations . . . and thus to be consistently skeptical and relativist." An attitude of generalized agnosticism "affirms everything it denies and denies everything it affirms" (31). Combining philosophical insights from Quine, Davidson, and Nagel, Botwinick appears to construct generalized agnosticism into the following complex of epistemological elements: (1) a preoccupation with "the middle" that continually defers the fixity of meaning and therefore "recoils before any particular version of reality"; (2) an acceptance of circularity (our conclusions have no alternative but to replicate our premises); (3) an attitude of "consistent skepticism" that is itself skeptical of skepticism as a consistent scheme; and (4) a rejection of the *explanadum-explanans* distinction that is linked to a view that assigns "philosophical centrality" to language rather than to "reality in the large sense," or to causal factors in the world (6, 33).

Botwinick does not want to knock a notion out of our heads so much as formulate the sort of notion we should take toward what is in our heads. His inventive construction and defense of generalized agnosticism delivers a kind of all-purpose "unitary epistemological model" (117) that is simultaneously advanced as a comprehensive worldview (characterized by openness and the acceptance of uncertainty); a political theory (linked to the practice of participatory democracy); and a critical hermeneutics deployed on a range of theorists from Rousseau, Habermas, and Strauss to Freud, Wittgenstein, and Lyotard (chapters 4–9). As a critical hermeneutics, generalized agnosticism queries how various theorists grapple with skepticism and relativism, assesses the nature of reflexivity (or "the requirement to be utterly consistent") in their writings, and considers the implications these matters have for their politics (90–91).

Although Botwinick offers some insightful, if debatable, secondary interpretations of the theorists he addresses (including an attempt to read Leo
Strauss as a liberal democrat), these chapters do not do much to shore up his
initial and expressly political assertion in the name of democratic theory, that
a generalized-agnostic approach provides "an epistemological backdrop in
which the naturalness and inevitableness of [political] participation . . . seem
especially persuasive and compelling" (54). It is to this claim that I wish to
return, for here Botwinick moves generalized agnosticism to the field of action
and appears to be prepared at least to gesture toward the conditions and limitations of a "participatory and procedural" democratic politics in the real existing (that is, democratizing) world, without succumbing to the constraints of
vacant conceptual distinctions and the deflections of philosophical binaries (5).

Despite these good intentions, however, Botwinick does not get there.
Tellingly, his consistent skeptical (generalized-agnostic) approach, which is so
assiduously constructed at the levels of epistemological formulation and
hermeneutical deployment, deserts him when he shifts to theorizing actual
(democratic) politics. I think this is because Botwinick's concept of participatory democracy is framed by what he calls the meeting of "two salient types
of political theory in the 1990s" (34)—and there is no need, by now, to bela-
bor the obvious. "The convergence of the epistemological limitations of liberalism and communitarianism," Botwinick (34) writes, "leads to primacy
being assigned to participatory democracy as overcoming these limitations"
(34). Generalized agnosticism is thus deemed to "be suggestive of a coalescence (or merging) between liberalism and at least some forms of communitarianism. . . . It might suggest a participatory democratic society" (170). The
epistemological model thus arrives on the scene at an opportune "historical"
moment of a "convergence," "coalescence," or "merging" between liberalism
and communitarianism (57). What generalized agnosticism offers is a way for
us to think ourselves through this convergence, into the new revolutionary
mentality of a "postmodernist liberal communitarianism" (55) that carries
with it a "real-world analogue" of "political participation" (89, 59).[15]

The idea that a participatory democratic society might emerge out of a
generalized-agnostic approach to the theoretical coalescence of liberalism and
communitarianism seems to me extremely problematic for at least two reasons. First, its underlying premise holds that once we get our epistemology
right (even if it is an epistemology that harbors no illusions about getting anything right), we will get our *praxis* and our politics right. Botwinick registers
this intellectualist assumption when he anticipates the "real-world analogue"
of participatory democracy that will be forwarded by "epistemological inves-
tigations" that unearth the "deep continuities" between liberalism and communitarianism (57). We are now on the ground of complex questions
concerning the relations among philosophy, political theory, and politics that I

cannot address here, and Botwinick is well aware of them. He acknowledges that "there is an inescapable move from 'pragmatism' to 'theory' and 'logic,'" if only for purposes of exposing their limitations and underscoring the virtues of pragmatism. "It is a question," he writes (31), "simply of what we want to leave hanging—whether pragmatism without foundations or theorizing that opens a gap between thinking and reality." Botwinick quite consciously chooses to go the latter route. Nevertheless, I think it highly improbable that a "logic" (31), even a sophisticated "multivalued logic" (69), can be fashioned for politics from Botwinick's call for "the suspension of the law of the excluded middle" and the "legitimizing of circularity" (69, 33). "The final term of a political logic," as Sheldon Wolin (1960, 65) observes in reference to Plato, "is not *q.e.d.*, because finality is the most elusive quality of a political solution." I submit that this insight holds for any attempt formally to "epistemologize" politics, no matter how open to fluidity the epistemology may be.

Second, I find Botwinick's generalized-agnostic approach to participatory democracy problematic because its political significance is nullified by a mundane but devastating fact: in the name of participatory *praxis*, the substantial epistemological apparatus of generalized agnosticism is placed in the service of the reductive formulation "liberalism *and* communitarianism" that bears about as much connection to political reality as refusing to believe in gravity bears to never drowning in water. At least Plato's Forms, built on an even more substantial epistemological apparatus and born of an even more resolute determination to order politics through epistemology, were mobilized in response to the real crisis of disintegrating concepts in everyday Athenian political discourse. The only "crisis" to which Botwinick's generalized agnosticism responds (and from which his participatory democracy issues) is that of a manufactured struggle between phrases that have precious little connection to anything except a narrow slice of the world of academic political theory discourse.

Oddly enough, Botwinick presents his epistemological model as an alternative to the very "false dichotomizations and distortions of . . . diverse arguments" that his concept of participatory democracy ends up presupposing under the dichotomy liberalism and communitarianism (xii). When even a theorist as self-reflexive, agnostic, and suspicious of dualisms as Botwinick uncritically accepts the construct "liberalism *and* communitarianism" as a starting point for theorizing democracy, we can be sure that this "false dichotomization" is hegemonic in our field. The consequences of recapitulating this dichotomy are not trivial for theorizing democracy. At the very least, the repeated invocation of this binary category effectively blocks access to the kind of freely creative, intellectually adventurous, and conceptually versatile explorations of politics that mark both first-order contributions to democratic theory of the sort we find, for example, in Tocqueville or Mill, as well as in superb critical reappraisals of historical and contemporary thought. Compare, for example, the historical richness of John Dunn's interpretation of Locke, or the interpretive astuteness of Patrick Riley's studies of Kant, or the careful precision of Thomas McCarthy's recent commentaries on Rawls, to the polemics on Locke, Kant, and Rawls that so often masquerade today under the title of "liberal and communitarian theory."

Moreover, the fixation upon liberal:communitarian threatens to turn "democracy" into little more than the third factor of an *already* reductive conceptual binary that *already* suppresses the real problems involved in theorizing contemporary democratic social and political life rather than posing and specifying them. Making "democracy" the final term in a (now) trinary relationship requires the "combination" of dualisms at the level of concepts, the "convergence" of oppositions at the level of action, the "reconciliation" of contrary impulses at the level of psychology, and the "coalescence" of partisan standpoints at the level of politics. This triangularizing operation, insofar as it culminates in the resolution of previously supposed contraries, seduces us into believing that "having it all" is what democracy (and equality) are about—a belief that Tocqueville brilliantly assessed as one of the essential elements of, and the chief dangers in thinking among, democratic peoples. Conceptual triangularization also invites us into viewing democracy as some sort of "solution": the answer to our political ills, the achievement of the "center," the apex of bipartisan interaction, perhaps even the triumph of a progressive sort of "localism," if not the political moment that finally approximates in a politics of meaning as perfectly deliberative discourse.

But this notion of democracy as bipartisan solution is nothing but a mystification. Its promise of combination and reconciliation represents the fantasy of a nonideological stance from which politics can pursue "consensus" by means of "conversation."[16] Its promise of convergence invites the illusion of politics as a condition of finality and a state of being wherein, at long last, "we can all just get along." And its promise of coalescence does more to pacify and subdue the citizen than it does to specify democracy as a problem to be posed, and thereby engaged, by citizens themselves. Ultimately, of course, the fantasy states that accompany the triangular political theorizing of democracy also do much to secure the position of the powerful, especially, perhaps, those who are in positions powerful enough to make triangularization itself a practice of politics.

Democracy as Security

From a disputation. A: My friend, you have talked yourself hoarse.
B: Then I stand refuted. Let us not discuss the matter any further.
                                                    —Friedrich Nietzsche

Let us dispense, then, with A and B. What would an analysis of democracy that did not theorize by binary look like? Zolo's work, which he characterizes as a "realistic approach," is one such example. *Democracy and Complexity* hearkens back to the "essential lesson" of the first generation of democratic pluralists in political science, as well as to Machiavelli, Hobbes, Weber, and the Italian elitists, namely, "that the salient characteristic of all political decision-making is its lack of impartiality, and the randomness of its morality" (ix). Zolo (1992, ix) thus eschews the entire train of contemporary theorizing that he finds represented in Habermas and Rawls, who are themselves the heirs of "the ethico-political prescription of classical democracy in the old European tradition." He is as unmoved by the ontology of rationality, the moral autonomy of the individual, and the concept of the sovereign subject as are the critics of liberalism. But he is also seemingly unswayed by the promises and possibilities of postmodernism or the new pluralism, or any "academic exercises incapable ever of making the transition from paper to reality" (73). The latter category appears to include a vast array of doctrines (including radical democracy and all forms of socialism), and thinkers (for example, Arendt, Macpherson, Barber, Pateman, and Poulantzas), whose "alternative models" are judged in light of "the increase of differentiation and social complexity in modern democracy" and found wanting (62).

Instead, Zolo proposes to rethink democracy by relocating it in the "neo-classical doctrine" of political science and reexamining its fortunes, particularly as they were defined in the theories of Schumpeter, Lipset, Dahl, Plamenatz, Aron, and Sartori. Presumably, this is a route to reality.[17] With this task in mind, he offers an effective crash course in the "descriptive" theory of democratic government for theorists who want to brush up on the so-called empirical theory of democracy that continues to play a leading role in political science. But Zolo is not out to engage in an exercise in nostalgia or a mere reaffirmation of neoclassical doctrine. His realistic approach appreciates certain basic premises of (Schumpeterian) political pluralism, including a "minimalist" definition of democracy that places its focus on the competitive nature of the procedure for access to political power, and an emphasis upon the function of leadership (or "elites"), while at the same time decisively rejecting the "epistemological fiction" of Schumpeter's neopositivist methodology (84).

Yet in the end, the neoclassicists really fare no better in Zolo's estimation than the defenders of direct or classical democracy. Despite the staying power of the theories of Schumpeter and his fellow revisionists, they are plagued by an "insufficient realism" that is aggravated by a defunct model of the polyarchic political market (113). The upholders of democratic pluralism, Zolo (150) argues, "can be seen today to be just as ambiguous, rudimentary and unrealistic as, fifty years ago, the classical liberal-democratic doctrine appeared to Schumpeter." The reason for this gets to the heart of Zolo's critique: in general terms, Schumpeter's weak realistic analysis does not take "clear note" of the "eclipse of citizenship" in modern technological societies, especially in the context of "the massive increase of the means of mass communication" (152–153). Zolo's particular call, then, is neither for a new pluralism nor an adventurous postmodernism but rather for political philosophy to "turn its most central attention to the political effects of mass-media communication," and the problems raised by communication research (153). Under the Machiavellian title "the principality of communication," Zolo (156) begins the task of assessing the long-term political effects of the means of mass communication that are the agencies "not simply of political socialization, but also . . . of the production and social distribution of knowledge."

Unlike Marx's valiant fellow, Zolo believes in gravity. The "democratic system" is pervaded by the relentless processes by which media communication is produced, the subterranean operation of procedures that govern the forces of communication, and the heavy, distorting effects of the "functional code" that is the medium of electronic communication (159). These threats to citizenship are far beyond what Kelly calls "the expansion of the empirical state" (in Beiner 1995, 93). Instead of leading to new modes of participatory democracy—a kind of electronic agora—the new techniques of interactive communication (teleconferencing, automated feedback programs, two-way cable television, and so on) have served a "narcotizing dysfunction" whereby the "cognitive differential" between transmitting agents and receiving subjects multiplies rather than diminishes (166–167). In Zolo's world, the subject is as decentered and as detotalized as it is in Mouffe's, but with this significant difference: it is constructed not at an intersection of "new identities" but rather at an intersection of telematic forms, media forces, and symbolized stimuli that are generating something akin to an "anthropological mutation" in human affairs (170).

In this world, democracy is not a question of the recognition of differences, the celebration of heterogeneity, or the proliferation of "life-narratives"—we should be so lucky. The gravitational pull that long-term exposure to the media exerts upon the average citizen has induced, Zolo effectively argues (170), "narcosis, cognitive dependence, dissociation and 'political silence.'" The question is: What is to be done? Can a democratic polity, where narcotized, dissociated individuals learn to act as citizens, be extracted from a complex democratic "system" of the sort Zolo describes? Given the ubiquity of the power frameworks and media effects that constitute the internal dynamics of complex modern social systems and subsystems, it seems unlikely. Given the "external risks" of demographic explosion; mass movements of populations and the racist reactions they provoke; disparities among rich "democratic" and poor nondemocratic countries; the diffusion of nuclear, chemical, and biological weapons; terrorism; ecological disequilibrium; and the persistence of a myriad of military threats, it seems almost impossible (178).

In the wake of such global circumstances, the only "fresh perspective" Zolo (181) can offer to theory is a model of the political system as "a social structure which fulfils the essential function of reducing fear through the selective regulation of social risks." This Parsonian spin on Hobbes may be realistic, but it is hardly very edifying. Under its spell, we might anticipate, as Zolo does (181), the "dissolution" of Aristotelian political philosophy, as well as the end of the "organicistic and consensualistic model" of political community, which, he adds, "today is reduced to being the object of the futile academic nostalgia of the North American 'communitarians.'" But what do we get in return? A conception that ties democracy's crucial "promise" to "the protection of social complexity against the functional predominance of any particular subsystem" (182), and its "laical functions" to the "organization of particular interests, the mediation of conflicts, the guarantee of security and the protection of civil rights" (180). In this vision of gravity without grace (including the grace that marks the civic *virtù* of that other Machiavellian, the republican citizen), Zolo has produced a democracy effectively devoid of an action context of citizen politics and subordinated to the demands of security, administration, and organization. Perhaps, looking squarely into the face of the future, this is the price that a realistic approach to democracy must pay. But that is neither an excuse to return to the false blandishments of comforting phrases nor an invitation to deceive ourselves about realism's costs.

Part Two

The Second Sex and
The Human Condition

Chapter 4

Debating de Beauvoir

Contemporary Western feminist theory is a great deal more than a footnote to Simone de Beauvoir, but little of it addresses issues that she did not anticipate perceptively in 1949. For all practical purposes, Beauvoir's celebrated declaration of gender—"One is not born but rather becomes a woman"—frames the field of feminist scholarly inquiry. In feminism, who else but Beauvoir has earned the accolades "prophetess extraordinaire," "greatest source of inspiration," and "Mother of Us All" (O'Brien 1981, 65; Schwarzer 1984; 67; Ascher 1987, respectively)? *The Second Sex* ([1949] 1974)—which Beauvoir's U.S. publisher declared "the classic manifesto of the liberated woman" and Beauvoir herself called her "most important [text] for women" (Wenzel 1986)—has likewise enjoyed a totemic status within feminism. In 1970 Shulamith Firestone (1970, 7) declared it "the definitive analysis" of sexism; more recently, Dorothy Kaufmann (1986, 128) has observed that "*The Second Sex* is where contemporary feminism begins."

Even Totem Mothers, and certainly Great Texts, are vulnerable to the forces of circumstance, however, and to the slings and arrows of generational critique. One generation's icon is often another's relic. No one was more aware of this than Beauvoir herself. When she was asked in 1977 what effect her manifesto would have on future generations, she replied, "I think that *The Second Sex* will seem an old, dated book after awhile. But nonetheless . . . a book which will have made its contribution. At least, I hope so" (in Jardine 1979, 236). In the first instance, Beauvoir did indeed prove herself prophetic. Consider a recent remark from a feminist philosopher, reported by Margaret A. Simons (1986, 167): "Why read *The Second Sex*? It's out-of-date, male-identified and just Sartrean anyway!" Another feminist philosopher (Seigfried 1990, 308) recently argued that a "misogynist biological explanation" guides *The Second Sex*; yet another (Card 1990, 291) contends that *The Second Sex* "was not intended to rock the heterosexual boat but, on the contrary, to calm it." This apparent "crusade against Beauvoir-style feminism," as Rosi Braidotti (1991, 168) terms it, has occasioned something of a split in the generational ranks of academic feminists: the older generation pays homage; the younger attacks. The increasingly heated nature of the confrontation has led one second-generation feminist (Kaufmann 1986, 131) to warn that "third generation daughters . . . would do well to keep alive the connection with our first generation Mother, even as we move beyond her limitations."

Is *The Second Sex* hopelessly out-of-date? If so, has it nonetheless made its contribution? Or, in predicting both the demise of *The Second Sex* and its contribution, did Beauvoir at once underestimate the resiliency of her text and overestimate the degree of interpretive consensus about it within feminist theory itself? To respond to such questions adequately, we need first to begin in 1952, with the legacy of Beauvoir and the legend of *The Second Sex*—part icon, part relic—in North American feminism.

In a sense, Beauvoir's legacy on North American shores has always been equivocal. Some of the equivocations attend the English translation of *The Second Sex* by the retired Smith College professor of zoology Howard M. Parshley. Parshley deserves credit for pressing the American publisher Alfred Knopf to pursue the copyright to Beauvoir's masterpiece. As Simons (1983) has pointed out, however, his 1952 translation (still the only English version) is filled with philosophical misinterpretations that fail to do justice to the complexity of Beauvoir's phenomenological existentialism. Parshley apparently thought that philosophical sophistication was not a necessary prerequisite for reading *The Second Sex*. He notes in the preface, "Mlle de Beauvoir's book is, after all, on woman, not on philosophy; the reader who is indifferent to existentialism or even in opposition to it will nevertheless gain pleasure and profit in plenty" (in Beauvoir 1974, vi–vii). But Parshley's own appreciation of Beauvoir's philosophical vocabulary had its own limits. He translated "*la réalité humaine*" as "human nature"—a mistake that led to Beauvoir's later comment (in Simons 1989, 20), "I have never believed . . . in human nature. So it's a serious mistake to speak of 'human nature' instead of 'human reality,' which is a Heideggerian term." Other equally problematic translations include Parshley's rendering of "*l'expérience vécue*" as "woman's life today," a reading that robs the expression of its phenomenological reference to actuality or "lived experience." Furthermore, the meaning of "being-for-itself" ("*pour-soi*") is confused with "in–itself ("*en–soi*"), thereby making incomprehensible a fundamental existential distinction. Simons reports that the text also suffered from Parshley's heavy editorial hand; large sections of the original were deleted, apparently without Beauvoir's full knowledge or acquiescence. Missing, for instance, is the account of women's history (the names of seventy-eight women are not included), most of the discussion of the women's rights struggle in England, a large section of the chapter on the married woman, and crucial aspects of the analysis of socialist feminism. As Simons (1983, 562) observes, "Parshley obviously finds women's history boring [but] he was quite content to allow Beauvoir to go on at length about the superior advantages of man's situation and achievements." Debts to Parshley notwithstanding, it thus bears mention that the text that was to become a mainstay of early women's studies in the United States and Canada was in many significant respects *not* the text Simone de Beauvoir wrote.

Translation is one thing, however, and reception quite another. Yet here too the fortunes of *The Second Sex* in North America were mixed. Compared with France, where public reaction was immediate and Beauvoir was caught amidst a succès de scandale, the response in the United States and Canada was considerably less intense. The social and ideological milieu of the United States in the early 1950s without question influenced the future of *The Second Sex*. In a social environment that heralded the return of middle-class women to domesticity, Beauvoir's existentialist ideas and her unrelenting exposure of women's oppression were, quite frankly, out (not to mention ahead) of their time. Her leftist sympathies and growing reputation as a defender of socialist regimes were also anathema in a country barely emerging from McCarthyism, arming for the cold war, and persistently paranoid. One ostensibly progressive weekly, *The Nation*, actually warned its readers about "certain political leanings" of the author of *The Second Sex* (Dijkstra 1980, 290).

Even if *The Second Sex* had met with a more hospitable political climate, it would have foundered on the rocks of American culture. Although it was taken seriously by a handful of American intellectuals (including Elizabeth Hardwick, Irving Howe, and C. Wright Mills), the book proved too dense and demanding to stir much sustained attention or debate in the United States. Hardwick (1953, 322), for instance, complained about the book's "bewildering inclusiveness," of which she noted, "there is hardly a thing I would want to say contrary to her thesis that Simone de Beauvoir has not said herself." In a culture where, as Alexis de Tocqueville once observed, less attention is paid to philosophy than in any other country in the West, any work of intellectual density was sure to encounter difficulty. A demanding existentialist tome on "feminine existence" was, perhaps, doomed from the start. It is not surprising, then, that reviews of *The Second Sex* in mainstream U.S. newsmagazines were vacuous and superficial. *Newsweek* (of 12 February 1953) described Beauvoir, for example, as "an alarmed male mind." The book was declared "a singular mixture of pedantry, nonsense, quotations from novels, case histories, and psychological, anthropological and other works." *Time* (of 23 February 1953) appeared more preoccupied with the heft of the volume than its content, which perhaps accounts for its caption under the picture of a sedate Beauvoir: "Weight 2¾ lbs." The reader was left to puzzle over either the gross enormity or the pitiful frailty of the author's reproductive labors.

The peculiar absence of genuine politically committed intellectual life in the United States and the pervasiveness of the "tyranny of opinion" were characteristics of postwar American society that Beauvoir herself had noted in her narrative travelogue, *America Day by Day* ([1947] 1952). *The Second Sex* was no more immune to these American cultural characteristics than any other erudite political-philosophical text from the Continent (although it is worth noting that Beauvoir herself did not consider *The Second Sex* an "academic" work!). In any case, and as Sandra Dijkstra (1980, 293) cogently argues, even by the early 1960s, when the economic and social conditions of women's lives and the feminist movement in the United States had caught up with Beauvoir's critique, *The Second Sex* still needed a "translator" who could boil down its ideas and throw its theory into more readable "journalese." By this time the feminist movement in the United States had acquired its own manifesto in the form of *The Feminine Mystique* (1953) by Betty Friedan.

Friedan's book was in many ways far less radical than Beauvoir's, but it was also more accessible and in the end better suited to the reformist, essentially middle-class political culture of the United States. Perhaps it was also better suited to the pragmatic, unphilosophical character of the American feminist movement. Friedan eventually acknowledged Beauvoir as "an intellectual heroine of our history," but gave her only a passing mention in *The Feminine Mystique*. It reads: "When a Frenchwoman named Simone de Beauvoir wrote a book called *The Second Sex*, an American critic commented that she obviously 'didn't know what life was all about,' and besides, she was talking about French women. The 'woman problem' in America no longer existed" (Friedan 1963, 14). Friedan appears to be dismissing the unnamed critic and defending Beauvoir even as she writes off Beauvoir's relevance to the United States by advancing the critic's comment. Beauvoir's apparently marginal influence upon Friedan (or at least upon *The Feminine Mystique*) is instructive, however, not only for what it reveals about the impact of the French feminist manifesto upon its American counterpart but also for what it indicates about Beauvoir's significance in a larger sense. Despite the legacy of Beauvoir as guide and guru, as well as the legend of *The Second Sex* as the "Bible" of American feminism, both appear to have had a rather minimal impact upon the feminist movement in the United States. Like the Bible, *The Second Sex* seems to have been much worshiped, often quoted, and little read. When viewed in this light, Beauvoir herself appears less as a "first generation Mother" to American feminism than as a far-distant, eccentric French aunt.[1]

Beauvoir's marginal influence in feminist politics was to no little degree a consequence of her almost lifelong ambivalence about feminism as a political movement. *The Second Sex* ([1949] 1974, xv) begins, after all, with the curious line, "Enough ink has been spilled in the quarreling over feminism, now practically over, and perhaps we should say no more about it." Accordingly, *The Second Sex* places its hopes for transformation not on a feminist movement but on socialism and "brotherhood." In concluding her manifesto with an explicit appeal to socialist development, Beauvoir signaled the position that defined her approach to "the woman question" over the next two decades: women's struggle for liberation should take place as a part of leftist movements, not outside of them. Beauvoir became an active feminist only, in fact, in the 1970s when the Mouvement de Libération des Femmes emerged in France. When asked why she had finally joined the Women's Liberation Movement, she replied, "I realised that we must fight for the situation of women here and now, before our dreams of socialism come true; . . . even in socialist countries, equality between men and women has not been achieved" (in Schwarzer 1984, 32). Nevertheless, even after her conversion Beauvoir remained something of an enigma to activist, second-wave feminists in the United States. On the one hand, she opposed reformist feminism (which she called conservative) and was not much impressed by Friedan (with whom she had an unpleasant meeting in 1975). On the other hand, as Schwarzer (1984) notes, she was quite hostile to separatism (she maintained a special dislike far SCUM, the Society for Cutting Up Men) and rejected any feminism that celebrated women's "difference." All the while in France she advocated radical feminism and revolt.

Beauvoir's influence upon feminism as a political movement in North America appears, then, to be somewhat more questionable than her fame would seem to suggest. But how does her legacy fare in the face of second-wave feminist texts and theorists? Even a cursory glance at some of the classics of second-wave feminist theory indicates that here too the impact of Beauvoir and *The Second Sex* is more equivocal than the legend implies. In *Sexual Politics* (1969), for example, Kate Millett leaves Beauvoir virtually unmentioned, and this despite some obvious similarities between her emphasis on literary texts and Beauvoir's discussion of "the myth of woman in five authors" in *The Second Sex*. Notwithstanding Shulamith Firestone's dedicatory page to "Simone de Beauvoir, who endured," her book, *The Dialectic of Sex: The Case for Feminist Revolution* (1970), offers no sustained analysis of Beauvoir's work, even though much of it reads like a series of footnotes to arguments in *The Second Sex*. In *Gyn/Ecology: The Metaethics of Radical Feminism* (1978), Mary Daly remarks on Beauvoir's *The Ethics of Ambiguity* ([1948] 1991), but is unusually silent about *The Second Sex*.[2] Beauvoir is also left unmentioned in two more recent and highly influential academic texts in American feminist social science. Nancy Chodorow (1978, 7) exempts *The Second Sex* from her analysis of gender-role differentiation and women's moth-

ering although she begins with a claim in the Beauvoirian spirit: "The reproduction of mothering [is] a central and constituting element in the social
organization and reproduction of gender." Beauvoir seems to have had equally little impact upon psychologist Carol Gilligan (1982), whose enormously
influential text *In a Different Voice: Psychological Theory and Women's Development*
(1982) instead pursued a "difference theory" of female propensities toward caring, particularity, and other-directedness, in contrast, as we have seen, to male
inclinations toward abstract justice and generalization.

There are, of course, some important exceptions to the second-wave feminist neglect of Beauvoir. These exceptions primarily involve Canadian and
British socialist feminists working at the intersection of Marxism and feminism
as well as in sociology, political economy, and psychology. The American feminist Zillah Eisenstein (1979a) also paid tribute to Beauvoir as a "pioneer in
feminist materialism," but she did not proceed to explicate this rather curious
claim in any detail. The socialist feminist attentiveness to *The Second Sex* is particularly intriguing because Beauvoir herself later acknowledged that she
should have provided a materialist, not an idealist, theoretical tradition for her
analysis of woman as man's "Other." Nevertheless, Juliet Mitchell (1971),
Sheila Rowbotham (1973), and Michèle Barrett (1980) critically assessed a
number of the theoretical positions taken by *The Second Sex*. The Canadian
feminist Mary O'Brien did as well. In her aptly titled chapter "Sorry We
Forgot Your Birthday," O'Brien advanced a reassessment of Beauvoir's analysis
of the social relations of reproduction. She (1981, 65) began, however, by noting that Beauvoir's attempt to lay a theoretical foundation for feminism "simply has not stimulated a theoretical dialogue: instead, her work has been almost
immune from the creative critique for which it cries out."

Whatever one makes of what O'Brien called the "feminist evasion" of the
theoretical implications of Beauvoir's work during the second wave, there is
no doubt that Anglo-American studies of Beauvoir took a dramatic turn in
the 1980s. At least ten books on her life and work (mostly by British authors)
appeared between 1981 and 1990. Interviews by Jardine (1979), Wenzel
(1986), Simons (1989), Bair (1990), and Schwarzer (1984), to name only a few,
reintroduced Beauvoir firsthand to North American academic audiences.
Critical assessments of her thought multiplied over the decade in journals of
feminist studies as well as in literary and political theory. A number of scholarly publications in the United States devoted special issues to Beauvoir's life
and work, among them *Feminist Studies* (1980), *Social Text* (1983), *Hypatia*
(1985), and *Yale French Studies* (1986). Beauvoir's death in 1986 was obviously
the occasion for more retrospectives on her writings and a catalyst for numerous biographical efforts—most notably perhaps, Bair's major work *Simone de
Beauvoir: A Biography*. But neither Beauvoir's newfound feminism, her seemingly inexhaustible willingness to sit for interviews, nor her death fully
explains the increase in serious American feminist analyses of *The Second Sex*

over the past decade. To explain this phenomenon fully we need to turn our attention back to France and to feminist theorizing itself.

To no small degree, the transformation in Beauvoir studies coincides with what might be called the *resituation* of academic feminist theorizing in the 1980s. During that time, a new generation of feminists and "feminisms" developed as materialist, historical, and social modes of analysis lessened and psychological and philosophical approaches to gender, sex, and culture gained ground. The new feminisms situated themselves primarily within the domains of literary, cultural, and discourse studies and variously appropriated the tools of psychoanalysis, poststructuralism, semiotics, deconstruction, genealogy, and post-Marxist critical theory.[3] Amid these new directions, feminist theorists resurrected and reread *The Second Sex* with special attention to Beauvoir's assumptions concerning sex, the construction of gender, and the concept of woman. Primary among these readers were a number of influential French thinkers (including Luce Irigaray, Hélène Cixous, Julia Kristeva, and Michèle Le Doeuff), and it is within the context of their work that we can locate what Braidotti calls the crusade against Beauvoir-style feminism.[4] Whatever else one makes of these French philosophical critiques of Beauvoir (which are as often implicit as explicit), they have certainly brought the feminist neglect of her thought to an end. Indeed, a whole new level of debate about Beauvoir's feminism has begun in both French and North American feminist theory.

Although it is impossible to do justice here to the complexity and range of the new feminist critiques of *The Second Sex*, at least three interrelated lines of criticism can be distinguished. The first takes up the question with which *The Second Sex* itself begins: What is woman? Beauvoir's now-famous quasi-Hegelian response involves positing woman as the Other to man, and as defined only in relation to and by man. "She is defined and differentiated with reference to man and not he with reference to her," Beauvoir ([1949] 1974, xix) writes. "She is the incidental, the inessential as opposed to the essential. He is the Subject, he is the Absolute—she is the Other." Beauvoir's analysis of gender oppression rests upon a very radical thesis indeed: that our notions of the female body, femininity, women's nature, and the conditions that underwrite these identities are entirely masculinist social constructions. The radical nature of this argument explains Beauvoir's apparently profound antiessentialism and her marked hostility to any feminism that returns to biological, natural, or social-psychological arguments in order to retrieve and elevate the concept of woman. Integral to the thesis of *The Second Sex* is the claim that women should not attempt to salvage such irreversibly infected ideas or pursue the practices (particularly marriage and maternity) that sustain them. Hence we find Beauvoir's unrelentingly savage portrayal of the female body as a biologic "fate," an "imprisonment," and a "passive instrument." Women, Beauvoir argues, must overcome the female situation of "immanence," "participate in full humanity," and achieve universality.

Beauvoir's analysis of the Other has come under intense scrutiny from "difference" feminists who want to endorse rather than transcend female "otherness" and assimilate it. Depending upon the difference feminism at issue, the concept of woman is adumbrated in terms that privilege woman's standpoint, maternal *jouissance*, motherhood, the female body, feminine eros, or the feminine as symbolic expression. The differences among these difference feminisms notwithstanding, viewed from a gynocentric perspective Beauvoir does appear to be an "alarmed male mind" with a fundamentally misogynist perspective on female sexuality and maternity. One American critic (Hartsock 1983, 288) writes, for instance, that "the ground on which [Beauvoir] constructs her theory memorializes the male rather than female experience of differentiation from the mother and the male struggle to 'achieve' masculinity." Another (Dallery 1990, 273) notes how in *The Second Sex* "female eroticism is effectively and linguistically repressed and, therefore, devalued in the metaphors of 'mollusk,' 'bog,' 'nature,' 'swamp,' 'hole' and 'slime.'" At stake in difference feminism, then, is a presumably anti-Beauvoirian project that involves the redeployment and not the transcendence of woman as a (social, psychological, and moral) category.

The second anti-Beauvoirian line of critique springs from the new feminisms' sweeping suspicion of Western Enlightenment philosophies (or what is sometimes called "the Enlightenment project of modernity") and their twentieth-century variants. Sartre's existentialism is taken as one such Enlightenment variant. This critique of Beauvoir begins with the assumption that whatever else she might be, she is Sartre's philosophical disciple and at most a Sartrean revisionist. Le Doeuff (1980, 279 f.) makes this point strongly, writing that "*The Second Sex* is [a] labor of love and [Beauvoir] brings as one of her morganatic wedding presents a singular confirmation of the validity of the Sartrean philosophy—'your thought makes it possible to think the feminine condition; your philosophy sets me on the path of my emancipation.'" An important critical claim follows from this reading of Beauvoir-as-Sartre. It is that Beauvoir's existentialist ethic of freedom—which is focused on the individual's (that is, woman's) overcoming of immanence—posits a naive conception of the transcendent subject and subjectivity. Thus Beauvoir's conception of women's emancipation is undermined by an existentialist reading of the subject as an autonomously constituting being who at any moment is free to create herself anew. Furthermore, this criticism contends, in failing to theorize the problematic gender subtext underlying Sartre's notion of the transcendent subject, Beauvoir mistook as universal what was actually a masculinist ideology of emancipation. What this means, the American political theorist Susan Hekman (1991, 44) argues, is that "for de Beauvoir, women must become like men, that is, constituting subjects, if they are to attain freedom." Another critic (Walzer 1988, 153) writes that Beauvoir "simply assumes that all liberated women will be like existentialist men." Thus, so this criticism goes, Beauvoir's humanism identifies "the human" with Western masculinity.

The third line of critique that distinguishes the new feminist interest in Beauvoir focuses on the assumptions about race, class, gender, and sexuality that inform the analysis of women's experiences and women's oppression in *The Second Sex*. When *The Second Sex* is analyzed from this "diversity" perspective, Beauvoir's account of women appears insufficiently attentive to class and racial inequality and burdened by heterosexist assumptions. Regarding the problem of race and class, Elizabeth Spelman (1988, 77) argues that Beauvoir takes "the lives of white middle-class women to be paradigmatic for the situation of 'women'"—a mistake that flows from problematic assumptions about how to investigate both gender and power. With regard to the problem of sexuality, the philosopher Claudia Card (1990, 290, 292) contends that in *The Second Sex* Beauvoir not only "incidentally" formulated her position on lesbianism but also created an invidious theoretical distinction between homosexuality and heterosexuality by recognizing the former as a "choice" and the latter as "fundamental," as a *Mitsein*. Although Card raises the question of Beauvoir's sexuality from a textual and philosophical position, an equally significant strand of the literature approaches the question in psychoanalytic and literary contexts and with Beauvoir's own autobiographical writings in mind (Evans 1986; Marks 1986; Simons 1986). Regardless of their emphasis, central to most of these studies is Beauvoir's relationship with Sartre and at least the implicit presumption that this heterosexual relationship, for good or ill, dominated her life and her identity as a woman.

Adding to these already lively debates over Simone de Beauvoir are three articles that appeared in the feminist journal *Signs* (1992) on the occasion of the fortieth anniversary of the English translation of *The Second Sex*. Each of the contributions, by Sonia Kruks, Linda M. G. Zerilli, and Margaret A. Simons, respectively, takes direct issue with one or more of the three critiques outlined above. At the same time, all expand the already contested terrain of Beauvoir studies. Because these articles point toward recuperations of Beauvoir (especially with regard to problem of subjectivity) I want to offer a brief summation of their respective arguments here.

In "Gender and Subjectivity: Simone de Beauvoir and Contemporary Feminism," Kruks (1992) makes a case for the philosophical sophistication of Beauvoir's theory of the subject and its significance for feminist theory. In Beauvoir's writings, Kruks (1992, 92) argues, "[W]e find a nuanced conception of the subject that cannot be characterized as either Enlightenment or postmodern: rather, it is a conception of the subject as situated." Thus, "Beauvoir can both acknowledge the weight of social construction, including gender, in the formation of the self and yet refuse to reduce the self to an 'effect'" (92). Central to Kruks's reading of "situated subjectivity," then, is the contention that Beauvoir "quietly subverted" (98) both Sartre's conception of the "walled city subject" (98) and his conception of freedom by complicating the notion of otherness. Unlike Sartre, Kruks argues, Beauvoir distinguishes two different kinds of relations of otherness: those between social equals and those that involve social inequality. The latter relation, where reciprocity is replaced by a dyad of oppression and subjection (ruler over ruled), is the condition of woman's otherness. It is not only that woman is the Other; "she is the *unequal* Other" (101). From this perspective, Kruks argues, Beauvoir can accommodate a notion of oppression that denies the possibility of choice and transcendence. Thereby she radically departs from the Sartrean notion of the absolute subject and instead pursues a conception of "situated" subjectivity that complicates rather than dichotomizes the relation between immanence and transcendence. "In so doing," Kruks contends, "[Beauvoir] breaks free of any kind of Enlightenment notion of the subject, although . . . she certainly does not thereby intend to 'get rid of the subject itself'" (101). (The quote within the quote is from Butler 1986).

On a more general theoretical level, Kruks's appropriation of Beauvoir as a "dialectical realist" is an attempt to move beyond the current "either/or" impasse in feminist philosophies of the subject in which Enlightenment accounts of "constituting," action-coordinating selves vie for position against poststructuralist theories of the subject as a "discursively constructed" entity. By rereading Beauvoir's existentialism as dialectical and her feminism as a theory of woman's situatedness, Kruks makes a powerful appeal for a more adequate feminist theory of freedom that mediates between action and power, choice and necessity, self and subjectivity.[5]

Kruks's argument for Beauvoir's relevance to contemporary feminist theory finds complementarity in Zerilli's (1992) article, "A Process without a Subject: Simone de Beauvoir and Julia Kristeva on Maternity." In particular Zerilli argues for the continued relevance of *The Second Sex* to feminist debates concerning the representation of motherhood and female subjectivity. In her provocative rereading, Zerilli rejects the claim that in *The Second Sex* Beauvoir recapitulates a masculinist ideology of horror toward the female body and maternity. In contrast to the difference feminists who take Beauvoir's savage critique of maternity at face value, then, Zerilli suggests an alternative textual approach that concentrates upon Beauvoir's rhetorical uses of the maternal body in *The Second Sex*. In this reading, *The Second Sex* becomes a "sophisticated and underappreciated feminist discursive strategy of defamiliarization" (112) through which Beauvoir "speaks deviously" in the words of the dominant discourse, exposes man's horror of the female body, and radically subverts the "masculinist idea of the mother" (113) even as she speaks it. "Thus, rather than betraying the feminist debate over the mother-daughter relation," Zerilli concludes, "Beauvoir actually advanced it, recasting it as a social relation wrought in the terrible context of a patriarchal culture rather than as a natural relation already given in every woman's biological destiny" (130).

The interpretive hermeneutics that guide Zerilli's article allow her both to appropriate certain elements of contemporary French feminist theory in analyzing *The Second Sex* and to contest some current French feminist readings of Beauvoir. If Kruks's Beauvoir is a "dialectical realist," then Zerilli's Beauvoir is a rhetorical warrior who employs something like the strategy of *parler femme* in her text in order to subvert the patriarchal discourse of maternity.[6] Although Zerilli wisely resists reading Beauvoir as a proto-poststructuralist, she suggests that Beauvoir's feminism did help establish an imaginative space for rethinking the maternal and a position that warns against reviving masculinist myths. Once appreciated, these contributions invite the reconsideration of Beauvoir's place in contemporary French feminism. Zerilli undertakes this task by comparing the theoretical similarities that inform Beauvoir's view of the maternal body those of the French feminist Julia Kristeva, so as "to clarify the political meaning of their differences" (113). In her conclusion Zerilli contends that "Beauvoir refuses both the nonsubject of the Kristevan maternal and the masterful subject of modernity because she understands how the one can work to buttress the other." Thus, like Kruks, Zerilli contests the "either/or" by offering a reading of Beauvoir that simultaneously questions the coherence of the antihumanist feminist critiques and also distances *The Second Sex* from Sartrean existentialism. "Beauvoir," she writes, "advances an alternative theory of subjectivity that places her at odds with both Kirstevan postmodernism and Sartrean existentialism."

The final essay in the *Signs* collection, "Lesbian Connections: Simone de Beauvoir and Feminism" by Simons, shifts from Beauvoir's philosophy of subjectivity to Beauvoir as an actual living, breathing subject. At stake in Simons's biographical study is the issue of Beauvoir's sexuality and her sexual and emotional relationships with women, including Zaza, her friend in childhood; Stepha, a governess to Zaza's younger siblings; José Le Core, a student with Beauvoir at the Sorbonne; a series of students (Olga, Védrine, and Natasha); and Sylvie Le Bon, whom Beauvoir called "the ideal companion of my adult life" (155). Drawing upon some recently released journals and letters that Beauvoir wrote between 1938 and 1945, Simons challenges "the heterosexual gender identity so carefully constructed by Beauvoir's biographers and critics" (140), arguing for a reading of Beauvoir's life and texts that confronts directly the issue of Beauvoir's lesbian identity. The case Simons presents for "lesbian connections" is compelling. The material she brings to light is sure to reignite debates about who Beauvoir was—as friend, lover, teacher, feminist, and philosopher—and in what fashion we might judge, if judgment is required, the relation between her life and work. With this in mind, Simons concludes her essay by reconsidering Beauvoir's discussion of lesbianism in *The Second Sex* and challenges what Card identifies as the heterosexism of Beauvoirian feminism. The ambiguous Beauvoir of Kruks's and Zerilli's readings—that is, the Beauvoir who resists any simple theoretical categorization, especially in terms of "either/or"—is continued here on the level of biography. For, as Simons notes, "Beauvoir's life demonstrates her ability to redefine her gender identity to include the love of both women and men" (160). How Beauvoir enacted this identity within the context of a patriarchal culture—and with what real human consequences—are matters that will no doubt occupy feminists for some time to come.

However Beauvoir fares in the current theoretical climate of feminist studies, these three articles spur the scholarly pursuit of her ideas and quiet the nostalgic rhetoric that positions the icon against the relic, the "first-generation Mother" against the "Has-Been." Instead of succumbing to either homage toward or dismissal of the symbolic Beauvoir, feminist theorists should continue to pursue the serious, critical assessments of Beauvoir's feminism that have already begun to appear.

Chapter 5

The Woman Question in Arendt

Hannah Arendt, perhaps the most influential political theorist of the twentieth century, continuously championed the *bios politikos*—the political life of action—as the domain of human freedom. In her major work, *The Human Condition*, Arendt appropriated a version of the Aristotelian distinction between the "mere life" of necessity and "the good life" of political association in order to characterize the crisis of the contemporary age in the West. What we are witnessing, she argued, is the eclipse of the public realm of politics and the emergence of an atomized society bent on sheer survival. Arendt's political vision was decisively (if only metaphorically) Hellenic: the classical Greek polis was her model of the public; Pericles, the Athenian statesman immortalized by Thucydides, was her exemplary citizen-hero; and the quest for freedom as glory through "self-revelation" in plurality was her political vision.

A political theory so seemingly indebted to the ancient Greek culture of masculinity and warrior heroes, and to the classical tradition of Western thought, was bound to meet with resistance in the feminist writings of the 1970s and 1980s, as participants in the "second wave" began to pursue a woman-centered theory of knowledge and debunk the patriarchal assumptions of "male-stream" Western political thought. Thus Arendt was not spared the critical, anticanonical gaze of feminist theory. For Adrienne Rich (1979) and Mary O'Brien (1981), *The Human Condition* was simply another attempt to discredit "women's work," to deny the value of reproductive labor, and to reassert the superiority of masculinity. Pulling few punches, Rich (1979, 212) argued that Arendt's work "embodies the tragedy of a female mind nourished on male ideologies"; and O'Brien (1981, 99 f.) called Arendt "a woman who accepts the normality and even the necessity of male supremacy." For both Rich and O'Brien, Arendt's sins were not simply those of omission. By elevating politics and "the common world of men," they contended, Arendt reinforced the legitimacy of "paterfamilias on his way to the freedom of the political realm," and denied the truly liberatory potential of the female realm of reproduction and mothering.

Other scholars, however, drew some distinctively feminist dimensions from Arendt's political thought. In *Money, Sex, and Power*, Nancy Hartsock (1983, 259) noted the significance of Arendt's concept of power as collective action, and her appreciation of "natality," or the human capacity for beginning anew, as promising elements for a feminist theory "grounded at the epistemological level of reproduction." Hanna Pitkin (1981, 303–326) observed that *The Human Condition* is located within "a framework of solicitude for the body of our Earth, the Mother of all living creatures." So Arendt, she argued, could hardly be described as hostile in principle to women's concerns. More recently, Terry Winant (1987, 124) found in Arendt's work the missing element in recent attempts to address the problem of grounding the feminist standpoint.

These differing feminist interpretations of Arendt's political theory serve as the organizational framework of this essay. With the critical attacks of Rich and O'Brien in mind, I contend that *The Human Condition* does, in fact, exhibit substantial theoretical limitations when it comes to gender. These limitations render it a far less powerful account of politics and human freedom than it otherwise might have been had Arendt been attentive to the situation of women in the human condition. Unlike Rich and O'Brien, however, I am not inclined to dismiss *The Human Condition* as hopelessly "male-stream"; nor do I think "the necessity of male supremacy" follows from Arendt's theoretical presuppositions. This essay also contends, then—in line with Hartsock and others—that Arendt's work has much to offer feminist thought, especially in its attempts to articulate a vision of politics and political life. Unlike Hartsock, however, I argue that an "Arendtian feminism" must continue to maintain a conceptual distinction between political life on the one hand, and reproductive processes on the other, and also recognize the problematic nature of a feminist politics grounded in what Arendt called "labor." Before proceeding to these arguments, I must outline in brief Arendt's conceptual reconstruction of the *vita activa* (as contrasted to the *vita contemplativa*) and its three primary elements: labor, work, and action. These elements form the core of her theory in *The Human Condition*. They are also the target of much feminist debate.[1]

"And Who Are We?":
The Human Activities of Labor, Work, and Action

In chapter 1 of *The Human Condition* (1958), Arendt begins by designating three fundamental human activities. Each corresponds "to one of the basic conditions under which life on earth has been given to man" (7). The three activities and their "corresponding conditions" are labor and life, work and worldliness, and action and plurality; together they constitute what Arendt calls the *vita activa*. Arendt envisions labor, work, and action not as empirical or sociological generalizations about what people actually do, but rather as existential categories that reveal what it means to be "in the presence of other human beings" in the world (22). These "existentials" do more than disclose that human beings cultivate, fabricate, and organize the world. In an expressly normative way, Arendt wants to judge the human condition, and to get us, in turn, "to think what we are doing" (5) when we articulate and live out the conditions of our existence in particular ways. Underlying *The Human Condition* is the notion that human history is a narrative of continuously shifting "reversals" within the *vita activa* itself. In different historical moments from the classical to the contemporary age, labor, work, and action have been accorded higher or lower status within the hierarchy. Arendt (79) argues that some moments of human experience—namely, those in which speech and action have been understood as the most meaningful human activities—are more glorious and free than those in which either "the labor of our body or the work of our hands" (a phrase she borrows from John Locke) have been elevated within the *vita activa*. Hence her reverence for the age of Socrates, Pericles, and the public realm of the Greek *polis* and her dismay over ensuing events within Western history and political thought (particularly in Locke and Marx) as political action in the public realm increasingly diminishes, displaced by "the social" and the activities of work and then labor. The critique of the modern world that *The Human Condition* advances rests on the claim that we are now witnessing an unprecedented era in which the process-driven activity of labor dominates both earth and world. As a result we live in a condition of world alienation, where automatically functioning jobholders have lost all sense of what constitutes true freedom, real action, and collective public life.

When Arendt calls "life" the condition of labor, "worldliness" the condition of work, and "plurality" the condition of action, she means to associate a corresponding set of characteristics with each. Labor (*animal laborans*) corresponds to the biological process of the human body and hence to the process of growth and decay in nature itself. Necessity defines labor, insofar as laboring is concentrated exclusively on life and the demands of its maintenance. Labor takes place primarily in the private realm, the realm of the household, family, and intimate relations. The objects of labor—the most natural and ephemeral of tangible things—are meant to be consumed and, therefore, they are the least worldly. They are the products of the cyclical, biological life process itself, "where no beginning and no end exist and where all natural things swing in changeless, deathless, repetition" (Arendt 1958, 96). *Animal laborans* is also distinguished by a particular mentality or mode of thinking-in-the-world. It cannot conceive of the possibility of breaking free or beginning anew; "sheer inevitability" and privatization dominate it. Hence, Arendt (131) refers to the "essential worldly futility" of the life process and the activity of *animal laborans*.[2]

In contrast to labor, work (*homo faber*) is the activity that corresponds to the "unnaturalness" of human existence. If "life" and the private realm locate the activity of *animal laborans*, then "the world" locates *homo faber*. Work is, literally, the working up of the world, the production of things-in-the-world. If *animal laborans* is caught up in nature and in the cyclical movement of the body's life processes, then *homo faber* is, as Arendt (1958, 144) puts it, "free to produce and free to destroy." The fabrication process, with its definite beginning and predictable end, governs *homo faber* activity. Repetition, the hallmark of labor, may or may not characterize work; at least it is not inherent in the activity itself. The objects of this activity, unlike those of labor, are relatively durable, permanent end products. They are not consumed, but rather used or enjoyed. The "fabrications" of *homo faber* have the function of "stabilizing" human life, and they bear testimony to human productivity (136–137).

Insofar as we are all *homo faber*, human beings think in terms of gaining mastery over nature and approach the world itself as a controllable object, the "measure of man." This tendency to objectify things and persons in the world is a foreboding of, in Arendt's (1958, 157) words, "a growing meaninglessness, where every end is transformed into a means," and even those things not constructed by human hands lose their value and are treated as instruments at the behest of the "lord and master of all things." The corresponding mentality of *homo faber*, then, is an instrumental attitude concerned with the usefulness of things and with the "sheer worldly existence" made possible through human artifice. Understood as an existential "type," *homo faber* is that aspect of human beingness that places its confidence in the belief that "every issue can be solved and every human motivation reduced to the principle of utility" (305).

The capacity that Arendt calls "action" stands in sharp contrast with but is not unrelated to the activities of labor and work. In order to act, human beings must first have satisfied the demands of life, secured a private realm for solitude, and also have a stable world within which they can achieve solidity and "retrieve their sameness . . . their identity" (137). At the same time, human beings possess extraordinary capabilities that neither labor nor work encompass. They can disclose themselves in speech and deed, and undertake new beginnings, thereby denying the bonds of nature and moving beyond the means-end confines of *homo faber* (190). Without action to insert new beginnings (natality) into the play of the world, Arendt writes, there is nothing new under the sun; without speech, there is no memorialization, no remembrance (204). Unlike either labor or work, action bears no corresponding singular Latin synonym (although the Greek *politikon zōon* comes close, Arendt did not use it. Perhaps this is because Arendt means for action to capture an aspect of human life that is fundamentally plural and collective, rather than solitary or distinguished by an atomized conception of persons). This collective condition where speech and action materialize Arendt calls "the human condition of plurality" (7).

Plurality is perhaps the key concept in Arendt's understanding of action. She uses it to explore the situation humans achieve when they "gather together and act in concert," thus finding themselves enmeshed within a "web of relationships" (1958, 244). In general terms, plurality is the simultaneous realization of shared equality and distinctive, individual differences. Arendt (175) calls it "the basic condition of both action and speech." Without equality, individuals would not be able to comprehend each other or communicate; without distinctiveness, they would have no need or reason to communicate, no impetus to interject themselves as *unique* selves into the shared world. Plurality, then, is the common condition in which human beings reveal their "unique distinctiveness." Arendt presents this in terms of a paradox: "Plurality is the condition of human action because we are all the same, that is, human, in such a way that nobody is ever the same as anyone else who ever lived, lives, or will live" (8). Thus, plurality promotes the notion of a politics of shared individual differences through self-revelatory speech and deeds. Because Arendt introduces plurality as a political and existential concept, she also locates this common condition in a discernible space that she calls "the public," or "the space of appearances" (52, 204). The public exists in stark contrast to the private realm; it is where the revelation of individuality amidst collectivity takes place. The barest existence of a public realm "bestowed upon politics a dignity," Arendt writes, "that even today has not altogether disappeared."

Arendt's concept of plurality as the basic condition of action and speech allows her to reconceptualize politics and power in significant ways. Put simply, politics at its most dignified is the realization of human plurality, the activity that simply is the sharing of the world and exemplary of the human capacity for "beginning anew through mutual speech and deed" (1958, 9). Arendt understands power as "an acting together" that "preserves the public realm and the space of appearance" (204). Without it, she writes, "the space of appearance brought forth through action and speech in public life will fade away as rapidly as the living deed and the living word." Conceptually, Arendt distinguishes power from force, strength, and violence (as well as authority). Thus tyranny is "the always abortive attempt to substitute violence for power" while "mob rule is an attempt to substitute power for strength" (203). When Arendt characterizes action as the only activity entirely dependent on "being together" and "the existence of other people," linking it to power, she intends to posit the existential difference between politics on the one hand, and labor and work on the other.

Finally, Arendt theorizes action as a way of getting us to consider yet one other dispositional capacity humans possess—something she variously calls common sense, judging insight, or "representative thinking." In an often-cited passage in the essay "Truth and Politics," Arendt (1969, 241) offers the following description of political thought as representative:

> I form an opinion by considering a given issue from different viewpoints, by making present to my mind the standpoints of those who are absent; that is, I represent them. This process of representation does not blindly adopt the actual views of those who stand somewhere else, and hence look upon the world from a different perspective; this is a question neither of empathy, as though I tried to be or to feel like somebody else, not of counting noses and joining a majority but of being and thinking in my own identity where actually I am not.[3]

Representative thinking, or what Arendt also calls the "process of opinion formation," can be distinguished from both the process logic of *animal laborans* and the instrumentalism of *homo faber* insofar as it is guided by a respect for persons as distinctive agents, as "speakers of words and doers of deeds." In order to flourish, the public realm requires this way of thinking; it proceeds from the notion that we can put ourselves in the place of others, in a manner that is open, reflexive, and aware of individual differences, opinions, and concerns. In this order of thinking, as Susan Bickford (1996, 83) puts it, "We do not exactly leave ourselves behind; rather, we let others in in order to be with them . . . in a way that gives voice to difference." I will return to this notion of representative thinking at the end of this chapter.

Where Women Are (and Are Not) in *The Human Condition*

The feminist critic who approaches *The Human Condition* for the first time is likely to conclude that Arendt's magnum opus, with its generic male terms of reference, its homage to classical Western political thought, and its silences about women make it just one more entry in a long line of allegedly patriarchalist Western philosophical texts. There are some grounds for these suspicions: Arendt mentions women only twice (aside from a few footnotes) in her lengthy discussion of the classical conception of the private realm. She tells us, without further comment, that in the sphere of the Greek household, men and women performed different tasks, and she acknowledges, briefly, that women and slaves "belonged to the same category and were hidden away" because their lives "were devoted to bodily functions" (1958, 72). Arendt's development of a conceptual history of labor and work is also remarkably silent on the sexual division of labor in the family and on the way in which unexamined assumptions about gender structured understandings of labor and work in both classical and modern thought. The bulk of her commentary on this matter is limited to one sentence about how the roles of men and women were understood in the classical sphere of the Greek and Roman household: "That individual maintenance should be the task of the man and species survival the task of the woman was obvious, and both of these natural functions . . . were subject to the same urgency of life" (30).

Also missing from *The Human Condition* is any commentary on the historical status of women as second-class citizens and their systematic exclusion, until the twentieth century, from electoral politics and the institutions of modern Western democracy. Even those historical moments in which women found ways of inserting themselves into public life, most notably, perhaps, in the suffrage movements of the late nineteenth and early twentieth centuries, go unmentioned by Arendt, although she frequently cites other examples of what we might call action "at the level of the people" in the modern age. For a theorist who grants priority to citizen action and political equality, and forwards the public realm as the domain of freedom, this lack of historical and political commentary on the situation of those human beings called "women" is striking indeed. In short, Arendt seems to have little interest in thinking about male domination and female subordination, or what Beauvoir called the situation of woman as the "unequal Other" within the human condition. Butler (2000, 81 f.) is correct to note that this neglect has implications for Arendt's theorizing as well. It prevents her from considering how there might be a "prepolitical" despotism, or how the "political" must be expanded to include those who were not permitted "into the interlocutory scene of the public sphere," or how the boundaries of the public were secured through the "production of a constitutive outside." Even if one contends that Arendt does acknowledge such realities (especially how the classical household of women, slaves, and children was structured in order to make possible the leisure necessary for political realm) she still withholds any direct comment about the justice or injustice of such arrangements in which some living beings are kept in darkness, deprived of or denied the only conditions (politics, plurality, power) that, by Arendt's own lights, render them fully human and free.

Nevertheless, the feminist critic is well advised to give *The Human Condition* a second look. Like other allegedly "male-stream" texts in political thought, Arendt's work is an enriching, not simply a frustrating, site for feminist inquiry. Partly this is because of its scope and complexity; *The Human Condition* admits of no definitive interpretation, although some interpretations are better than others. Moreover, it offers some promising directions for feminist speculation by way of the concepts of labor, work, and action. In this sense, although a feminist analysis never emerges in *The Human Condition*, the materials for one are always threatening to break out. What these materials are and how they might be appropriated by feminist political theory are my concerns in what follows. With this in mind, what I want to suggest is that, as a text for feminism, *The Human Condition* is *both* noticeably flawed and powerfully illuminating.

Without question, Arendt understands politics as existentially superior to both labor and work. Thus she has often been interpreted as devaluing the latter and therefore as having contempt for women, the poor and working classes, or, in her own words, "the vast majority of humankind" (1958, 199) who have been relegated to the activities of labor and work. On this score it is worth repeating that *The Human Condition* thematizes labor, work, and action *not* as constructs of class or social relations but rather as properties of the human condition that are features of human life itself and within the range of every human being. Thus the assumption that Arendt denigrates women and workers because she takes them to represent the lower existential categories of *animal laborans* and *homo faber*, respectively, is based on a conceptual error. Neither ontologically nor normatively do the existential categories of labor and work align with "women" on the one hand and "workers" on the other. (Although as I shall argue later, there is a way in which *animal laborans* can be understood as gendered female.) Nor does the category of action (or politics) align with (some) men. This is a difficult idea, however, and so many feminist theorists have misunderstood Arendt's meaning that a brief example from *The Human Condition* might help by way of clarification.

When Arendt (1958, 219) praises the modern labor movement in her chapter on action, she writes, "[W]hen the labor movement appeared on the public scene, it was the only organization in which men acted and spoke *qua* men—and not *qua* members of society." If we interpret this claim under the assumption that Arendt reduces the labor movement to *animal laborans*, then we will miss completely the significant feature that she accords to the working class as a political movement in a particular time and place in history. However briefly, in the modern age this movement's distinctly political identity exercised itself in the actualization of speech and action ("*qua* men") in the public realm.[4] Therefore, Arendt allows: "From the revolutions of 1848 to the Hungarian revolution of 1956, the European working class, by virtue of being the only organized and hence leading section of the people, has written one of the most glorious and probably the most promising chapter of our recent history" (215). If we take this example seriously, we can see that Arendt's concept of action does not limit politics to the bourgeoisie, or to "paterfamilias on his way to the freedom of the public realm," as O'Brien (1981, 101) charges. Nor is the working class relegated to the category of *homo faber*. The fact that, historically, the public realm has been a domain of exclusion (as Arendt recognizes) does not mean that *The Human Condition* perpetuates this reality at the normative level of her theorization of political action. Indeed, as the example of the working class shows, the political realm is, for Arendt, the conceptual stand-in for any and all humans who organize and act in plurality in history. It is the capacity for action, not the exercise of the activity of labor, that Arendt wants to emphasize here, not because she denigrates labor or dismisses the working class but rather because she forwards an action concept of politics and an ontology that privileges "the plurality of agents" (20).

In other words, "world alienation" is not for Arendt (1958, 257) a regrettable matter of rising masses or threatened aristocracies, but has to do with the fact that the collective human capacity for exercising power through shared word and deed is rapidly disappearing, succumbing ever more steadily to "the rise of society" and an existence governed by the instrumental calculations of *homo faber* and the process mentality of *animal laborans*. Thus she writes (to return to the example of the labor movement), "The political significance of the labor movement is now the same as that of any other pressure group; the time is past when, as for nearly a hundred years, it could represent the people as a whole . . ." (219). Arendt's target here is not "class," much less the workers of the world united, but rather certain forces (what she sometimes calls "the social") that have devoured and co-opted the labor movement, thereby advancing "the withering of the public realm" (220). The possibilities for freedom and the conditions required for its existence are compromised, if not obliterated, in the face of the sheer survivalism and automatic functioning that mark the modern world.[5]

Although Arendt has been accused of romanticizing the public realm and ignoring the brutality and patriarchalism that attend politics, she is, in fact, not wholly inattentive to the historically grounded relationships that have structured the activities she posits as fundamental to the human condition. From the beginning, she argues, some have sought ways to ease the burden of life by forcibly assigning to others the toil of *animal laborans*. Those who have been regularly reduced to the status of "worldless specimens of the species mankind" have made it possible for others to transcend "the toil and trouble of life" by standing on the backs of those they subordinate (1958, 118 f.). Arendt also acknowledges that the freedom of the "man of action"—the speaker of words and doer of deeds in the public realm—is made possible because of others who labor, fabricate, and produce. The man of action, as citizen, thus "remains in dependence upon his fellow men" (144). Now Arendt does not pursue a sociological account of the structural conditions that have made these arrangements possible in both classical antiquity and the modern age. But it is surely not accurate to say that she has no sense of the coercive and oppressive conditions that have historically included some and excluded others from the benefits of action in the public realm.[6]

Likewise, Arendt cannot be accused of completely overlooking the manifestations of patriarchal power within the historical development of the public and private realms. Although she literally renders the discussion as footnotes, she provides in small print some illuminating insights into various dimensions of patriarchal history. She reports, for instance, that the terms *domi-*

nus and paterfamilias were synonymous throughout "the whole of occidental antiquity" (1958, 28 n. 12). The realm of the ancient household was, literally, a miniature patria—a sphere of absolute, uncontested rule exercised by the father over women, children, and slaves. Only in the public realm did the paterfamilias shed his status as ruler and become one among his equals, simultaneously ruling and ruled. Only he was able to move between public and private as both citizen among citizens and ruler over those not fit or eligible for admission to the public realm.

In her subtext discussion of the Greeks' etymological distinction between labor and work (*ponos* and *ergon*), Arendt (1958, 83 n. 8) notes that Hesiod considered labor an evil that came out of Pandora's box. Work, however, was the gift of Eris, the goddess of good strife. Earlier she also observes that for Aristotle, "the life of woman" is called *ponetikos*—that is, women's lives are "laborious, driven by necessity, and devoted, by nature, to bodily functions" (72 n. 80). Following the poet and the philosopher, Western patriarchal history begins by counting painful labor (*ponon alginoenta*) as "the first of the evils plaguing man," and by assigning to women and slaves the inevitable and ineliminable task of carrying out this labor, according to their respectively less rational and irrational natures (48 n. 39). These are the tasks that, for the Greeks, occupied and defined the private realm and were forced into hiding within the interior (*megaron*) of the house. Here Arendt observes that the Greek *megaron* and the Latin *atrium* have a strong connotation of darkness and blackness (71 n. 78). Thus the realm of women and slaves is, for the ancients, a realm of necessity and painful labor, "the dark and hidden side of the public realm" (64). In its toil and trouble, the private realm symbolizes the denial of freedom and equality and the deprivation of being heard and seen by others. In its material reality, it makes possible the Greek male's escape from the "first evil" into the life of political association.

As Arendt implies in the footnotes, then, for the realm of freedom and politics to exist and take on meaning, it needed an "other"—a realm of necessity and privacy against which it could define and assert itself. That this realm of the other (what Butler refers to as "the constitutive outside") and the human practices that distinguish it were constructed and assigned behind the backs of women is something that feminist theorists and historians have brought to light in powerful detail, across a variety of fields of inquiry. In those footnotes in *The Human Condition*, Arendt too presents some striking etymological and conceptual insights to further this case, although she does not accord them centrality in the text or in her own theorizing of the human condition. But these footnotes are tantalizing nonetheless for feminist theorists who are interested in how in classical antiquity the private realm and its practices came to be gendered "female" and so decisively established as the domain of women that the grip of this identity persisted well into the modern age (and still remains a powerful symbolic feature of contemporary claims about who women are). To the extent to which *The Human Condition* acknowledges the problem of women's subordination (if only in its margins), it helps us to identify what bell hooks (1984, 43) calls "the sexism perpetuated by institutions and social structures," and understand how constructions of gender organize human practices and legitimate relations of domination.

Let us move past Arendt's footnotes, however, and now turn back the text, for there is another way in which *The Human Condition* addresses the meaning of women's lives, although not explicitly and perhaps rather deviously. Consider again some of the characteristics that distinguish the situation of *animal laborans*: enslavement by necessity and the burden of biological life, a primary concern with reproduction, absorption with the production of life and its regeneration, painful effort, and a focus on "the natural metabolism of the living body," (1958, 100), on nature, fertility, and natural life processes (8, 88). Labor assures "not only individual survival, but the life of the species," and, finally, there is the elemental happiness that is tied to laboring, to the predictable repetition of the cycle of life, and from just "being alive" (111, 119). Labor's condition is life, and "the force of life is fertility" (108). Unlike the productivity of work, Arendt writes, "the productivity of labor power produces objects only incidentally and is primarily concerned with the means of its own reproduction; since its power is not exhausted when its own reproduction has been secured, it can be used for the reproduction of more than one life process, but it never "produces" anything but life" (18). In this passage Arendt is referring to Marx's introduction of the term *Arbeitskraft* (labor power), but what will stand out more immediately for the feminist theorist is the emphasis upon "reproduction," "life process," and the "life of the species." In short, the *animal laborans* is female.[7] The activity of labor that Arendt captures so vividly is invested, in other words, in the female body and in women as reproducers, childbearers, preservers, and caretakers within the household domain. Thus the activity that Adrienne Rich (1979, 205) celebrates as "world-protection, world-preservation, world-repair" is absorbed within *The Human Condition* by the category of *animal laborans*. Being "submerged in the over-all life process of the species" and identified with nature have been women's lot; being tied to biological processes has been women's destiny; facing the "essential worldly futility" of the life cycle, within the darkness of the private realm, has been women's challenge. The cyclical, endlessly repetitive processes of household labor—cleaning, washing, mending, cooking, feeding, sweeping, rocking, tending—are the activities through which something called "womankind" has been symbolically structured and actually secured in history.

It is indeed curious that Arendt never makes the womanhood of *animal laborans* a matter of explicit acknowledgment in her text, even though she decisively reads women through the category of labor, the lowest activity in the existential hierarchy of the *vita activa*. But let's speculate anyway: what insights might Arendt's persistently female *animal laborans* carry for feminist political thought?

Turning Operations

As we have seen, part of Arendt's critique of contemporary world alienation involves her belief that political action, as a space of appearance where citizens engage with one another in speech and deed, has nearly disappeared as an existential feature of human life. As her emphasis on plurality indicates, Arendt means more by political action than voting, lobbying, or pursuing interest-group activities. Indeed, the fact that we need to clarify the difference between voting or running for office and the active self-revelation of equals and peers in the public realm is proof to Arendt that we have ceased to think "what we are doing" as we appropriate categories of consumption and production, buying, selling, and exchange, in order to confirm to ourselves who we are. In Arendt's terms, the mentalities of *animal laborans* and *homo faber* dominate our self-understandings. Thus the answer to the question "And who are we?" is more frequently expressed in terms of "what" we are—what we own, what we want, what identity we wish to claim, to what social or cultural groups we belong—answers that reflect the dead end of "the last stage of laboring society" (1958, 322). We are obsessed with security, wealth, family, possessions, things, and entertainment but at a loss to comprehend the human condition as a being-in-the-presence-of-others in the world. We do not imagine ourselves, much less do we act, in plurality, or think very often in terms of a political "we" rather than an isolated and self-centered "me." Our ability to grasp political association as a public happiness has diminished; "mere" life overrules everything else, the body eclipses the body politic. This "society of jobholders," Arendt writes, "demands of its members a sheer automatic functioning, as though individual life had actually been submerged in the over-all life process of the species and the only active decision still required of the individual were to let go, so to speak, to abandon his individuality . . . and acquiesce in a dazed, 'tranquilized,' functional type of behavior" (322).

In reflecting upon these matters, Arendt (1958, 320) calls this condition "the victory of the *animal laborans*." Although it is not easy to say precisely what she means by this, at the very least it involves a profound human loss. Perhaps her argument is best summed up in terms of her own concepts: in the modern age, "the force of the life process itself" (321) predominates and "the capacity for action," still faintly flickering, is now only "the exclusive prerogative of the scientists" (324). The human capacity for speech and deed, and the knowledge that comes with acting in concert, are now submerged under the imperatives of "making a living" and the dictates of "a consumers' society" (126–127). To assure "the continuity of one's own life and the life of the family" (321) is all that is necessary. Action and its condition of plurality, once the highest elements of the *vita activa*, have been devoured by "the smooth functioning of a never-ending process" that marks labor and its condition of life (135). Everything is sacrificed to "abundance"—the ideal of the *animal laborans* (126).

Arendt intends for this indictment to cover philosophers and political theorists of the modern age as well as ordinary human beings. She includes Marx, Kierkegaard, Nietzsche, and Bergson among those for whom political freedom and the worldliness of action have lost their meaning, or at least been radically transfigured. Hence the ultimate point of reference in their writings is not politics, action, or plurality but rather "life and life's fertility" (1958, 313). And at least in the cases of Kierkegaard and Nietzsche, the alternately agitated or aesthetic "I" replaces the politically engaged "we." Thus Kierkegaard "wants to assert concrete and suffering men," while Nietzsche "insists on life's productivity," and Marx "confirms that man's humanity consists of his productive and active force, which . . . he calls labor power" (Arendt 1969, 35). In so doing, each of these theorists exerted what Arendt calls "turning operations" on the *vita activa*, questioning the traditional hierarchy of human capacities (action, work, labor) and consequently reversing the order of their normative priority, so that ultimately in their respective rebellions, labor displaces work and work displaces action.

A similar turning operation now seems to characterize certain elements of contemporary feminist theory, where the temptation to valorize "women's experience"—with heightened attention to nature, reproduction, birth, the biological body, and the rhythmic processes of life itself—takes form in positions that privilege an epistemology grounded in specifically female practices and a generalizable womanhood. Consider, for example, O'Brien's (1981) emphasis on birth and reproduction as a starting point for a feminist theory of material relations, Hartsock's (1983) attention to the body's "desires, needs, and mortality" as a primary element in feminist epistemology, Rich's (1979) concentration on "housework, childcare, and the repair of daily life" as the distinctive feature of women's community, Ruddick's (1989) claim that daily nurturance and maternal work give women special insights into peace, and Kristeva's case (in Jones 1984) for the subversive potential of gestation, childbirth, and motherhood. Although these arguments are variously materialist, maternalist, and semiotic in their theoretic predispositions, they have in common a perspective that defends the moral and subversive possibilities of women's role as reproducer, nurturer, and preserver of vulnerable human life. O'Brien (1981, 209), for one, envisions a feminist theory "which celebrates once more the unity of cyclical time with historical time in the conscious and rational reproduction of the species. It will be a theory of the celebration of life in life rather than death in life." Within this celebratory feminist vision we might notice the happy, contented face and the speechless activity of the *animal laborans*.[8]

The temptation to theorize from the standpoint of women's bodies, and with an emphasis on fertility, reproduction, childbirth, and the cyclical processes of daily life, bears a compelling logic in feminism. As *The Human Condition* itself shows (and reenacts), women have been construed in terms of bodily processes and the so-called imperative of "nature." Feminist theory, in its world-disclosing or critical guise, confronts these putatively natural attributes and interrogates them.[9] In O'Brien's words (1981, 208), feminist theory has made "the private realm . . . where the new action is," not only through its powerful slogan "the personal is political" (which is another kind of turning operation) but also in its painstaking efforts to probe the dimensions of women's subordination in the private realm of the household and family. However, in the process of unmasking the manifold faces of violence, force, and strength in "women's sphere," many feminist theorists have, in effect, elevated the *animal laborans* as the central feature of women's identity and feminist politics. Guided by a reading of *The Human Condition* and Arendt's categories of the *vita activa*, we might consider whether this feminist maneuver poses problems for a feminist theory of politics and, if so, why.

"Who Are You?"

Unavoidably, when feminist theorists locate emancipatory or interventionist possibilities in "female reproductive consciousness" and the female body, they grant some warrant to the very patriarchal arrangements that have historically structured the *vita activa*. Of course, feminists appropriate these arrangements in order to assert the dignity of women; but at the same time their reinscription of the female as the progenitor and protector of "life" simply reinforces traditional gender roles and a sexual division of labor that have, since ancient times (as Arendt shows), linked women to the sphere of the private and men to the sphere of the public. If paterfamilias is still on his way to the public realm in these theoretical perspectives, then materfamilias is still bound to the private. By way of their transvaluation of women's bodily processes and women's work, then, these feminist operations (re)produce a universalized, constricted, deindividuated view of the subject "woman" (tied as she is to the *animal laborans*). In these sorts of feminisms, however, once the *animal laborans* is accorded a preeminence that makes "the celebration of life in life" the highest feature of human experience, there is a substantial loss. As the Arendtian narrative reveals, when *animal laborans* emerged victorious in the modern age, reversing yet again the complicated relationships among labor, work, and action, a world picture of the human experience of speaking and acting in the presence of other human beings in the world—the actualization of power and plurality—began to disintegrate. At a more prosaic but no less significant level, the feminist theorists that join in celebrating what Kristeva once fashioned as the "cycles, gestation, [and] the eternal recurrence of a biological rhythm which conforms to that of nature" repeat this conceit of the modern age.[10] As these feminisms submit to the worldless (and wordless) embrace of the *animal laborans*, the boundless, open, interlocutory space of appearances shrinks from their worldview, leaving them with no resources for theorizing power, political action, or human plurality.

To put this in slightly more philosophical terms, in these *animal laborans* feminisms the identity of women is located as a uniform and homogeneous sin-

gularity of "woman," a maneuver that is itself bound by the ontological principle of "One over Many." As a result, to borrow one of Arendt's metaphors, an
"empty space" unfolds between the expressed commitment to freedom that
these feminisms presuppose, on the one hand, and freedom's actualization as a
feminist politics, on the other. *Animal laborans*, "swing[ing] contentedly in
nature's prescribed cycle," cannot fill this space (Arendt 1958, 106). In the articulation of politics as the mutual engagement of diverse, heterogeneous, multifaceted peers in a public realm, however, Arendt shows us what can. It is those
"speakers of words and doers of deeds" whose particular and distinctive identities shine forth in the space of appearance. Accordingly, Arendt invites feminist theory (which in some of its manifestations is still searching for a totalizing
answer to the question "Who are you?") to initiate a project of political space
that is expressly inspired by an action concept of *politics*.

For an Arendtian, then, the goals of a truly political feminism should be just
the opposite of *animal laborans* feminisms. First, to release "women" from the
straitjacket of a universalized and uniform subjectivity, and, second, to free feminist theory itself from its quest for certainty about "who you are." This quest
for certainty—which privileges knowing over doing—is at once quixotic and
distracting; it merely aggravates the fruitless desire for "safety first," as John
Dewey (quoted in Barber 1996, 49) aptly put it, and encourages the misleading
hope "to find a realm in which there is an activity which is not overt and which
has no external consequences." Instead, Arendtian political theory urges feminist theory toward a space of appearance where certainty ends and a politics
that is overt and consequential begins. In this world, it is the static category of
the "what" called "women" that disintegrates, as the "living flux of acting and
speaking" (Arendt 1958, 187, 178) manifests itself in a multitude of different
answers to the question "Who are you?"—answers that reverberate through
speech and reveal the diversity of human persons within the political space.

A feminist theoretic turn to plurality would require the abandonment of
certain epistemological longings that underlie some current feminist perspectives, including the *animal laborans* feminism that is under microscope here. In
particular, the quest for univocality, certainty, and a fixed standpoint on
women's reality would have to go. As Wendy Brown (1995, 40) remarks, however, "dispensing with the unified subject does not mean ceasing to be able to
speak about our experiences as women, only that our words cannot be legitimately deployed or construed as larger or longer than the moments of the
lives they speak from; they cannot be anointed as 'authentic' or 'true' since the
experience they announce is linguistically contained, socially constructed,
[and] discursively mediated." (We might also, following Arendt, add "uniquely
self-revelatory" to the list.) Brown's observation moves in an Arendtian vein; it
effectively shifts the subject of woman from the arena of philosophical and
epistemological certainty to the realm of speech action, where an individual may
well reveal "who" she is by way of a linguistic appeal to the "experience of

women." But by its very nature, this speech act already specifies and individuates within a multivocal public sphere that accommodates the self-revelations of many speakers of words, over the truth posit of a univocal "One." In the Arendtian public realm, feminism can felicitously replace its search for a legitimizing truth with a speech–action concept of politics, and repair from the demands for a systematic knowledge into the space of appearance, where equal voices share in the unpredictable and exhilarating activity of opinionated speech.

Of course, an Arendtian politics that is true to its name must make some adjustments of its own if it wishes to achieve a harmonization of differences with feminism instead of speaking simply from a position of, to use the current phrase, "hegemonic domination." "Political thought is representative," Arendt (1958, 241) writes. And this Arendtian insight applies as much to the activity of theorizing different theorists' standpoints as it does to "the process of opinion formation" on any given problem in politics. Accordingly, I want to conclude by briefly considering two viewpoints, conjured through an exercise in "textual" representative thinking, that we should keep in mind while pondering an Arendtian politics of freedom for feminism.

The first viewpoint involves space, specifically the relation between the public and the private realms. Insofar as an Arendtian politics privileges the speech and action of all human beings as equals and peers in the public realm, it (implicitly) invites the question "Who, then, will tend to the private?" (Every citizen, it seems, still needs a "wife.") It may be that, as Sheldon Wolin (1996a, 38) writes, "the very idea of equality is transgressive of the social and political boundaries that have formed the precondition for political exclusion"; but a political theory that forwards equality and erases exclusion does not necessarily resolve the problem of the private—of who should occupy and tend to the realm that has been existentially abandoned in favor of a spontaneous politics. This is partly the old and familiar problem of "who's got the time"—Arendtian politics, just like democratic socialism, takes up too many evenings, not to mention mornings, afternoons, and nights—but it is also a problem about how to dismantle previously gendered spaces while still retaining the spaces themselves.[11]

Theoretical and practical responses to this problem, which feminist political theorists have long recognized, generally fail to move much beyond calls for "equal parenting" (if the private realm is taken to mean the family) or emancipatory appeals for a kind of simple sex role reciprocity (if the private realm is associated with women, and the public with men). Thus, Hanna Pitkin (1984, 481) writes, "Women should be as free as men to act publicly; men should be as free as women to nurture.... A life confined entirely to personal and household concerns seems ... stunted and impoverished, and so does a life so public or abstracted that it has lost all touch with the practical, everyday activities that sustain it." Similarly, Susan Okin (1979, 195) argues, "Only when men participate equally in what have been principally women's realms ... and when women participate equally in what have been principally men's realms of . . . production [and] government . . . will members of both sexes develop a more complete *human* personality than has hitherto been possible." These formulations are well-intended but hardly satisfactory, insofar as they tend to call "freedom" and "equality" back into service for purposes of reasserting, albeit in a more liberating way, the very discursive and spatial formations (public men/private women) that an Arendtian politics is concerned to overcome. So the problem of public and private still awaits an adequate specification, if not a political solution, within the context of an expressly Arendtian feminist politics.

The second viewpoint that we need to keep in mind involves the problem of political action and formulates a challenge to the politics of Arendtian politics itself. Significantly, Arendt's phenomenological conception of politics places emphasis on speech and "voice," human capacities that have also been central to many gender studies (see Gilligan 1982), as well as to feminist political theorizing (see Young 1997; Benhabib 1992a; Bickford 1996; Fraser 1986, 1989a), and in various deliberative or discursive or communicative models in democratic theory. The Arendtian case for speech (which is actually concerned with "self-revelation" rather than communication or deliberation) rests on two claims concerning the human condition: first, that it is within the range of all human beings to insert themselves into the public realm through speech; and second, that the speech activity of diverse individuals in the public realm represents the actualization of freedom. From the standpoint of a feminism that is committed to theorizing what Iris Marion Young (1986b) calls a "politics of difference" or Wendy Brown (1995, 51) (contesting Young) calls a "politics of diversity," an Arendtian speech concept of politics that takes its own start from the notion of a multifaceted, highly differentiated space within which a complex and diverse "we" engages in the activity of shared, individuated discourse is helpful indeed. But from the standpoint of a feminism also committed to a politics that actually works to dismantle the hegemonic structure of "the master's house" (rather than just talking or speechifying about it), the Arendtian concept of politics leaves much to be desired as a program for direct political action.

What this viewpoint forces an Arendtian politics to recognize (notwithstanding its considerable phenomenological glories) is what is truly at stake politically. Wolin (1996a, 44) puts the point bluntly when he writes, "heterogeneity, diversity, and multiple selves are no match for modern forms of power" (that is, "power" in the conventional, non-Arendtian, sense). Perhaps this is true even when those selves are organized into action formations of solidarity, although certain remarkable phenomena of the past two decades (which I will invoke again in these pages)—including Polish Solidarity, Tiananmen Square, Charter 77 in Czechoslovakia, "People Power" in the Philippines—would seem to indicate that sometimes, at least, the modern forms of authoritarian or dictatorial power are no match for the collective and united power of the people. The problem for Arendtian politics, however, is not that it cannot accommodate these events (to the contrary, they seem almost paradigmatic representations of what Arendt means by politics). The problem is that Arendtian politics cannot theorize them in terms of the strategic articulation of ends and the decisive disposition of means. (This is a problem that I consider in detail in chapter 8.) And a concept of politics that cannot countenance Machiavellian forms of maneuver is probably a concept that a feminist emancipatory project should not fully embrace. It may be, to borrow an early feminist credo, that one cannot use the master's tools to dismantle the master's house. But if you are not given any tools at all, the master's house will most likely remain intact.

My argument for *The Human Condition* as a possible starting place for a feminist theory of politics is not, therefore, an endorsement of Arendt's theory *tout court*. Indeed, a feminist reading reveals more than a few inadequacies in Arendt's major work. Still, feminism—in both its political theoretical moment and its praxis—needs a calling back to politics. In this respect, *The Human Condition* gives feminist thought ground on which to stand and deliver upon its commitment to political freedom. Because *The Human Condition* articulates freedom as the raison d'être of politics and presents power as speech and action in plurality, it indicates a pathway out of the opaque thicket that has for some time now trapped feminist political theory in thorny, redundant, and politically uninspiring debates about the nature and meaning, construction and deconstruction, of "the subject as woman." For academic feminism, which has so vividly illuminated the distortions of gender embedded in existing social formations but not yet advanced a transformative vision of politics, *The Human Condition* marks a theoretical space in which to begin anew, as we try to imagine and actualize better political worlds.

Chapter 6

The Arendt Question in Feminism

Hannah Arendt was not invited to the Dinner Party, but Judy Chicago did count her as one of the nine hundred and ninety-nine "women of importance" in her story. In many respects, Arendt was unprecedented: "a major political philosopher of our time, a woman greatly respected in the intellectual establishment" (Rich 1979, 211); "the central political thinker of this century whose work has reminded us . . . of the loss of public space" (Benhabib 1993, 98); "one of the most powerful figures" in the tradition of civic republicanism (Phillips 1991, 46); "the political theorist who wrote most powerfully on [the theme of public and private] in our time, and who tried hardest to renew our access to politics as . . . a 'public happiness'" (Pitkin 1981, 326). For those who keep track of such things (with Young-Bruehl 1982, 272, 392), Arendt was also exceptional: the first woman to give the Christian Gauss seminars at Princeton University (1953); the first woman appointed to the rank of full professor at Princeton University (1959); one of only a few female academicians to receive honorary degrees at a dozen American universities; one of the very few to be awarded the prestigious Lessing Prize of the Free City of Hamburg (1959), the Emerson-Thoreau Medal of the American Academy (1969), and the Sigmund Freud Preis of the Deutsche Akademie für Sprache und Dichtung (1967). Arendt's friend Mary McCarthy (1976, 5) thought her a goddess—a "chthonic goddess, or a fiery one, rather than the airy kind . . . enacting a drama of mind." At her funeral in 1975, Arendt's friend Hans Jonas (1976, 4) said, "She has set a style of inquiry and debate which will ensure that no cheap formula for the human predicament will pass muster, so long as her example is remembered."

Yet the woman who is arguably the most influential theorist of action, participatory politics, and the public realm in the twentieth century appears to have had no discernible influence upon the second-wave feminist movement in either North America or Europe, in either its theory or its public, political practice. In part, no doubt, the gulf between feminism and Arendt—at least in the United States—was occasioned by the pragmatic rather than theoretical character of the American feminist movement itself, and probably by Arendt's (1968, 72) own personal reluctance to "venture into the public realm." An academic political theorist who located her origins not in the left but in "the tradition of German philosophy" (1978, 246), Arendt was an unlikely source of inspiration for the activists of American feminism, in any of their ideological varieties. Even in its theoretical vein, however, feminism was unlikely to find in Arendt a line compatible with the idea that "the personal is political." As Anne Phillips (1991, 113) notes, "When Hannah Arendt defines politics in terms of the pursuit of public happiness or the taste for public freedom, she is employing a terminology almost opposite to that adopted within the contemporary women's movement."

Certainly the gulf between feminism and Arendt was enforced by her unwavering inclination to distance herself from women's liberation in general. As Elisabeth Young-Bruehl (1982, 273) writes, Arendt "became uneasy whenever she saw the 'woman problem' generate either a political movement separated from others or a concentration on psychological problems." "What she wanted for women and from women," Young-Bruehl continues, "was attention paid to questions about political and legal discrimination." Like Rosa Luxemburg, whom she greatly admired "for who she was and what she did," and Simone de Beauvoir, whom she brusquely dismissed as "not very bright,"[1] Arendt was unsympathetic to a politics that divorced "women's issues" from a broader range of emancipatory concerns (Brightman 1992, 330). Like the two other most famous female political theorists of the twentieth century, Arendt was by no means free of conventional, patriarchal attitudes. She was "suspicious of women who 'gave orders,' skeptical about whether women should be political leaders and steadfastly opposed to the social dimensions of Women's Liberation" (Young-Bruehl 1982, 238).[2]

Nonetheless, feminism has smiled more benevolently upon Luxemburg's and Beauvoir's antifeminist traces than it has upon Arendt's. In practical terms at least, and especially in the United States, Luxemburg's influence has in any case always been negligible. Too heroic a Sparticist, too little a womanist, and muted by time, Luxemburg left a legacy that is informed less by her politics than by her brutal death in 1919 at the hands of creatures she would have called "another zoological species."[3] Beauvoir's is, of course, a different and more definitive story (see chapter 4). Her opposition to the women's move-ment (which relaxed considerably in the 1970s) was fully eclipsed as a matter of comment by *The Second Sex* ([1949] 1974), the totemic postwar manifesto that gave birth and impetus to the cause of female liberation in Western Europe and earned Beauvoir the dubious but unparalleled title "first-genera-tion Mother" (Kaufmann 1986, 131). Arendt is yet another matter. A German-Jewish émigré from fascist Europe to the United States, her life story has aspects of bravery to rival Luxemburg's[4] and, later, works of singular mean-ing and importance that easily equal and perhaps surpass all of Beauvoir's. But as Maria Markus (1987, 76) notes, during her lifetime Arendt was "almost totally ignored" by feminists. After her death, however, and as her work began "its uncertain, always adventurous course through history" (Arendt 1968, 71), things took a different turn. The influential poet Adrienne Rich (1979, 212) declared *The Human Condition* "a lofty and crippled book." Not long after, the indomitable midwife-turned-theorist Mary O'Brien (1981, 9) leveled a scorching attack upon "such female male supremacists as Hannah Arendt," in her widely read book *The Politics of Reproduction*.

Even in less virulent and loftier theoretical reaches, the feminist reception of Hannah Arendt has been on the whole an often polemical and hyperbolic affair that has probably generated more heat than light on her work. The polemics, as we shall see, are partly symptomatic of some tensions within fem-inist theorizing itself, and thus they reveal as much about certain theoretical presuppositions in contemporary academic feminism as they do about Arendt.[5] Nevertheless, it is also true that Arendt's ideas seem to invite among feminists an intensity of response that few other female thinkers—and surely none of her stature—have received.

In what follows in this chapter, my instincts are both critical and pro-grammatic. First, I want to explore one particular arena of feminist commen-tary that aligns some of Arendt's most unforgiving critics[6] against some of her most enthusiastic defenders.[7] I shall show that regardless of their specific views, the commentaries in this arena are driven by a shared feminism of "difference" that genders Hannah Arendt. That is, they reproduce gender as the primary category of their critiques of both Arendtian theory and of Arendt the theo-rist. Ironically, under the weight of this powerful analytical category, these commentaries miss what I take to be the true "gender subtext" of Arendt's the-ory; and they miss the way in which Arendt's action concept of politics dis-places the binary of gender as well. My second and more programmatic aim is to suggest that in Arendt's most systematic political text, *The Human Condition*, we can uncover a conceptual strategy that rejects gender in favor of a politics of "unique distinctiveness" and action as self-revelation in speech. In elaborat-ing upon this Arendtian strategy, I will consider a variety of recent feminist commentaries that are concerned either with bringing Arendt to feminism as a political movement or with bringing feminism as an "identity politics" to

Arendt in ways that do not necessarily endorse the presuppositions of difference feminism.[8] By and large, these commentaries are critically attuned to the problem of action and to the conditions that might constitute a genuinely Arendtian politics. Whether this augurs well or ill for feminism is, of course, itself an interpretive question, and what follows from it remains to be seen.

The Gendering of Hannah Arendt

The activity of textual interpretation and the reception of any author always take place against the background of particular but invariably complex historical, ideological, and practical realities. Much hinges not only upon the texts that are available to or selected by interpreters but also upon the discursive context within which the practice of interpretation transpires. Although a full accounting of the background against which the feminist reception of Arendt initially unfolds is impossible here, we should note that from the start it is shaped by one specific text and a specific discursive context.

In the years immediately following Arendt's death most secondary studies of her work focused primarily, if not exclusively, upon the text that appeared in Europe under the title *Vita Activa* and in the United States as *The Human Condition* (1958). Given the scope and power of almost all of Arendt's writings, it was not altogether predictable that the text she wanted to call *Amor Mundi* (Love of the World) would become her most widely read and interpreted work (see Young-Bruehl 1982). From a contemporary political perspective, *The Origins of Totalitarianism* (1951) is more vivid and compelling; Young-Bruehl (1982, 244) is right to say that "no one who wishes to study totalitarianism can ignore it." *Eichmann in Jerusalem* (1963) is stunning and courageous; *Rahel Varnhagen* (1974) maneuvers deftly at the intersection of biography, gender, class, and ethnicity. *On Revolution* (1965) is the work Justice William O. Douglas (in Young-Bruehl 1982, 472) foresaw as a "classic treatise"; and *Between Past and Future* (1969) is the text that Arendt herself thought was the best of her books (in Young-Bruehl 1982, 473). Yet it is in *The Human Condition* that the panorama upon which the conceptual schematic of Arendt's thinking unrolls more vividly and completely than anywhere else. To borrow Mary McCarthy's (1976, 8) metaphor, *The Human Condition* is the "vast surveyor's map of concepts and insights" in which the main elements of Arendt's rich and complex valuation of the conditions of human existence are explicitly and systematically put forward for the first and last time. So in this sense, *The Human Condition* is also a map to the hidden treasure of Arendt's own thinking, as well as a guide to all of the rest of her work.

The concepts that constitute Arendt's map appear in ones, twos, and threes; sometimes they multiply into fours and sixes. One term constitutes the text-map itself: the *vita activa*. Three others—conditions, activities, and spaces—establish its outer boundaries. A complex of related concepts—some binaries, others not—emerge inside: earth, world, private, public, social, household, polis, society, worldliness, worldlessness, labor, work, action, natality, mortality, plurality, *animal laborans*, *homo faber*, process, life, necessity, means-end, instrumentality, fabrication, action, speech, freedom.[9] Arendt's concepts assume spatial, geometric relations to each other; they are variously parallel, transverse, orthogonal, and homologous, but always circumscribed, delimited, and specified. Arendt wants to refocus our attention on certain distinctions that have transformed over time and have also become blurred. Hence the concepts in *The Human Condition* take on various temporal relationships that she poses as "reversals." For example, in the classical age the human capacity for action enjoys existential priority over the capacity for work; in early modernity, work triumphs over action; in late modernity, labor and life are victorious over action and work. Increasingly, "the social" invades the public world, *animal laborans* overwhelms *homo faber*, and freedom falls prey to necessity. Arendt's concepts are fluid; they mix and match, intermingle, separate, change position, appear, disappear, and reappear along a narrative course that is itself a tale of cyclicalities, lineations, reversals, dead stops, and boundless possibilities. What this adds up to is an exceedingly dense and complex, always provocative, and often frustrating text that has focused the scholarly attention on Arendt for the past fifteen years. Feminist theory and scholarship are no exceptions.

The background for the reception of Arendt is also set by what might be called the dominant discursive context of feminist theorizing in the United States in the late 1970s and early 1980s. Against the increasingly dreary landscape of the androgyny debates, Marxist feminist arguments over capitalist patriarchy and socialist feminism, and radical Beauvoirian proclamations about childbearing and child rearing as "the heart of woman's oppression" (Firestone 1970, 72), a new perspective on "the woman question" emerged. We now have a series of terms that identify it: "feminist standpoint theory"(Hawkesworth 1989); "standpoint epistemology" (Harding 1986, 292); "cultural feminism" (Alcoff 1988, 408); "gynocentric feminism" (Young 1990); or "difference theory" (Fraser 1992a). The difference feminists, who cast rather romantic figures against the grain of oppression studies, were determined to reassert the concept of "woman" as the starting point for academic feminism. They were also skillful purveyors of rhetoric who often relied on attractive phrases and striking images (including maternalism) to advance the celebration of female difference (Zerilli 1991). Accordingly, difference feminism advanced insights drawn from psychology, epistemology, and moral philosophy and undertook to counterpose certain so-called female attributes or values (such as motherhood, connectedness, caring, reciprocity, and other-directedness) against certain so-called male attributes or values (such as violence, domination, competitiveness, power, and self-centeredness). As Nancy Fraser (1992a, 6) argues, difference feminism holds that "in some respects, women really [are] different from men, and . . . the differences [are] to women's credit."

At least two analytical presuppositions are embedded in the discursive

context of difference feminism. First, the binary of gender is simply repro-
duced and treated unproblematically. Female:Male or Women:Men, to paraphrase Parveen Adams and Jeff Minson (1990, 83), "simply mark the always
already given gender in the category of humanity." This static polarity is taken
as a structural premise and simply read off history, society, discourse, language,
a text—whatever the target of analysis happens to be. Second, the binary carries with it a heavily weighted normative dimension that formulates the
female (or "women") positively and the male (or "men") negatively. Thus the
conditions for emancipation are constructed out of the struggle between these
differently weighted gender identities, and women's liberation is resolutely
connected to the victory of the female side of the gendered opposition. The
female side carries with it a host of secondary conceptual terms (naturally
posed against their male opposition): life (death), nature (culture), reproduction
(production), birth (death), the body (mind), the household (*polis*), the maternal (paternal) and, finally, perhaps the most decisive duality in feminist political theory: private (public).

Next I shall consider what happens when a feminist interpretation driv-
en by an analytically gendered and normatively weighted binary conceptual
framework meets a vast surveyor's map like *The Human Condition*, with its proliferating (mostly) nonbinary concepts. We should not forget that the deploy-
ers of the binary framework are themselves females who bring a feminist
celebration of women's difference to their work. Thus what is at stake in the
initial interpretive feminist context of Arendt studies is both the gendering of
The Human Condition and the gendering of Hannah Arendt. The question at
issue in difference feminism is (and can only be) this: Is Arendt a woman who
thinks like a woman, or a woman who thinks like a man? The verdict, as we
shall see, ultimately depends upon the way in which the gender binary is read
off of Arendt's major theoretical text.

Phallocentric Arendt

Adrienne Rich and Mary O'Brien set the initial tone for the feminist reception
of Arendt, and both of them, in effect, declare that Arendt is a woman who
thinks like a man. Rich and O'Brien also bring decisive interests to bear upon
The Human Condition. In keeping with the strategy of difference feminism, they
posit a feminist emancipatory politics of "women's work" (Rich) or "reproductive consciousness" (O'Brien) over and against a male politics of the public or
political realm, which the engulfing metanarrative of Western "male-stream
thought" or "male ideology" supports.[10] From this vantage point, *The Human
Condition* is, to say the least, a deeply flawed book, and not only because Arendt
barely alludes to the condition of women in the human condition and thereby
shows contempt for the efforts of women in labor.[11] The problem also involves
Arendt's celebration of "the common world of men" (Rich 1979, 208), especially in the form of "Paterfamilias on his way to the freedom of the political

realm" (O'Brien 1981, 101). In this glorification of the public [man] over the private [woman], Rich (212) sees "the tragedy of a female mind nourished on male ideologies"; and O'Brien (100) reads "a woman who accepts the normality and even the necessity of male supremacy."

Since there is much at issue for both Arendtian political theory and feminist politics in these views, it is worth considering how Rich and O'Brien arrive at their reading of *The Human Condition* as a masculinist text and Arendt as a male ideologue. As difference feminists, both bring to *The Human Condition* a perspective that is substantively geared toward gaining access to the true nature or meaning of women as human beings.[12] Methodologically, they follow a strategy that places Arendt's text under the logic of a binary interpretive schema that posits a static gender polarity as its core analytical category. From this "difference" starting point follow at least three interpretive moves that have some significant consequences for the conceptual integrity of *The Human Condition* as a political theory. First, Arendt's text must be approached from an analytical prospect fixed upon being, nature, and subjectivity, and not upon "doing," "activities," and interaction, which is where Arendt (1958, 7) herself begins. Thus, O'Brien (1981, 100) characterizes Arendt's discussion of the *vita activa* in terms of "the two natures of man."[13] Second, O'Brien poses the problem of human nature as a binary male:female opposition that effectively erases Arendt's (1958, 7 f.) commitment to a tripartite notion of activities (labor:work:action) with its corresponding "basic conditions" (life:worldliness:plurality) and substitutes the category nature:society. So activities become subjectivities, and a triplet becomes a doublet.[14] As a result of these two moves, O'Brien (1981, 100, 121) can argue that Arendt supports an "action metaphysics" that simply recapitulates Aristotle's justification of male (society) over female (nature), and "polis life" (man's second nature) over "bodily need and species continuity" (man's first nature). Following hard upon the logical must of the gender binary, O'Brien's third move seizes the Arendtian spatial category that best accommodates the logic she imposes, and that is the category public:private. Thus the one obvious pairing in Arendt's conceptual map is hypermagnified in O'Brien's analysis, while all other conceptual configurations are blurred, if not altogether erased, even as O'Brien (1981, 110) criticizes the "artificiality" and "literal thoughtlessness" of Arendt's own analytical categories.[15] Under the category "private/female" O'Brien reloads her terms "first nature/body/species life"; under "public/male" she reloads "second nature/uniqueness/politics." Keeping in mind Arendt's privileging of the public realm of politics, O'Brien (1981, 101) now suggests that "Arendt stands in a long line of social and political thinkers who, in failing to analyze the significance of reproductive consciousness, are able to find all kinds of ontological, metaphysical and ultimately ideological justifications of male supremacy."

As a result of these three moves, O'Brien reads the hierarchy that Arendt establishes in the *vita activa* not as the existential superiority of action (plural-

ity) over labor (life) and work (worldliness), but as the superiority of one ontological realm (Male Public) over another (Female Private).[16] In O'Brien's hands,
Arendt's *vita activa* is transmuted from an Existenz category that reveals three differentially illuminated human activities within the human condition into an
ontological category that assigns two differentially weighted gender subjectivities (women:MEN) to human nature, and two differentially weighted realms
(private:PUBLIC) to human life. Moreover, Arendt's action concept of politics
is rendered as "patriarchy and the doctrine of potency, the creations of a brotherhood of fathers acting collectively to implement their definitions of manhood
in social and ideological forms" (O'Brien 1981, 103–104).[17] O'Brien (1981, 110,
9) does not have to go far to conclude, then, that the "ideology of male supremacy" infects *The Human Condition* and that Arendt herself is a "female male-
supremacist." Rich (1979, 212) follows suit and denounces "the power of male
ideology to possess such a female mind, to disconnect it as it were from the
female body which encloses it and which it encloses."

What follows from these adamantly dismissive views is, in essence, a series
of feminist contestations over the gender of the mind that thinks in Hannah
Arendt's gendered female body. As the text most representative of that mind,
The Human Condition remains the source of feminist inquiry into the gender-
ic allegiances of Arendtian thinking, and (following O'Brien) the Greek *polis*
becomes a popular excavation site for evidence of Arendt's phallocentrism.[18]
Nowhere, perhaps, are the phallocentric possibilities of Arendt's *polis* envy
more vividly rendered than in Hanna Pitkin's (1981, 338) depiction of the
Arendtian public sphere as a bunch of "posturing little boys clamoring for
attention . . . and wanting to be reassured that they are brave, valuable, even
real." Although "Arendt was female," Pitkin avers, "there is a lot of *machismo* in
her vision . . . the men she describes strive endlessly to be superhuman."[19]
Along these same lines, Wendy Brown (1988, 61) praises Pitkin's "marvelous
account" and forwards a critique of Arendtian politics that bears numerous
similarities to O'Brien's. Like O'Brien, Brown imposes a binary category that
erases Arendt's tripartite construction (*animal laborans:homo faber*:action) and
maps a gender dichotomy with masculinist preferences upon Arendt's text. In
the machismo of Arendtian politics, Brown (1988, 148, 27) argues, we find the
celebrated image of the Greek *polis* and its "strutting young men in restless
pursuit of honor" who "stomped the ground that fed them [and] suppressed
and violated their connectedness with others and with nature." This machismo is enshrined in what Brown (180) takes to be the dichotomy Arendt constructs between *animal laborans* (life, body, necessity, and "woman") and action
(politics, freedom, and "manhood"). By locating freedom in the realm of politics, Arendt fulfills the phallocentric desire for release from the realm within
which "Woman" has been traditionally configured: bodily maintenance, necessity, and life. Thus Brown (29) arrives at O'Brien's conclusion, although from
a different direction.[20] Arendt's public realm reasserts an "unapologetic attach-

ment to a politics of manly deeds liberated from concern with life and the lives of others," and Arendt herself exhibits an "extraordinary level of horror at 'the natural.'"[21] Like Rich, Brown notices "something perilously close to pathology" in Arendt's attempt to situate action in a "free space" outside the (female) body. What Arendt cannot admit, Brown (196) says, is that "the body is the locus or vehicle of action, hence of freedom."

Gynocentric Arendt

For other feminists, the female body as a locus of freedom is precisely what Arendt's thinking mind embraces, and a gynocentric project is something that *The Human Condition* supports. Thus Terry Winant (1987, 146) finds Arendt useful for a philosophy that "takes the side of woman and sticks to it," and Nancy Hartsock (1983, 253 f.) concludes that "Arendt remains an interesting and important example whose work indicates some of the beneficial theoretical effects women's experience of both connection and individuation may have. . . . She has, despite her adherence to the Homeric model, reinterpreted it in ways much more congruent with women's than men's experience." If the feminists who read a phallocentric Arendt magnify the Greek *polis* of posturing boys, then these commentators redefine Arendtian concepts as gynocentric images that contest Pitkin's bracing metaphor and, in the words of Jean Bethke Elshtain (1986, 110), "stir recognition of our own vulnerable beginnings and our necessary dependency on others, on (m)other." Within this context, nothing takes on more importance for Elshtain and the (m)others than the Arendtian concept of "natality," which along with "life," "mortality," "worldliness," "plurality," and the "earth," Arendt (1958, 11, 9) deems a "condition of human existence." In Arendt's phenomenology, natality contrasts to mortality, and marks the human capacity for "beginning something anew" or "acting," not ending.[22]

Hartsock, Winant, Elshtain, and Ruddick appropriate natality or birth in various ways, but all of them find in this category a gynocentric Arendt whose feminist theory (a) is unique to political theorists as women and to "women's experience" with motherhood (Hartsock 1983, 225–226, 237); (b) invites us to counter the massive denial of "'the female'" and restore "commemoration and awe" for "the birth of new human beings" (Elshtain 1986, 110); (c) provides a context for "a maternal history of human flesh" that celebrates "a birthgiving woman's labor" and "the child who has been born" (Ruddick 1989, 209–211); and/or (d) brings to a feminist "standpoint" insights concerning "a multiplicity of 'mother tongues'" and "cultural and discursive birthplaces" (Winant 1987, 127). In arriving at this gynocentric Arendt, all of these views link political natality primarily to the domain of *animal laborans* (that is, to the biological process of the [female] human body or to activities involved with "vital necessities" like caring and tending for vulnerable human life). This is an inventive move that certainly rescues Arendt from the clutches of hateful machismo, and it goes a long way to correct O'Brien's and Brown's insistence upon the violence inherent in Arendtian power politics. (For her part, Elshtain [1986, 110] goes a rather exceedingly long way, casting Arendt as a kind of redemptive figure and finding in Arendtian politics a "pacific image that evokes love, not war." Given Arendt's [1958, 242, emphasis added] view of love as "the most powerful of all *antipolitical* human forces," this is a little difficult to sustain.)

Whatever their advances, however, these gynocentric interpretations proceed from conceptual assumptions that are no less problematic than those which drive the phallocentric readings of Arendt. Most problematically, perhaps, they resolutely erase the very distinctions between labor:action and political:metaphysical upon which Arendt insists. Nowhere is this erasure conceptually more evident and mistaken than in Hartsock's (1983, 259) appropriation of an Arendtian concept of power "grounded at the epistemological level of reproduction." To ground Arendtian politics in reproduction and thereby make *animal laborans* (for example, biology, metabolism, birth, birthgiving, parturition) the source of power is to blur labor:action (power) so thoroughly as to make its uniquely Arendtian aspect unrecognizable. Moreover, although the gynocentric difference feminists have a better grasp of Arendt's action concept of politics than do Rich, O'Brien, and Brown,[23] we should notice that in the end, they release the very same analytically gendered and normatively weighted binary against *The Human Condition* as do those who charge Arendt with phallocentrism. The only difference lies in that with the aid of the reconstituted concept of natality, they gender Arendt along the feminine side of the binary rather than the masculine side. The key to this gendering lies in accepting natality as the central category of politics (as Arendt does) and then configuring it literally as women's experience in giving birth and mothering, or figuratively as a feminist concept derived from women's "life activity" (as Arendt does not). As a result of this natalization, Arendt can be coded as a woman who thinks like a woman in a female body, rather than a woman who thinks like a macho man.

In what I have characterized as the difference feminist struggle between phallocentric and gynocentric accounts of the Arendtian public realm, we might also notice two looming images of Arendt herself, ironically not unlike the images she thinks came to characterize the myth of Rosa Luxemburg. On the one hand, there looms the "propaganda image" of the patriarchal male supremacist; on the other, there looms the "sentimentalized image" of the good-woman-as-mother (Arendt 1968, 36). As Arendt (1958, 38) says of Luxemburg so we might say of Arendt: "Her new admirers have no more in common with her than her detractors." This is because Arendt's admirers and detractors both bring to "the vast surveyor's map" nothing more than projections of a problematic interpretive schema that is wedded to a static binary of gender. In so doing, they render little justice to *The Human Condition* and perhaps even less to Arendt herself. We need to turn elsewhere than to difference feminism, then, for more promising and emancipatory receptions of Arendt's political thought.

Displacing the Gender Binary

Even those feminists who do not share the analytical presuppositions of difference feminism often find it necessary to acknowledge that Arendt's distinction between public and private is "historically invidious" (Honig 1992, 222), "astounding" in its "denial of the 'women's issue'" (Benhabib 1992a, 115), or at least inappropriately viewed as a "preferred state of affairs" (Fraser 1989a, 160). In effect, the public:private distinction is often taken as evidence that Arendt is far less compelling as a theorist of gender than she is, in Bonnie Honig's (1992, 215) words, "as a theorist of a politics that is potentially activist." But Arendt's conceptual map is contested terrain. Some (nondifference) feminists see the Arendtian public:private as a key to problems of exclusion and to the historical condition of women in particular.[24] Thus Joanne Cutting-Gray (1993, 50 n. 1) argues that "as early as 1933 Arendt saw that the private sphere to which most women are relegated devalues their potential because it valorizes the life process."

I shall return to some of these feminist interpretations momentarily. But as a first response to these projects, I suggest that the "woman issue" notwithstanding, *The Human Condition* carries a far more provocative gender subtext than most feminists have noticed to date.[25] In this provocative (and perhaps unintended) subtext, Arendt not only thematizes gender as a dominant category of modernity; she also displaces it through an action concept of politics. In order to appreciate how Arendt does this, we need to move away from the category public:private and repair instead to the tripartite category labor:work:action (that is, to the triplet that difference feminists reduce to the doublet PUBLIC/freedom/politics/male:PRIVATE/necessity/labor/female). By recovering the Arendtian triplet, we will discover that the two concepts that Arendt does relentlessly gender as feminine and masculine are not "private" and "public" but *animal laborans* and *homo faber*. Once we understand this, we can also see how the third concept, action, is existentially superior as the embodiment of freedom to both the biological cyclicalities of earth's and nature's "servant," *animal laborans*, and the means-end fabrication of "earth's lord and master," *homo faber* (Arendt 1958, 139).[26]

Arendt's gendering of the *vita activa* takes form in what Pitkin (1981, 340) calls "a pair of inappropriate attitudes or states of mind, both connected with the social: the attitudes of expedient utility [*homo faber*] and of 'process' thinking [*animal laborans*]." If we look to the subtext of Arendt's text, we might notice that the social realm is not only "a historically emergent societal space specific to modernity" (Fraser 1992a, 160) but also a symbolic order within which the two attitudes of mind that Pitkin identifies are repeatedly inscribed and represented as feminine and masculine signifiers (or as what Arendt in other contexts calls *feminini generis* and *masculini generis*; see Arendt 1968, 45, and Young-Bruehl 1982, 272). Thus, the crisis of modernity, which Arendt (1958, 126–135) brilliantly casts as the struggle between worldless technological automatism and the world of work, is also a matrix of social attitudes relentlessly driven by the binary of gender. From this Arendtian perspective we might think of the difference feminists as thoroughly in the grip of modernity's favorite symbolic category.

As the subtext of Arendt's text unfolds, the gender binary *animal laborans:homo faber* appears as a complex and multifaceted relationship in at least three aspects.[27] From the first aspect, the relationship is (mutually) beneficial. Thus, "nature and the earth constitute the condition of human life" (1958, 134); but at the same time, "*homo faber* [comes] to the help of the *animal laborans*" by making "the effort of its sustenance and the pain of giving birth, easier and less painful than it has ever been" (121). From a second aspect, the relationship is (mutually) oppositional. *Animal laborans* threatens to "consume," "devour," and subjugate *homo faber* by sucking him into "an enormously intensified life process" (132). When this happens, "the ideals of *homo faber*" are "sacrificed to abundance, the ideal of *animal laborans*" (126). At the same time, with the "huge arsenal" of implements and tools that he uses to "erect the world," *homo faber* tears materials "out of the womb of the earth" and does unspeakable violence to *animal laborans* (155). Thus, "the work process takes matter out of nature's hands without giving it back to her in the swift course of the natural metabolism of the living body" (100). Arendt (1958, 100) suggests that both *animal laborans* and *homo faber* exercise violence toward each other (labor "consumes" man-made things; work "violates" nature, and so on) and both are destructive (labor from the standpoint of the world, work from the viewpoint of nature). But nowhere does Arendt (139) more vividly encompass the violent character of the labor:work relationship than when she represents *homo faber* as the male supremacist whose ideology of instrumental fabrication carries with it "both violence and violation" over the life process of the female body of *animal laborans*. In this vivid encounter between nature and artificer, labor and work, Arendt captures in *homo faber*'s mentality the fear "of being consumed by the life process, by natural necessity and the body"—the fear that Brown (1988, 31 n. 29) mistakenly assigns to Arendt herself. Here as well, Arendt recognizes precisely what O'Brien (1981, 103) claims she overlooks: that "violence is needed to overcome the imperiousness of biological necessity."

With these first two aspects in mind, I want to suggest that Arendt is engaged in a double project. By (indirectly) affiliating *animal laborans* with the female and *homo faber* with the male, she sets up a conceptual structure that simultaneously embodies and unmasks the pervasive gender norms of modernity.

In the temporal story that Arendt tells of the *vita activa*, the reproductive-birthing-consuming fertility of the female *animal laborans* eventually triumphs in the modern world over the productive-violating-fabricating artifice of the male *homo faber*. But it would be a mistake to find here the celebration of female difference. For whatever the reversals within this opposition, the gender-symbolic *animal laborans:homo faber* is in its totality for Arendt (1958, 308 f.) a "restricted frame of reference." Taken together, neither "the driving necessity of biological life and labor nor the utilitarian instrumentalism of fabrication and usage" (174) foster the condition where freedom appears as the actualization of speech and action in a space of appearances in the world. Indeed, both *animal laborans* and *homo faber* do much to defeat such a space of appearances, and thus they threaten freedom itself. From a third aspect, then, the *animal laborans* and *homo faber* are, despite their opposition, in alliance against an alien power. What Pitkin (1981, 341) calls "the twin dangers of process and expediency"—the automatism of labor and the instrumentalism of work—conspire in the modern world to obliterate the human capacity for action.

If in the temporal dimension of Arendt's *vita activa*, *animal laborans* appears to have triumphed in modernity over *homo faber* and action, then in its existential dimension, which concerns "the basic conditions under which life on earth has been given to man," action is victorious over both labor and work (1958, 7). Action requires *animal laborans* and *homo faber* for, in order to act, human beings must first satisfy the demands of life and achieve stability, not only to protect "man from nature" but also to "build the world of the human artifice" within which action can take place (137, 230). Yet action also triumphs existentially over labor and work because its corresponding condition of plurality and its coequal element of speech actualize in human life the acting together in concert of unique and distinctive persons who are speakers of words and doers of deeds. This solidarity born of unique distinctness, spontaneity, and new beginnings (natality) Arendt also calls politics. In Arendt's theory, then, the action concept of politics sets off an existential experience that is profoundly different from either the singular collectivity of *animal laborans*'s repetitive labor or the collective singularity of *homo faber*'s instrumental work.[28]

If we keep in mind *The Human Condition*'s gender subtext, then for feminism Arendt's recovery of action is significant on at least two levels. On the level of theory, action is a category that can release feminism from the generic-genderic force of the familiar bifurcation that divides all human capacities relevant to agency into masculine:feminine (*animal laborans:homo faber*). In its gender subtext, Arendtian theory distances freedom from the static language (*langue*) of gender identity and locates it instead in acts of personal speech-revelation (*parole*) that resolutely resist the control of predetermined, descriptive, bifurcated signifiers. Once released from the tenacity of such signifiers, feminist theory in its action-coordinating mode is free to reimagine an account of agency that is, among other things, not committed to a gendered telos of the human condition. In keeping with Arendt's (1958, 205) emphasis upon freedom as the "who-ness of acting" and not the "what-ness of Being," feminism might theorize human persons as sui generis, and thereby liberate subjectivity (feminist theory's current *bête noire*) from the damaging and unnecessarily repressive scrutiny of the binary of gender.

On a practical-normative level, Arendtian action is a category that can serve to revivify feminism as a politics committed to the spontaneity and unpredictability of persons acting together in concert as speakers of words and doers of deeds. By refusing to collapse the labor of *animal laborans* (as woman) into the politics of action, the Arendtian subtext renounces the restrictive language and the nostalgic celebration of "women's traditional capacities" (or the female body) in order to open capacities, as speech-acts, to their full emancipatory potential. Like other social movements in modernity, feminism has had its difficulties distinguishing politics as an action concept from the power of the patriarchal state or (to recall O'Brien) as paterfamilias in the public realm. But in the displacement of the gender binary, Arendt not only leaves the celebration of woman (*animal laborans*) out of politics; she also releases politics from the stultifying grasp of *homo faber* and the negative formulations "masculinity," "patriarchy," and "paterfamilias." As a result, Arendtian theory invites a rebirth in the feminist understanding of politics as "a kind of theatre where freedom could appear," beyond the phallocentric:gynocentric divide (Arendt 1969, 154).

The (De)Gendering of Arendtian Politics

From the vantage point of the radical gender subtext and the action concept of politics that I have identified in *The Human Condition*, we might now assess how a new wave of feminist readings have appropriated Arendt's thought for feminist projects. These readings are not interested in gendering the mind and body of Hannah Arendt; nor do they summon the spirits of machismo and maternity to Arendt's corpus. Rather, they seek to bring Arendtian theory to bear upon a conceptual problem that bedevils much contemporary theoretical feminism, and upon which the meaning of a "feminist politics" itself hinges: the identity of the female as woman. Since many recent feminist interpretations appropriate Arendt in order to address the gender-identity question, I shall sketch first how academic feminism writ large has brought "the politics of identity" to the political movement called feminism. Then I shall consider how feminists have brought the politics of identity to Arendt.

In academic feminism writ large, the politics of identity is not a unified domain of inquiry but rather a multifaceted enterprise that has unfolded in three discrete (if not dialectical) moments, as the cunning of gender and the concept of woman work their way through feminist inquiry. In the first moment, the problem of identity is formulated in a fashion that resurrects the epistemological assumptions of *difference* feminism for expressly political purposes. Thus it grounds feminist action-coordination in "women's life activity" or a privileged epistemological "feminist standpoint" (Hartsock 1983, 226). Feminist politics is linked to the distinctive character of women as a group and to the undifferentiated subjectivity of (certain) persons as women. In the second moment, the politics of identity takes shape in feminist appeals to diversity, with an aim toward hybridizing and complicating "women" in terms of an identity complex of race, class, ethnicity, culture, sexual identity and/or sexuality, and so forth, that may be open to "choosing" (Alcoff 1988, 432). In effect, *diversity* feminism posits "woman" as a "relational term" and a "positional perspective" from which a feminist politics can emerge (Alcoff 1988, 434).[29] In its third moment, the feminist politics of identity theorizes its own negation by designating "women" an "undesignatable field of differences, one that cannot be totalized or summarized by a descriptive identity category" (Butler 1991, 160). Thus *deconstructive* feminism disrupts all of the univocal and stable social categories that difference and diversity feminisms embrace and instead poses the term "women" as a "site where unanticipated meanings might come to bear" (Butler 1991, 160; also Brown 1995).

Just as the initial receptions of Arendt developed against the dominant discursive context of difference feminism, so many recent commentaries map upon Arendt's thinking one or another of the moments I have just sketched in the feminist discourse of identity. From a difference position that reaffirms gender as the "self-conscious development of [women's] own latent tradition" (Lane 1983, 115) or "women's power" and "material life activity" (Hartsock 1983, 253, 261) or "a community of speaking women" (Yaeger 1988, 277), Arendtian politics is celebrated as a context within which distinctive persons are reaffirmed as "women." In this vein, Patricia Yaeger (1988, 276) recovers Arendt's figuration of the polis and imagines "a nexus of women 'combining and covenanting,' 'acting and speaking together.'" Ann Lane (1983, 115) suggests that Arendt's concept of politics is uniquely suited to "the meaning of women's hidden tradition . . . of doing rather than making." Thus Arendtian politics provides a "regenerative potential" within which (the unitary subjectivity) "women" can achieve liberation.[30]

From a diversity position that complicates gender with other socialdescriptive categories, Arendtian politics is sometimes redeemed as (sympathetic to) the idea of a "multiplicity of publics" or "subaltern counterpublics" that promote "intercultural communication" (Fraser 1992b, 126). In this context, Arendtian plurality absorbs gender into a hybrid of cultural identities "woven of many different strands" (126). Hence, the Arendtian public becomes "publics" wherein the "what-ness of Being" is, in all of its multiculturality, discursively revealed. In another guise, diversity feminism folds the politics of identity into biographical questions of Arendt's own Jewish-female-ness, read through the critical categories of "pariah" and "parvenu" that inform her analyses of anti-Semitism, totalitarianism (1978), and Zionism (1973), as well as her studies of Rahel Varnhagen (1974) and her essay on Rosa Luxemburg (1968). Taken as a whole, this complex of elements allows diversity feminists to move beyond *The Human Condition* and seize the pariah category as a useful device for complicating various contexts of difference (Markus 1987), exclusion (Ring

1991, 1997; Lane 1983), and marginalization (Moruzzi 1990) in ways that either elide, assimilate, or hybridize gender into an identity complex.

Whether they complicate gender or simply reaffirm it, diversity and difference feminists all take possession of Arendt in order to mobilize descriptive characteristics—or the "what-ness" of group identity—in the interests of a liberatory feminist politics. But in this gendering of Arendtian politics, they also reconfigure Arendt's action concept of politics beyond recognition. Specifically, these feminist readings blur the very distinction between a "what" and a "who" upon which Arendtian politics rests. In doing so, they miss the emancipatory point: for, as we have seen, Arendt locates freedom in the "who-ness of acting" (speech), not the "what-ness of Being." Arendtian action, understood as the displacement of the binary of gender (*animal laborans:homo faber*), decisively forfeits the "description of qualities [one] shares with others," in favor of the existential display of "unique distinctness" in the company of peers, which is the locus of freedom itself (Arendt 1958, 179, 181). Thus Arendt (181) argues that once one becomes a "what" in an action context, a person's "specific uniqueness escapes us" and freedom disappears.[31] If we take this point seriously, and in relation to the gender subtext of *The Human Condition*, then it seems that an emancipatory Arendtian feminism must reject both the reaffirming strategy of difference feminism that posits the generic-genderic "woman" and the complicating strategy of diversity feminism that posits a hybridized subjectivity ("everyone is *mestizo*") as gender-race-class-ethnicity-sexuality under the rubric of social or cultural positionalities (Fraser 1992b, 141 n. 27). For insofar as both of the latter feminisms reduce action to the reclamation of a particular descriptive social or cultural category/categories and freedom to identity "standpoints" or a complex of "positions," they fundamentally misconstrue the raison d'être of Arendtian politics.[32] Thus the feminist freedom that these feminisms promote in the name of Arendt is not, in view of Arendt's action concept of politics, freedom at all.

There is a third alternative, however. In response to difference and diversity feminisms, Joanne Cutting-Gray and Bonnie Honig bring a deconstructive conceptual sensibility to Arendt's action concept that comes closer, I think, to the spirit of an Arendtian feminist politics. Implicitly at least, both Cutting-Gray (1993, 49) and Honig (1992, 216) pose Arendtian action as the displacement of gender (and unitary subjectivity) and recommend to feminism a politics that dismantles the "inhibiting polarities" of gender and contests "(performatively and agonistically) the prevailing construction of sex and gender into binary and binding categories of identity." By degendering Arendtian politics, deconstructive feminism rescues Arendt's action concept from difference in a way that does not commit it to diversity. Thus Cutting-Gray (1993, 49) notes that "identities like 'Jew' or 'Woman' are historically constituted" and should not be closed to dialectical resistance. Similarly, Honig (1992, 231, 227;

also 1995) calls for resistance to "the violent closures" imposed by "some Jewish and feminist politics of identity," and she unleashes Arendt's theory of action against any concept of "a political community that constitutes itself on the basis of a prior, shared and stable identity" and threatens to "close the spaces of politics."

In effect, deconstructive feminism aims to restore the Arendtian who-ness of acting over the what-ness of Being. Hence it recommends a politics of "alterity" (Cutting-Gray 1993, 36)[33] or an "agonistic politics of performativity" (Honig 1992, 225) and urges feminism to disrupt an identity politics of (*femin:masculin*) generis in favor of the sui generis. Along these lines, Honig (1992, 231) rereads Arendtian space(s) agonistically, as both external and internal "sites of critical leverage" within which (communities) and (self) rupture, fragment, and proliferate. In Honig's challenge to proliferate, the sturdy "what-ness of Being" is repeatedly confounded by what Arendt (1958, 178) calls the "startling unexpectedness" of the disclosure of "who." At the same time, the who's univocal identity is strategically opened to an unpredictable flux of multiple significations and unanticipated meanings. Somewhat similarly, in the name of "a genuine feminist politics of alterity," Cutting-Gray (1993, 49) recommends a "plurality to the female political subject" that embraces "unique difference" and the irreducible particularity of "otherness." By emphasizing uniqueness, particularity, and contingency rather than sameness, generality, and fixity, Cutting-Gray argues, Arendtian politics prepares feminist politics "for the dissolution of the female as any set identity."[34] Consequently, both Honig and Cutting-Gray appropriate Arendt in order to disrupt the solid positionalities of "identity" with an evanescent politics of irreducible "identities" (Honig) and radically pluralized otherness (Cutting-Gray). In deconstructive feminism, the meaning of Arendt's action concept of politics as the overcoming of gender (or any and all complexes of "what-ness") is effectively preserved and feminist identity politics is released to the full Arendtian flux of "[r]esistibility, openness, creativity and incompleteness" (Honig 1992, 217; cf. Cutting-Gray 1993, 48-50).

Existentially Speaking

The strength of deconstructive feminism rests in its appropriation of Arendt's action concept for purposes of freeing identity (and the term "women") from restrictive categories that reduce acting to being and "efface difference for the sake of an equality of sameness" (Honig 1992, 244 f.). Once it is opened to the equivalent of a play of "resignifications" (Butler 1991, 161), Arendtian politics becomes a powerful theoretical starting place for the articulation of an action-coordinating feminism that maintains the category "women" as the critical focus of its politics, *but does not assert it as the political identity of its agents.*[35] For in its recovery of Arendtian action, deconstructive feminism dismantles the fixity of identity-in-kind in favor of "identities"; thereby it makes it impossible for "women" to serve as the unexamined posit of an action-coordinating feminist politics.[36]

In its Arendtian deconstruction of the stability of "what-ness" into the instability and fragmentation of disclosing "who-ness," feminism's third identity moment introduces a new set of complexities into feminist politics. For given the "coeval and coequal' relationship that Arendt's (1958, 189) action concept of politics forges with an action concept of speech, deconstructive feminism's disclosure of the "who-ness" of Arendtian politics is also, and unavoidably, an encounter with how "who-ness" gets disclosed—or with what it means collectively to speak—in the Arendtian public realm. Thus in Honig's deconstructive feminism, we find not only an agonistic Arendtian politics but also a dramatic picture of political speech as agon in the Arendtian space—as a verbal game of struggle, dispute, competition, and contest wherein, perhaps, the very terms of political discourse explode and fragment even as they are uttered. Now, if we have gained anything from the linguistic turn of the twentieth century, we have learned that the link between a theory of language (or speech) and a theory of politics is not trivial. So the agonistic account that Honig offers of Arendtian speech-acts directly raises for feminists the question of what constitutes truly emancipatory speech, or expressive collective interaction, in the public space of politics. In responding to this question, Seyla Benhabib has explicitly challenged Honig's formulation with an alternative conception of what constitutes the Arendtian public space. Thereby she opens the possibility of yet another feminist struggle over the Arendtian public realm.

As part of a larger project that is directed to the ethical content of an action politics and "models of public space," Benhabib (1992a, 1993) poses a (Habermasian) communicative concept of "associational public space" as an alternative to the (Nietzschean) disruptive concept of "agonistic public space" that Honig purportedly supports.[37] Although Benhabib (1993, 110) traces both of these models in Arendt, she deems the agonistic one "at odds with the sociological reality of modernity." But Arendt's so-called associational model, which seems to have a close affiliation with what Benhabib (1992a, 95; 1993, 110) describes as Habermas's "discourse model," is an appropriate starting point "for the feminist transformation of public life." Benhabib (1993, 102) understands the associational model in terms of "common action coordinated through speech and persuasion" that takes place in any space that is "the object and location of an 'action in concert.'" In such spaces she (1992a, 89) imagines speech not as agonistic verbal performativity but rather as "a conversation of justification" that unfolds in accordance with a norm of "egalitarian reciprocity." In casting Arendtian politics under the spell of Habermas, Benhabib encourages a feminist politics wherein speech "acts" in the interest of proliferating *issues* in a public space, rather than proliferating identities. Unlike Honig (1992, 220, 234 n. 40), whose Nietzschean agon focuses upon the performative "multiplicity" of the public and the self as a spectacular "event," Benhabib

(1992a, 95) imagines the Arendtian space as a context of procedural debate, where "the voice of persuasion and conviction" is governed by "the reflexive questioning of issues by all those affected by their foreseeable consequences."

While Honig commandeers Arendtian speech in the service of agonistic disruption and the "who-ness of acting," Benhabib (1992a, 95) notarizes it for purposes of sustaining the "spontaneity, imagination, participation and empowerment" that is the mark of "what our 'res publica' is all about." As a result, Benhabib's associationalism asserts something for feminism that Honig's agonism diminishes: the power of Arendt's concept of freedom as the politics of citizens speaking and acting in concert in the space of appearances.[38] In this associationalism, feminist theory might be able to find a way out of its current fixation on subjectivity and social recognition (wherein freedom is frequently formulated as the opening of spaces for the celebration of previously repressed group identities) and into a theoretical purchase that thematizes plurality over subjectivity and politics as collective action and deliberation over politics as group recovery and celebration. Yet at the same time, Benhabib's associationalism presupposes something that Honig's agonism deconstructs: the coherence of the gender identity of feminist performers in the public realm. Thus, even though she calls for a "feminized" practical discourse that challenges "unexamined normative dualisms as between justice and the good life, norms and values . . . from the standpoint of their gender context," Benhabib (1992a, 113, 110) posits an "elective affinity" between discourse ethics and "social movements like the women's movement" that derive out of "a postconventional and egalitarian morality." By assigning to the women's movement a normative position of superiority, Benhabib does not displace gender so much as reinforce it.[39] In this sense, then, Benhabib is correct to see Honig's agonistic model as at odds "with the sociological reality of modernity." For it is precisely modernity's favorite "reality"—the binary of gender—that Honig subverts in her deconstructive appropriation of Arendtian politics, and Benhabib does not.

The details of the exchange between Honig and Benhabib notwithstanding, in the exchange itself we might note the return of a dichotomy to the feminist receptions of Hannah Arendt. Only in its more recent incarnation, the dichotomy does not pose Arendtian politics in terms of a phallocentric:gynocentric attitude but rather as a Nietzschean:Habermasian orientation toward the politics of Arendtian speech. (Thus the identity of an *Arendtian* Arendtian politics of speech in the public realm—an Arendtian politics as sui generis—remains for the moment an open interpretive question.) Although it may be premature to spot a new feminist binary lurking in the agonistic:associational formulation of Arendtian public speech and space, the reading of the category off the Arendtian corpus confirms that Arendt's political theory continues to be a locale upon which academic feminism plays out its dominant discursive struggles, whatever those struggles may be. Even more important, howev-

er, we might see in the agonistic:associative struggle the continuing contemporary fascination with what Pitkin (1981, 336) calls, not entirely facetiously,
"that endless palaver in the [Arendtian] *agora*"—a fascination with the way in
which public speech takes place.

Indeed, what looms large on the current stage of feminist political theory are debates over models of discourse (as a symbolic system or a social practice) and disagreements about the dynamic that constitutes the emancipatory
quality (or qualities) of democratic political speech. Is it consensus or resistance?
Procedure or aesthetics? Communication, negotiation, argumentation, agonism, persuasion, debate, disruption, discourse, deliberation, theatricality, story-
telling, or dialogue? Insofar as the Arendtian action concept of politics places
speech at its center and Arendtian speech is hermeneutically open-ended, it
brings these dilemmas in all of their ambiguity not only to the question of
what constitutes a feminist politics, but also to the discursive activity of feminist theorizing itself.

Yet in the end, as Pitkin (1981, 346) reminds us, "my fellow citizens are
less an audience before whom I try to present a memorable image of self, than
fellow actors in collective self-definition, determining along with me not our
image but who we shall be, for what we shall stand." With this observation,
Pitkin ultimately takes Arendtian politics to task not for machismo but for failing to encompass adequately the "for what shall we stand" question: the question of what politics and public discourse are *about*, rather than the question
of how they "appear." In her critique of Arendt, Pitkin reminds us that
speech-acts and the presentation of the self (whether as agonal or associative)
do not exhaust the activity of politics. Nor should they exhaust the feminist
activity of theorizing about politics. Politics is not only the action context of
speaking, which Arendt decisively redeems as freedom. Politics is also the
action context of doing, the strategic practice of pursuing ends and determining means that Pitkin (1998, 280) redeems in the question of *justice* as "what
is to be done?" and in *action* as "just do it!"

If strategic action does indeed reside in the question of justice, then justice is something that Arendtian politics—whose focus on freedom resolutely
downplays the "what-ness of doing" in favor of the "who-ness of speaking"—
is unable to accommodate. But the focus on what is to be done, and doing it,
is a political imperative nonetheless. Feminists would do well to maintain this
focus, even as we continue to struggle within the Arendtian flux.

Part Three

The Politics of Politics

Chapter 7

Working in Half-Truth
Habermas, Machiavelli,
and the Milieu Proper to Politics

The international association of writers (PEN) held its Sixty-First World Congress in Prague in 1991, five years to the month after the "revolution of the Magic Lantern" and the whirl of events that marked the beginning of the end of the Communist regime in Czechoslovakia, and a rebirth of politics. The general political theme of the PEN congress posed a problem to politics, insofar as it raised questions about the role of the intellectual, and about the relationship of the intellectual to the professional politician. As Timothy Garton Ash (1995, 34 f.) reports, the problem was not merely a matter of academic debate but had itself become politicized in the Czech Republic "around the . . . magnetic polarity between the two Václavs, now better known as President Havel and Prime Minister Klaus." Ash, who was himself an invited speaker at the congress, sought to clarify the problem by positing the following distinction:

> The intellectual's job is to seek the truth, and then to present it as fully and clearly and interestingly as possible. The politician's job is to work in half-truth. The very word party implies partial, one-sided. (The Czech word for party, *strana*, meaning literally "side," says it even more clearly.)

Ash's formulation put him at odds on one end of the polarity with Prime Minister Václav Klaus, who was also present at the congress and spoke in favor of the proposition that there is no clear dividing line, or special status, that the intellectual enjoys over the professional politician. In fact, Klaus found Ash's (1995, 35) notion that politicians work in half-truth "incredible," and he accused Ash, author of *The Magic Lantern* (1990), of delivering a "political" speech against politicians, from the side of a partisan (and perhaps morally self-righteous) "intellectual."[1] On the other end of the polarity, Ash's formulation was also at odds with President Václav Havel's view of politics (in Ash 1995, 37–38) as "work of a kind that requires especially pure people, because it is especially easy to become morally tainted." "The way of a truly moral politics," Havel continues, "is neither simple nor easy." With this in mind, Havel opened the PEN congress by acknowledging the distinctive position of the intellectuals and calling upon his "dear colleagues" to take responsibility and "have an impact on politics and its human perceptions in a spirit of solidarity" (in Ash 1995, 34, 37). Herein lies his hope that "a new spirituality" might come to politics.[2]

Klaus and Havel hold different views about the role and integrity of the intellectual in politics. Nevertheless, we might notice a shared, as spoken, conviction between them concerning the possibilities for *purity* in politics. Klaus registers the conviction on the side of the politician, and by adamantly resisting both Ash's uneasy metaphor of "half-truth" and Havel's investiture of the intellectual over the politician as the morally superior seeker-of-truth. Havel registers the same conviction on the side of the intellectual, by arguing (against both Ash and Klaus) that in a corrupted age politics can be transfigured by the moral commitments of those intellects and writers who refuse to be dissuaded by "the lie" that "politics is a dirty business" (in Ash 1995, 37).[3] In this shared speech that commends itself to the purity of politics, the magnetic polarity between the two Václavs galvanizes into the form of a nearly Platonic political ideal. On this level, it matters not whether intellectuals are politicians or whether, by some dispensation of providence, politicians can become intellectuals. What matters is that both Václavs speak in the name of a politics that carries with it the imprimatur (if not the promise) of purity and truth.

Against this Václavian politics of truth, Ash (1995, 35 f.) deploys the alternative formulation of "working in half-truth" in order to distinguish "the professional party politician's job" from the intellectual's, especially as it is "reflected, crucially, in a different use of language." Here he amplifies what it means to work in the language of half-truth: "If a politician gives a partial, one-sided, indeed self-censored account of a particular issue, he is simply doing his job. And if he manages to "sell" the part as the whole then he is doing his job effectively.... If an intellectual does that, he is not doing his job; he has failed in it."

Ash (1995, 36) is anxious to insist that he is not casting the intellectual as "the guardian or high priest of some metaphysical, ideological or pseudoscientific Truth with a capital T." Thus, the difference between the role of intellectual and the role of the politician is not equivalent in any easy way to the epistemological divide between absolute Truth and relativism, or the metaphysical divide between objective reality and subjective experience. Whatever else they are, Ash's intellectuals are not Platonic philosopher-kings; although from the perspective of Platonic philosophy his politicians are surely sophists and rogues. The divide between Ash's truth-seeking intellectual and his partisan politician has rather more to do with the linguistic and ethical terrain on which they work, and not the upper ether of epistemology and metaphysics. If this terrain is organized along lines of "responsibility," then we might understand the divide between the intellectual and the politician as a matter of assuming, as Ash (1995, 36, emphasis added) puts it, "qualitatively different responsibilit[ies] for the *validity, intellectual coherence and truth*" of speech in each of these irreducible domains.

Some Machiavellian Presuppositions

Ash's observations raise many interesting issues about the nature and the role of intellectual activity, in and outside of politics. But I want to appropriate the formulation of "working in half-truth" in a Machiavellian spirit, in order to suggest that it captures not only an "elementary fact" about the job of the partisan party politician, as Ash (1995, 35) provocatively contends, but also something about the intrinsic impurity and partisanship of the peculiar domain of speech-action that is "politics itself." As we shall see, the "intrinsic impurity" thesis embodies a substantial challenge to certain modern theoretical approaches to politics, insofar as it carries with it at least two Machiavellian presuppositions. First, the intrinsic impurity thesis implies that as a field of reality, politics cannot be adequately contained under the formal rubrics of a modern legal-juridical or a constitutional-democratic political philosophy alone. Second, it implies that political speech is not as open to the possibility of "redemption" under the normative claims of validity, coherence, and truth as some philosophical modernists, deliberative democrats, and discourse ethicists appear to believe.

I am calling these presuppositions "Machiavellian" in less than a philosophical and more than a metaphorical sense. In the first instance, the limitations of a purely legal-juridical approach to politics are anticipated in Machiavelli's beastly advice in *The Prince* (1950, 65) concerning the "two methods of fighting, the one by law, the other by force." The former, Machiavelli observes, "is often insufficient," hence one must "have recourse to the second." Then follow his famous remarks upon the lion and the fox. In the second instance, Machiavelli anticipates the limitations of a concept of political speech as a practice of redeeming validity claims (especially with regard to sincerity) when he advises the prince that politics requires both the appearance of such qualities as sincerity and a "mind so disposed that when it is needful to be otherwise you may be able to change to the opposite qualities."

In short, a truly *virtúous* prince-as-political-actor must not only be always ready to *intend to deceive* others but also able to resist attempts by others to "redeem" the (sincere) intention behind the speech-act that deceives. In light of these Machiavellian insights, we might also bear in mind Foucault's (1984c, 374) observation that even the "best" theories and philosophies do not constitute very effective protection against disastrous political choices. We should reckon with the fact that there is an extremely tenuous link between a philosophical conception of (political) language as communication on the one hand and the concrete speech dynamics of strategic political actors who appeal to such principles on the other.[4]

The intrinsic impurity of-politics thesis that I am alluding to and the "political metaphysic without a philosophy"[5] that it represents are not especially *en vogue* in political theory today. Theorists who are committed to leveling the "genre distinction" between politics and culture, or politics and society, or the personal and the political, or the "spheres" of public and private, will find suspect the effort to endow politics with a special kind of intrinsicality, although some may find the ambiguities embedded in the notion of "half-truth" appealing.[6] Theorists who are engaged in philosophical efforts to rationalize politics in terms of justice and equality, or "the basic intuitive ideas" of constitutional democracy, will find the moral implications of working in half-truth troubling, although they may appreciate the effort to distinguish politics as a form of action or a mode of procedure. At the highest political philosophical reaches of the latter group we can find John Rawls's theory of justice and political liberalism. In Rawls's view, the basic intuitive ideas of democratic politics include the notion that society is a fair system of cooperation (not conflict) between free and equal persons. Behind the idea of "person" are two moral powers that Rawls (1985, 233) identifies: a capacity for a sense of justice, and a capacity for a conception of the good.

An even more important example of the philosophical effort to rationalize politics is Jürgen Habermas's influential discourse theory of deliberative democracy. Habermas (1990) conceives of the basic principles of the democratic constitutional state in relation to a normative conception of democratic deliberation among rational and reasonable agents who have themselves adopted the moral point of view. In both Rawls's and Habermas's philosophies, the normative structure of constitutional democracy is invested with a Kantian respect for individuals as free and equal persons, and for the impartiality of laws that all can agree to on that basis. Because I think that Habermas's political philosophy of discourse ethics provides the most powerful theoretical vindication of the practical attitude that I have been calling a "Václavian politics of truth," I will consider it more fully below, and in relation to the Machiavellian position on politics that I will proceed to defend.

Habermasian Discourse Ethics

Over the past two decades, Jürgen Habermas has developed a strong link between a philosophical conception of language (as communicative rationality) geared toward the redemption of validity claims and the concrete dynamics of politics as speech-action. He unites the two in a discourse theory of politics as deliberative democracy, where the public use of reason is distinguished by the enactment of procedures (validity relations) through which participants (as free and equal citizens) achieve agreement through critical discussion, or at least engage in "action oriented toward reaching understanding" (Habermas 1990, 133). Habermasian citizens are truth seekers insofar as, in Habermas's words (1987, 115), "the sphere of validity relations is . . . internally differentiated in terms of the viewpoints proper to truth, normative rightness, and subjective truthfulness or authenticity."[7] In short, Habermas's defense of rationality and reasonableness, and his equally compelling conception of politics as democratic deliberation, are both directed toward identifying and rooting out of politics "distorted communicative" conditions. In clarifying the relation between speech and politics, Habermas (1996, 12, emphasis added) notes, "[D]iscourse theory has the success of deliberative politics depend not on a collectively acting citizenry but on *the institutionalization of the corresponding procedures and conditions of communication.*" The "procedures and conditions" to which Habermas refers emerge out of a theory that (a) thematizes a "terrain of argumentation" in which validity claims are made; (b) assumes that all speech presupposes a "background consensus" among participants; and (c) anticipates that the validity claims inherent in the performing of a speech-action can be "vindicated" or "redeemed" (*Einlosen*) when the background consensus among interlocutors breaks down or is challenged.

Although Habermas certainly recognizes that communicative action is a never-ending aspect of human interaction, there is nevertheless a sense of purification, if not finality, implicit in his understanding of what constitutes any given instance of X questioning what Y is saying. This orientation toward purification is evident in Habermas's vocabulary of "vindicating" and "redeeming" validity claims. An act of *vindication* involves (a) clearing someone or something of accusation, censure, suspicion, and so forth; (b) supporting or maintaining, as a right or claim; and (c) serving to justify. (Although the obsolete usage in which vindicate means "avenge" or "punish" is telling.) In addition to its theological connotation as salvation from sin, *redemption* carries a propertarian reference, for example, regaining possession by paying a price; an ethical reference, for example, fulfilling an oath or a promise; and a reference to setting free, rescuing, or ransoming from hostile forces. Therefore, the negotiation and resolution of breakdowns in speech-communication appear, in Habermas's thinking, to take on the character of a cleansing from "suspicion" or "sin" that aligns rather nicely with the "new spirituality" that Havel commends.

Habermas links linguistic intersubjectivity as *practical discourse* to the vindication of validity claims that all citizens make (either implicitly or explicitly) as speakers. Therefore, discourse theory reconstructs four claims that are potentially redeemable in every statement a speaker utters, and grounded in the very character (or the "universal pragmatics") of our linguistic intersubjectivity: (a) intelligibility (or comprehensibility); (b) truth (regarding the propositional content); (c) justifiability (or appropriateness, in terms of the norms invoked); and (d) truthfulness (or sincerity, in the sense that the speaker does not intend to deceive the listener). Undistorted communication (and hence the success of deliberative politics) is thus secured in procedures and conditions in which interlocutors can, if necessary, redeem the four validity claims to intelligibility, truth, justifiability, and truthfulness that are themselves embedded in every speech-act.

The premise behind the highly specialized discussion that Habermas (1990, 134) calls "practical discourse" is the desire to *reach agreement* on the basis of "rationally motivated approval of the substance of an utterance." Discourse ethics establishes what Habermas (58) calls a "fundamental idea": interactions are *communicative* "when the participants coordinate their plans of action consensually, with the agreement reached at any point being evaluated in terms of the intersubjective recognition of validity claims." Thus "Anyone who seriously engages in argumentation," Habermas (1993, 31) contends, "must presuppose that the context of discussion guarantees in principle freedom of access, equal rights to participate, truthfulness on the part of participants, absence of coercion in adopting positions, and so on. If the participants genuinely want to convince one another, they must make the pragmatic assumption that they allow their 'yes' and 'no' responses to be influenced solely by the force of the better argument." Again, Habermas deploys these as *anticipatory* suppositions that are constitutive of a practice that, without them, would degenerate "at the very least into a surreptitious form of strategic action" (31). As such, these suppositions forward something that is quite a bit more than a "mere de facto acceptance of habitual practices" and quite a bit less than an externalized, transcendent Ideal.

To clarify this point, Habermas (1990, 58) draws his now-well-known distinction between two types of social interaction—*communicative* and *strategic*:

> Whereas in strategic action one actor seeks to *influence* the behavior of another by means of the threat of sanctions or the prospect of gratification in order to *cause* the interaction to continue as the first actor desires, in communicative action one actor seeks *rationally* to *motivate* another by relying on the illocutionary binding/bonding effect (*Bindungseffekt*) of the offer contained in his speech act.

In other words, actors are *strategic* if they "are interested solely in the *success*, that is, the *consequences* or *outcomes* of their actions (Habermas 1990, 133–134). As such, strategic actors "will try to reach their objectives by influencing their opponent's definition of the situation, and thus his decisions or motives, through external means by using weapons or goods, threats or enticements." At issue in strategic situations, Habermas (133) suggests, is the meshing of "egocentric utility calculations" in which the degree of cooperation is determined by the "interest positions" of the participants. By contrast, actors are *communicative* if they "are prepared to harmonize their plans of action through internal means, committing themselves to pursuing their goals only on the condition of an agreement . . . about definitions of the situation and prospective outcomes" (134).

The normative and procedural implications of Habermas's analytic distinction are instructively sketched by Simone Chambers (1996, 99):

> As opposed to strategic action, where participants are primarily interested in bringing about a desired behavioral response, in communicative action, participants are interested in bringing about a "change of heart." For example, in strategic action participants often attempt to sway each other by introducing influences unrelated to the merits of an argument, for example, threats, bribes, or coercion. . . . Communicative actors are primarily interested in mutual understanding as opposed to external behavior. . . . Only the "force of the better argument" should have the power to sway participants.

This distinction between "pure" communicative action and strategic action that Chambers delineates raises many difficulties, not the least of which is its adherence to an idealized model of communication that, as Habermas himself acknowledges, does not fit a great deal of everyday social interaction (McCarthy 1991, 132). Machiavelli's (1950, 56) famous riposte to those thinkers who "have imagined republics and principalities which have never been seen or known to exist in reality" seems pertinent here, for the idealized model that Habermas imagines and the distinction that supports it appear to dismiss the Machiavellian insight that "how we live is so far removed from how we ought to live, that he who abandons what is done for what ought to be done, will rather learn to bring about his own ruin than his preservation." I will return to this point as it relates to politics later.

For now, it is important to underscore that Habermas relies upon the communicative:strategic distinction to do at least two things: first, to show that on the level of linguistics, communicative action enjoys an "originary" priority over strategic and all other modes of linguistic usage, which are themselves "parasitic" (Rasmussen 1990, 38) or "derivative" (McCarthy 1991, 133) upon the former.[8] Second, on the level of political theory, Habermas introduces the distinction in order to limit the exercise of threats and coercion (or strategic action) by enumerating a formal-pragmatic system of discursive accountability (or communicative action) that is geared toward human agreement and mutuality. Despite its thoroughly modern accoutrements, communicative action aims at something like the twentieth-century discourse equivalent of the chivalric codes of the late Middle Ages; as a normative system it articulates the conventions of fair and honorable engagement between interlocutors. To be sure, Habermas's concept of communicative action is neither as refined nor as situationally embedded as were the protocols that governed honorable combat across European cultural and territorial boundaries and between Christian knights; but it is nonetheless a (cross-cultural) protocol for all that. The entire framework that Habermas (1993, 160) establishes is an attempt to limit human violence by elaborating a code of communicative conduct that is designed to hold power in check by channeling it into persuasion, or the "unforced" force of the better argument.[9]

At its most abstract normative level, discourse theory formulates what Habermas calls an "*ideal speech situation.*" This formulation has come in for its share of criticism, especially on the grounds that it posits an unrealizable, utopian ideal that bears no relevance for judging actual communicative contexts. The terms of this debate between Habermas and his critics involve highly complex methodological and philosophical issues in the reconstructive sciences, and I am in no position to negotiate them today (or, I suspect, any other day).[10] But let us agree for now that what Habermas (1993, 146) calls "the ideal moment of unconditionality" is neither a utopian blueprint nor a hypostatized configuration, and that philosophy can explicate this moment beyond what he (revealingly) calls "the provinciality of the given historical context."[11] The question I want to ask is: How meaningful is it to conceive of politics as open to the philosophical achievement of a discourse ethics?

The Milieu Proper to Politics

In responding to this question, I want to return to the intrinsic-impurity thesis that has been lying in wait here under the label of a Machiavellian politics of half-truth. For once we move from the subterranean contours of language philosophy to the "provincial" or existential terrain of politics; we are on the Machiavellian's field of actual historical reality. Hence, Machiavellian politics does not focus its challenge to Habermasian discourse ethics at the level of the reconstructive science of language, or the theory of communicative action that this science supports.[12] Indeed, the Machiavellian is quite content to allow the philosophers and underlaborers of discourse ethics—those who journey deep into the construction of language, normativity, and the logic of discourse—to go about their business. The aim of a Machiavellian endeavor, as Althusser (1999, 52) expresses it, is "not to imagine, dream, or hit upon ideal solutions," but rather "to think the conditions of possibility of an impossible task, to think the unthinkable." For the Machiavellian, that is, attending to philosophical or "utopian" matters is just so much fiddling while Savonarola burns.[13]

Where the Machiavellian thesis takes its stand against Habermasian discourse ethics is within "the milieu proper to politics," or what the phenomenologist Maurice Merleau-Ponty (1964, 211, 214) imaginatively terms (in deference to Machiavelli) that "knot of collective life in which pure morality can be cruel and pure politics requires something like a morality." This shifting of the terms of the debate from the Habermasian to the Machiavellian highlights the distance between a formal *theory* of practical discourse on the one hand and the concrete complexities of the phenomenal world of politics and political speech on the other.[14] From this vantage point of politics, the Habermasian appears all too modern, and *Diskursethik* seems politically naive, if not practically irrelevant. But what is the "range of phenomena," as Wolin (1960, 211) puts it, that Machiavelli perceived as uniquely peculiar to politics, and how is it resistant to the categories of Habermasian discourse ethics?

With this question in mind, we might note (at least) three levels of action where Machiavelli situates politics in *The Prince*.[15] Each of these levels involves the exercise of what we might call "instituting" and "constituting" acts. On the first and grandest level, Machiavelli's (1950, 94) action concept of politics comes to life at the end of the treatise, with the exhortation to "liberate Italy from the barbarians." From this vantage point, politics is the activity that aims at the fate of the state, the whole community, or the collectivity that is a people, and for a period of time that is in principle indeterminate and open to the vicissitudes of fortune (Machiavelli 1950, 92–93; see also Castoriadis 1992, 255).[16] Politics in its grandest sense thereby undertakes the initiation of innovations or even, at its most transformative, a "new system" (Machiavelli 94) or "order of things" (21). Under these circumstances, Machiavelli writes, it is sometimes necessary for the prince "to disturb the existing condition and bring about disorders . . . in order to obtain secure mastery," as Alexander VI did in Italy (25). It is one of the paradoxes of politics that sometimes acting contrary to a goal enables one to reach it. Disorders can bring order.

However, disorders can undermine order as well. Hence, on a second level, politics demands the astute exercise of power and an acute sense of what works in practice (*verita effettuale*), always with a view toward avoiding ruin. Machiavelli (1950, 14) offers this "general rule" to the prince: "[W]hoever is the cause of another becoming powerful, is ruined himself; for that power is produced by him either through craft or force; and both of these are suspected by the one who has been raised to power." Implicit in this observation is the fundamental view of politics as an arena of conflict and struggle where the political actor must anticipate and detect (as only the prudent person can) "the evils that are brewing" (11). The prince must be prepared to "remedy disorders" that are not of his own making, through violence if necessary and before they become insoluble (8).[17] Yet no certainty attends the politician's capacity to anticipate and counter disorder. "This is found in the nature of things," Machiavelli (84 f.) writes, "that one never tries to avoid one difficulty without running into another, but prudence consists in being able to know the nature of the difficulties, and taking the least harmful as good." As Merleau-Ponty (1964, 212) observes, "power is always described in *The Prince* as questionable and threatened." The world cannot be made unequivocally safe; nothing predestines it for a final harmony.

The achievement of secure mastery, equivocal though it may be, requires a background consensus that Machiavelli repeatedly characterizes as the support of the people (1950, 38–39, 67, 68, 70, 71, 81; also Merleau-Ponty 1964, 212). "And let no one oppose my opinion in this," he warns (38), "by quoting the trite proverb, 'He who builds on the people, builds on mud.'" Yet this collective consensus is not "interpretive understanding," much less the *end* or goal of politics in Machiavelli's view. Rather, consensus is a means (perhaps the most significant means) that allows politics (as the activity that aims at the fate of the collectivity) to continue. In Merleau-Ponty's (1964, 212) words, consensus is "the crystallization of opinion, which tolerates power, accepting it as acquired." On a third level of action, then, politics imposes upon the politician the imperative to maintain the consensus that is the support of the people, or at least to work to avoid its dissolution, which can happen at any time. Thus, Machiavelli (1950, 69) reiterates, "Well-ordered states and wise princes have studied diligently not to drive the nobles to desperation, and to satisfy the populace and keep it contented, for this is one of the most important matters that a prince has to deal with."

I have located the milieu proper to politics on these three levels of action in order to illuminate a primary Machiavellian point. On all three levels of instituting and constituting acts, from the grandest and most visionary (that is, the institution of new modes and orders) to the gravest and most elementary (that is, the anticipation and remedy of evils) to the grittiest and most rudimentary (that is, the maintaining of consensus between politician and public), *politics is an irreducibly strategic concern and a domain of strategic action.* Our basic political commitments notwithstanding, this is the case in princedoms as well as republics, oligarchies as well as democratic regimes, Communist and post-Communist nations, provincial states and global empires. Although there is much that must be said by way of evaluation and critique about how ideals get articulated, power organized, consensus sought, and tensions managed in these various state and global formations, there is no prior or more basic "truth of the matter" than the presence of strategic interests in the power struggle that is politics, whatever the hegemon or regime (Machiavelli 1950, 56).[18]

The strategic quality of politics embodies no necessary distinction between ruler and ruled, or politicians and citizens. As Berlin (1982, 55) succinctly notes, in reference to Machiavelli's views, "The subjects or citizens must be Romans too . . . if they lead Christian lives, they will accept too uncomplainingly the rule of mere bullies and scoundrels." When it comes to the pursuit of objectives, the feasibility of different courses of action, the struggle for competitive advantage, the contest for mastery, and the likelihood of success, there is no a priori or predetermined division between the "strategic" or active state and the "nonstrategic" or inert citizenry. Indeed, the very division between the ruler and the ruled is often the outcome of strategic struggles between participants in politics. Once the line is drawn, the relationship between the ruler and the ruled may be the continuation of this struggle in a different, but always strategic, form. Or, to follow Aristotle, the relation between ruler and ruled may also dissolve, amid struggle, into a situation of citizenship that entails the simultaneity of ruling and being ruled, of equals and peers who share rulership as a self-governing people. Thus, when Machiavelli counsels the prince against perceiving (much less treating) the people as "mud," he also conveys the notion that the strategic domain that is politics extends into the people itself—even if the means of containment and control of the subjects differ from princedom to princedom, and the possibilities for transforming princely subjects into republican citizens differ from state to state or regime to regime.

In identifying the strategic dimension of struggle that is politics, however, I do not mean to suggest that politics is fundamentally a context of domination, force, coercion, aggression, threat, or accusation.[19] Of course no one recognized better than Machiavelli that these means and even worse ferocities may be called for in certain situations. Witness Caesare Borgia's brutal slaying of his minister Remirro (Machiavelli 1950, 27); Ferdinand's "pious cruelty" toward the Moors (82); Severus's expeditious and bloody dispatch of Julianus, then Nigrinus, and then Albinus (72 f.). "For it must be noted," Machiavelli (9) contends in one of his more chilling remarks, "that men must either be caressed or else annihilated . . . the injury that we do to a man must be such that we need not fear his vengeance." Nevertheless, politics in a Machiavellian sense is not reducible to violence any more than it is reducible to the honest delegation of individual wills or the intersubjective mutuality of reciprocal understanding. Part of the intransigence of politics, as Machiavelli makes clear, involves its refusal to transform or restore itself into the philosophical desire for an ethical ideal. Yet politics also resists being factored into the basest of basic functions. Machiavelli can therefore maintain in equilibrium a relation that the Habermasian attempts to break. Thus, he writes (22): "[T]he character of peoples varies, and it is easy to persuade them of a thing, but difficult to keep them in persuasion. And so it is necessary to order things so that when they no longer believe, they can be made to believe by force."

What Machiavelli asks us to recognize, in other words, is that politics alternately tenses and relaxes somewhere in-between pure persuasion and pure force. This "collective knot" (to return to Merleau-Ponty's [1964, 211] telling phrase) of "vested interests and expectations, privileges and rights, ambitions and hopes, all demanding preferential access to a limited number of goods" (to borrow Wolin's [1960, 221] apt phrase) loosens and constricts in a milieu that is neither pure manipulation (where humans are treated as "means") nor pure communication (where humans are treated as "ends" in themselves). Within this in-between, reliance upon pure persuasion can be a disastrous thing; witness Savonarola—unarmed prophets fail (Machiavelli 1950, 22). But also within this world, pure violence can only be episodic and force intermittent, used and not used "according to the necessity of the case," lest power fall to ruin under the weight of human hatred and contempt (Machiavelli 1950, 56, 61).

With this in mind, we might now return to the political naivete of *Discursethik*, which begins by presupposing precisely what the Machiavellian considers not only naive but self-defeating: that it is meaningful to conceive of politics and political speech as open to the vindicative powers of rational claims to validity, coherence, and truth, or practically useful to ask participants "to exclude from [their] conversation all strategic and instrumental attitudes toward interlocutors" (Chambers 1996, 100). The Machiavellian throws the coherence of this "intellectualist" presupposition into question by maintaining, in the name of politics, that those who rely upon the consensuality of communicative rationality must necessarily come to grief among so many who are not communicative or, more accurately, always and inevitably strategically communicative and communicatively strategic.[20] Let me now try to say precisely what all of this might mean by returning at last to the intrinsic impurity and partisanship of political speech.

The Intrinsic Impurity of Political Speech

Just as the work of politics tends to generate a good many needs for which deeds of varying extremity are required, so political speech, the activity of articulating and justifying these needs and the deeds that spring from them, may prove impenetrable to discourse ethics, if not agonizing to communicative actors of the Habermasian kind. What "kind" of actor is this? Simone Chambers (1996, 99) offers a succinct characterization of the participants in Habermasian practical discourse: "In discourse a participant must recognize his dialogue partner as responsible and sincere in her desire to reach agreement, even if he disputes the validity of her claim. A sincere interest in reaching authentic agreement presupposes that participants are not interested in deception, manipulation, misdirection, or obfuscation." Similarly, Seyla Benhabib (1990, 359) writes of "good partners" in moral conversation and notes, "In conversation, I must know how to listen; I must know how to understand your point of view; I must learn to represent to myself the world and the other as you see them. If I cannot listen . . . the conversation stops, develops into an argument, or maybe never gets started." As a theory of deliberative democracy, Habermasian discourse ethics projects precisely this kind of moral conversation upon political speech, if only to enable the communicative actor to identify and challenge instrumental and strategic effects in situations of political interaction with a view toward approaching truly rational agreement if not absolutely securing it.

Now it is important to recognize that the Machiavellian does not deny the moral value of the notion of sincere interest in reciprocal conversation, nor even rule out the possibility of its realization in certain domains of social interaction. The Machiavellian simply denies the translatability of moral conversation into the practice of political speech and, moreover, warns against developing the capacity "to assume the moral point of view" (Benhabib 1990, 359) as a mode of being (as opposed to acting) in politics.[21] "If men were all good," as Machiavelli (1950, 64) puts a related point, "this precept would not be a good one; but as they are bad, and would not observe their faith with you, so you are not bound to keep faith with them." This is not so much a theory of human nature as it is an observation about human conduct in the milieu proper to politics and political speech.

Because the politician's world and hence the politician's speech cannot be readily separated from any of the elements that Habermas links to strategic action (the attempt to reach objectives by influencing others' definitions of a situation, the purposeful pursuit of outcomes and consequences, the use of "weapons, goods, threats or enticements" to achieve the "success" of a policy, plan, or operation), political speech cannot be cleansed of the elements that present gratuitous obstacles to Habermasian moral conversation. In the political world, if speech is mostly convention and convention is mostly aimed at securing certain strategic ends, then claims to validity, coherence, and truth, not to mention "sincerity" and "truthfulness," have to be understood not only as "redeemables" but also as potential rhetorical tools, or "reliables" that enable political actors to go about their work, if not their life.[22]

To put this otherwise, the Machiavellian thesis holds that it is necessary for those who wish to maintain themselves in politics to learn, among other things, how *not* to be open to the argumentative redemption of validity claims, and to use this knowledge and not use it, according to the necessity of the case.[23] I take the import of Machiavelli's advice as underscoring the importance of both adaptability and strategic calculation in political speech. The effective political rhetorician, whether citizen or politician, speaker or hearer, recognizes that political speech is (quite often and necessarily) the rhetorical art of *strategically* deploying claims to "truth" and *instrumentally* appealing to "sincerity" while *calculatingly* disguising the fact that one is acting strategically, instrumentally, or calculatingly. Success in the domain of half-truth hinges on one's ability to grasp validity claims as reliable techniques of persuasion and to deploy them effectively in response to problematic contexts. It also requires cognizance of the fact that one is doing so.[24] The political actor must be cognizant, that is, of *working* in half-truth, as opposed to "being," in some constant or consistent characterological sense, "half-truthful" (or, for that matter, a "liar" or a "truth teller"). Working in half-truth is a skill, an art, and a mode of acting, not a mode of being.

In politics, the effective strategic deployment of claims to validity, coherence, and truth and the activity of effectively resisting their "redemption" does not necessarily take place in an ethical vacuum, even though it may be a moral one. Indeed, the skillful appeal to moral notions of "reciprocity" or "mutuality" and the rhetorical manipulation of moral values that one does not necessarily believe may, if successfully delivered, mark the difference between order and disorder, security and chaos, freedom and enslavement—even the polity's life or death. "A certain prince of the present time, whom it is well not to name," Machiavelli (1950, 66) writes, "never does anything but preach peace and good faith, but he is really a great enemy to both, and either of them, had he observed them, would have lost him state or reputation on many occasions."

This does not mean that truth or truth seeking and truth telling have no currency in politics or that politics is the graveyard of communicative principles. Although the prince should discourage unsolicited advice, Machiavelli (1950, 88) argues, "[the prince] ought to be a great asker, and a patient hearer of the truth about those things of which he has inquired; indeed, if he finds that any one has scruples in telling him the truth he should be angry." Politics and political speech are not inherently immune to the deployment of validity claims, or even to their discursive redemption. Yet Machiavelli (87) also reminds us of the peculiar complexity of these matters in politics by offering this telling observation:

> There is no other way of guarding one's self against flattery than by letting men understand that they will not offend you by speaking the truth; but when every one can tell you the truth, you lose their respect. A prudent prince must therefore take a third course, by choosing for his council wise men, and giving these alone full liberty to speak the truth to him, but only of those things that he asks and of nothing else; but he must ask them about everything and hear their opinion, and afterwards deliberate by himself in his own way, and in these councils and with each of these men comport himself so that every one may see that the more freely he speaks, the more he will be acceptable.

The compulsions of politics are formed by certain necessities that make it analytically difficult to establish nice distinctions, and practically impossible to sustain them. The Habermasian's distinction between communicative and strategic speech-action seems, in this respect, especially ill adapted to the fugitive quality of politics, where the elements of the communicative and the strategic are intricately entangled and intertwined. To return to Machiavelli's example: if one of the imperatives of the political world is to avoid surrounding oneself with flatterers, then is not the politician's enlistment of those who "speak the truth" both a communicative and a strategic goal? It is communicative because "speaking the truth," as Machiavelli describes it, is not a mere game; it is a genuinely discursive activity where the politician asks for and hears the opinions of his or her interlocutors "in full liberty," and with a view toward shared counsel. Yet at the same time this communication is not an end-in-itself. It is strategic, not only in content but also in form. For "speaking the truth" is a scenario that the politician creates, manages, and participates within, in order to "guard against the plague" of flatterers and mitigate "the risk of becoming contemptible," thereby achieving some measure of success in maintaining power (Machiavelli 1950, 87). There is in this sense an entanglement of, if not a complementarity between, strategic and communicative action in politics.[25]

A Greek Interlude

Perhaps one of the most compelling textual examples, outside the field of literature, of how strategic and communicative elements intertwine in political speech is presented by the Greek historian Thucydides (1982) in the narrative of the debate between Cleon and Diodotus over the matter of Mitylene, a colony that had partly revolted against Athens in the fourth year of the Peloponnesian War and appealed for alliance with Sparta. The exchange between the two politicians concerned the fate of the Mitylenians, whom the Athenians were at first determined to annihilate by putting the whole adult male population to death and making slaves of the women and children. But having reflected, as Thucydides (1982, III [171]) puts it, upon "the horrid cruelty of a decree which condemned a whole city to the fate merited only by the guilty," the Athenians were moved to reconsider the matter. An assembly was called, and many views were expressed, most notably by Cleon, son of Cleaenetus, and Diodotus, son of Eucrates, whose opinions, Thucydides states, "were the ones that most directly contradicted each other" (180). With a view toward persuading the demos to uphold its earlier decision to slay and enslave the Mitylenians (thereby sustaining his own imperialist ambitions), Cleon, a great rhetorician, launches a series of speech maneuvers. Not the least of these maneuvers is this great rhetorician's rhetorical attack on rhetoric and rhetoricians themselves (1982, III [38]). In Cleon's speech, Thucydides offers a brilliant example of how the principles of communicative action can be rhetorically deployed in the service of strategic ends. Thus, Cleon (whom Thucydides describes as "the most violent man at Athens") charges the Athenian demos with what we might call certain failures in communicative competence and discursive democracy:

> [you] go to see an oration as you would to see a sight, take your facts on hearsay, judge of the practicability of a project by the wit of its advocates, and trust for the truth as to past events not to the fact which you saw more than to the clever strictures which you heard; you are the easy victims of new-fangled arguments, unwilling to follow received conclusions.

In short, Cleon castigates the demos for surrendering to distorted communicative processes, following procedures and conditions of communication that move them further away from truth and closer to the untrammeled reign of *doxa*. Cleon also accuses the demos of betraying "strategic" rather than "communicative" sensibilities. Thus, "the first wish of every man among you is that he could speak himself, the next to rival those who can speak by seeming to be quite up with their ideas by applauding every hit almost before it is made, and by being as quick in catching an argument as you are slow in foreseeing its consequences . . . you are very slaves to the pleasures of the ear" (173). Cleon's appeal to the demos to be more like "the council of a city" than "the audience of a rhetorician" is not, however, a case for genuinely deliberative democracy in the Habermasian communicative sense. Rather, his appeal is instrumentally calculated to blunt the force of what he fears (rightly, as it turns out) will be Diodotus's more skillful rhetoric geared toward playing upon the demos's change of heart and persuading the Athenians to spare the Mitylenes.

Thucydides (176) has Diodotus begin by warning the demos against speakers who rely on coercion (a barely veiled, strategic reference to Cleon) as well as haste and passion, for: "haste usually goes hand in hand with folly, passion with coarseness and narrowness of mind." The speaker who attempts to sway the people by resorting to "well-aimed calumny" or "charge[s] of dishonesty" against others, or by accusing another of "making a display in order to be paid for it," Diodotus warns, deprives the city of its advisers by instilling fear in honorable persons and threatening to ruin their reputations. Thus Diodotus tells the assembly that "The good citizen ought to triumph not by frightening his opponents but by beating them fairly in argument. . . . In this way successful orators would be least tempted to sacrifice their convictions to popularity, in the hope of still higher honors" (176 f.). If ever there were a classic example of a critique of strategic action (including reliance upon bribes, threats, coercion, sanctions, gratifications, and so on) in favor of the "force of the better argument" (Chambers 1996, 99), then Diodotus's opening appeal for fair argument seems to be it. But context is all (even given its "provinciality"); and we must remember that Diodotus is speaking at a moment of intense crisis where the question is "what is to be done?" Speed is of the essence if the Mitylenes are to be spared; the Athenian ships charged with carrying out the death decree are already well on their way toward the colony. Thus Diodotus's appeal to the demos for what Chambers (1996, 99) calls a "change of heart" (that is, the aim of communicative action), is at the same time inextricably intertwined with an effort to bring about what Chambers calls "a desired behavioral response" (that is, the aim of strategic action) namely, the Athenians' rescinding of the death decree. The compelling and paradoxical element in Diodotus's speech is that even as he calls for fair argument (communicative action) and criticizes underhanded rhetorical ploys (strategic action), he is making a strategic effort to induce the Athenian demos to reject Cleon's advice and do something that he, Diodotus, wants them to do, and quickly. Thus the very appeal to "the force of the better argument" is itself part of a larger strategic maneuver that Diodotus undertakes in order to undermine Cleon, change the heart of the Athenians, effect a desired behavioral response, save the lives of the Mitylenes, and win the debate. [26]

One other point about the provincial context surrounding the Mitylene debate is worth making: whatever his political commitment to something like communicative action as the basis for democratic discourse, Diodotus also understands that he is speaking within an already corrupted situation where, to use the Habermasian terms, validity claims can neither be vindicated nor redeemed. Thus he says to the Athenian demos that in the city, "Plain good advice has thus come to be no less suspected than bad; and the advocate of the most monstrous measure is not more obliged to use deceit to gain the people, than the best counselor is to lie in order to be believed" (177). As a result, Diodotus avers, the city "can never be served openly and without disguise, he who does serve it openly being always suspected of serving himself in some secret way in return" (177). Whether Diodotus thinks that this statement accurately reflects the reality of discourse in Athens is perhaps less important than what Thucydides has him doing in stating what he states, at this particular moment, within this particular struggle over the fate of the Mitylenians, against this particular opponent, Cleon. Diodotus wants to win the argument, of course. To do so, in part, he paints the picture of a corrupt discursive context and thereby (attempts to) inoculate himself against the very charges that he anticipates may be forthcoming against him from Cleon and his allies, not to mention from the demos itself. "[Y]ou visit the disasters into which the whim of the moment may have led you, upon the single person of your advisor, not upon yourselves," Diodotus tells the Athenians, thus hoping to prevent exactly that from happening to him. At this point in the exchange it becomes very difficult to discern whether Diodotus is appealing to communicative principles in strategic terms or utilizing strategic rhetoric in an effort to reassert a communicative context, or both, or neither. Perhaps that is just the point, however. In this key, politics is a complicated mix of the communicative and the strategic, of mutual understanding and pressure, of the force of the better argument and the manipulative exercise of rhetorical tricks in the service of specific interests.

In sum, the brilliance of this piece of political literature has to do with Thucydides's recognition of the way strategic action supervenes upon communicative action in political speech. In the domain of political speech-struggle that Thucydides brings to life in the agonal contestation between Cleon and Diodotus, the "end" is mediated not only by an immediate and urgent question of life or death but also by the clashing ambitions and vested interests of the participants in the debate, which include not only Cleon and Diodotus but also other politicians and the Athenian demos. Under these circumstances (which might be understood not as incidental to but, to varying degrees, *inherent in* politics) we must (at the very least) recognize the tension between communicative and strategic action that is embedded in political speech. At the very least, we might recognize that the "resolution" of this tension never admits of the achievement of "pure" communicative action or the banishment of strategic action, but rather takes place along a continuum of "more or less." Indeed, Thucydides's history might be read as representing various nodal points along this continuum in its narrative of the complex unfolding of speeches and events that mark the politics of the Athenian democracy and Peloponnesian War.

Postscript

The paradoxes of politics tend to wreak havoc with the principles of communication because, as Merleau-Ponty (1964, 219) observes, "politics is a relationship to men rather than principles."[27] Thus in politics an openness toward the opinions of others is sometimes not a condition of mutual respect but antithetical to it. It may be a peculiarity of the political domain that "when everyone can tell you the truth, you lose their respect," but it is a peculiarity that discourse ethicists ignore to their peril (Machiavelli 1950, 87). One might say, then, that speaking the truth is an indispensable element in politics, but not the goal of it. To make communicative action, or the enactment of principles of discourse ethics, or moral conversation, the end or goal of politics is to mistake the nature of working in half-truth and thereby misconstrue "the milieu that is proper to politics" itself.[28]

The supervenience of strategic (speech) action on communicative (speech) action in politics to which I have been alluding is what I also think Ash (1995, 36) meant to convey when, in the aftermath of the PEN congress, he referred to the "qualitatively different responsibility" that the intellectual has for "the validity, intellectual coherence, and truth of what he says and writes," as opposed to the politician, who invariably works in half-truth. The point is not that the intellectual lives in a communicative world of validity, coherence, and truth while the politician does not. (Although Habermas's ideal communication situation *might* stand a better chance of realization in a scholarly conference or perhaps a graduate seminar, as opposed to a press conference, an election campaign, an assemblage of political organizers, a city council hearing open to the public, or a faculty meeting of just about any academic department.) The politician also inhabits a world of validity, coherence, and truth. Yet validity, coherence, and truth take on different colorations working in the context peculiar to politics—where strategic imperatives and the exercise of power, conflicts of interest, and drives of ambition are ineliminable aspects of collective action. Hence, it is one thing to encourage (or insist upon) the intellectual's responsibility to keep providing us with various practical (or even imaginary) means for judging the health or sickness of the body politic

and thereby speaking truth to power, and quite another to expect the politician—or the citizen—to "live" them while working in half-truth.

Whatever we make of the philosophical status of *Diskursethik*, we might
notice in Habermas's theorizing an attitude or orientation that is fundamental
to a strain of Western thought generally, and perhaps particularly in the
German tradition from Immanuel Kant to Karl Marx, and quite contrary to
the disposition toward politics I have been calling Machiavellian. The philosopher Bernard Williams (1993, 164) describes this attitude as indicative of theorists who think that "Somehow or other, in this life or the next, morally if
not materially, as individuals or as an historical collective, we shall be safe; or,
if not safe, at least reassured that at some level of the world's constitution there
is something to be discovered that makes ultimate sense of our concerns."
Isaiah Berlin (1982, 76, 68) registers a similar and even broader claim when he
identifies the "one major assumption" of Western thought, "That somewhere
in the past or the future, in this world or the next, in the church or the labo-
ratory, in the speculations of the metaphysician or the findings of the social sci-
entist, or in the uncorrupted heart of the simple good man, there is to be
found the final solution of the question of how men should live." In this
regard, Berlin maintains that Machiavelli "lit the fatal fuse" that finally "split
open" this rock upon which "Western beliefs and lives had been founded."

Yet, whatever its power against the alleged naivete and intellectualism of
the Habermasian, the Machiavellian thesis is also vulnerable to a modern form
of critique. Insofar as Machiavelli "did not seek very energetically to define" a
power which would not be unjust (Merleau-Ponty 1964, 221), we might take
the Machiavellian thesis as "machiavellian"—as little more than a premodern
nihilistic relativism incapable of furnishing any norms for politics beyond
either strategic efficiency or perhaps perspectival art (see Dietz 1986). Without
question, Machiavelli's "tough-minded wisdom" accepted politics as a field of
struggle for which our best preparation is to study "war and its organization
and discipline" (Machiavelli 1950, 52). This pre-Clausewitzian thesis, as
Charles Taylor calls it (1988, 223 f.), holds that the arbiter of politics is "a kind
of power which is no respecter of truth," and puts one in mind of Foucault
(see Ingram 1994). And Foucault has drawn on Nietzsche, as Taylor (1988, 223
f.) points out, to present the will to truth itself as a manifestation of the will
to power. From this purchase in postmodernity, then, we might imagine a
series of grapnels, first from Clausewitz, then Nietzsche, then Foucault, heaved
over modernity, and thrown back to the Florentine.

I am not sure, along with Taylor (1988, 224), whether Machiavelli really
did suspend the question of truth and displace the values of humanism, as at
least Nietzsche and Foucault tried to do.[29] But the contestation between premodern and postmodern will have to wait another day. In any case, it is true
that Machiavelli gives us no clear guidelines or philosophical principles as to
how to choose the lesser of evils among powers in politics, or the relatively

best, much less the "good" and the "best." His distinction between cruelties "well-committed" and "ill-committed" does not seem, to moderns, to offer much by way of guidance for political work (Machiavelli 1950, 34). But perhaps neither definitive nor moral guidelines are available from "outside" the action context of politics, and that is the point Machiavelli wants us to grasp. Even so, as Wolin (1960, 223) writes:

> There was no hint of child-like delight when Machiavelli contemplated the barbarous and savage destructiveness of the new prince, sweeping away the settled arrangements of society and "leaving nothing intact." There was, however, the laconic remark that it was better to be a private citizen than to embark on a career which involved the ruin of men.

Whatever we might count as the "civilizational norms" that modern constitutional democracy has bestowed upon us, I do not believe they offer any excuses for misconceiving or deceiving ourselves about that "knot of collective life" that is politics. Machiavelli, who lived within the historical moment of a dazzling and dynamic Renaissance, a "rebirth" of politics, understood this very well. He thought through the human condition of political existence accordingly.

Chapter 8

The Slow Boring of Hard Boards
Weil, Arendt, and the Work of Politics

It is the law as in art, so in politics, that improvements ever prevail;
and though fixed usages may be best for undisturbed communities,
constant necessities of action must be accompanied by the constant
improvement of methods.

—Thucydides

We are just now beginning to take the measure of the astonishing revolutionary events that heralded the final decade of the twentieth century and initiated the capacity of millions of citizens to act in concert for the power of
democratic self-realization. For political theory, the challenge in the aftermath
of 1989 is to advance understandings of democracy and political life that
attempt to recover an emancipatory potential in modernity and meaningfully
confront what Václav Havel (1990, 136), now president of Czech Republic,
calls "the practical task of organizing a better world." In many respects, I think
that the most promising source for this enterprise lies in public realm theory,
perhaps particularly in the theories of Hannah Arendt and Jurgen Habermas.[1]
Both of these thinkers sustain a deep critical commitment to a politics of citizen interaction, reciprocal understanding, self-realization, and human dignity
in a realm where, as Arendt (1958, 25 f.) puts it, "speech and only speech
[makes] sense."

The compelling quality of Arendt's and Habermas's public realm conceptions of politics has much to do with their adaptations of a venerable conceptual strategy that has its roots in Aristotle and draws a palpable distinction
between the human activities of "work" (*technē*) and "interaction" (*praxis*).
With this strategy in hand, public realm theory inventively juxtaposes a theatrical image of the space of appearances (Arendt) or a communicative
metaphor of the public sphere (Habermas) against an instrumentalist reading
of manipulative work processes. Thereby, Arendt and Habermas effectively particularize politics as a vibrant and unique human activity and develop a critique aimed at freeing human beings from the technical domination and
violence to nature that they resolutely associate with work. They also invest
freedom or emancipation in expressly noninstrumental, linguistically mediated modes of human action in the world.[2]

My inclination is to support attempts to locate freedom in a politics of
speech or communicative interaction. Thus I do not wish to contest the turn
in public realm theory that allows intersubjective understanding to achieve, as
Axel Honneth (1982, 45) writes, "the status in the theory of emancipation
which social labor had had in Marxian theory."[3] Nevertheless, I think that the
conceptual strategy that Arendt and Habermas so brilliantly employ in order
to counter modern theories of action as social labor is a double-edged sword;
for even as the conceptual dichotomy between work and interaction provides
public realm theory with a valuable analytical device for distinguishing
between human activities, it undercuts the effective theorizing of politics as a
human practice. The dichotomy work:interaction seems especially to foreclose
what Max Weber (1946, 128) had in mind when he called politics "the strong
and slow boring of hard boards"—a sustained, purposeful activity that meets
obstacles and undertakes acts of transformation in the world. This conceptual
inadequacy in public realm theory is not, I think, a minor matter. If our most
praxis-oriented theories cannot deliver an action-coordinating concept that
appreciates the purposeful nature of human struggle as politics, we should
hardly be surprised to find the "project of modernity" (Rasmussen 1990, 7–8)
undermined, if not defeated, by other alternatives, including the seductive
"affirmative nihilism" (Villa 1992, 719) of certain late-twentieth-century
postmodernisms.

We need, then, to rethink the action concept of politics in public realm
theory. To pursue this task in this chapter, I shall turn again to Arendt's theory
of action,[4] not only because it presents public realm theory in what is perhaps
its most exemplary anti-instrumentalist form but also because it has played a
role in at least one of the most dramatic emancipatory events of our time.[5] To
provide an instructive critical perspective, I turn to a contemporary of
Arendt's, the French thinker Simone Weil. Compared to Arendt, Weil has
received relatively little attention as a social and political theorist; but she is
surely Arendt's equal as a diagnostician of modernity.[6] Indeed, from the per-

spective of quite different theoretical traditions, Weil and Arendt present nearly identical and equally powerful critiques of technological determinism
modernity.

Yet unlike Arendt, Weil draws a distinction between technology and instrumental action that refuses to reduce all forms of instrumentality to violence or
purely manipulative processes. As a result, Weil's concept of work as *methodical
thinking* embraces something that Arendt's conceptual strategy rejects: a liberatory form of instrumentality. A liberatory form of instrumentality is precisely what
public realm theory must be ready to accommodate if it is to be practically prepared for the challenge posed by the world events of 1989 and beyond. Arendt's
public realm theory in particular needs to discover a more "neighborly affinity"
(in Hans–Georg Gadamer's evocative phrase) between work/interaction and
instrumentality/politics than the current agonistic-versus-discursive debates over
Arendtian politics allow.[7] With this in mind, I tentatively propose the idea of a
methodical politics in order to suggest that Weil's notion of work (instrumentality
as purposeful performance) is potentially compatible with Arendt's notion of
interaction (politics as theatrical performance). If this affinity is indeed possible,
then public realm theory might be more adequately equipped to deliver on its
promise as an emancipatory project of (post)modernity.

Automatism and the Shattering of the World

Simone Weil's and Hannah Arendt's very different theoretical assessments of
freedom in modernity nevertheless arise out of nearly identical diagnoses of
the times. In a very general sense, they were both part of a generation of twentieth-century social and political theorists who lived their formative intellectual lives in interwar Europe, in an epoch when the Enlightenment's summer
bloom was past and modernity's polar night proceeding.[8] Equivocal humanists
and ambivalent modernists, both Weil and Arendt bear the traces of darkness
before the face of universalized forces of domination. Yet in their arguments
we can also find purposes that place them within a context of twentieth-century thinkers struggling to redeem the modern project of freedom. Weil's and
Arendt's respective analyses are, in this sense, efforts to respond to the sterile
passivity of modernity, the degradation of the human person, and the suppression of individuality by appealing to thought-action accounts of freedom that
are aimed at recovering what technological forces have taken away.
Consequently, Weil and Arendt share a kind of hope in their concern to identify forms of human activity that disclose the reality of the world, so that
human beings as individuals may actualize "relations worthy of the greatness
of humanity" (Weil 1973, 104) and guarantee that "human life can be at home
on earth" (Arendt 1958, 134).

Like many intellectuals of their time, Weil and Arendt understand the crisis of the modern age as a period of profound fragmentation and deformation
accelerated by "the frenzy produced by the speed of technical progress" (Weil

1973, 54).[9] Like others, they situate the modern crisis in relation to the after-math of the Industrial Revolution, wherein the imperatives of economic con-quest, mass production, routinized labor, and relentless consumption gradually usurp the activities of fabrication and workmanship (Weil 1973, 115; Arendt 1958, 124 f.). More uniquely, however, they both confront what Arendt (1958, 150) vividly terms the shattering of "the very purposefulness of the world" as the consequence of something they call *automatism*. Automatism is the third stage in human production, and the most recent feature of the productive rela-tions of advanced, consumer capitalism (Arendt 1958, 4, 147–149; Weil 1973, 52). Automatism, Weil (1973, 52) argues, follows a principle that "lies in the possibility of entrusting the machine not only with an operation that is invari-ably the same, but also with a combination of varied operations." Arendt (1958, 151) draws the implication that "we call automatic all courses of move-ment which are self-moving and therefore outside the range of willful and purposeful [human] interference." Assessing automatism as a complex of ele-ments, Weil and Arendt identify the same three elements as problematic.

First, automatism (or automation) involves the appropriation of *homo faber* (roughly, work) activity by forms of mechanized industrial production that substitute reflexive, bodily processes for experiential work that distinguishes between ends and means, operation and product (Arendt 1958, 149–151; Weil 1977). Under the pressure of automatic machines, Arendt argues, the defining features of *homo faber* are in jeopardy. The distinction between means and ends no longer makes sense; tools and instruments "lose their instrumental charac-ter"; the standards of utility and beauty are replaced by "basic functions"; the act of fabrication is subsumed in consumption; and *homo faber's* driving atti-tude—the "conscious human effort to enlarge material power"—is neutralized in a stream of never-ending processes (1958, 137, 145, 152). As Weil (1973, 92; 1977, 57) notes, under automatic machines, "thought draws back from the future" into a "perpetual recoil upon the present" in which human beings are "reduced to the condition of automata."

Second, automatism simultaneously supplants and recuperates the rhythms of nature, thereby invoking a form of species existence that mimics the natu-ral life cycle, elevates basic functions, and deflates the social value of human creativity and worldly artifice. As a result of technical developments, Weil (1973, 83) writes, "humanity finds itself as much the plaything of the forces of nature, in the new form that technical progress has given them, as it ever was in primitive times." Arendt (1958, 132) elaborates: "The danger of future automation is less the much deplored mechanization and artificialization of natural life than that, its artificiality notwithstanding, all human productivity would be sucked into an enormously intensified life process and would follow automatically, without pain or effort, its ever-recurrent natural cycle." Automatism is not only an obstacle to individual freedom; it is also a specific organizational form of the human species that, paradoxically, liberates action from the constraints imposed by the pains and dangers inherent in earlier forms of life by mutating action into an extramundane repetitive process.

Within this situation, a third element arises in the complex that identifies the modern age: the dissolution of the world of the senses and appearances into a pseudoworld (Arendt 1958, 153) that produces pseudoideas (Weil 1973, 110). Rather remarkably, both Weil and Arendt identify algebraic physics as the prime producer of a nongenuine, counterfeit world (Arendt 1958, 264–273, 285–288; 1969, 265–290; Weil 1968).[10] Physics proceeds by stripping away the subjective effects of the human senses with a view toward an objective theory of physical particles in fields of force. It thereby manifests a loss of confidence "in the phenomena as they reveal themselves of their own accord to human sense and reason" (Arendt 1969, 272). Weil (1968, 32) argues that for physics even to be possible, perceptual appearances and the world as a mediating medium must be considered *negligible*: "The negligible is nothing other than what has to be neglected in order to construct physics. . . . What is neglected is always as large as the world." The neglect is furthered by algebraic formulae and equations that dissolve all real human relationships into "logical relations between manmade symbols" (Arendt 1958, 264 f., 284; Weil 1968, 37). Once in the world of these symbolic relations, "one inevitably loses sight of the relationship between sign and thing signified," and a form of mechanized petrification sets in (Weil 1973, 93). Hence even as algebraic formulae advance the processes of technology and automation, the formulae themselves proceed automatically and become "impenetrable to the mind," stifling the human capacity to think (Weil 93; also see Arendt 1958, 5).[11]

Weil's account of automatism, which she calls the triumph of "the blind collectivity" (*une collectivité aveugle*), is written in the turbulent and authoritarian climate of Europe in the early 1930s and replete with images of grinding mechanisms, vast crushing forces, and a domain of control in which "there is no means of stopping the blind trend of the social machine towards an increasing centralization" (1973, 120). Arendt's account of automatism, which she calls the victory of *animal laborans*, is written in the relatively placid but paranoid consumer atmosphere of the United States in the 1950s and appropriates metaphors of the biological life cycle to characterize "the reckless dynamism of a wholly motorized life process" that is inherently futile and worldless (1958, 132). These temporal and metaphorical differences are more matters of degree than kind, however, given Arendt's (1958, 93, 322) references to motors and machines and Weil's (1973, 63) inclination to view automatism as the pressure of nature and necessity upon human action. What they share is an account of advanced society as a domain of endlessly repetitive, artificially natural cyclicalities.

How *Homo Faber* Works

Before the deadly and dehumanizing forces of automatism, Weil and Arendt seek to identify the practical context within which human beings as individuals can actualize freedom as a mode of thought in action and thereby regain a sense of being at home in the world. In doing so, they both reject the modernist strategy—so often associated with the liberal historicist outlook of the nineteenth century—that finds freedom in the domination of nature and necessity. They also reject the romantic reaction of the early twentieth century, with its yearning for submergence within nature and necessity. The metaphysical picture behind both Weil's and Arendt's accounts is that of an all-pervading necessity that forms the fabric of the world but wherein freedom, as the *recognition* of necessity, is nevertheless a human possibility (Arendt 1958, 121; Weil 1973, 85).

Given their shared view of automatism as a process that destroys the experience of work as a causally efficacious relationship between human beings and the world, we might expect that both Weil and Arendt would link freedom in some way to working in the world. In fact, in her magnum opus,[12] Weil (1973, 104) wholly situates the practical context of freedom in "a civilization in which labour would be sufficiently transformed to exercise fully all the faculties," in what we might call the "purposeful performance" of work as self-determination. In *The Human Condition*, Arendt wholly situates the practical context of freedom elsewhere. Even as she pays homage to Weil's *Factory Journal*, which she deems "the only book in the huge literature on the labor questions which deals with the problem without prejudice or sentimentality," Arendt (1958, 131 n. 83, 183) entrusts freedom to "men's acting and speaking directly *to* one another," or to what we might call the "theatrical performance" of politics as self-revelation.[13] These different strategic moves and their implications for the practical context of freedom are directly related to the different ways in which Weil and Arendt think about how *homo faber* works. The practical political inadequacy of Arendtian public realm theory originates here as well. But to see this, we need first to consider how Weil thinks *homo faber* works as *homo methodus*[14] and how Arendt thinks *homo faber* works as *homo fabricatus*.

Homo Methodos

In Weil's theory of action, "work" is a critical concept that designates a normative and emancipatory form of human activity. Loosely following Marx, she uses the term to distinguish both a human form of reproduction and a value sphere within which the human species gains access to reality. Thus, when labor is "sufficiently transformed to exercise fully all the faculties," it forms "the human act *par excellence*" (1973, 104). But Weil also objects that in Marx, "the locus of the process of freedom was transferred from the individual to the species" (McLellan 1990, 72).[15] There is an insistence upon individual subjectivity in Weil's concept of work, and it takes form in the "garden contrast" (Winch 1989, 96) between work, "wherein only efforts exclusively directed by a clear intelligence" determine the expenditure of the working subject's effort, and "blind operations" (*d'opérations aveuglés*), where "the mind is weighed down" and movements are beyond control of the intelligence (Weil 1973, 98, 94). Here Weil introduces the idea that if human beings are to escape the humiliation foisted upon them by automatism, they must recover the capacity for methodical thought (*la pensée méthodique*). This is the driving theme of her magnum opus, and the focus of her thought–action account of freedom as well.[16]

For Weil, methodical thinking is a kind of activity in which the subject independently conceives of, coordinates, and carries out physical efforts or undertakings in the external world.[17] Such action is analogous, she argues, to solving properly a problem in arithmetic or geometry. Thus, "a completely free life would be one wherein all real difficulties presented themselves as kinds of problems, wherein all successes were as solutions carried into action" (1973, 86). The analogy to mathematical problem solving posits freedom as the activity of enacting a solution (success) in response to a problem, once identified. When freedom is realized in work, then, it is as a mode of instrumental action in which the subject determines his or her own activity as *homo methodus*, according to his or her own problem-specifying and problem-solving initiative. Thus, Weil (1973, 85) writes, "the absolutely free man would be he whose every action proceeded from a preliminary judgment concerning the end which he set himself and the sequence of means suitable for attaining this end."

On its face, the analogy Weil constructs between methodical thinking and problem solving has its drawbacks—not the least of which involves its appeal to mathematics (Winch 1989, 96–99).[18] There is another drawback evident here as well, for with its overt appeal to means and ends, Weil's analogy appears to connect freedom with something like the Weberian notion of purposive-rational (*Zweckrational*) action that reduces life activity to specific instrumental properties. But this is not, in fact, the case. Indeed, if we view purposive-rational action as (1) geared toward the production of objects, (2) directed toward the domination of nature, (3) governed by technical models, and (4) driven by "success" in the securing of a goal or an end, then Weil's concept of methodical thinking must be taken as an action type of considerably different practical and normative magnitude than this.

To see how this is so, we might first return to the problem orientation that Weil establishes as the context within which methodical thinking takes place. Unlike concepts of work that take object production as their primary context, Weil's concept places the human appropriation of "means" within a kind of thought-action experience through which the subject perceives the world not as a construction site but as a domain of obstacles, challenges, or perplexities requiring identification, and open to possible (re)solution. The emphasis thereby shifts from the making of things to the conscious identification of, and response to, "things thrown forward" or problems (Greek *pro*, forward + *ballein*, to throw). The kind of work activity Weil (1973, 104) has in mind assigns a secondary status to the single end product of work and primary status to problem identification and the undertaking of a solution within a circumscribed context. Only within the context of responding to challenges, Weil (85) argues, does the subject "dispose[s] of his own capacity for action" and exercise "fully all the faculties" by bringing judgment to bear upon circumstances.

Weil also distinguishes the problem orientation that is methodical thinking from the purposive-rational urge to conquer or dominate nature. Here we might attend to the metaphors of high seas and sailing she often uses, in order to grasp how she distances work from an act of violent overcoming.[19] For example, "The intelligence is powerless to get its bearings amid the innumerable eddies formed by wind and water on the high seas; but if we place in the midst of these swirling waters a boat whose sails and rudder are fixed in such and such a manner it is possible to draw up a list of the actions which they can cause it to undergo. All tools are thus, in a more or less perfect way, in the manner of instruments for defining chance events" (1973, 89; cf. 88, 91, 101). In this image, nature is both a zone of danger and a domain of possibility, not an inert force to be wrestled under control. The kind of voyaging spirit that Weil has in mind is not that of "the Dutch sea-captain who would go through hell for gain, even though he scorched his sails" (Weber 1958, 57). In the latter case, the boat is a ship, and the ship and its sails are nothing more than expedients for the captain's ruthless pursuit of booty. Weil's sailor is occupied differently. Apparently immune to the daring of adventure and without port or destination, the sailor brings the boat to life simply in the activity of engaging the sea, in a methodical undertaking that risks intelligence, not temerity, against chance. In this image, the tools of work are not directed toward domination, nor are they mere conveyances. They are rather instruments through which the methodical thinker initiates and attempts to maintain a tentative equilibrium within circumstances that challenge and constantly change.

Because the methodical thinker must "continually use craft and strategy, set sails and rudder, transmute the thrust of the wind by means of a series of devices" (Weil 1973, 91), he or she cannot find freedom in a resting place or glory in victorious struggle. Indeed, Weil (85) argues, it matters little whether actions are "crowned with success." Failure can bring unhappiness, but it cannot *humiliate* if a human being resolutely acts "under control of the mind" by filtering an "undefined mass of possible accidents" into a "few clearly defined series" (88). This is also to say that such a person acts in full recognition of the powers of nature; hence Weil (1973, 107) appreciatively cites Bacon's dictum "We cannot command Nature except by obeying her." Only in this tentative equilibrium of body, mind, and universe, where freedom is as Nietzsche writes, "near the threshold of the danger of servitude" (1968, 92), can one locate the ineffable skill of methodical thought. Methodical thinking, it seems, values a particular form of navigation as a mode of acting in the world.[20]

When one has excluded from methodical thinking the urge to objectify, dominate, and secure success, it by no means follows that work is completely purposeless, goalless, meaningless—"a snake biting its own tail" (Nietzsche 1968, 81). Weil's exclusions invite us to comprehend work from a different aspect, but they do not erase purposefulness from the picture. The great stimuli, in fact, are problems that, once identified, arouse thoughtful attention. The more work "throws up such difficulties," Weil (1977, 59) argues, "the more the heart is lifted." The great engagement is in the conscious undertaking of a method or solution, "when wits are exercised, devices tried, obstacles cunningly eliminated." The great release has "nothing to do with welfare, or leisure or security"; it is actualized in the intelligent navigation of challenges and solutions carried into action (1973, 101). Only in this form of action does the subject challenge what Havel (1985, 34) calls "the *diktats* of automatism" through work that is problem-oriented but not objectifying, masterful but not dominating, and purposeful but not preoccupied by a single "end." Not surprisingly, then, Weil (1973, 85) argues that *all* human activities should "imitate the accuracy, rigor, scrupulousness which characterize the performance of work," lest they "sink into the purely arbitrary" and be submerged by forces beyond control. A neighborly affinity thus distinguishes the conceptual relationship she draws between work as methodical thinking and other human pursuits. This "purposeful performance" concept of human action is at the foundation of Weil's account of freedom.

Homo Fabricatus

When Hannah Arendt thinks about how *homo faber* works in the world, she, too, posits a notion of purposeful human performance against the endlessly repetitive, artificially natural processes of automatism. Thus she (1969, 42) argues, in a seemingly Weilian spirit, "Whenever men pursue their purposes, tilling the effortless earth, forcing the free-flowing wind into their sails, crossing the ever-rolling waves, they cut across a movement which is purposeless and turning within itself." But on closer inspection, Arendt's characterization of the sailor's activity bears little resemblance to Weil's example of the boat as an instrument for defining chance events. For Arendt (43) goes on to identify "purposeful human activities" as those which "do violence to nature." In this image, the sailor as seafarer is a violator who is disposed toward command and control of the natural environment, and the ship cutting across the waves is the instrument through which his domination over nature is extended. The image is powerful, but it also points to a more general problem in Arendt's thinking about how *homo faber* works.

In the tradition of German philosophy, and especially under the influence of Martin Heidegger, who in turn appropriated and transformed Aristotle's distinction between *praxis* (acting) and *poiēsis* (making),[21] Arendt conceptualizes work as an emblem of modernity. She also designates work activity not as a material relation among humans, instruments, and nature but as a kind of visionary nightmare rooted in "the utopian hope that it may be possible to treat men as one treats other material" (1958, 188). The theoretical result of this turning operation is Arendt's concept of *homo faber*, in which she installs the "typical attitudes" of a (masculinist) modern age: "his instrumentalization of the world, his confidence in tools and in the productivity of the maker of artificial objects; his trust in the all-comprehensive range of the means-end category; his conviction that every issue can be solved and every human motivation reduced to the principle of utility; his sovereignty, which regards everything as material and thinks of the whole of nature as 'an immense fabric from which we can cut out whatever we want . . .'; finally, his matter-of-course identification of fabrication with action" (305–306). With this breathtaking indictment, Arendt (1958, 139, 153) summons the spirit of heroic capitalism in modernity, in which all things are treated as means, all acts are oriented toward success, and man conducts himself as lord and master, a "destroyer of nature," who rips and cuts his materials "out of the womb of the earth" in relentless pursuit of the acquisition of goods.[22] With the nullity that is victorious capitalism still to come, Arendt conjures up *homo faber* as the last blast of a ruthless epoch that arose "from the great revolution of modernity" (307). But this conjurer's trick has its costs. In order to indict modernity, Arendt must make *homo faber* a powerful symbolic-conceptual category, and in order to do this, she must conceptualize the human activity of work in a constricted way. On a symbolic level, that is, Arendt's depiction of *homo faber* is a dramatic, expressive triumph, but on a conceptual level her analysis is a series of rigidifying moves that hammer out the normative content of work activity and destroy its emancipatory elements altogether.

Arendt's first move is, perhaps, the most devastating for an emancipatory-action concept of work. In this move, the notion of work as a causally efficacious and meaningful equilibrium between human beings and circumstances (of the sort Weil advances) is quickly resolved into nothing more than the devising of instruments and appropriation of tools for the making of things. Arendt's *homo faber* is simply the shell inside which we find that energetic constructor *homo fabricatus* (1958, 139–144, 305–307; 1969, 215–217). Situated within a world of artifice, the activity of *homo fabricatus* takes on an orientation that is exclusively directed toward the object. Hence Arendt's second move is to theorize fabrication as an act "where a clearly recognizable end . . . determines and organizes everything" (1958, 156 f.; 1969, 215). Under these auspices, the actual process of engaging in fabricating activity is "secondary and derivative" (307). *Homo faber*, Arendt contends, experiences processes "as mere means toward an end." The action structure of work, or what happens *in between* "the definite beginning and the predictable end" is thereby reduced to the negligible, while the end is granted existential priority (144). In Arendt's third conceptual move, this already stunted notion of work as an objectifying means-end orientation now becomes a thoroughly negative formulation as well. The use of tools in the production of objects is secured to "the degradation of all things into means" (1958, 156), "the limitless devaluation of every-

thing given" (1958, 157; 1969, 216), and the "element of violation and violence" (1958, 139). This move to degradation, devaluation, and violence is
decisive. With it, Arendt surrenders the ability analytically to grasp the difference between instrumental action as utilitarian objectification and instrumental action as, in Weil's sense, purposeful performance.[23] As a result, she
conceptualizes all forms of means-end relations as necessarily and not just contingently connected to acts of violence, manipulation, and control.

Arendt's final move should come as no surprise. In the attitudes of the
modern age that she assigns to the means-end activity of *homo faber*, there is
no room for genuine interaction oriented toward teamwork or mutual subjectivity. The only company that grows out of workmanship, she argues (1958,
161 f.), "is in the need of the master for assistants or in his wish to educate
others in his craft," against which she opposes "the multiheaded subject," or
the teamwork of *animal laborans*. *Homo faber* appears only in the "exchange
market" and not in "the specifically political forms of being together with others, acting in concert and speaking with each other" (1958, 161; 1969, 217).
To appreciate the rather unimaginative and conceptually constricted nature of
(both sides of) this Arendtian opposition, we might compare it to an example that Weil (1973, 101) offers of purposeful performance as a form of interaction at work: "A team of workers on a production-line under the eye of a
foreman is a sorry spectacle, whereas it is a fine sight to see a handful of work-
men in the building trade, checked by some difficulty, ponder the problem
each for himself, make various suggestions for dealing with it, and then apply
unanimously the method conceived by one of them, who may or may not
have any official authority over the remainder. At such moments the image of
a free community appears almost in its purity."

This telling example is characteristically Weilian in its subjectivism (and its
yearning for absolute purity). Nevertheless, it realistically differentiates and
emancipates where Arendt's formulation congeals and confines. The human
situation that Weil's purposeful performance account challenges as contingent
and alienating (the herd-team of object producers) is one that Arendt deems
intrinsic to labor (as teamwork) and to work (as fabrication). Arendt, it seems,
can have no equivalent of Weil's problem-oriented, collectively methodical
builders. This is not only because she reduces work to an object orientation
that prohibits genuine relations with others but also because she reduces teamwork to the routinized performance of motions that prohibits speech, discussion, disagreement, and deliberation.

As the scenario of *The Human Condition* unfolds, then, *animal laborans* and
homo faber emerge in conflict with each other but also allied against freedom
and action (1958, 144–153, 188, 210). Both the automatism of labor and the
means-end instrumentality of work are symbolically opposed to, and normatively distinguished from, Arendt's action concept of politics. The symbolic
oppositions that Arendt establishes as labor:work:action give her public realm

theory much of its courageous character. But at the same time, Arendt's inability to conceptualize instrumental action within a richer situational context than *homo fabricatus* leaves her account of politics practically inadequate and vulnerable to what Weil (1973, 85) calls "an unconditional surrender to caprice."

The Theater Where Freedom Courageously Appears

"As long as we believe that we deal with ends and means in the political realm," Arendt (1958, 229) writes, "we shall not be able to prevent anybody's using all means to pursue recognized ends." Elsewhere (1953, 597) she argues, "If we insist on applying the category of means and ends to action and human relationships, we shall see that everything comes to stand on its head. . . . A bad deed for a good cause instantly makes our common world a little worse."

The alarm behind these words is neither trivial nor negligible. Out of the hubris of the modern age Arendt (1958, 228) detects a conviction that has spawned a myriad of twentieth-century horrors: man can know "only what he makes." The conviction can be historically located in Plato, "who was the first to design a blueprint for the making of political bodies" (227). What Plato enacted was a brilliant and devious conceptual maneuver that associated *archein* ("beginning") with "ruling" and eliminated *prattein* ("achieving"), thereby accomplishing a philosophical act of treachery against politics (188 f., 222 f.). The essence of politics became knowing how to rule. Thus, the *polis* became an object of order and manipulation, the perplexities of action were reduced to "problems of cognition," and the genuine plasticity of acting was hardened into the solidity of work, craft, and making. Consequently, Arendt (1958, 225) writes, "the most elementary and authentic understanding of human freedom disappeared from political philosophy."

When the conviction that "man is the measure," with its necessary degradation and objectification of all things, donned modern dress and invaded the realm of human affairs, politics became a means to be put to the purposes of particular ideological ends, into which history itself was drawn as consort. The prosaic dimension of a mentality "that forces one to admit that all means, provided that they are efficient, are permissible and justified to pursue something defined as an end" found inherent plausibility in the formulation of capitalistic economy (Arendt 1958, 229). Its murderous dimension took shape in the Leninist line of argument—"You cannot make a table without killing trees, you cannot make an omelet without breaking eggs, you cannot make a republic without killing people"—and reached its most virulent and horrific form in the totalitarian state (Arendt 1969, 139). This ideological orientation toward politics, with its ferreting out patterns in history, its distortion of all things into means for the pursuit of allegedly higher ends, its violent appeals to new orders and final solutions, and its utter contempt for human personhood and individuality, is what Arendt's action concept of politics courageously attempts to overcome. Consequently, Arendtian public realm theory risks a theatrical politics that "lies altogether outside the category of means and ends" against an ideological politics as the pursuit of ends that justify all means (1958, 207; cf. [1953c] 1994).

Outside the category of means and ends, Arendt (1958, 176 f., 202) heroically stakes freedom in the condition of "plurality," or the common situation in which human beings reveal their "unique distinctiveness" through acting and speaking together. In the phenomenal space "where I appear to others as others appear to me," Arendtian politics recovers the world that the tremendous cosmos of modern automatism threatens to obliterate. The world is recovered in "the living essence of the person as it shows itself in the flux of action and speech" (1958, 181, 198). Daring to enter the space of appearances, every individual leaves behind the concern with life, and finds in the courage to speak a personal identity and specific uniqueness brought to light. In this condition only, one is not a *what* but a *who*—a name, a physical presence, a living essence, a character-in-voice—"distinguished from any other who is, was or will ever be" (175; cf. 179–181). The "intercourse of the citizens of the polis" is the theater in which mortal actors seize reality as unique and distinct speakers of words and doers of deeds (1969, 222; 1958, 180).

Consequently, politics is the space of appearances in which, as Arendt declares, the "inner affinity of speech and action, *their spontaneity and practical purposelessness*" interrupt the "circular movement of biological life" and thwart the drive to calculate a trajectory of human affairs (1958, 177 n. 1, emphasis added; 1969, 43). In the name of this "inner affinity" that is freedom, an Arendtian politics bravely defies both the artificial, repetitive, cyclicalities of *animal laborans* and the durable, means-ends lineations of *homo faber*. In Arendtian public realm theory, then, the *polis* is neither a nostalgic yearning nor a perverse Hellenic fixation. It represents metaphorically what "politics" constitutes literally—"a kind of theater where freedom could appear" (1969, 154).

If one of the markers of an emancipatory political theory is its capacity to speak meaningfully about individuals as social and political beings and not just isolated subjects against nature, then Arendt's theatrical performance concept of freedom has some considerable advantages over Weil's purposeful performance concept. Primarily, it carries with it a sure grasp of the emancipatory value of speech as interaction in plurality and a vivid presentation of politics as the "web of human relationships" in which such interaction is actualized through speech (Arendt 1958, 178). In short, if "politics are wholly instrumental," as M. I. Finley (1983, 97) insists, then they can only be instrumental and *meaningful* if they are conceptualized as a *common* human enterprise and against the background of something like plurality in an Arendtian sense. To the extent to which Weil bears allegiance to a post-Cartesian philosophy of consciousness, she can do none of this—neither conceptualize action intersubjectively, nor theorize speech as the activity of mutual recognition geared toward some kind of understanding, nor present politics in the context of genuine commonality. (In fact, Weil does not seem to consider politics a genuine human activity at all. It does not even appear on the list of activities she thinks should imitate work.)[24] Interaction, in Weil's thinking, is at most the cooperation or the coordination of individualistic, disaggregated particulars, like her methodical builders. Speech, in Weil's thinking, seems to be at best a kind of "awkward substitute for sign language" (Arendt's phrase); it is simply the vehicle through which the builders advance the solutions they have pondered in work (Arendt 1958, 179). Consequently, Arendt's theory of action remains superior to Weil's—not only because it rescues politics within a context of interaction as speech but also because it makes freedom the raison d'être of politics itself (Arendt 1969, 154).

Yet in arriving at this powerful action concept of politics, Arendtian public realm theory also stands in danger of—in Weil's words (1973, 85)—sinking into the "purely arbitrary," for without a dimension of substantive purposefulness that finds positive expression in the vocabulary of "problem," "solution," "means," "end," and "method," Arendt's politics cannot embrace performance as the carrying out or active pursuit of purposes in the very world it strives to vitalize. Politics can encompass performance as public presentation, as in the act of performing a play, a part, or a piece of music; the performing arts "have indeed a strong affinity" with Arendtian politics (Arendt 1969, 154). But without a substantive purpose, Arendt's courageous political performer is constantly in danger of becoming only an actor, "concerned merely with the 'impression' he makes" (Weber 1946, 116). When this happens, the politics of the public realm threatens to become an unconditional surrender to caprice. Moreover, it leaves the theory behind it vulnerable to charges of aestheticism, sentimentalism, and self-defeat. Arendt's public realm theory is dangerously close to this surrender to the arbitrary and the capricious not because it rescues theatrical performance in the face of reductive and routinizing life processes but because it celebrates the "practical purposelessness" of speech and action and the transcendence of "mere productive activity" in politics as it does so (1958, 177, 180).[25]

By this I do not mean to redeploy the familiar claims that the Arendtian public realm is a talk shop full of speechifying, "the plaything of an already educated elite," or a kind of game playing "set apart from the real world" (Elster 1983, 98; Schwartz 1989, 30, 41; Udovicki 1983, 56). Arendt in fact anticipates that in a society that celebrates the artifice of *homo faber* and the life of *animal laborans*, her concept of politics (and action) would probably be taken as a narcissistic tribute to "idleness, idle busybodyness and idle talk" (1958, 208; cf. 159, 180). Accordingly, she is careful to assign certain a priori features to words and deeds (that is, they are "*about* some worldly objective reality") and to action (that is, it has a "specific content" and a "specific productivity") (1958, 182, 187, 190 f.). These comments obviously failed to inoculate Arendt's public realm theory against charges of irrelevance and elitism, but they indicate that she knew that politics was not simply acts of self-revelation—splendid, courageous, and immortalizing though they may be.

Still, the acknowledgments a theorist makes are one thing, and what the theory can conceptually vindicate is quite another. I am suggesting that Arendt's theory cannot conceptually vindicate either the emancipatory value of purposeful performance or the practical purposefulness of politics.[26] We can trace this conceptual failure in part to Arendt's thinking about how *homo faber* works. Had she initially differentiated between *homo fabricatus* and *homo methodus*, she might have recognized that there is nothing *necessarily* violent, dangerous, or ideological about the category of means and ends in politics. Rather, everything hinges upon the action context within which that mentality or mode of thinking exerts itself. But by assuming that the category of means and ends is necessarily (and not just contingently) afflicted with violent objectification, Arendt has to deny (or at least evade) the normative dimension of the active pursuit of substantive purposes in the space of appearances. Thus, although means-end activity is not excluded from Arendtian politics, it is always and only a negative formulation tied to fabrication.[27] Ultimately, Arendt (1965, 208–210) locates means-end activity in its least negative form in the "prepolitical" domain of legislation. In its most negative form, where it slides into something like automatism, it emerges in the "antipolitical" domain of administration (276–278). Accordingly, Arendtian public realm theory cedes the most important aspects of political activity as everyday life to charismatic founders on the one hand and administrative teams on the other. There must be another way to think politics.

Thinking Methodically in the Space of Appearances

Earlier, in considering the means-end category in politics, I suggested that everything hinges upon the action context within which this mentality or mode of thinking takes place. I now want to suggest that there is a richer conceptual context—beyond utilitarian objectification, rational capitalist accumulation, and/or Leninism—within which to think about the category of means and ends. Weil offers this alternative in her account of methodical thinking as (1) problem-oriented, (2) directed toward enacting a plan or method (solutions) in response to problems identified, (3) attuned to intelligent mastery (not domination), and (4) purposeful but not driven by a single end or success. Although Weil did not even come close to doing this herself, we might derive from her account of methodical thinking an action concept of politics. Methodical politics is opposed to the ideological politics Arendt deplores; but it is also distinct in important respects from the theatrical politics that Arendt defends.

Identifying a problem—or what the philosopher David Wiggins (1978, 145) calls "the search for the *best specification* of what would honor or answer to relevant concerns"—is where methodical politics begins.[28] It continues (to extrapolate from Weil's image of the methodical builders) in the determination of a means-ends sequel, or method, directed toward a political aim. It reaches its full realization in the actual undertaking of the plan of action, or the exercise of a way of doing itself. To read any of these action aspects as falling under technical rules or blueprints (as Arendt tends to do when dealing with means and ends) is to confuse problem identification and resolution with object making, and something methodical with something ideological. By designating a problem orientation to political activity, methodical politics assigns value to the activity of constantly deploying "knowing and doing" on new situations or on new understandings of old ones. This is neither an ideological exercise in repetition nor the insistent redeployment of the same pattern onto shifting circumstances and events. The problem orientation that defines methodical politics rests upon recognition of the political domain as a matrix of obstacles where it is impossible ever to secure an ideological fix or a single focus.

In general, then, methodical politics is best understood from the perspective of "the fisherman battling against wind and waves in his little boat" (Weil 1973, 101), or perhaps as Michael Oakeshott (1962, 127) offers: "In political activity . . . men sail a boundless and bottomless sea; there is neither harbour for shelter nor floor for anchorage, neither starting-place nor appointed destination."[29] Neither Weil's nor Oakeshott's is the perspective of the Platonist, who values the modeler, constructing his ship after preexisting formulas, or the pilot-philosopher who steers his craft to port by the light of immutable Forms fixed in a starry night. In both of the Platonic images (where the *polis* is either an artifact for use or a conveyance to safe harbor), a single and predictable end is already at hand. Neither Weil's nor Oakeshott's images admit any equivalent finality. The same is true of methodical politics, where political phenomena present to citizens—as the high sea presents to the sailor—challenges to be identified, demands to be met, and a context of circumstances to be engaged (without blueprints). Neither the assurance of finality nor the promise of certainty attends this worldly activity.

In his adamantly instrumental reading of politics in the ancient world, M. I. Finley (1983, 53) makes a similar point and distinguishes between a problem orientation and patterned predictability by remarking upon the "iron compulsion" the Greeks and Romans were under "to be continuously inventive, as new and often unanticipated problems or difficulties arose that had to be resolved without the aid of precedents or models." With this in mind, we might appreciate methodical politics as a mode of action oriented toward the identification of problems and the undertaking of solutions within a context of adventure and unfamiliarity. In this sense, it is compatible with Arendt's emancipatory concept of natality (or "new beginnings") and her appreciation of openness and unpredictability in the realm of human affairs.

There are other neighborly affinities between methodical and theatrical politics as well. Both share a view of political actors as finite and fragile creatures who face an infinite range of possibilities, with only limited powers of control and imagination over the situations in which they are called upon to act. From both a methodical and a theatrical vantage point, this perpetual struggle that is politics, whatever its indeterminacy and flux, acquires meaning only when "knowing what to do and doing it" are united in the same performance (Arendt 1958, 223). Freedom, in other words, is realized when Plato's brilliant conceptual maneuver is outwitted by a politics that opposes "the escape from action into rule" and reasserts human self-realization as the unification of thought-action in the world (223–225). In theatrical politics, however, the actual action content of citizen "knowing and doing" is upstaged by the spectacular appearance of personal identities courageously revealed in the public realm. Thus Plato's maneuver is outwitted in a bounded yet elastic space where knowing what to do and doing it are disclosed in speech acts and deeds of self-revelation in the company of one's fellow citizens. In contrast, methodical politics doggedly reminds us that purposes themselves are what matter in the end and that citizen action is as much about obstinately pursuing them as it is about the courage to speak in performance. So, in methodical politics, the Platonic split between knowing and doing is overcome in a kind of boundless navigation that is realized in purposeful acts of collective self-determination.

Spaces of appearances are indispensable in this context, but these spaces are not exactly akin to "islands in a sea or as oases in a desert" (Arendt 1965, 279). The parameters of methodical politics are more fluid than this, set less by identifiable boundaries than by the very activity through which citizens "let realities work upon" them with "inner concentration and calmness" (Weber 1946, 115). In this respect, methodical politics is not a context wherein courage takes eloquent respite from the face of life, danger (the sea, the desert), or death: it is a daily confrontation wherein obstacles or dangers (including the ultimate danger of death) are transformed into problems, problems are rendered amenable to possible action, and action is undertaken with an aim toward solution. Indeed, in these very activities, or what Arendt (1958, 154) sometimes pejoratively calls the *in order to*, we might find the perpetuation of what she praises as the *for the sake of which*, or the perpetuation of politics itself.

To appreciate the liberatory dimension of this action concept of politics as methodical, we might now briefly return to the problem that Arendt and Weil think most vexes the modern world: the deformation of human beings and human affairs by forces of automatism. This is the complex manipulation of modern life that Havel (1985, 83) describes as the situation in which everything "must be cosseted together as firmly as possible, predetermined, regulated and controlled" and "every aberration from the prescribed course of life is treated as error, license and anarchy." Constructed against this symbolic *animal laborans*, Arendt's space of appearances is the agonistic opposite of the distorted counterfeit reality of automatism. The space of appearances is where individuality and personal identity are snatched from the jaws of automatic processes and recuperated in "the merciless glare" of the public realm (Arendt 1969, 86). Refigured in this fashion, Arendtian citizens counter reductive technological complexes in acts of individual speech revelation that powerfully proclaim, in collective effect, "This is *who* we are!"

A politics in this key does indeed dramatically defy the objectifying processes of modern life—and perhaps even narratively transcends them by delivering up what is necessary for the reification of human remembrance in the "storybook of mankind" (Arendt 1958, 95). But these are also its limits. For whatever else it involves, Arendtian politics cannot entail the *practical* confrontation of the situation that threatens the human condition most. Within the space of appearances, Arendt's citizens can neither search for the best specification of the problem before them nor, it seems, pursue solutions to the problem once it is identified, for such activities involve "the pursuit of a definite aim which can be set by practical considerations," and that is *homo faber*'s prerogative and so in the province of "fabrication," well outside the space of appearances where means and ends are left behind (170 f.). Consequently, automatism can be conceptualized as a "danger sign" in Arendt's theory, but it cannot be designated as a problem in Arendt's politics, a problem that citizens could cognitively encounter and purposefully attempt to resolve or transform (322).

From the perspective of methodical politics, which begins with a problem orientation, automatism can be specified and encountered within the particular spaces or circumstances (schools, universities, hospitals, factories, corporations, prisons, laboratories, houses of finance, the home, public arenas, public agencies) upon which its technological processes intrude. Surely something like this is what Weil (1973, 123 f.) has in mind when she calls for "a sequence of mental efforts" in the drawing up of "an inventory of modern civilization" that begins by "refusing to subordinate one's own destiny to the course of history." Freedom is immanent in such moments of cognitive inventory, in the collective citizen work of "taking stock"—identifying problems and originating methods—and in the shared pursuit of purposes and objectives. This is simply what it means to think and act methodically in spaces of appearance. Nothing less, as Wiggins (1978, 146) puts it, "can rescue and preserve civilization from the mounting irrationality of the public province, . . . from Oppression exercised in the name of Management (to borrow Simone Weil's prescient phrase)."

Perhaps we have now gained some clarity on this picture of methodical politics, but a problem of value remains. Boards can be instruments of violence, and so can boats. So the problem, simply stated, involves the ethical constitution of the common context within which methodical thinking can take place. What normative prerequisites are necessary in order to guarantee that methodical politics does not disintegrate after all into the ideological politics that Arendt identifies as the objectification of human beings and adamantly deplores? Against what kind of background can a public realm politics of means and ends, problems and solutions, be secured as methodical and *ethical*? Perhaps this quintessential problem of politics (how to judge rightly the lesser evil, the relatively best, the ends that justify the means and the means themselves), is simply too much for Arendtian public realm theory to bear—hence Arendt's ultimate evasion of the category of means and ends in politics altogether. Or perhaps (as some thoughtful scholars argue), Arendt's condition of plurality itself provides the ethical dimension that a truly emancipatory politics—even a politics of means and ends—requires.[30] I cannot answer this problem of value here. In reflecting upon it, I am drawn to the advice that Weber (1946, 151) offers on a related problem in science: "If you remain faithful to yourself, you will necessarily come to certain final conclusions that subjectively make sense." Of course, this probably does not suffice. In any case, I must simply acknowledge that for now we have come to the limits of methodical politics.

The Plastic People of the Universe

Even if it could be scrupulously formulated as free and ethical, a methodical politics of problems, plans, possibilities, and purposes might still come to public realm theory at too great a cost. Ultimately, an Arendtian might argue, it threatens to reimprison human beings in the very existential "solidity" that theatrical politics (with its luminous sense of boundlessness, unpredictability, and irreversibility) is, in the first place, an attempt to overcome. It is true that one of Arendt's greatest accomplishments involves the rescue of politics from what Wolin (1960, 352 f.) calls its "sublimation" into organization and its "absorption" into nonpolitical institutions and activities. The spatial and temporal phenomena that are set forth with atomic-age urgency in Arendt's space of appearances defy the solidity, relentless automatism, and patterned predictabilities that weigh down human existence in the modern world.[31] Humanness is, therefore, regained in the thrills, the highs, and the almost apocalyptic energy of spontaneous word and deed, and in new beginnings (natality) that give rise to the totally unexpected.

That is why, when Arendt looks to history, she recaptures the "lost treasure" of action in those moments when politics is redeemed as the sudden, spontaneous release of numbers of people, whose "sheer momentum of acting-together" brings forth the cry for freedom: the American Revolution, the revolutionary councils that appeared in Europe in 1848, the Paris Commune of 1871, the "soviets" in Russia in 1917, the November revolutions in Germany and Austria after World War I, the revolt in Hungary in 1956, and the antiwar and civil rights movements in the United States. We can now confidently add to this list Charter 77, Worker's Defense Committee, Solidarity, Civic Forum, Public Against Violence, Tiananmen Square, a second Russian revolution, and the truly glorious spectacles of 1989: Warsaw, Prague, Budapest, Berlin. One can only wish that the curator of lost treasures had lived to witness them.

We do disservice to these moments of Arendtian action, however (and hence to politics itself) if we stake acting together solely on "sheer momentum" or the "spontaneity" of rare movements that burst out against the dark backdrop of modernity. To render as truly political only events that are public, spontaneous, and momentous is to underestimate the full complexity (and sometimes the brutality)[32] of human conduct in such events themselves—to see them, as Havel (1985, 49) puts it, "from the outside" and perhaps "chiefly from the vantage point of the system and its power structure." Charter 77 "came as a surprise" and appeared as a "bolt out of the blue," but, as Havel reminds us, it was neither a bolt out of the blue nor the result of a spontaneous political event. Its initial impetus was a small protest against the impending trial of the rock group The Plastic People of the Universe (formed in September 1968 under the leadership of Milan Hlavsa, shortly after Russian tanks rolled into Prague), whose rock festivals, music, and manifestos about an artistic underground "second culture" came to displease the communist authorities.[33] In 1976, after one such festival, the police made a sweep of the rock underground, arresting twenty-seven and seizing the Plastic People's equipment, along with many other people's tapes, photos, and books (Pareles 2001). The protest against the arrest, trial, and imprisonment of members of the band began with a campaign planned in detail and with "modest, internal steps" that culminated in the signing of a petition by seventy people (Havel 1990, 130–138). The action group Charter 77, which became a formal human rights movement, eventually emerged out of the opposition circles that the campaign for The Plastics had informally organized. As a document, the charter took form slowly during the late months of 1976, not in the merciless glare of the public but in what Havel (1985, 49) calls "that semi-darkness where things are difficult to chart or analyse." Its history has as much to do with the laborious organization of meetings, the meticulous crafting of language, the arduous collection of signatories, and the repeated drafting of copies of the original document as with the "explosion" that followed its release in the public realm. Even then, as Havel (1990, 139) understands it, the charter was neither a "one-shot manifesto" nor by any means a prepolitical act of legislation but rather a commitment "to participate in ongoing work."

Like Havel and in the spirit of Arendt's instruction that we must "think what we are doing," I have been thinking about what it means to consider politics as a kind of ongoing worldly work that necessitates, to return to Thucydides, "the constant improvement of methods" (1982, 41). I raise the example of Charter 77 not to diminish the beauty of an Arendtian politics of spontaneity but in order to propose a public realm theory that is better able to coordinate political action as purposeful and hence open to a broader range of significance "in the whole way of life" (Weber 1946, 77). In thinking about the same sort of things, Havel (1985, 90) warns that the global automatism of technological civilization poses a "planetary challenge" to the position of human beings in the world. If he is right, then those of us who take the project of emancipation seriously must do no less than face the challenge with all the means at our disposal and endeavor, in Simone Weil's (1973, 121) words, "to introduce a little play into the cogs of the machine that is grinding us down." As citizens, in other words, we must think methodically what is to be done.

Chapter 9

A Transfiguring Evening Glow
Arendt and the Holocaust

All efforts to escape from the grimness of the present into nostalgia for a still intact past, or into the anticipated oblivion of a better future, are in vain.

—Hannah Arendt

Hannah Arendt spent much of her life and a great deal of her writing in an effort to comprehend the destructive forces of the twentieth century, some of which, as she never ceased to remind us, were fundamentally unprecedented and incomprehensible in any ordinary or conventional sense. Within the domain of the social sciences, Arendt ([1950a] 1994, 234) argued, there are data which "respond to our commonly accepted research techniques and scientific concepts," and then there are data "which explode this whole framework of reference" and defy our categories of explanation concerning human social and individual behavior. In the face of such data, Arendt (242) noted, "we can only guess in what forms human life is being lived when it is lived as though it took place on another planet."

Arendt ([1950a] 1994, 235) thought that the line between the comprehensible and the incomprehensible, between human life on earth and some other planet, between human evil and absolute evil, was crossed in the final stages of totalitarianism when Nazi anti-Semitism transmogrified into the Holocaust, as

anti-Jewish legislation, the herding of Jews into European ghettos, and the establishment of forced labor camps mutated into the creation of death factories for
"the fabrication of corpses" undergirded by a methodical and mechanized program for the extermination and annihilation of human beings. Arendt insisted
that although the incomprehensible crime at issue was committed in its largest
measure against the Jews of Europe, it was in no way limited to the Jews or the
Jewish question (in Arendt and Jaspers 1992, 423). The deeds of horror perpe-
trated by the Nazi regime and totalitarianism "wherever it ruled" threatened to
destroy the very "essence of man" (Arendt 1951, viii); thus the incomprehensible Holocaust had to be reckoned with as a crime against humanity.

Over the past two decades, many scholars and writers have tried to confront
the Holocaust through philosophical, sociological, psychological, symbolic, literary, and religious formulations. Indeed, the literature is by now so voluminous
that there is a genre called "Holocaust studies" that locates it.[1] My aim in this
chapter is to explore Arendt's political theory, and particularly her most famous
text, *The Human Condition* (1958), within the specific context of the Holocaust.
I wish to suggest that approaching Arendt from this perspective not only underscores the originality of her theorizing totalitarianism but also illuminates the
depth and profundity of her contribution to our thinking through the most
fiercely inhuman and horrific event of twentieth-century Europe.

Facing Up to Reality

What does it mean to comprehend what is historically incomprehensible?
Spoken or unspoken, this question lies at the center of Arendt's thinking about
the Holocaust and the fate of European Jewry in the twentieth century. Arendt
(1951, viii) argued that we must begin by resisting the urge to make shocking,
outrageous, and unprecedented realities "comprehensible" in terms of reductive commonplaces. "The greatest danger for a proper understanding of our
recent history," she wrote ([1950a] 1994, 243), "is the only too comprehensible tendency of the historian to draw analogies. The point is that Hitler was
not like Jenghiz Khan and not worse than some other great criminal but
entirely different." Thus, comprehension does not mean "explaining phenomena by such analogies . . . that the impact of reality and the shock of experience are no longer felt," but rather requires "examining and bearing
consciously the burden which our century has placed on us—neither denying
its existence nor submitting meekly to its weight." Arendt (1951, viii) concluded that comprehension "means the unpremeditated, attentive facing up to,
and resisting of, reality—whatever it may be."[2]

The difficult task of comprehending totalitarianism and simultaneously
facing up to and resisting the absolute factual evil of the Holocaust posed at
least two problems of thinking for Arendt. The first concerned historiography.
In her reply to Eric Voegelin's review of *The Origins of Totalitarianism*, Arendt
([1953b] 1994, 402) stated that the problem was "how to write historically

about something—totalitarianism—which I did not want to conserve but on the contrary felt engaged to destroy." Arendt wanted to avoid an impulse that she thought characterized the "extraordinarily poor" scholarship of many contemporary historians of anti-Semitism. In recovering the history of a subject that they did not want to conserve, these historians "had to write in a destructive way." However, Arendt remarked, "to write history for purposes of destruction is somehow a contradiction in terms." Making the Jews "the subject of conservation" was no solution in these matters. In Arendt's view, to look at the events only from the side of the victims resulted in apologetics, "which of course is no history at all." Thus the problem that comprehending "the particular subject matter" of totalitarianism posed for Arendt was how to face the reality of certain "facts and events" (404) objectively and on their own terms without at the same time robbing them of their hellishness or appearing to neutralize or condone them.

This first, historiographic, problem led Arendt to criticize the standard approaches of the social sciences as well as political theoretical frameworks along the lines of Voegelin's. In each mode of inquiry, she argued, there was a failure to recognize "phenomenal differences" of factuality and "to point out the *distinct quality* of what was actually happening" in particular events. Thus certain "inarticulate, elementary, and axiomatic assumptions" that form the basis of social scientific presumptions regarding human behavior are absolutely unable to account for or perhaps even appreciate exceptions to the rule. Arendt [1950a] 1994, 234) noted, for example, that "utilitarian" presumptions about human behavior and institutions are utterly unable to understand the concentration camps, which were distinguished by the *absence* of utilitarian criteria, rendering them precisely the curious and seemingly "unreal" phenomena that they were. Similarly, theoretical frameworks that attempt to locate totalitarianism along a historical continuum of "intellectual affinities and influences" fail to appreciate that which is novel and unprecedented, thereby threatening to minimize truly radical breaking points within the human condition by making them appear as though they are merely aspects of "a previously known chain of causes and influences" ([1953b] 1994, 404 f.). Arendt further clarified her differences with Voegelin by establishing a distinction between her "facts and events" approach and his tendency to proceed by way of "intellectual affinities and influences." By way of the latter, Voegelin identified a "'rise of immanentist sectarianism'" in the late Middle Ages that, he argued, culminated in totalitarianism. Arendt vigorously eschewed such explanations, preferring to speak not of "essences" that precede a phenomenon's coming-into-being (for example, of an "essence of totalitarianism" in the eighteenth century) but only of particular historically traceable "'elements'" that eventually "crystallize" into totalitarianism. Arendt develops this approach in great detail in The *Origins of Totalitarianism* (which she obviously thought Voegelin had misinterpreted).

The second problem that Arendt faced in comprehending the absolute
evil of totalitarianism was on a different plane than historiography and in a different province than the historian's. On this plane, we move from what we
know of the event to how to remember it. In Lawrence Langer's words (1995),
this move "shifts the responsibility to our own imaginations and what we are
prepared to admit there." Arendt alluded to this problem in the very personal
and dedicatory letter that she wrote to Karl Jaspers as the preface of her book
Sechs Essays, published in Germany in 1948. Here too she was concerned with
factuality—but of another kind than the factual reality that she wanted to
identify and trace in the unprecedented historical reality of totalitarianism.
Indeed, this reality had less to do with totalitarianism than it had to do with
what Arendt called the "factual territory" that the Holocaust had created for
the Germans and the Jews. To Jaspers she wrote:

> The factual territory unto which both peoples have been driven
> looks something like this: On the one side is the complicity of the
> German people, which the Nazis consciously planned and real-
> ized. On the other side is the blind hatred, created in the gas
> chambers, of the entire Jewish people. Unless both peoples decide
> to leave this factual territory, the individual Jew will no more be
> able to abandon his fanatical hatred than will the individual
> German be able to rid himself of the complicity imposed upon
> him by the Nazis. ([1948] 1994, 214)

For the Jews, Arendt tells Jaspers, the decision to leave this factual territory "is
difficult to make." The difficulty has nothing to do with the miserable but
comprehensible saga of anti-Semitism and Jew-hatred in modern Europe; for
even in this hostile context, Arendt wrote that, "the possibility of communication between peoples and individuals" was alive. "One could defend oneself as
a Jew," she continued (215), "because one had been attacked as a Jew. National
concepts and national membership still had a meaning; they were still elements
of a reality within which one could live and move."

Leaving the factual territory of German complicity and Jewish hatred was
a different matter. It involved dealing with the construction of concentration
camps and "the fabrication of corpses." With Auschwitz, Arendt ([1948] 1994,
215) averred, "the factual territory opened up an abyss into which everyone is
drawn who attempts after the fact to stand on that territory." After Auschwitz,
the space one occupies if one "pulls back" from the abyss is "an empty space
where there are no longer nations and peoples but only individuals for whom it
is now not of much consequence what the majority of peoples, or even the
majority of one's own people, happens to think at any given moment." Thus we
might understand the second problem of comprehending the incomprehensible
that Arendt ([1946a] 1994, 198) faced as the problem of how to repair the empty
space where there are no longer nations and peoples but only individuals, in a

way that leaves the factual territory behind and national pasts surmounted, even despite the pervasiveness of what Arendt called "the image of hell."

By now it is commonplace to hold that Arendt took up the problematic task of comprehending the factual reality of totalitarianism and absolute evil primarily in two works that, in Dagmar Barnouw's words (1990, 162), "may turn out to be [Arendt's] most important achievements": *The Origins of Totalitarianism* (1951) and *Eichmann in Jerusalem: A Report on the Banality of Evil* (1963). Less well known is the fact that Arendt assumed the task of finding out and recording factual reality in many articles on Nazism, totalitarian terror, and extermination that she wrote between 1945 and 1955.[3] In *Origins* and *Eichmann* as well as the articles on Nazism, Arendt was primarily (and monumentally) concerned with what I have identified as the first problem of comprehending the reality of totalitarianism, and with telling "the real story of the Nazi-constructed hell"—her task was about finding out, witnessing, recording, and reflecting (Arendt [1946a] 1994, 200).[4] *The Human Condition* (1958), written between *Origins* and *Eichmann*, is a different matter.

The Human Condition as Response to Trauma

Like all great works of political theory, *The Human Condition* can bear, and indeed it has invited, a plenitude of possible readings, some of them contradictory and some better than others. Yet while it is often (and usually) read within the context of modernity and world alienation, the significance of *The Human Condition* in relation to *Origins* and *Eichmann*, and hence to the specific historical and political reality of the Holocaust under Nazism, has not been sufficiently recognized or explored by Arendt scholars. Usually, *The Human Condition* has been read outside, or at least beyond, the context of totalitarianism—perhaps as the nostalgic evocation of a finer past linked to the ancient Greek *polis* (for which Arendt is often criticized) or as the prospective hope for a better future that forwards a theory of participatory democratic (or republican) citizenship or (under the shadow of Heidegger) as a critique of mass society and technological determinism in Western civilization.[5] Despite the power of many of these interpretations, very few have approached Arendt's text in a way that specifies its relation to the task of comprehending what Barnouw (1990, 223) terms "the space and time in which a figure like Eichmann had been possible."[6]

In what follows, I want to sail against the prevailing interpretive winds and present a reading of *The Human Condition* that not only places it within the context of totalitarianism and the Holocaust but also understands it as a profound response to the trauma inflicted upon humanity by the Nazi regime. I also maintain that *The Human Condition* is situated quite differently in relation to these events than are *The Origins of Totalitarianism* and *Eichmann in Jerusalem*, because it is primarily concerned with the second problem of comprehending reality, with surmounting what Arendt ([1946a] 1994, 200) called "the facts

[that] have changed and poisoned the very air we breathe . . . [that] inhabit our dreams at night and permeate our thoughts during the day . . . and [are] the basic experience and the basic misery of our times." Shoshana Felman (1995, 334) clarifies the distinction I am drawing between "finding out" and "surmounting" in the following way:

> To *seek* reality is both to set out to explore the injury inflicted by it—to turn back on, and to try to penetrate, the state of being *stricken, wounded* by reality [*Wirklichkeit suchend*] and to attempt, at the same time, to reemerge from the paralysis of this state, to engage reality [*Wirklichkeit suchend*] as an advent, a movement, and as a vital, critical necessity of *moving on*.[7]

In reading *The Human Condition* as an attempt to undertake this second problem of comprehension, or what Felman calls the effort to "reemerge from paralysis," I will suggest that the act of political conceptualization that Arendt enacted there was a direct and personal effort to offer both Germans and Jews a way back from the abyss so that, as individuals, they might be guided out of trauma and brought together "from their dispersion."[8]

The Greek Solution
As a way of situating *The Human Condition* in response to the trauma of the Holocaust, I wish to begin with section 474 of Friedrich Nietzsche's text *Human, All Too Human* ([1878] 1996, 174).[9] Titled "The Evolution of the Spirit Feared by the State," the section concerns Thucydides, as well as the resistance and hostility with which the Greek *polis* met the evolution of culture. Nietzsche ended on a telling note that, as is often the case with his observations, carries dimensions of meaning and possibility beyond the immediate subject to hand. Nietzsche wrote:

> one should not invoke the glorificatory speech of Pericles: for it is no more than a grand, optimistic illusion as to the supposedly necessary connection between the *polis* and Athenian culture; immediately before night descends on Athens (the plague, the rupture of tradition), Thucydides makes it rise resplendent once again, like a transfiguring evening glow in whose light the evil day that preceded it could be forgotten.

In this complex statement about a great catastrophe that destroyed the body politic of a people Nietzsche cautioned against reading Thucydides's grand invention, the Funeral Oration of Pericles, in a way that stirs a nostalgic yearning for a still intact past that might be recovered and restored in some futuristic moment yet to come. The Athenian polis that Thucydides invents through the imagistic symbol[10] of the Funeral Oration is "no more," no more than a grand, evocative illusion: it bears no connection to the factual reality of a city-state called Athens that was dominated by the statesman Pericles in 431

B.C.E. By throwing the spatial status of the Funeral Oration into question, Nietzsche also refused a reading that confines its temporal status solely to a moment preceding the catastrophe (the plague, the rupture of tradition) that befell Athens. In one sense, the Funeral Oration is such an event: in the chronological sequence of Thucydides's narrative, it appears, Nietzsche says, "immediately before night descends upon Athens." In another equally important sense, however, the imagistic symbol of Athens that Thucydides (1982, 13) creates through Pericles's speech-act is offered in the aftermath of catastrophe, "not as an essay which is to win the applause of the moment, but as a possession for all time." It is Thucydides's powerful riposte to the devastating prior event that "spites healing and does not seek cure" (Felman 1995, 21). Thus in the evocative image of Athens rising resplendent, Thucydides fashions a dream for "the storybook of mankind" (Arendt 1958, 95) that crosses out of the horror and delirium of plague and war, exposure and vulnerability, destruction and death, allowing the vehemence of their cruelty to be undone. Nietzsche ([1878] 1996, 174) put this idea in terms of the provocative simile that finds Thucydides's transforming illumination of Athens to be "like a transfiguring evening glow in whose light the evil day that preceded it could be forgotten."[11]

With this remark, Nietzsche transfigured Thucydides the historian as bearer-of-witness into Thucydides the theorist-as-healer. With this act, the facing up to reality transmogrifies into the creation of a luminous and healing illusion that opens the possibility for a convalescence from pain and suffering, as well as a way toward moving on. In keeping with Nietzsche's rendering of the Funeral Oration as a grand optimistic illusion, I mean to suggest that Thucydides is engaged in a project of inventing an imaginary time and space, an imaginary Athens, that serves a significant purpose. It creates a contrary world that does not so much obliterate the established fact of evil (the plague, the rupture of tradition) as interfere with, counter, or block the human impulse to ruminate upon and incessantly rekindle the perpetual memory of hardship and evil, thereby fanning the flames of desire for retribution and revenge. The Funeral Oration deflects this injurious impulse by offering the intervening image or "countermemory" of Athens as glorious, magnificent: "the school of Hellas," where "the singular spectacle of daring and deliberation" are each carried to their "highest point" (Thucydides 1982, 110). The fixation upon "what was" is modulated by the liberating power of this imaginary world; the obsession with retribution is thereby deferred. By inventing an alternative world swept clean of horror, suffering, and degradation, Thucydides's solution offers not only the Athenians but all of humanity a way toward thinking themselves anew. It is thus "a possession for all time" (Thucydides 1982, 13). It offers a path toward forgetting the evil of the day before.

In much the same way that Nietzsche suggests that Thucydides was engaged in assisting in the convalescence of the Athenians, so I want to suggest that, in *The Human Condition*, Arendt is responding to the trauma of survival that faced the Europeans, and especially the Germans and the Jews, in the wake of the overwhelming deadliness of Nazism and the burning darkness of the extermination camps. In the aftermath of this ultimate evil, Arendt creates a powerful, iridescent image that counters the "reality of persecution" (1968, 17) that had annihilated the Jews and in its aftermath robbed the Germans of "all spontaneous speech and comprehension, so that now . . . they are speechless, incapable of articulating thoughts and adequately expressing their feelings" ([1950a] 1994, 253). Perhaps we should not be surprised to learn that the resplendent image that Arendt fashions in *The Human Condition* (1958, 207)— the image of the public realm and the "space of appearance"—draws its own light from the transfiguring glow of Thucydides's luminescent Periclean *polis*. As Arendt (1958, 205) observes, "Pericles's speech, though it certainly corresponded to and articulated the innermost convictions of the people of Athens, has always been read with the sad wisdom of hindsight by men who knew that his words were spoken at the beginning of the end." In Arendt's view, Thucydides places the Funeral Oration at a point in the narrative preceding the dark night of plague and the rupture of tradition. Arendt also holds to a version of Nietzsche's greater insight when she writes, "The words of Pericles, as Thucydides reports them, are perhaps unique in their supreme confidence that men can enact *and* save their greatness at the same time and, as it were, by one and the same gesture."

So let us not invoke the glorificatory speech of those warrior Greeks in the public realm in order to decry Arendt's alleged "nostalgia" for Hellas and a heroic past that could be a perfect future. For in truth, Arendt's image of the space of appearance is "no more" than a dream—a grand, optimistic illusion.[12] In what follows, I shall attend instead to the way this formulation functions when it is drawn into what Arendt (1969, 13) calls the gap of time between past and future, into "this small track of non-time" which "each new generation, indeed every new human being as he inserts himself between an infinite past and an infinite future, must discover and ploddingly pave . . . anew."

Inventions and Illuminations

The Human Condition is not directly or explicitly about totalitarianism, Nazism, or the extermination of the Jews. Nowhere in the course of this text does Arendt make any detailed or specific reference to these circumstances. Indeed, two other ominous events were the explicit impetus for this work: the launching of Sputnik (which Arendt [1958, 44] called an event "second in importance to no other"); and the advent of "automation" (which she saw as the harbinger of a "society of laborers without labor," liberated into nothingness). To begin the task of staking out a reading that places *The Human Condition* in relation to the Holocaust, I will draw upon two interpretive insights that justify the significance of what is "unspoken" in a work of art or a political theory text.

The first interpretive insight is the literary critic Harry Berger's (1988) compelling notion of the "conspicuous exclusion" of themes that are "saturatingly present" in great texts or artworks—but only as silence or *felt absence*.[13] Following this insight, a text or artwork can be read as holding certain themes at bay, but manifestly so. As Berger (1988, 442) writes: "Conspicuous exclusion makes us attend to what has been left out; the omitted item is not merely missing but *present-as-missing*. It is one thing for an artist merely to omit . . . or ignore something. But it is another for him to make a point of his omission, directing our attention to it." Berger suggests, for example, that the healing tranquility at the center of the paintings of Johannes Vermeer has the horrors of the seventeenth-century wars of religion as its indirect, conspicuously unstated background. Thus, "a whole set of anecdotal, allegorical, and narrative values hovers about Vermeer's painting. But none of them is firmly developed, articulated, or nailed down" (448). Berger locates the "felt absence" of war in the roaring lions that are carved into the filials that Vermeer bathed in the window light, and also in the maps of the bloodily contested Netherlands that adorn the walls where young women read in serene and intimate rooms (456). When Vermeer is viewed in this way, the achievement of his paintings becomes all the more remarkable. As Lawrence Weschler (1995, 56) has remarked, "It's almost as if Vermeer can be seen to have been asserting or *inventing* the very idea of peace" amid the horrors of a tremendously turbulent juncture in the history of his country and continent.

The second interpretive insight involves a brief but telling observation that Karl Jaspers made to Arendt in December 1960, upon having read *Vita Activa* (the German title for *The Human Condition*). Allowing that he grasped "the overall picture" of the book much more easily and quickly in the German than in English, Jaspers noted (in Arendt and Jaspers 1992, 407):

> What appeals to me so strongly in this book is that the things you explicitly state you will *not* talk about (right at the beginning and repeatedly thereafter) exert such a palpable influence from the background. That makes the book in some strange way very transparent for me. There is nothing quite like it today. All your important and concrete discussions are carried by another dimension. Therefore, despite their great seriousness, they become "light" in all their reality. Your many pertinent insights and illuminations and the historical profundity of your explanations provide concreteness and solidity.[14]

Jaspers did not proceed to specify what he thought the other dimension of *The Human Condition* was, the things that exerted their palpable influence from the background of the text in an indirect, unspoken, yet illuminating way. But if we consider his remark in relation to Berger's notion of conspicuous exclusion, then we might imagine that adumbrated around the edges of Arendt's great achievement is a theme that is saturatingly present but only as *felt absence*—a theme that is withheld but at the same time palpable. Thus, just as Berger's insight invites us to see more in Vermeer's art than may immediately meet the eye, so Jaspers's remark opens the possibility that there is more in *The Human Condition* than the things explicitly stated or directly addressed.

We might take these insights, then, as cautionary comments against reading *The Human Condition* too closely to the surface, or in a manner that misses the depth and profundity of certain "concrete discussions" (as Jaspers puts it) because it fails to see a dimension of meaning that is, at once, demonstrable and undisclosed in that text. For example, in the "prologue" to her book (1958, 4) Arendt indicates one thing that she will not discuss, and some "preoccupations and perplexities" to which her book "does not offer an answer." The topic undiscussed is the background against which she says the book was written, namely, the "modern world" born with the first atomic explosions. The preoccupations and perplexities left unanswered are initiated by the two "threatening" events of Sputnik and automation. All three of these phenomena (the birth of the modern world, space exploration, and automation) conspire toward a deeper issue, however. They introduce the specter of a rupture between "knowledge" (in the sense of scientific and technical know-how) and "thought." The possibility of such a rupture, Arendt notes (1958, 3), threatens to turn humanity into "helpless slaves" and "thoughtless creatures," "at the mercy of every gadget which is technically possible, no matter how murderous it is."

Arendt's reference to the murderousness of certain human scientific and technical inventions of the modern world was not, I think, written solely in the face of the lurid glow of nuclear apocalypse. When Arendt wrote explicitly in *The Origins of Totalitarianism* (1951, 443) that "a victory of the concentration-camp system would mean the same inexorable doom for human beings as the use of the hydrogen bomb would mean the doom of the human race," she invoked another type of murderous technology that lingered, palpable but unspoken, in the background of *The Human Condition*. This is the dimension of meaning that suffused Arendt's project, and also gave rise to the "light" that Jaspers found at the center of *The Human Condition*, both in the sense of illumination (where light is a metaphor perhaps for truth) and in the sense of a defiance of gravity (where light is a metaphor for the release from weight or pain).

What I want to contend, then, is that the depth and profundity of Arendt's concept of the "space of appearance" can be fully appreciated only in terms of the features of a phenomenon that is saturatingly present but conspicuously held at bay in *The Human Condition*. The phenomenon is the "hellish experiment" that Arendt thought opened the abyss to the Holocaust, to the most extreme form of totalitarian evil: the SS concentration camps, where the whole program of extermination and annihilation of the Jewish people was enacted and the crime against humanity was carried out. This hellish experiment is what a great deal of *The Human Condition* is all about and what Arendt's luminescent invention of "the space of appearance" is meant to counter. Of course, not directly; but this does not mean that we cannot see the horrors of a human-made hell both subtly insinuated and ultimately overcome in Arendt's text.[15] In what sense, then, is the Holocaust palpable but unspoken in *The Human Condition*?

Labor and Work *in extremis*

As many of Arendt's commentators have noted, in *The Human Condition*, the concepts of labor (*Arbeit*) and work (*Werk*) can bear, and indeed they invite, a plenitude of possible meanings, some of them contradictory.[16] At their most basic level they designate, along with action, the fundamental human activities within the *vita activa*; each corresponds to one of the basic conditions under which, Arendt (1958, 7) writes, "life on earth has been given to man." As we have seen previously, the human condition of labor is life itself; the human condition of work is worldliness; and the human condition of action is plurality.

Yet even at this very basic level we would be mistaken to suppose that the *vita activa* is simply a conglomerate of three fundamental units (labor-work-action) that are things-in-themselves or enduring phenomena with particular definitive features or side effects. This is partly because Arendt theorized the activities of labor, work, and action as externally bound to and connected by each other in sometimes compatible and sometimes incompatible ways. Equally importantly, however, Arendt took the more radical step of internally differentiating these concepts so that each presupposes a multiplicity of interconnected elements that defy attribution in terms of a settled meaning or unified synoptic picture. The concept of labor or *animal laborans*, for example, is the sum of the following multifarious elements:

> the blessing of life as a whole, nature, animality, life processes, (human) biology, (human) body, (human) metabolism, fertility, birth, reproduction, childbirth, femaleness, cyclicality, circularity, seasons, necessity, basic life needs (food, clothing, shelter), certain kinds of toil, repetition, everyday functions (eating, cleaning, mending, washing, cooking, resting, and so on), housework, the domestic sphere, abundance, consumerism, privatization, purposeless regularity, the society of jobholders, automation, technological determinism, routinization, relentless repetition, automatism, regularization, nonutilitarian processes, recyclability, dehumanizing processes, devouring processes, painful exhaustion, waste, destruction (of nature, body, fertility), and *deathlessness*.

The concept of work or *homo faber* is the sum of the following multifarious elements:

> the work of our hands, the man-made world, fabrication, (human) artifice, (human) creativity, production, usage, durability, objectivity, building, constructing, manufacturing, making, violation,

maleness, linearity, reification, multiplication, tools and instruments, rules and measurement, ends and means, predictability, the exchange market, commercialism, capitalism, instrumental processes, utilitarian processes, objectifying processes, artificial processes, vulgar expediency, violence, predictability, deprivation of intrinsic worth, degradation, disposability, destruction (of nature, world), and *lifelessness.*

As I have arranged them here, the features that Arendt assigned to labor and work can be viewed as points along a single continuum that shade from the human condition "under which life on earth has been given to man" into a condition *in extremis* under which life on earth is taken away. Near the end of the continuum, labor manifests itself in extremis in the form of dehumanizing automatic processes and compulsive repetitions that displace human death while work manifests itself *in extremis* in the form of dehumanizing fabricating processes and instrumentalized objectifications that violate human life. Now, along this continuum we might find the automatic processes of *animal laborans* and the instrumental processes of *homo faber* in the nullity that is advanced capitalism in late modernity. This is indeed what many readers of *The Human Condition* do when they (quite reasonably) interpret this text as an Arendtian critique of late-modern, postwar, technological consumer society, and (variously) approach Arendt's concept of action as an attempt in the face of this nullity to revitalize a deliberative or democratic or agonistic or destabilizing politics.[17]

Yet I think that if we stop here we will miss the monumental theme that Arendt is holding at bay, but conspicuously so, in *The Human Condition*, and perhaps overlook the palpable significance of Arendt's concrete discussion of action as well. For the two forms of extremity that she warned of—labor as routinized deathlessness and work as the objectified violation of life—have hitherto coupled in human experience, although only once and with terrible and traumatic consequences that defy comprehension. This coupling occurred in the "hellish experiment" of the SS extermination camps where, existentially speaking, the obliteration of human life was effected before it was actually ended. "Extermination," Arendt wrote ([1950a] 1994, 236), "happens to human beings who for all practical purposes are already 'dead.'" The "skillfully manufactured unreality" of the human beings sealed off inside these camps was, at once, an existential condition of being dead and yet not annihilated, alive and yet not living (1968, 445). Death-yet-not-death, life-yet-not-life.

The already-deadness/still-aliveness of the inmates had to do with another existential feature of the extermination camps—an extreme isolation that was carried to perfection hitherto unknown in human experience. In their complete dehumanizing isolation, Arendt ([1950a] 1994, 239) observed, "the camps were separated from the surrounding world as if they and their inmates were no longer part of the world of the living." It was as if the human beings there had dropped off the face of the earth, into a life "removed from earthly purposes," for their departure from the world was not announced; nor were they even pronounced dead. The status of the inmates to those in the world of the living was such that it was "as though they had never been born" (1968, 444 f.). Arendt thought that the horror of life in the concentration camps could "never be fully embraced by the imagination for the very reason that [this horror stood] outside of life and death."

This existential condition of extermination was furthered by the development of certain new technological processes under which mass murder was mechanized, the death rate of inmates was regulated, and torture was "strictly organized" and efficiently calculated in a way that perpetuated dying without inducing death—that is, until "depopulation" was ordered so as to make room for "new supplies" (Arendt [1950a] 1994, 238). "The concentration-camp inmate has no price," Arendt noted (1968, 444), "because he can always be replaced; nobody knows to whom he belongs, because he is never seen. From the point of view of normal society he is absolutely superfluous." There was, then, a paradoxical nonutilitarian utility to these camps. On the one hand, they were utterly useless to the Nazi regime either for the purpose of winning the total war or for the exploitation of labor; on the other, the undefined fear that the camps inspired was more essential to the preservation of the regime's power "than any other of its institutions" (1968, 456; [1950a] 1994, 236). It is in this nonutilitarian utility that we find the obscene coupling of labor and work *in extremis* where the routinized fabrication of corpses commingled with the instrumental cyclicality of extermination, human beings came face to face not with life on earth but with living death on some other planet. Thus Arendt observes in *The Human Condition* (1958, 229): "We are perhaps the first generation which has become fully aware of the murderous consequences inherent in a line of thought that forces one to admit that all means, provided they are efficient, are permissible and justified to pursue something defined as an end."

In an even more mundane and terrible sense, labor and work were also operative in the extermination camps. The "work camp" was the identity that served to mask the real function of the death camps. *Arbeit Macht Frei* was the brightly illuminated sign over the large gate to Auschwitz. Nevertheless, as Arendt (1968, 444) writes, "The concentration camp as an institution was not established for the sake of any possible labor yield; the only permanent economic function of the camps has been the financing of their own supervisory apparatus. . . . Any work that has been performed could have been done much better and more cheaply under different conditions." (Notice Arendt's own commingling of the terms "labor" and "work" in these sentences.) Pierre Vidal-Naquet ([1985] 1992, 109) contributes importantly to this subject when he notes that "Concentration camp labor *also* served the ends of exhaustion and control . . . [and] also had the characteristic of being indefinitely replenishable." Although some camps (Chelmno, Sobibor, Belzec, Treblinka) were directed solely toward extermination, Vidal-Naquet observes that "Maidanek and (above all) Auschwitz . . . were living proof that extermination could go on side by side with exploitation of forced labor . . . between exploitation and extermination there was a tension, never a break." In *The Origins of Totalitarianism,* Arendt elaborates the effects of this extreme situation exacted upon the human person. The disintegration of human personality was accomplished in three moves in the extermination camps: first, the "juridical person" was destroyed at the moment of arbitrary arrest (447); second, the "moral personality" was destroyed and "human solidarity" utterly corrupted through the techniques of enforced isolation and living "in absolute solitude" (451); and finally, the destruction of "the differentiation of the individual, his unique identity " (453), beginning with "the monstrous conditions in the transports to the camps" and ending with the permanence and institutionalization of torture and the relentless processes of extermination.

As Primo Levi writes (1961, 49) of Auschwitz: "we have learnt that our personality is fragile, that it is much more in danger than our life; and the old wise ones, instead of warning us 'remember that you must die' would have done much better to remind us of this greater danger that threatens us." These are "the evil tidings," Levi remarks, "of what man's presumption made of man in Auschwitz."

When in *The Human Condition* Arendt affirmed the existential superiority of action over labor and work, I do not think that she was extolling the posturing hero (much less vanity and vainglory) in some sort of existential confrontation with mortality and death. Indeed, Arendt remarks upon the peculiar modern inability to appreciate the earnest aspiration to an "earthly immortality" as anything more than vanity. She also attributes the tendency to "look down upon all striving for immortality as (nothing more than) vanity and vainglory" to the "shock" of the philosophers' discovery of the eternal (1958, 56, 21). Her concept of action and her invocation of glory are decidedly more human and far more courageous than that. What action and glory attempt to counter is not death as such; what Arendt (1958, 97) called "the two supreme events of appearance and disappearance" (birth and death) merely delimit (although supremely) the time interval within which the other events of nonbiological life—this mortal, human life of action and speech—take place. To the contrary, it seems that what Arendt is attempting to confront and counter by asserting and, yes, inventing the "space of appearance" was the existential unreality of "death-yet-not-death, life-yet-not-life": the living death and deathly life that was the horrific specter of the Holocaust.

"Wherever People Gather Together": Reinhabiting the Empty Space

"If art is to survive the Holocaust—to survive death as a master," Shoshana Felman writes (1995, 39), "it will have to break, in art, this mastery, which insidiously pervades the whole of culture and the whole of the esthetic project." We might say the same here not only of political theory but of all works of "outstanding permanence" that, in Arendt's words (1958, 168), release "the world-open and communicative" human capacity for thought. I now want to turn to Arendt's concept of politics and the imagistic symbol of the space of appearance, in order to consider how they create both a healing illusion and a disruptive countermemory, attempting thereby to reach over the abyss created by Auschwitz and break the mastery of the Holocaust.

Arendt's concept of action (politics) carries within it a multitude of dimensions and meanings. Yet unlike her concepts of labor and work, "action" does not threaten to destroy itself or point toward the precariousness of extremity. In the voluminous secondary literature that has developed around Arendt's political theory, the concept of action is usually affiliated with the notion of a public space of freedom and equality that comes into being when citizens speak together and act in concert; hence many of Arendt's commentators take their purchase on Arendtian politics from a perspective that casts it as the active engagement of citizens in the public realm.[18] But if we look closely, we can see that the concept of action is also the sum of the following multifarious elements:

> the web of human relationships, the realm of human affairs, the space of appearance, being together in the presence of others, being seen and heard by others, the sharing of words and deeds, the spontaneous beginnings of something new, the active revelation of unique personal identity, the distinction of each human person, courage, boldness, esteem, dignity, endurance, the shining brightness once called glory, boundlessness, inherent unpredictability, the human capacity for *power* generated by action in concert, the human capacity for *freedom* born of acting, the distinctly human condition of *living on earth and inhabiting the world.*

The tendency of Arendt's contemporary commentators to construe her concept of action primarily in terms of participatory citizen politics (whether in the form of agonal contestation or deliberative communication, classical republicanism or radical democracy) tends to occlude two elements that are profoundly important to reading *The Human Condition* in the context of dark times. The first element involves the phenomenal nature of the space of appearance itself. "Wherever people gather together," Arendt (1958, 199) writes, "[the space of appearance] is potentially there, but only potentially, not necessarily and not forever." The "peculiarity" of the space of appearance hinges upon action and speech; wherever humans are together in the "manner of speech and action," there the space of appearance might emerge, in all of its evanescence and reality. But unlike the spaces that are the work of our hands, Arendt (199) notes, the space of appearance does not survive "the actuality of the movement which brought it into being." This space is fragile (yet also resilient) and prone to disappearing, not only with "the dispersal of men—as in

the case of great catastrophes when the body politic of a people is destroyed"—
but also with the "arrest of the activities themselves" (199 f.). So when Arendt
identifies the "empty space" that is the aftermath of Auschwitz, she is tracking
both the dispersion of human beings initiated by a great catastrophe, and the disappearance of the very activities that allow the space of appearance (potentially)
to manifest itself in the world: action and speech.

The second element that is often overlooked in Arendt's concept of action
is the phenomenon of self-revelation, or what she (1958, 182) also calls "the
disclosure of the acting and speaking agent" in the space of appearance. We
might say that self-revelation is precisely what crystallizes in the space where
human beings gather and that spontaneous acting and speaking are the capacities through which the unique human person discloses his or her individuality, as sui generis. In a particularly telling passage in *The Human Condition*
(1958, 179–180) Arendt underscores the significance of action as the revelation of the unique and distinct identity of the agent:

> In acting and speaking, men show who they are, reveal actively
> their unique personal identities and thus make their appearance in
> the human world. . . . This disclosure of "who" in contradistinc-
> tion to "what" somebody is—his qualities, gifts, talents, and short-
> comings, which he may display or hide—is implicit in everything
> somebody says and does. . . . Without the disclosure of the agent
> in the act, action loses its specific character and becomes one form
> of achievement among others.

It is the "who-ness" of acting, the "agent-revealing capacity" of action and
speech, that Arendt repeatedly invokes in her concrete discussion of politics in
The Human Condition.[19] The space of appearance is the realm within which "I
appear to others as others appear to me," through the disclosure and the exposure of myself—my uniquely individual, irreducible, and distinctively human
self—through word and deed (1958, 198). Arendt finds in the willingness to
act and speak at all, to "[leave] one's private hiding place and [show] who one
is," a kind of "courage and even boldness" that are usually assigned to the hero
(186). The existential significance that she grants to the space of appearance is
such that, "[t]o be deprived of it means to be deprived of reality; which,
humanly and politically speaking, is the same as appearance" (199).

From one perspective, it is difficult to appreciate Arendt's image of
self-revelation in the space of appearance as adequate to the task of capturing
what politics requires or entails. As Arendt herself admitted about the Greek
concept of action,[20] so I am tempted to say of Arendt's action concept of politics (as I elaborated in chapter 8): it is overly attuned to subjective individuality, and stresses the urge toward collective self-disclosure at the expense of
many other factors in political action, including the dimension of strategic or
instrumental purposefulness that Arendt so resolutely opposed as an aspect of

the political. From a different perspective, however, I believe that there is a better way to make sense of the unique and sui generis conception of self-revelation in the space of appearance that Arendt creates in *The Human Condition*. This has little to do with the expectations that one might wish to impose upon a concept of politics or a political theory generally, but rather with a healing illusion that is inseparable from the historical reality of the Holocaust, even as it cannot and does not in any way "redeem" that event with meaning or succumb to the human desire for redemptory "closure."[21]

We can appreciate the power and luminescence of Arendt's concept of the space of appearance, with its reclamation of self-disclosure, only if we draw it into the gap between past and future, and recognize what it invites us, in collectivity with others, to overcome. The luminosity of this space, where the reality of the living being is fulfilled in the ordinary glory of speaking and doing in concert with others, is the absolute counter to the disintegration of personality (the juridical, the moral, the identity of each unique individual) that was the insidious achievement of the extermination camps, where the end result was "the reduction of human beings to the lowest possible denominator of 'identical reactions'" (1968, 447). In Arendt's imagistic symbol of the space of appearance, with its great glorification of "the paradoxical plurality of unique beings" there is illuminated a way over the abyss (1958, 176). For in this powerful image Arendt does nothing less than bestow upon us the world picture, and the promise, of human persons rising resplendent in word and deed, within a space where we gather together and rescue ourselves from our dispersion. It is a space that strives to subvert, counter, and overcome a factual territory as assiduously invented and dark as its obverse is suffused with light. With this concept of the space of appearance we might say that Arendt ([1946b] 1994, 186) returns us to the modern will to create a human world that, to borrow her own language, "can be a home within a world which is no longer a home." Or, to put this differently (but still in Arendt's words), in the midst of the "fluid contour" of Being, the concept of the space of appearance traces an island "on which man, no longer threatened by the dark inexplicable aura . . . finally can have free rein" ([1946b] 1994, 186).

Perhaps it is not too much to say (although it may indeed be saying too much) that the grand, optimistic illusion of the space of appearance offers a new beginning to the sufferers and survivors of a trauma that is still very much with us, and has left so many stranded still in the factual territory of complicity and hatred. "Our yearning anticipates landfall," writes Augustine, "throws hope as an anchor toward that shore" (in Wills 1999a, xiii). Can the idea of the space of appearance, the image of a phenomenal space of participating persons, offer a way to think anew what we are doing? Might we contemporary Athenians, aided by the gift of a great thinker, step into this space in our own imaginings, relating ourselves to people, things, and relationships so that the evil day, with its old meaning and its legacy of grievances and guilt, can be surmounted? Can we participate in this optimistic illusion so that the "empty space of individuals" is once more infused with plurality and life? I have no answers to these questions, but one thing does seem clear. Through the human "movement of transcendence in thought," that is *The Human Condition*, Hannah Arendt ([1946b] 1994, 187) subverted evil in a manner that was utterly devoid of both gratuitous moralizing and self-righteous condemnation. This is itself a kind of miracle. But this miracle was fully in keeping with the one that she thought saves the world: the human capacity to bestow upon human affairs the two essential characteristics of human existence: faith and hope.

Notes

INTRODUCTION

1. The quotes within the quote are references to Sidney Hook.

2. Arendt's determination to turn to politics, action, and human affairs is underscored in an interview that she gave to the journalist Gunter Gaus for the publication *Zur Person* in Munich, 1965. Arendt remarks, "The expression 'political philosophy,' which I avoid, is extremely burdened by tradition. When I talk about these things, academically or nonacademically, I always mention that there is a vital tension between philosophy and politics. That is, between man as a thinking being and man as an acting being. . . . There is a kind of enmity against all politics in most philosophers, with very few exceptions. Kant *is* an exception. This enmity is extremely important for the whole problem, because it is not a personal question. It lies in the nature of the subject itself . . . 'I want no part of this enmity' . . . I want to look at politics, so to speak, with eyes unclouded by philosophy" (Arendt 1994, 2). (The quote within the quote is Gaus's.) As a matter of categorization, Arendt did not locate Thucydides, Augustine, Machiavelli, or Tocqueville, among others, within the tradition of Western "philosophy."

3. Foucault, the theorist perhaps most associated with the problem of "the subject," introduces the "crisis of subjectivation" (or "a difficulty in the man-

ner in which the individual could form himself as an ethical subject") in a chapter titled "The Political Game" (Foucault 1986, 81–95). Whatever responsibility Foucault might bear for the proliferation of academic inquiries into "the subject," his own theorization of what he calls "subjectivation" is decisively situated within a historical political context that poses problems to politics. Unfortunately, Foucault's historical-political orientation has not carried through in many of the contemporary efforts to thematize "the subject" in political theory.

4. Although the sources for Arendt's use of "turning" are not entirely clear, it seems likely that they are somewhat indebted to Heidegger's analysis of the historicity of Being in the tradition of Western thought, and also to his later writings and lectures. One of these lectures, titled "The Turning," was given in December 1949 in Bremen, and was repeated without alteration in 1950 in Buhlerhohe. Arendt does not wholly appropriate a Heideggerian vocabulary, nor does she adopt without alteration a conceptual structure that privileges *poiēsis* over *praxis*. However, in *The Human Condition* (1958) Arendt does exhibit a Heideggerian sensibility toward disclosing a certain "coming-to-pass" that makes use of the notions of reversal, inversion, return—in short, of turning operations. For an elaboration of these matters, see Villa (1996).

5. Quite clearly, however, Aristotle (1962, 99) writing in the face of the imperial expansion of Macedonia and Persia, is troubled by the problem of at what point, exactly, a polis as a political community loses its identity, since the form of association as "an association of citizens" is not infinitely elastic; nor is it ultimately unrelated to the physical identity and the population of the city or place. Thus he raises the important issue of "how large a *polis* can be and yet remain a single *polis*" but leaves this problem unresolved. As Barker remarks, however, "[Aristotle] seems to incline to the view that a very large *polis* cannot possess a real identity" (in Aristotle 1962, 99 n. 1).

6. Consider, for example, Mueller's (2000, 223) observation that "Arendt has been the subject of a remarkable renaissance in Germany. . . . There is now a growing literature and recognition of her possible importance for the Berlin Republic." Mueller goes on to argue that Arendt's political theory is important for two reasons in particular: first, "1989 is interpreted through Arendt's theories, both as an historical moment in which nonviolent revolutionaries spontaneously brought about something entirely new. . . . The GDR revolutionaries experienced the power they could constitute by acting together . . . and they realized what it meant to constitute a public space and to move in this public space." The second reason for Arendt's importance involves mobilizing Arendt's categories against "the familiar categories and strategies of nationalism and geopolitics on the right, and antifascism on the left" (224).

CHAPTER 1

This chapter is a revised and considerably expanded version of an earlier article (see Dietz 1987).

1. For some idea of the wide-ranging nature of feminist critiques of liberalism, see Eisenstein (1981); Elshtain (1981); Jaggar (1983); Nicholson (1986); and Okin (1979). On social contract theory, see Pateman (1980, 1988); Brennan and Pateman (1979); and Shanley (1979). On liberal "rational man," see Hartsock (1983), Lloyd (1984); and Young (1989). On Hobbes, see Di Stefano (1983). On Locke, see Butler (1978); Clark (1979); and Pateman (1975). On Mill, see Annas (1977); Krouse (1982); and Ring (1985). On liberal moral theory, see Blum (1982); Benhabib (1992b); Young (1986a,1990); and Tronto (1993). On the public:private dichotomy, see Pateman (1983); Okin (1979, 1990a); Boling (1996); and Phillips (1991).

2. As Macpherson (1977, 2) rightly points out, one of the prevailing difficulties of liberalism is that it has tried to combine the idea of individual freedom as "self-development" with the entrepreneurial notion of liberalism as the "right of the stronger to do down the weaker by following market rules." Despite attempts by contemporary libertarian liberals including Nozick, Riker, Buchanan and Tullock, and others to reconcile market freedom with self-development freedom, a successful resolution has not yet been achieved. For his part, Macpherson argues that the two freedoms are profoundly inconsistent, but he also asserts that the liberal position "need not be taken to depend forever on an acceptance of capitalist assumptions, although historically it has been so taken." The context of liberalism in the United States has surely been defined by capitalism and its complementary ethic. However, as Macpherson continues, liberalism is not necessarily bound (theoretically or politically) to what he calls the "capitalist market envelope."

3. In identifying "camps" I want to avoid the standard ideological and textbook classifications of feminist theories (for example, "liberal," "conservative," "socialist," or "radical") and focus instead upon specific feminist thinkers and theorists who have articulated theoretical (if not highly systematic) action alternatives to liberal notions of politics and citizenship, thereby explicitly thematizing the political in ways that might combine liberal, socialist, conservative, or radical elements without being reducible to any or all of them. Radical feminism is difficult to discuss in this context because it has not developed a coherent or consistent political position on the issues that are of concern to me here. For a helpful critique of some of radical feminism's political theoretical failings, see Jaggar (1983, 286–290) and Cocks (1984).

4. Now some fifteen years since this essay first appeared, I think it is fair to say that Marxist feminist theories have diminished considerably in academic feminism, although Marxian approaches remain of significant importance in many feminist theoretic projects geared toward genealogy, postcolonialism,

post-Marxism, subaltern studies, and critiques of technology. For earlier incarnations and debates, see Dalla Costa and James (1972); Eisenstein (1979a); MacKinnon (1981); Rowbotham (1972); Hartmann (1981); Sargent (1981); and Hartsock (1983). More recently, see Weeks (1998).

5. See, for example, Elshtain (1982a, 1982b, 1982c); Ruddick (1980, 1983b); and Hartsock (1983). The latter incorporates both Marxist and maternalist elements in her feminist standpoint theory.

6. These matters have been instructively addressed and assessed by Tronto (1987).

7. The alternative conception introduced here—of politics as participatory and citizenship as the active engagement of peers in the public realm—has been of considerable interest to political theorists and historians over the past twenty years and has developed in detail as an alternative to the liberal "negative liberty" view. Perhaps the leading contemporary exponent of politics as popular action in plurality is Arendt (1958, 1965). Also see Barber (1984); Cohen and Rogers (1983); Hanson (1985); Goodwyn (1976); Pateman (1970); Walzer (1980); Mansbridge (1980); and Wolin (1960). The short-lived journal *Democracy* (1981–1983) remains an important source for thinking about democratic politics of the kind I support here.

8. I am concerned to clarify these appeals to citizen and citizenship in response to some objections that appeared after the first version of this essay was published in 1987. Narayan (1997) and Young (1989), for example, take issue with the idea of citizenship as an ideal, and with my (alleged) "insistence that citizens should leave behind particular affiliations and experiences," an argument that, they argue, tends to reinforce privilege (Narayan 1997, 56). Although Phillips (1993, 82) is not unsympathetic, she too suggests that I share "the implicit ideal of citizenship as transcending localized and interest-driven claims." Narayan also objects to my tendency to restrict political activity to "a dialogue among members 'of a shared community'" since this "has the unsettling effect" of excluding from the political domain a "huge array of modern political struggles." To the first charge I plead not guilty, since the purpose of my appeal to citizenship was an effort to move this concept out of the domain of an abstracted ideal and situate it instead in the realm of concrete, phenomenal, and contextualized political action where the citizen is thematized as an expressly individuated, unique, and distinctive acting being (following Arendt 1958). Indeed, I am trying to move away from universalizing abstractions ("liberal individual," "mother") that beckon toward the "transcendence" of locales, interests, and the like, not reconstitute them. On the matter of political activity as a dialogue among members of a shared community, I am more vulnerable. Thinking back over this locution, I concluded that the appeal to "shared community" moved my argument for politics in an overly communitarian, or perhaps republican, direction as Phillips (1993, 83) interprets it. I have tried to correct this misunderstanding in this revision, by attempting to distinguish

more clearly my democratic conception of citizenship from either a communitarian or a republican one. In chapter 7, I will also indicate the drawbacks of formulating politics primarily in terms of discourse ethics and the "dialogue" of free and equal beings.

9. The difficulties here may also involve certain problematic developments in the discourse of democratic theory; for example, the shift of focus from participatory democracy to matters of deliberative democracy and discourse ethics, and various efforts at the conceptual level to reduce democratic politics to the effective synthesis of liberalism and communitarianism. See chapter 3 for an extended discussion of these matters.

10. See Katzenstein (1998) for an excellent study of contemporary feminist activism, organization, and protest that situates and explores the politics of power within the institutions of the American military and the American Catholic Church. Although Katzenstein is concerned with the problem of equal access and opportunity, her research is primarily geared toward understanding what we might call the action dimension of, in her words, "unobtrusive mobilization" and civic associationalism among women (acting as citizens) inside these institutions. We (that is, North American academic feminist political theorists) must also remember, in looking for instructive examples of feminist political action, that feminism is a global movement and includes, in Pollitt's words (2001a, xxiii) "indigenous women's movements [that] flourish around the globe." She goes on to observe: "It is African women who are organizing against clitoridectomy, Iranian women who are fighting unfair divorce laws and subverting Islamic dress codes, Jordanian and Pakistani women who are protesting 'honor killings' and the tacit permission given to these crimes by the legal system." We might now add to this list women in Afghanistan who for many years covertly and bravely resisted the oppression of the Taliban regime and are now on the streets, demanding democracy and calling for the recovery of human rights.

CHAPTER 2

This chapter is a revised and expanded version of a previous essay (see Dietz 1985).

1. See among others, Rowbotham (1972); Eisenstein (1979a); Dalla Costa and James (1972); Edmond and Fleming (1975).

2. According to Ann Crittenden (2001), motherhood is the single biggest cause of poverty for women.

3. For a compelling but nonetheless problematic attempt to make a case for extending family values and relations of "caring and sharing" into the economic sphere, see Folbre (2001).

4. In an important book, Joan Tronto (1993, 118–119) calls attention to the difference between conceptualizing care as a "disposition" and care "as a

practice." To think of care as a disposition or an emotion, she argues, makes it easy to sentimentalize it, to privatize it, and to gender it in conventional ways that assume that women are more emotional than men, therefore more caring. Thus "unless we understand care in its richer sense of a practice," Tronto rightly contends, "we run the risk of sentimentalizing and in other ways containing the scope of care in our thinking." Elshtain's social feminism is somewhat ambiguous on this matter. On the one hand it offers a description of caring (and maternal thinking) as a practice (Elshtain 1989, 225), while on the other hand it refers to women in the private realm in terms of "anticipative and reverential attitudes," calling up the emotional and dispositional "other" to the arrogant, rational male public. It is the latter move that lends to Elshtain's social feminism its sentimentalizing (and sometimes condescending) tone, reinforcing what Tronto (119) calls a "traditional ideology" and "traditional gender roles and the association of women and caring."

5. As the current so-called Mommy Wars reveal, mothers themselves have difficulty agreeing upon what constitutes appropriate maternal thinking and maternal practice. The conflict appears to center upon the question of whether "employed" or "stay-at-home" mothers are more likely to raise better, more perfect children. This issue is the source of some increasingly deep-seated resentments (not to mention guilt, anger, bad conscience, and embarrassment) especially among middle-class, white suburban "Moms." Whatever the reciprocity and mutual sense of obligation that may arise from caring for children, maternalism does not seem to generate these same virtues among mothers in relation to each other as adults. Meanwhile, as the distraction of the Mommy Wars rages on—"(You let your child have milk from the store? *My* child drinks nothing but organic goat milk from flocks tended by Apollo himself!)" (Pollitt 2001b, 10)—real efforts to transform the status of the economy of child care and day care systems in this country remain a low priority of government.

6. Actually, Elshtain's social feminism bears a more complex and sympathetic relation to Aristotle, or at least to Aristotelianism as a political ethics, than her criticism of Aristotle as a kind of sexist progenitor of Western political thought may suggest. Behind Elshtain's social theory lies a commitment to communally accepted basic norms and civic virtues that aligns it with the communitarianism of many contemporary neo-Aristotelians. Thus Elshtain is no less interested in thematizing an ethical culture than was Aristotle; indeed she seems to embrace a "communitarian" perspective that owes much to his mode of political philosophizing or at least to his emphasis on the primacy of ethos, character, and habituation in human life.

7. This is important because Elshtain (1989, 226) regularly insists that at the level of theory, social feminism seeks to "break out" of "a rigid public and private dichotomy, even as one recognizes and seeks to preserve some version of a public-private distinction." I am not sure exactly what this means, but the statement reveals the conceptual ambiguities in Elshtain's thinking about the

efficacy of a public-private framework, which sometimes she wants to reject and other times wishes to mobilize as part of a positive project for social feminism's effort to restore ethos to the *polis*.

8. Although I cannot develop this argument here, it is worth considering whether, contrary to much existing scholarship, Aristotle is best interpreted as deploying a dichotomy of public:private in his political thought. In Book I of the *Politics*, for example, the "associations" that Aristotle (1962, 4) delineates are the family, the village and "the final and perfect association," the *polis*. He proceeds to discuss the separate "arts" of "household management" (18) and "acquisition of property" (19), both of which are contrasted to the activity of citizenship or "the right of sharing in judicial or deliberative office" (96). These categories roughly track the spheres of the household, the economy, and the *polis* (or political association). What is not evident in Aristotle's analysis (or in Barker's translation) is any explicit reference to the categories of "public" and "private," although we know that the Greeks used the term *idion*—from which our word "idiot" is derived—to distinguish "one's own," outside the world of the common, and the term *koinon* for what is communal. But it is not clear to me that these terms exactly track the modern dichotomy between "private" and "public." In any case, how Aristotle's theory (and much of subsequent Western political thought) came to be identified in feminist theory with the dichotomy of public:private is not entirely clear. Arendt (1958) surely contributed importantly to this conceptual strategy, however.

9. Elshtain is not the first theorist to notice and appropriate the figure of Antigone for political or social theoretic interpretive purposes. Most famously, see Hegel (1967). More recently, see Steiner (1982); Nussbaum (1986); Benhabib (1992a); Hartouni (1986); Euben (1997); and Butler (2000, 88), who notes her disagreement with Elshtain's interpretation insofar as in her view "there is no uncontaminated voice with which Antigone speaks. This means she can neither represent the feminine over and against the state nor can she represent a version of kinship in its distinction from state power."

10. Some of the more insightful critiques of Aristotle on the matter of inclusion/exclusion include Bickford (1996); Okin (1979); Williams (1993); and Yack (1993). For the "elitist or egalitarian" approach to understanding Aristotle's politics I am indebted to Hanna Pitkin's lectures in political theory at the University of California at Berkeley in the 1970s.

11. On this matter I differ from Butler (2000, 82) who identifies "kinship" as the "mediating link" between the public and private spheres. What I wish to argue (following Aristotle's concept) is that "politics," not kinship, is this "in between" public and private. Thus Antigone, by speaking and acting in defiance of Creon (as well as the Theban norms of citizenship), enters into a space that decisively disrupts the relation of "ruler over ruled." In the name of particular cultural norms (the ritual burial of the dead, the honor accorded to fallen warriors, family honor, and so on) Antigone upsets not just "the vocab-

ulary of kinship," as Butler contends, but also the vocabulary of *kingship* that relies for its legitimacy on the structure of ruler over ruled.

12. In a more recent essay Elshtain (1989) modifies parts of "Antigone's Daughters," especially by way of emphasizing that Antigone's "transgressive" actions throw her into the flux between private and public. This allows Elshtain to escape the spatially bounded formalisms of her earlier essay (that is, the persistent references to male public and female private) in favor of a more dynamic reading of Antigone's persona and performance that does not simply take them to be reflections of "familial and social imperatives and duties" (230). The latter theme by no means disappears, however.

13. For a more detailed sociological analysis of the mother-child relationship that is informed by object-relations theory, see Chodorow (1978). Dinnerstein (1977) offers a provocative and original approach by exploring the negative psychodynamics of mothering and recommends democratizing the family, not "familizing" the polity.

14. These general descriptions of the mother-child relation are, of course, mediated by history, culture, context, and time and cannot be applied universally or transhistorically to all societies past and present. See, for example, Aries's (1962) still important (but increasingly disputed) study of childhood as a historically changing phenomenon in the West.

15. For other arguments against the use of family as a metaphor or model for political arrangements, also see Locke's *First Treatise of Government* (1690). For a contemporary view, see Acklesberg (1983).

16. As Butler (2000, 81 f.) points out, Arendt casts the private sphere as both protective (for those who were a part of the public sphere) and despotic (for those trapped inside the private), although Arendt expends little theoretical energy assessing the implications of such a situation for women, children, and slaves. Arendt did not explain, Butler observes, "how there might be a pre-political despotism, or how the "political" must be expanded to describe the status of a population of the less than human, those who were not permitted into the interlocutory scene of the public sphere" (81). For further discussion of this matter in Arendt, see chapter 5.

17. For a discussion of why love, goodness, and the Christian virtues in general are "anti-political," see Arendt (1958).

18. In aiming this critique at the theoretical level of social feminism's intentions I do not mean to imply that at the practical level mothering is utterly devoid of developed orientations that might usefully be called upon when particular, individual mothers enter the domain of politics. What I have in mind is not love or intimacy but rather things like the cognitive capacity to juggle a number of different demands simultaneously; the practical capacity to exhibit patience and understanding in moments of chaos that do not respond to control; and the willingness to undertake drudge work for no immediately evident gain. To the extent to which these capacities can be said to develop

out of mothering, mothering develops orientations that are useful in the practice of citizenship. But the argument remains tricky, not only because not all mothers can or do acquire these capacities in real life (thus there is a gap between the normative ideal and the actual activity that involves real mothers) but also because these capacities may develop in other professions as well: elementary school teachers, brain surgeons, intensive care nurses, air traffic controllers, and private detectives might also generate this mix of capacities without being mothers. Thus mothering may or may not be "the most important job in the world" (Crittenden 2001), but there is no reason to think that it is a special province for the development of potentially political traits.

19. Although I am not convinced by Boling's (1996, 119) efforts to defend "the values of the caring mother," as a basis for feminist democratic action, I am grateful to her for forcing me to clarify my views of the relation among mothering, democratic citizenship, and feminism. In looking over my earlier argument, I think that I leaned too readily in the direction of dictating the terms of a feminist political consciousness and its attendant political vocabulary while at the same time underplaying the significance of political actions undertaken by female citizens self-identified as mothers. This gave my recommendations the air of "theorizing by fiat" and led me to indulge in the same tendency to impose unilaterally terms of female political identity that I criticize in Elshtain's social feminism. I have tried to correct that problem in this version, without changing my basic views.

20. Feminist historians have, for some time, been concerned to recover and assess examples of women's collective political action and political identity within existing democratic contexts. See, for example, Evans and Boyte (1982) and Evans (1980) for analyses of women's political action that is not causally invested in "family first" explanations or maternal proclivities. Also see Tilly (1981) for a study of women's collective action outside formalized political structures and Katzenstein (1998) for a study of women's collective action inside formalized institutions (in the U.S. military and the American Catholic Church).

CHAPTER 3

1. The books under discussion are Beiner (1995); Bridges (1994); Botwinick (1993); Mouffe (1993); Phillips (1993); and Zolo (1992).

2. Tracing the recent conceptual history of the formulation "liberalism and communitarianism" is beyond the scope of this essay. The originary moment of the binary appears to be the late 1970s and early 1980s, when a number of distinguished North American theorists—including Alasdair MacIntyre, Carole Pateman, Michael Walzer, Charles Taylor, Amy Gutmann, and Richard Rorty—began to formulate responses to John Rawls's *A Theory of Justice* (1971). The debates that emerged posited the alternative concept of

"community" and the notion of a "habituated self" shaped by constitutive attachments against the deontological ethic of a liberal "unencumbered self," both of which Michael Sandel (1982) codified in the book that was the first, and probably should have been the last, promulgation of these two "alternatives." See Kautz (1995) for an example of how this binarism frames political theorizing, and Taylor (1989) for an insightful critique of its cross-purposes and (over)simplifications.

3. "Team L" and "Team C" are Taylor's (1989) felicitious characterizations.

4. Phillips (1993, 67), for example, remarks upon the dangers of moving between opposite sides of "a false divide" and producing "an over-simple dichotomy," but continues nonetheless to mobilize the dichotomy and call for a "middle way" across the divide. Beiner (1995, 12) worries about being "locked into a choice between two mutually exclusive alternatives," neither of which he finds satisfactory; nevertheless he accepts the alternatives as given. Carens (in Beiner 1995, 243–245) confesses, "Some may feel that I have wrenched [Nozick, Rawls, and utilitarianism] out of context," but he proceeds to counter "liberal theory" with a stated preference for Walzer's "communitarian critique."

5. These phrases proliferate in all of the works under discussion, but the following one from Phillips (which appears under the subtitle "Can We Manage without Abstraction?") is typical of the vagueness that attends so much theorizing by phraseology: "The liberal distinction between an essential 'man' and contingent person has served us reasonably well, for, while it buried class and sexual difference as irrelevant and boring, it nonetheless gave us standards of impartiality without which equality is hard to conceive" (1993, 49). The polemical "us and them" tone has the effect of muting more pertinent and concrete theoretical issues, such as to what thinker, text, or theory does the phrase "liberal distinction between essential man and contingent person" actually refer? Why is this distinction liberal? What "liberal" text or thinker dismisses "class" and "sexual difference" as "irrelevant and boring"? What "standards of impartiality" issue from the idea of an "essential man" in any case?

6. In her succinct overview of generational transformations in political science, Kirstie McClure (1992, 115, 121) identifies this development as "third-generation," "postmodern," and "post-Marxist" pluralism. I am referring to much the same phenomenon but situating it instead within the context of the binary *liberalism:communitarianism* that McClure does not consider. My implicit contention is that once the new pluralism is understood in the latter context, and as part of a "combinative" strategy that seeks to reconcile or synthesize liberalism and communitarianism, it appears less radical and more retrograde than may initially be the case.

7. One does not have to be an exceptionally historical or political thinker to recognize the mistakenness of the claim that liberalism (and liberal political theorists) has been oblivious to the human phenomena of social heterogeneity, diverse particulars, and individual difference. (See, for example, Mill

[1854]). But perhaps a political and historical sensibility helps insofar as it can mitigate the reductionism that comes from assigning precedence to (quasi) philosophical and metaphysical terms like "universalism" or "particularism." Rawls (1985) himself may have assisted in the resurrection of political and historical sensibilities by way of his reassessment of justice as fairness as "political not metaphysical," thereby redirecting theoretical attention away from philosophical categories and toward the cultural and historical context of liberalism, if only analytically. This is a move that Mouffe and Bridges appreciate and attempt to build upon: Mouffe (1993, 123) emphasizes "the whole range of institutions characteristic of political liberalism" and Bridges (1994, 112 f.) calls for a "rhetorical turn" that situates liberalism within the context of a "civic culture." Yet even with such clarifications, the discussion of liberalism and liberal political thought remains curiously ahistorical and decontextualized in this literature, and seemingly unable to escape the grip of the "metaphysical" vocabulary of universal and particular.

8. By way of introduction to his book, Beiner (1995, 15, 18, 19) also (briefly) asserts the salutary alternative of a "civic" republican perspective on citizenship that is not reducible to either "the purposes of individuals" or "the goals of subcommunities" but rather transcends the "two opposing extremes" between "the individual and group identity" in the name of a "robust civic involvement." But Beiner's call to "republicanism" and civic identity remains here at the level of a stated rather than a developed alternative to what he calls the "universalizing and particularizing antipodes" of liberalism and nationalism (he rather curiously aligns the latter with communitarianism).

9. Most of Mouffe's arguments in these essays presume some familiarity with the theory of the subject as a decentered, detotalized agent constructed at the intersection of a multiplicity of subject positions that is developed at greater length in *Hegemony and Socialist Strategy: Towards a Radical Democratic Politics* (Laclau and Mouffe 1985). But the essays in Mouffe (1993) also mark an expansion of the previous work insofar as they seek to recover certain institutional and ethical principles of liberalism (that is, liberty and equality) for the purposes of theorizing democratic procedures and democratic politics.

10. Wolin (1996b, 23). Although it would be impertinent to align "the new pluralism" of democratic political theory with "the new progressivism" of the (previous) Clinton administration and the currently ineffectual Democratic Party, it seems important not to overlook the rhetoric of antiliberalism that these two movements with attenuated ties to the "center" share in common. When democratic theorists as well as Democratic politicians begin to sound like Irving Kristol (who has recently identified the "real cold war" as the war against the "rot and decadence of contemporary liberalism"), we may need to take stock of what is going on. Nor should democrats underestimate the ideological significance of the relation between attacks upon liberalism and "liberal doctrine" and the systematic dismantling of Medicare, Medicaid, welfare, affir-

mative action, birth control and abortion rights, environmental standards, public health, working families (and so on), a process now under the sway of a regime that promulgates and feeds off the empty and cold-hearted rhetoric of "compassionate conservatism."

11. Mouffe's (1993, 123) position on liberalism, although surely debatable, is fairly clear; she wants to defend "the whole range of institutions characteristic of political liberalism," as well as the principles of liberty and equality, but reject liberal individualism and "rational universal consensus." Her position on communitarianism is another matter; sometimes it seems compatible with the idea of a participatory civic republicanism (20, 28, 36, 57, 63) that she wishes to defend in the name of "radical and plural democracy" (8, 72, 82, 100, 105). At other times it appears to equate with "a substantive notion of the common good and shared moral values," which she decisively rejects (83).

12. Although I find the Machiavellian side of Mouffe's agonistic pluralism inventive and appealing, the Schmittian side is considerably less so, not in the least because its view of politics as an implacable "friend-enemy" polarity seems decidedly un-Machiavellian, if not ominously totalitarian. As Zolo (1992, 45) argues (in criticism of Schmitt), "politics in a modern sense only begins at the point at which . . . polarization is overcome . . . [it is] not a zero-sum game which expresses itself in a struggle without rules, having no possibility of mediation or of compromise, and affording no solution except in the total defeat, i.e. violent suppression, of the enemy."

13. Beiner, Botwinick, and Bridges all use the term "postmodern" in idiosyncratic ways that have little to do with the diverse twentieth-century thinkers (for example, Foucault, Derrida, Lacan, Lyotard, Kristeva, Irigaray, Rorty, and Butler) and theories that are usually associated with postmodernism. Their references to postmodernism in fact seem more aligned with "multiculturalism," a theoretical orientation that differs in many respects from postmodernism, whatever that term may mean in any general sense.

14. In fact, with the exception of a few footnotes to Rawls, Bridges hardly acknowledges any previous scholarship in this book and offers no list of references or bibliography. He thus appears to be wholly unindebted to the previous work in the field from which his argument could have benefited, and certainly unaware of the vast number of excavators that have already come and gone from the territories that he is mining to exhaustion.

15. Botwinick's (1994, 191–197) discussion of the future shape of society ultimately rests on a different set of "two contrasting ideal types of politics" than liberalism:communitarianism. The pairing he proposes is a Hobbesian "spatial" politics that privileges a "Priority of Political Obligation," on the one hand, and a Platonic "temporal" politics that privileges a (more relevant) "Priority of Justice," on the other. I will leave to those who are interested the task of assessing the significance of this dualism, and the theoretical persuasiveness of Botwinick's (1994, 170, 224) claim that both Plato and Hobbes are

"pathbreakers to postmodernist society" who "point toward participation as the appropriate supreme political value."

16. See Botwinick (1993, 231), for example, whose concluding chapter calls for "Conversation: The Ethics of Participation" and draws explicitly upon Oakeshott's metaphor as part of the "appropriate vocabulary for articulating our sense of being" in the postmodern age. The increasing attention that is being paid in democratic theory to "deliberative democracy," a theme that is rapidly replacing liberalism and communitarianism as the most repetitive in the literature, might itself be understood as an outgrowth of the liberalism:communitarianism picture and as part of what constitutes democracy theorized in "reconciliatory" terms. For a good example of the range of issues that attend the "deliberative democracy" debates, see Benhabib (1996a).

17. At the core of Zolo's realist approach is the idea that "the general function of a modern political system is that of reducing fear through a selective regulation of social risks and a competitive distribution of 'security values,'" and the premise that "the central categories of the political code are the inclusion/exclusion principle and the asymmetric power/subordination relation" (55). Zolo's "reflexive epistemology," like Botwinick's, argues for uncertainty and circularity and suggests that the "point of arrival in every cognitive process consists . . . in the propositions of linguistic communication" (9). Unlike Botwinick, however, Zolo (1992, 8) distances this epistemological position from postmodernism as well as from "internal realism" and "radical constructivism."

CHAPTER 4

1. The question of Beauvoir's intellectual impact upon the American feminist movement is complicated, of course, and requires far more in-depth study of the leaders and participants in the movement, as well as the role of academic feminists, than I can develop here. Still, it is instructive that at least two respected historians of American feminism (Evans 1980; Echols 1989) emphasize the significance of Friedan's work but make no substantive mention of Beauvoir.

2. In a recent essay, Simons (1998) takes exception to my observation that Beauvoir's influence upon the American feminist movement (especially in the texts of well-known feminist writers and theorists) appears to have been rather minimal. Simons infers (incorrectly) that "according to Dietz we should discount Beauvoir's influence because it was unacknowledged by Millett and unsurpassed by Firestone" (69). My point however was about the *extent* of Beauvoir's scholarly influence at the theoretical level of feminist writings, not that we should "discount" it. None of the interviews that Simons proceeds to quote undermine my basic claim: namely, that the influence of *The Second Sex* as a philosophical text in academic and theoretical feminism (as opposed, perhaps, to its popular impact on grassroots and consciousness-raising groups in

the United States) proceeded at a surface level, if at all. Beauvoir's regard for Firestone, which Simons reports, is not evidence of Firestone's attention to *The Second Sex* in *The Dialectic of Sex*. Simons cites a very revealing BBC interview that simply reinforces this, at least with regard to Millett, who allowed that she had probably "cribbed" Beauvoir in *Sexual Politics* and was "cheating all over the place" by not acknowledging Beauvoir's influence (69), something Beauvoir herself apparently thought. This confession simply substantiates my observation that Millett did indeed "leave Beauvoir virtually unmentioned" in her book, whatever else we might want to make of her later confessional about her personal indebtedness. My concern here, at any rate, is with the actual written texts of Daly, Millett, Firestone, and so on, not with anecdotes about the authors' verbal acts of homage, however ardent or sincere they might have been.

3. The new "feminisms" have in turn given rise to a series of influential essays that delineate and assess the diverse range of theoretical positions that now constitute "feminist theory." For example, see Scott (1986); Fraser (1989b); and Hawkesworth (1989).

4. There are some important exceptions to the "anti-Beauvoir" crusade in contemporary feminist theory. They include French theorists who emphasize the historical and social reality of women's experiences (Christine Delphy and Monique Plaza), the French neohumanist historian Elisabeth Badinter, and the French feminist philosopher Monique Wittig. For two especially interesting retrievals of Beauvoir by American feminist philosophers, see Butler (1987) on gender identity and Singer (1990) on Beauvoir's ethical discourse of freedom.

5. Kruks elaborates this argument and seeks a renewed appreciation of existentialism and phenomenology in her recent book, *Retrieving Experience: Subjectivity and Recognition in Feminist Politics* (2000).

6. Zerilli (1991) also deploys this strategy and elaborates upon the French feminist idea *parler femme* in her interesting response to Elshtain and me.

CHAPTER 5

This chapter is a revised and expanded version of a previous essay (see Dietz 1991).

1. See chapter 6, where I again take up these matters by way of a more detailed conceptual discussion that is informed by an assessment of the varied contemporary feminist receptions of Hannah Arendt. I am indebted to Bonnie Honig (1995, 3) for formulating the distinction between the "Woman Question in Arendt," and the "Arendt Question in Feminism" that became the titles for chapter 5 and chapter 6, respectively.

2. See Pitkin (1981) and (1998) for instructive clarifications of the relationship among labor, work, and action and their associated "mentalities."

3. See Bickford (1996) who illuminates the meaning of this passage with considerable sensitivity, and Disch (1994) who thematizes it in the suggestive terms of "situated impartiality."

4. Of course, here the reference to "men" (which is a standard locution for Arendt, as it is for most political thinkers before contemporary feminism interrogated this category) is particularly misleading, since Arendt wants to associate speech and action in the public realm with a *human* (and existential) capacity, not simply with men. Her use of "men" unfortunately obscures the more important insight: when the labor movement exerted itself as "the people"—as "the actual political body" (1958, 219)—it escaped the bonds of a singular social identity and achieved freedom (if only briefly). Arendt's conception of the labor movement covers not only (white, working-class) men but also all men and women, all of whom Arendt includes as "the people" and allows for as citizens in the public realm. Given Arendt's frequent tendency to represent citizens with the word "men," however, it is not surprising that she has been interpreted as recapitulating (and endorsing) a notion of the public realm that includes only men. And as I noted earlier, Arendt leaves unremarked examples of women's movements in the public realm; this does not help to alleviate the sense that she is limiting the idea of political action to men.

5. I cannot pursue Arendt's meaning of "the social" here, but see Pitkin (1998) for a magisterial and definitive analysis of how this concept plays out in Arendt's thought.

6. In a powerful (and rarely noted) passage concerning "wealth accumulation" in the modern age, Arendt (1958, 256–257) identifies three stages of alienation that reduced "the laboring poor" to the existential condition of *animal laborans* and accelerated the "eclipse of a common public world": the first stage is marked by "cruelty" and expropriation, which deprived the poor of "the twofold protection of the family and property"; the second substituted "class membership and national territory" for family and property; and the "last stage in this development" began the process of replacing "nationally bound societies," further advancing "the process of world alienation" started by "expropriation and characterized by an ever-increasing progress in wealth." (Arendt anticipates what we now call "globalization.")

7. Correspondingly, the *homo faber* is gendered male. I take up the relationship between *animal laborans* and *homo faber* in more detail in chapter 6. Here I am primarily concerned with how Arendt's text connects women, or at least the female, to *animal laborans*.

8. "[O]nly the *animal laborans*," Arendt (1958, 134) writes, "and neither the craftsman nor the man of action, has ever demanded to be 'happy' or thought that mortal men could be happy."

9. Although Arendt herself is read by Rich (1979), O'Brien (1981, 206), and others as showing "contempt and indifference" for women's experiences in her assignment of the *animal laborans* to the lowest rung on the ladder of the *vita activa*, it is important to note that she often confirms the indispensability and the significance of labor in the human condition. Thus, "life itself depends on labor," and "the blessing of life as a whole [is] inherent in labor" (1958, 87,

107). Furthermore, the holding of labor in contempt is something that Arendt locates in history and therefore problemizes in relation to the "reversals" that constitute the transformations in the *vita activa*. In ancient times, Arendt notes, "Contempt for laboring, originally arising out of a passionate striving for freedom from necessity . . . spread with the increasing demands of *polis* life upon the time of the citizens" (81). That Arendt realizes this does not mean she endorses it.

10. More recently, Kristeva seems to have moved away from a feminist worldview that (in effect) celebrates the *animal laborans* and anything like "group identity." Some of these changes are directly related to Kristeva's fairly new recognition of the centrality of Arendt's thought for her own thinking through matters of narrative, language, and politics. See, for example, the remarkably insightful essay "Hannah Arendt, or Life Is a Narrative" (in Kristeva, 2000). Given this work (and her most recent book [2001]), I think that Kristeva no longer fits the mold of *animal laborans* feminism, thanks in part to her reconsiderations of Arendt.

11. The problem may be even more complicated than this, if we remember that Arendt does not posit the "public" and the "private" realms as a fixed or static relation, or conceptualize the public:private as somehow ontologically prior to the *vita activa*. To the contrary, the private and public realms are in as complex a relation to each other, and to the activities of labor, work, and action, as those activities are to each other. For example, the triumph of *animal laborans* in the modern world also marks the absorption of the public by the private, which itself has been transformed and mutated by the rise of "the social," an operation that Pitkin (1998) represents through the powerful imagistic metaphor of "the blob." Consequently, if we follow Arendtian theory through, the problem may be that there *is* no longer a meaningful way even to ask a question like "who will tend to the private?" because that question has been rendered superfluous by the blurring effects of modern social formations that have effaced whatever clear distinction there once may have been between a so-called public and a so-called private realm. Nevertheless, at the level of practical politics, we continue to live (and talk) as though that distinction makes sense. But perhaps it does not make sense. For an even more complex and important assessment of the current state of the "private/public sphere," see Bauman (1999, 107) who assesses the private/public sphere as one from which "'the public' has recoiled, seeking shelter in politically inaccessible places, and 'the private' is about to redraw in its own image." Bauman continues: "To make the *agora* fit for autonomous individuals and autonomous society, one needs to arrest, simultaneously, its privatization and its depoliticization. One needs to reestablish the translation of the private into the public."

CHAPTER 6

1. Arendt gave some advice to her friend William Phillips on the occasion of his *Partisan Review* interview with Beauvoir, or "the Prettiest Existentialist," as Janet Flanner called her. Responding to Phillips's complaint about Beauvoir's "endless nonsense," Arendt advised, "Instead of arguing with her, you should flirt with her." See Brightman (1992, 330).

2. In her essay on Rosa Luxemburg, Arendt (1968, 44) appreciatively remarks that Luxemburg expressed "distaste for the women's emancipation movement, to which all other women of her generation and political convictions were irresistibly drawn." In the face of "suffragette equality," she continues, Luxemburg "might have been tempted to reply, *Vive la petite différence*." Young-Bruehl (1982, 238) suggests that this "maxim," along with an urge to be independent, constituted Arendt's "motherly advice" to young women as well. Yet whatever *la petite différence* signified in terms of a woman's intimate relations with a man, Arendt obviously recoiled when it was congealed into the social identifier "woman" in order to represent someone as "exceptional" within her kind. The complex social history of the Jews of Germany provided Arendt with this particular frame of reference. So strong were Arendt's views on this matter that she initially threatened to refuse the invitation to become a full professor at Princeton, according to Young-Bruehl (1982, 272) "because the university stressed the 'first woman' aspect in their report to the *New York Times*." Arendt in turn responded by placing herself within a category that denied the exception in favor of the "kind": *feminini generis*.

3. this is the phrase Arendt (1968, 55) herself uses in discussing Luxemburg's brutal murder.

4. For an account of Arendt's refugee flight to France and her subsequent detention and escape from an internment camp at Gurs, whose remaining inmates later died in Nazi concentration camps, see Young-Bruehl (1982, 152–166), and Arendt (1978, 57–60).

5. Other evaluations of feminist approaches to Arendt include Lane (1983) and Markus (1987). For a more extensive review of the literature, see Benhabib (1993).

6. In particular, Rich (1979); O'Brien (1981); and Brown (1988).

7. In particular, Hartsock (1983); Elshtain (1986); Winant (1987); and Ruddick (1989).

8. In particular, Pitkin (1981); Lane (1983); Fraser (1992b); Honig (1992); Cutting-Gray (1993); and Benhabib (1992a, 1993).

9. As Young-Bruehl (1982, 318) notes, Arendt wrote numerous topical essays in which she employed the "complex schematism" articulated in *The Human Condition*, but "she seldom paused to recapitulate its main elements," and this "paved the way for many misunderstandings." The proliferation of conceptual distinctions and categories that Arendt put forth in her initial

schematism also paved the way for misunderstandings of *The Human Condition* itself, as we shall see. For a different account of *The Human Condition* as a conceptual configuration of layers of mutually reinforcing "binaries," see Honig (1992, 223).

10. See Rich (1979, 205–207), and O'Brien (1981, 93, 101), also chapter 5. Rich, a lesbian feminist poet and essayist, was active in the antiwar movement and became one of the most influential cultural feminist thinkers of the 1970s. O'Brien comes to political theory with, as she puts it (1981, 11), "the sensibilities of a woman and a midwife." But she also arrives trailing remnants of a socialist feminist perspective analytically indebted to Marx, methodologically attuned to (formal) dialectics, and academically directed toward the study of social and political thought. O'Brien's perspective is primarily theoretical and critical, and her framework links a Marxist analysis of labor as emancipatory activity to a difference feminism of women's labor as reproduction—literally, to labor as birth. Thus, she contends (1981, 92), "[B]irth is a subject and object of an integrative feminist philosophy." For a sympathetic account of O'Brien that is equally critical of Arendt, see Held (1990).

11. Rich (1979, 206, 212) and O'Brien (1981, 100). As I shall argue shortly, *The Human Condition* contains a gender subtext, but that does not necessarily suppose that it also contains an adequate theorization of how women have fared within the reversals of the *vita activa*. Thus O'Brien and Rich are correct to notice the androcentrism of Arendt's analysis; that is, how Arendt relegates the struggles of women "to footnotes" (Rich 1979, 204). The latter is literally the case (see chapter 5).

12. Since O'Brien offers the more explicit and systematic theoretical critique of Arendt, I focus my attention in what follows primarily upon her argument in *The Politics of Reproduction*. Given O'Brien's (1981, 58–59, 115) emphasis upon feminist political *praxis* and reproduction as a "process," it may seem that my characterization of her strategy as an "ontological politics" misrepresents her feminist philosophy. Indeed, she argues that it is Arendt's phenomenological analysis of the *vita activa* that bears insuperable "ontological burdens" to which her own theory is presumably invulnerable. Nevertheless, despite her objection to the "generic apartheid" of such categories as public:private, and her call for "the abolition of the phony wall between public and private, first nature and second nature, continuity and discontinuity," O'Brien grounds her notion of a feminist political *praxis* in a "feminist principle" that is animated by "woman's reproductive consciousness" and "reproductive labor." The latter, she says, "is a synthesizing and mediating act" that "confirms women's unity with nature experientially and guarantees that the child is hers." Unlike women, men are "naturally alienated from their children" and possess a "splintered and discontinuous" rather than "continuous and integrative" reproductive consciousness. Thus on a metaphysical and ontolog-

ical level, O'Brien recapitulates through the category "reproduction" the very gendered oppositions she apparently wants to demolish in *praxis*.

13. To appreciate what a disastrous initial move this is for O'Brien's analysis, we might recall the explicit disclaimer with which Arendt (1958, 9 f.) begins her conceptual analysis: "To avoid misunderstanding: the human condition is not the same as human nature, and the sum total of human activities and capabilities which correspond to the human condition does not constitute anything like human nature." Starting from the perspective of an *Existenz* philosophy that theorizes "doing" not "being," Arendt (10) dismisses the question of human nature or essence as something "only a god could know and define . . . and the first prerequisite would be that he be able to speak about a 'who' as though it were a 'what.'" O'Brien misses this crucial point because her analysis is captured by a singular conceptual category and a philosophical strategy that grants priority to the idea of being over doing, subjectivity over interaction, and "what" over "who." This is the category of woman. As a result, she erroneously assumes that the concepts that Arendt designates as labor:work:action are sociological categories of humans as male:female beings, rather than concepts that designate potential human capacities, or mentalities embodied in human capacities, as Arendt intends.

14. In a subsequent response to my argument here, Pitkin (1998, 168) interestingly points out that O'Brien is not alone "in distorting Arendt's triadic scheme into a gendered, dichotomous contrast; Arendt herself does so as well, in the second chapter of *The Human Condition*, where the orderly explication of the conceptual triad is interrupted by the introduction of both the social as Blob and the ancient Greeks." Pitkin goes on to suggest (rightly in my view) that "the structure of Arendt's book is not simply and uniformly triadic," a position she seems to think characterizes my reading of *The Human Condition*. But nowhere do I mean to assert that a "simple and uniform" triad structures Arendt's text, only that O'Brien and others persistently miss triads because of their fixation on a *dyadic* gender construct. Indeed, I think that one of the most intriguing features of *The Human Condition* lies in its proliferation of concepts and categories that regularly disrupt the triadic structure including in ways that, as Pitkin writes, "profoundly reflect Arendt's ambivalences about autonomy, ambition, and gender." These matters, which I do not even begin to consider here, are at the heart of Pitkin's very important book.

15. In order to understand what O'Brien loses by erasing the Arendtian configuration of labor:work:action in favor of the conceptual (gendered) dualism public:private, we should remember that Arendt (1958, 160) assigns a "public" realm both to *homo faber* (work) and to action (politics). Arendt (1958, 87) also identifies an "actual historical development that brought labor out of hiding and into the public realm." Thus, public and private (and social) cut across labor, work, and action in a variety of ways. Because she misses this, O'Brien cannot appreciate Arendt's critique of the predominance of the pub-

lic realm of the "exchange market" in modernity. Nor can O'Brien grasp Arendt's action concept of politics as a counter to the very sphere her own "politics of reproduction" is meant to challenge: the sphere of (economic, cap-italist) production.

16. For her part, Rich does not appear to have a secure understanding of the way in which *vita activa* operates in Arendt's theory. Commenting upon Arendt's failure to consider women's condition, she (1979, 212) writes, "The withholding of women from participation in the *vita activa,* the 'common world,' and the connection of this with reproductivity, is something from which [Arendt] does not so much turn her eyes as stare straight through unseeing." But it may be Rich who has the vision problem. From an Arendtian perspective her claim is incoherent, because the *vita activa* is neither a catego-ry of "participation" nor a "realm" that some humans are allowed into and oth-ers denied. Rich seems to be confusing *vita activa* with Arendt's notion of "action" (politics). The latter, however, is only one part of the *vita activa* as Arendt conceptualizes it (1958, 7–11). (See chapter 5.)

17. O'Brien (1981, 103) also argues that from this perspective of politics, Arendt indirectly sanctions the continuing violence of "paterfamilias," who must maintain the "separation of public and private." Given Arendt's anti-instrumentalist action concept of politics and her condemnation of violence as antipolitical, this is perhaps O'Brien's most astonishing (and wrongheaded) claim.

18. Regardless of their sympathies, almost all feminist interpreters seize upon the Greek *polis* image that Arendt employs of the public realm. I suspect that this is partly because of the provocative quality of the image itself, but also because feminist interest in Arendt's work develops alongside a significant amount of feminist scholarship on the representation of women in ancient polit-ical thought, the social history of women in classical Greece, and the symbolic significance of goddess worship in ancient cultures. As for Arendt's (1958, 196) own views, it is important to remember that she is not concerned "with the his-torical causes for the rise of the Greek city-state," but rather with how the *polis* (as a metaphor for politics) functions as a "remedy" for the "frailty" of human action. This claim was not enough to inoculate the Arendtian public realm con-cept against charges of irrelevance, nostalgia, or romanticism in the general lit-erature, or masculinism in feminist commentary. For an alternative interpretation of the role of the Greek polis in Arendt's thinking that does not charge her with an archaizing worldview, see chapter 9.

19. Pitkin's influential essay is a common reference point for many fem-inist interpretations of Arendt. See, for example, Hartsock (1983); Markus (1987); Hansen (1987); Brown (1988); Ring (1991); Honig (1992); and Benhabib (1993). A considerable portion of these commentaries (for example, in Hartsock, Brown, Benhabib, and Ring) is directed toward negotiating the metaphor of the posturing boys, with a view toward securing a fix on Arendt.

In a sense, then, Pitkin's essay provides a second scene upon which the (often) hyperbolic gendering of Arendt is played out. Matters are further complicated by the fact that Pitkin (1981, 338–339, 341) renders her formulation of Arendtian "machismo" in a deliberately provocative way that sets up an Arendtian macho politics of superhuman male immortals initially, only to reject this reading of Arendtian politics later. Some commentators recognize the conceptual implications of Pitkin's rhetorical shift (Hartsock, Benhabib); others apparently do not (Brown).

20. That is, Brown (1988, 14, 205) rejects "a prefigured conception of masculinity" grounded in some biological "maleness," and she distances herself from feminist projects tied to "revaluing reproductive work" and "childrearing." Thus she conceptualizes gender as a textual and symbolic construct open to interpretive critique, rather than as a mode of consciousness or a "process" linked to reproduction, as O'Brien does. Nonetheless, her feminist project is grounded in an interpretive binary of gender that consistently formulates "life" and "body" positively and "manhood" and "politics" negatively. Hence, for Brown (1988, 31), the *vita activa* represents Arendt's "fear of being consumed by the life process, by natural necessity and the body (also see Zerilli, 1995). Brown reads this as an unfortunate vestige of Arendt's being "a female intellectual prior to the days of the 'second-wave' women's movement"—by which I take her to mean that second-wave feminism reunited woman, life, and body in an appropriate and meaningful way. So perhaps she celebrates a kind of female difference after all (although her later work decisively rejects any such move). (See Brown 1995.)

21. It is worth noting that Brown (1988, 24–27), like O'Brien, tends to (mis)read the *vita activa* through the category of human nature, and the fundamental activities of labor, work, and action as sociological entities that identify people in terms of class, occupation, or gender. So, even as she correctly interprets Arendt as arguing that speech and action in the public realm "embody defiance of the incorrigible fact of [human] mortality," Brown mistakenly concludes that Arendt deems people who have historically been denied access to the public realm as "*animal laborans*," "idiotic," and "deprived." This mistake is so pervasive in the feminist critiques of Arendt that it bears repeating (as I did in chapter 5), that the concepts labor:work:action do not function as empirical, historical, or sociological generalizations in her theory, much less as validations of some historical status quo. They are existential categories intended to reveal what it means to be human and in the presence of other human beings on earth and in the world. It is from this existential imperative to "think what we are doing" that Arendt theorizes the world alienation of nearly all individuals as *animal laborans* in the modern age. (See Pitkin 1981, 342; Hinchman 1984b).

22. Although natality is "intimately connected" to all three human activities of labor:work:action, it bears its closest connection, Arendt argues, not

with labor or work, but with action (politics) in its aspects of spontaneity, unpredictability, and irreversibility, which neither the automatic processes of *animal laborans* nor the means-end lineations of *homo faber* allow. For Arendt (1958, 9, emphasis added) natality is "the central category of *political*, as distinguished from metaphysical, thought." Natality exhibits itself as freedom in the realm of action and speech, not in the realm of biological life, metabolism, and growth. Insofar as the gynocentric-difference feminists reassign natality to the (female) body and motherhood, they mistake Arendt's meaning. For a somewhat different perspective on Arendtian natality that is nevertheless sympathetic to Elshtain and Ruddick, see Jones (1993, 173–185). For a nongynocentric perspective that is closer to Arendt's meaning, see Yaeger (1988, 94–96).

23. This is especially true of Hartsock, who offers a number of interpretive corrections to formulations like O'Brien and Brown's. For example, in contrast to Brown (1988, 25) who argues that Arendt reenacts Plato's pathology toward the body, Hartsock (1983, 213–214) correctly insists that Arendt "rejects Plato's argument that the body is merely a shadow of the soul" in favor of a "Homeric" view of the primacy of the body and "embodied action." Relatedly, against O'Brien, Hartsock recognizes that what Arendt views with horror "is not nature itself but the failure to differentiate oneself from the world of nature." Finally, and in an *Existenz* spirit that both Brown and O'Brien fail to appreciate, Hartsock (1983, 217) casts the polis not as a form of machismo but as "a guarantee against the futility of individual life" that Arendt finds in the automatic processes and artificial cyclicalities that distinguish modern world alienation.

24. See, in particular, Markus (1987, 82). Also see Lane (1983); Hansen (1987); Cutting-Gray (1993); and Benhabib (1993).

25. Here I am deliberately distinguishing between, as Susan Okin (1990, 15) puts it, an analytical focus "on either the absence or the assumed subordination of women in a political theory" and a focus on "the gendered structure" of a society, a culture, a theory, or a text. In turning to the second focus, I find *The Human Condition* far more positively illuminating for feminist purposes than it is on the first. I have already noted in chapter 5 such a subtext in Arendt's concept of *animal laborans* that is symbolically if unintentionally gendered as female. Arendt often refers to *animal laborans* as "he." (For example 1958, 118, 133, 139). But she also refers to *animal laborans* as an "it." (For example, 1958, 118, 121, 144). Sometimes, on the same page *animal laborans* is both "he" and "it" [1958, 118], but never "she." In what follows, I wish to amplify the gendered subtext of *animal laborans* in relation to *homo faber* but suggesting that the former is actually gendered female in Arendt's theory, and the latter is male.

26. On this score, I respectfully disagree with Joan Landes (1992, 114 f.) who contends that "although [Arendt] is nowhere concerned either with

women or with the gendered construction of subjectivity . . . [she] addresses the performative dimension of human action and human speech" in a way that is useful for feminists. To the contrary, I shall argue that Arendt's "performative" concept of action-speech is useful for feminists precisely because at once it is posed against and displaces the gendered subjectivity of *animal laborans* and *homo faber*.

27. The gender binary of *animal laborans:homo faber* is complex in another way as well. Both are good examples of Arendtian concepts that, no matter how externally differentiated, are internally loaded with numerous (and sometimes contradictory) dimensions of meaning. It is little wonder, for example, that Arendt's feminist critics have had difficulty sustaining a coherent account of labor, for this term as *animal laborans* carries (at least) the following connotations: nature, animality, (human) biology; (human) body, fertility, birth, reproduction, childbirth, cyclicality, seasons, basic life needs (food, clothing, shelter), certain kinds of toil, repetition, "everyday" tasks (eating, cleaning, mending, tending, washing, cooking, resting, and so on), housework, the domestic sphere, abundance, the blessing of life as a whole, the female; but also life:death, pain:pleasure, necessity, routinized processes, consumption, (economic) demand, "automatism," automation, technological determinism, the society of jobholders, and the nullity that is advanced capitalism in late modernity (also see chapter 9). Given Arendt's otherwise discerning sense for conceptual distinctions, it is odd that she could reduce so many irreducible aspects of human experience into one specifically gendered category—unless that is precisely what she wants us to think about.

28. Within the *vita activa*, action carries with it no singular or unitary Latin equivalent such as *animal laborans* is to labor and *homo faber* is to work. This is because Arendt designates action not as an "identity" (animal, man) but as a context of collective performativity that reveals identities in plurality.

29. Not all diversity feminists adopt Linda Alcoff's distinctive formulation of gender, race, class, and ethnic identity as "choices" or "positions" from which woman can constitute herself. But her argument has had considerable influence on those feminist theorists and philosophers who are inclined to focalize identity in terms of what Alcoff (1988, 432) calls "immediately recognizable oppressed groups" such as "Jewish people," "black men," "women of all races," and the like. Such individuals, Alcoff continues, "can practice identity politics by choosing their identity as a member of one or more groups as their political point of departure." Acting out such choices constitutes what Alcoff calls "positionality." For a related perspective on the politics of "social group differences," see Young (1990).

30. When Lane (1983, 115) refers to "the self–conscious development of [feminists'] own latent tradition," she seems to mean women's moral distance from the construction of "the modern capitalist and technological state." Although Lane rejects any sort of essentialist view of women's traditional

activities, she comes rather close in this notion to confusing exclusion with a collectively superior morality, grounded in the identity of "women." Furthermore, by automatically reading "women" out of the capitalist picture, Lane preempts the need to approach gender, morality, and politics in advanced capitalist societies from an analytical perspective that is highly attuned to the particularities and complexities of discrete historical and social contexts (all of which include and construct women, in various ways).

31. I emphasize the "action context" because I do not mean to suggest that Arendt undervalues the "what-ness of Being" over the "who-ness of acting" in all possible contexts. The relationship she establishes between these two things is complex. On at least two occasions, Arendt herself had recourse to expressions of "Being": when she called herself *feminini generis* (see note 2 above); and when she observed in her address (1968, 17) on the occasion of accepting the Lessing Prize, "I cannot gloss over the fact that for many years I considered the only adequate reply to the question, Who are you? to be: a Jew. That answer alone took into account the reality of persecution." What do these appeals to gender and ethnicity mean, especially in light of Arendt's critique of the "what-ness" that obliterates the unique distinctiveness of the agent? Perhaps a clue lies in the Lessing Prize address (1968, 18), where she clarifies that in the extreme situation of Nazism it was imperative to acknowledge "not a special kind of human being . . . [nor] a reality burdened . . . by history . . . but a political fact through which my being a member of this group outweighed all other questions of personal identity." Thus in the totalitarian context of the Third Reich, identifying oneself as a Jew is an act of purposeful will, a response to the political fact of "a hostile world." Arendt (1958, 179) also suggests that in a different world, where the space of appearances flourishes, and action and plurality are actualized, "such an attitude would seem like a pose." In this latter world, expressing oneself in terms of a solidified group identity impedes rather than enhances the solidarity that springs from the "disclosure of 'who,'" or personal identity. Thus, Arendt wants to free the person from the group in the action context of speech-politics; but in dark times, when political speech is silenced, she insists upon the individual's responsibility to confront political reality, embrace the language of Being (or group identity), and speak. For somewhat different treatments of Arendt's relation to Jewish and female identity, see Honig (1995); Disch (1995); Zerilli (1995); Kaplan (1995); Benhabib (1996b); Bernstein (1996); and Ring (1997).

32. I do not mean to suggest that the difference and diversity feminists completely erase the significance of the "who-ness of acting" or the revelation of personal identity through speech in Arendtian politics. Hartsock (1983, 215), for example, appreciates that "for Arendt, human plurality results in the 'paradoxical plurality of unique beings.'" Fraser (1992b, 141) acknowledges "the salience of discourse" in the "construction" of "cultural identities"; Ring (1991, 445) recognizes that "display of individuality" is integral to Arendtian

action; and Markus (1987, 78) notes Arendt's concern for "'*Who*' *we are.*" Nevertheless, none of these accounts confronts the problematic relationship that Arendt herself establishes between the "what-ness of Being" and the "who-ness of acting." Thus "women's life activity" (Hartsock), "cultural identities" (Fraser), or the "pariah" as a "group identity" (Ring, Marcus) rest rather uncomfortably alongside Arendt's (1958, 180) action concept which rejects a politics of (descriptive, social, passive) identity in favor of a politics of "the unique and distinct identity of the agent" as disclosed in (performative, political, active) speech and deed. Markus (1987, 78) even obfuscates Arendtian natality when she takes it to define "'*what*' we are in a society." Arendt (1958, 246 f.) clearly associates natality with action, "the one miracle-working faculty of man" that is aligned with "originality and unprecedentedness," not with predictable social or behavioral categorizations.

33. There is a problem of conceptualization in Cutting-Gray's appropriation of "alterity" as "distinctness," however, and it makes hers a less fully deconstructive feminism than Honig's (1992, 50 n. 2). Arendt (1958, 176) notes that alterity or "otherness" is possessed by everything that "is"—it *transcends* "every particular quality." As such, alterity distinguishes the human as species-being but not as a unique person who is "alive." Only "distinctness," which humans reveal in and through expression and communication, secures each one of us as sui generis (176–181). By collapsing distinctness into alterity (otherness), Cutting-Gray (1993, 49) forfeits the very concept she needs for a more radical (and genuinely Arendtian) insistence upon the irreducible multiplicity of our distinct "identities." As a result, when she targets "all who have shared in the historical condition of otherness" as one of the aspects of "a genuine feminist politics of alterity," she sounds more like a diversity than a deconstructive feminist.

34. Similarly, Honig (1992, 227) notes that Arendt would have been wary of "any proclamation of homogeneity in 'women's experience' or in 'women's ways of knowing'" or in any feminist politics that "relies on a category of woman that aspires to or implies a universality that belies . . . significant differences and pluralities within—and even resistances to—the bounds of the category itself."

35. I am not arguing that recourse to the term "woman" has no part in the speech-action of a feminist politics, only that it must be rejected as an "identity" posit that is prior and "politically paramount" (Alcoff 1988, 432). It seems not only inevitable but also necessary that in the domain of speech-action (politics) feminists will have to deploy descriptive identity categories. First, these categories are integral to the critical activity of unmasking existing conditions, institutions, relations of power, policies, and ideologies that systematically exclude or overtly oppress human beings by explicitly or implicitly imposing group identities that are formulated negatively. Second, descriptive terms are a part of the strategy and rhetoric of speech-action (pol-

itics) itself. Depending upon the action context, self-revelatory speech that makes an appeal to a particular group identity may be a more effective tactic than speech that eschews such utterances as an absolute rule. Nevertheless, purposeful appeals to "what-ness" (for example, "as a middle-class, heterosexual Catholic woman, I . . ."; "we Hispanics"; "all gay African-Americans") are speech-acts that an Arendtian deploys warily at best, in recognition of the havoc they wreak upon spontaneity and the damage they inflict upon the unique distinctiveness or the "who-ness" of the speaker. (For a powerful critique of identity politics and their implications for feminist theory, see Brown 1995; 1998).

36. What I mean to imply in this reference to "identities" is a paradox of deconstructive feminism: even as it seeks to disrupt "identity," it stays fixated upon it. Honig (1992, 231 f.), upon whom my discussion of deconstructive feminism will now focus, demolishes "identity" as a congealed term of political discourse; but it remains a conceptual a priori in her political critique insofar as, ruptured and proliferated, it comes back around in the form of "identities." Whether Honig is simply appropriating Arendt's action concept as a critical tool against difference and diversity-identity feminisms, or whether she thinks that the proliferation of identity/identities is and must be what politics is all about, is not entirely clear. Her concluding remarks (on 232) appear both to separate and to align "matters of identity" and "politics," thus leaving uncertain what she takes to constitute the action content of politics as performative. This may be a subset of a larger problem, since the actual "action content" of Arendtian politics is, as we shall see in chapter 8, a long-standing matter of debate (see Pitkin 1981).

37. Honig (1992, 232) clearly aligns Arendt more on the "Nietzschean" than the "Habermasian" side, as does Benhabib, although she recognizes Arendt's distance from Nietzsche as well. In any case, it is not obvious to me that Honig shares Benhabib's (1993, 105) notion of public space as "a sphere that comes into existence whenever and wherever all affected by general social and political norms of action engage in a practical discourse." Insofar as she posits Arendtian "space" not only in/as political communities but also as "sites of critical leverage" "within the frame of . . . 'identities' themselves," Honig (1992, 231) treats "space" as also a site of *internal* disruption wherein the agent subverts his or her own "identity" performatively. On this account, then, speech is presumably the act whereby the agent discloses this internal disruption-resistance publicly. Hence while Honig makes speech problematic both inside the agent and in the act, Benhabib makes it problematic only as the agent in the act (that is, in the agent's already given engagement in collective, practical discourse). Two rather different theories of language/speech/agency/self seem to be driving Honig's and Benhabib's different Arendtian sensibilities, and I think that in some ways both of them distort aspects of Arendt's thought. But pursuing this matter is beyond the scope of this chapter.

38. Benhabib is not the only commentator to find in Arendt's public realm theory a source for a critical and emancipatory account of what constitutes a specifically feminist politics. Other studies use particular Arendtian concepts to analyze gender or women in historical publics and public spheres—for example, Landes (1988); Ryan (1990); Fraser (1992b)—or to clarify the nature of republicanism and "engendering democracy" (Phillips 1991); the problem of authority (Jones 1993); or the possibilities of feminist citizenship (see chapter 1).

39. Apparently, gender is a sociological reality that Benhabib is willing to question in the name of feminist politics, but it is not something that her discourse model actively displaces or thoroughly subverts. By congealing feminism as a politics into the category "women's movement," and linking the latter with a normative ideal indebted to Gilligan (1982), Benhabib simply reaffirms the validity of gender difference on the level of social movements. Thus her "ethics of dialogue" is an odd notion: on the practical-normative level, it allows for challenges to conventional gendered arrangements, but at the level of social theory, it designates a form of human interaction ("the women's movement") in terms of a gendered ideal.

CHAPTER 7

1. In fact, Ash (1995, 35) reports, Klaus misquoted his (Ash's) distinction by finding "incredible" the notion that politicians "*live* in half-truth." As Ash proceeds to clarify, "what I said was that politicians *work* in half-truth. The phrase characterizes the professional party politician's job, not his life." Klaus's misquotation was revealing, insofar as it reprised Václav Havel's pre-1989 formula "living in truth" and thereby jumbled the meaning of both Havel's and Ash's perspectives on politics.

2. The phrase "new spirituality" comes from a speech that Havel made in Tokyo in April 1992, where he took issue with "a British friend" (Ash himself) and resisted the either/or of "independent intellectuals" and "practicing politicians" (Ash 1995, 37). Identifying a "historic challenge," Havel (in Ash 1995, 37) speculated upon the possibility of introducing a "new dimension into politics" that would draw a "new wind, [a] new spirit, a new spirituality . . . into the established stereotypes of present-day politics." It is up to intellectuals, among others, Havel concluded, "to demonstrate whether my British friend has shown foresight, or has simply been too influenced by the banal idea that everyone should stick to his own trade."

3. In a speech delivered on this theme at New York University in October 1991, Havel acknowledged that "in politics, as anywhere else in life, it is impossible and pointless to say everything, all at once, to just anyone." But he immediately qualified this remark by adding, "This does not mean having to lie. All you need is tact, the proper instincts, and good taste. . . . I have discovered that good taste is more useful here than a degree in political science" (in

Ash 1995, 37). I will refrain from remarking upon the important insight involved in at least the last part of Havel's observation.

4. Foucault (1984c, 373 f.) amplifies this point on principles when he recounts coming across a text devoted to *Fuhrertum* by Max Pohlenz, the philosopher, who "heralded the universal values of Stoicism all his life." "You should read the . . . book's closing remarks on the *Fuhrersideal* and on the true humanism constituted by the Volk under the inspiration of the leader's direction," Foucault remarks to his interviewer; "Heidegger never wrote anything more disturbing." He also adds, "Nothing in this condemns Stoicism . . . needless to say." Maurice Merleau-Ponty (1964, 219) expresses a similar insight when he asks, "Has not history shown even more clearly after Machiavelli than before him, that principles commit us to nothing, and that they may be adapted to any end?" This point is also made powerfully by Arendt (1963, 135–137) in her discussion of Adolf Eichmann's frequent references, during his trial, to Kant's moral precepts and particularly to the categorical imperative, according to which Eichmann claimed he lived his own life.

5. In his definitive essay "Machiavelli: Politics and the Economy of Violence," Sheldon Wolin (1960, 211) introduces this phrase in order to characterize Machiavelli's theory. "To possess a political metaphysic without a philosophy," Wolin argues, "may initially strike us as paradoxical or trivial . . . but in discarding philosophy [Machiavelli] was freed to create something new: a truly 'political' philosophy which concentrated solely on political issues and single-mindedly explored the range of phenomena relevant to it." Wolin amplifies this point by asking, "What would be the implications if man's whole existence were defined by a world of fleeting sense impressions and phenomenal flux, a world having precious little in the way of a firm foundation for knowledge?"

6. I hasten to add that by emphasizing the "intrinsicalness" of politics I mean to specify it along the lines of an action concept (as I proceed to do in chapter 8), but not in a way that focalizes a spatially bounded "sphere" or "realm" that is (in either an Arendtian or Rawlsian sense) "public" rather than "private" or "social." Since all of these realms (however they are delimited) are both externally and internally open to struggle, conflict, and the play of relations of power, they might be understood as (actual or potential) sites of strategic maneuver as well as dissensus, dispute, deception, manipulation, half-truth—that is, as political. Specifying the site of such struggles is impossible in advance for, as Isaiah Berlin (1969, 130 n. 1) observes, "the possibilities of action are not discrete entities like apples which can be exhaustively enumerated." For an example of how the private realm (of familial, marital, intimate, reproductive, sexual, and gender relations) exhibits the overall effect of strategic positions and maneuver as politics, see Machiavelli's domestic comedy *Mandragola* (1957). Also see Ian Shapiro (1994, 127–130) for an intelligent discussion of how politics can be specified and at the same time understood as

"ubiquitous to human interaction" and "permeat[ing] every facet of human interaction."

7. That is to say, Habermasian citizens are not truth seekers with a capital T since, for Habermas, truth is not an objective transcendent aspect of some metaphysical reality. Rather, truth is the outcome of agreement reached through critical discussion or rational consensus. Still, politics is truth-seeking insofar as discourse theory has the success of deliberative politics depend on the institutionalization of certain procedures geared toward the achievement of consensus.

8. Because the Machiavellian thesis that I am developing operates on the terrain of political action and not the philosophy of language, I will not pursue this aspect of Habermas's distinction between communicative:strategic action here. But it is important to note that, to date, Habermas has not developed the linguistic "priority" of communicative over strategic speech-action to any sufficient degree, or adequately addressed the charge that linguistic communication cannot be so easily separated from purposive activity. As Jonathan Culler (1985, 137) notes, "To understand 'Could you close the window' is to grasp that it could be used to get someone to close the window as well as to inquire about their abilities." The problem this example raises is that in the absence of an account that can show how strategic action possesses a "derivative" status (Rasmussen 1990, 40), the positing of communicative consensuality as "primary" is likely to boil down simply to a matter of preference for its norms as better, or more appealing, or more "basic" to language. But that is precisely what has to be shown.

9. The analogy between the chivalric codes and Habermas's theory of communicative action ultimately breaks down on a substantial point: the strict protocols that governed medieval combat themselves presupposed a shared normative consciousness and an existing communal ethos in which the question of *honor* (among other significant norms and practices) was taken very seriously. Constructed in the context of the technicization of the modern world, Habermas's "code" presupposes no equivalent ethos; it relies instead upon theoretical criteria and knowledge of the correct norms that are, for Habermas, part and parcel of the very nature of language itself. For a discussion of the dilemmas that attend Habermas's theoretical grounding of a philosophical ethics without ethos, see Gadamer's letter to Bernstein (in Bernstein 1983, 261–265); also see Ronald Beiner (1989).

10. In a 1990 interview with Torben Hviid Nielsen, Habermas (1993, 163) regretted what he called his "dubbing" of certain conditions under which idealizing presuppositions would be fulfilled as an "ideal speech situation" because it suggests a "kind of hypostatization" that he resolutely rejects. Habermas (164 f.) goes on to allow that he even hesitates to call the communication community "a regulative idea in the Kantian sense," since these conditions must be satisfied to a sufficient degree "here and now" if we want to

engage in argument at all. He then (165) tries this "paradoxical" formulation: "the regulative idea of the validity of utterances is constitutive for the social facts produced through communicative action" insofar as it "transcends the limits of social space and historical time '*from within the world.*'"

11. Habermas makes this argument in response to Albrecht Wellmer's contention that discourses are always social, historical, and *institutionalized.* That is, institutions impose obligations regarding argumentation that are constructed within the institutions themselves. Habermas (1993, 31) agrees that institutions (such as "courts, university seminars, and parliamentary hearings") carry "practical obligations"; but he also distinguishes the former from the "transcendental constraints" that characterize the "general pragmatic presuppositions" that *presuppose* institutionalized argumentation. These presuppositions differ from institutional norms insofar as they do not impose obligations to act rationally; rather the presuppositions "*make possible* the practice that participants understand as argumentation." In a Machiavellian mode, I will leave this universalizing idea behind and follow Cornelius Castoriadis (1992, 253) in allowing that: "It is actual historical universality with which we are concerned when we confront the political question, not 'transcendental universality.'"

12. Habermas maintains that his discourse ethics, based on a theory of rationality that is itself based on language, is open to falsification by scientific evidence; hence, he opens his argument to empirical falsification. This draws Habermas's theory into a number of difficult issues, none of which I will consider here. But see Alford (1985) and Rasmussen (1990).

13. Girolamo Savonarola, Dominican monk, political ruler of Florence, and unarmed prophet, was hanged (and his body burned) as a heretic by the Florentine citizenry in 1498. Shortly thereafter, the republic was restored and Machiavelli assumed office in the second chancery, and was named secretary to the Ten of War.

14. Beiner (1989, 239–240) makes a related and equally valuable point in his defense of Gadamer's neo-Aristotelian ethics against Habermas's appeal to universal postulates of linguistic reason. As he concludes, "the dispute between Gadamer and Habermas ultimately comes down to a question of the relative priority of theory and prudence," or science over *phronesis*. See also Aryeh Botwinick (1993, 76, 77), who contends that Habermas's philosophy-of-language theorizing "raises the specter of an unbridgeable gap between theory and practice—since even the most detailed and elaborate of theoretical texts cannot substitute for the context of decision-making and application that confront an agent at the moment of practice, the moment of actual doing or responding." But see my discussion of Thucydides's text *The Peloponnesian War* (1982), a text which I think comes as close to succeeding in this elaboration as anything else in political theory.

15. Machiavelli writes of politics in an age in which the entire chivalric system is nearly collapsed, and to no little extent because of certain techno-

logical advances that mark the "premodern" world, in between medievalism and modernity. The elaborate conventions on ransom giving and taking (how one knight accepted the surrender of another, the promise of "safe quarter" to the surrendering knight, and so on) disintegrated as a result of material developments (first in archery and later in artillery and gunfire) that reduced face-to-face combat and, with it, the possibility of capture and ransom (Meron 1993). The accompanying breakup of the unified Christian culture of Europe, the Crusades (where chivalric norms were not extended to infidel Arabs) only hastened the process, which may have reached its climax in 1415 on the fields of Agincourt (Weschler 1996). Thus, in contrast to both the medievalism of the Christian chivalric and the modernism of the Habermasian communicative codes, Machiavelli asserts a mode of conduct that can only be known by understanding the codeless code of politics—a realm that, as Benedetto Croce wrote (in Berlin 1982, 53), has its own laws against which it is futile to rebel, "which cannot be exorcized and banished from the world with holy water," nor tempered, I might add, with a reconstructive science of language.

16. For many of these formulations, I am indebted to Castoriadis's (implicitly Machiavellian) discussion of politics, which he terms "the activity that aims at the transformation of society's institutions in order to make them conform to the norm of the autonomy of the collectivity" (1992, 254), and uses to counter what he takes to be the excesses of Habermas's theory of communicative action and ideal speech situation. Insofar as he stresses the institutional context of intersubjective communication, Castoriadis (1992, 254–255) echoes Wellmer's critique of Habermas's argument; but he also challenges as "totally inadequate" Habermas's efforts to found a theory of social action on the ideas of communicative action, interpretive understanding, and an ideal speech situation. The latter, Castoriadis argues (256), are "only the atmosphere indispensable to *political* life and creativity—and their very existence depends upon instituting acts. The *end* or *goal* of these acts goes far beyond the establishment of an ideal communication situation, which is only part of that end, and really just a mere means."

17. As both Berlin and Wolin argue, Machiavelli believes in a permanent "economy of violence" (Wolin 1960, 220)—the need for a "consistent reserve of force always in the background" (Berlin 1982, 66). Wolin (1960, 221, emphasis added) links Machiavelli's view of violence to the nature of the context in which power was exerted: "the tightly-packed condition of political space which mocked any *merely verbal attempt* at translating power into simple direction or supervision of the affairs of society." The metaphor of a "tightly-packed condition" that Wolin associates with politics recalls Merleau-Ponty's "collective knot," and both in turn capture the constricted milieu of conflicting ambitions, demands, fears, hatreds, hopes, and vested interests that is politics.

18. How these strategic interests are theorized is a broader question that is not predetermined by my argument. However, I endorse Shapiro's (1994) warning not to thematize strategic interests too reductively, especially solely in terms of game theory or rational choice. Machiavelli's (1950, 91) observations about fortune (*fortuna*) as "the ruler of half our actions" remind us that strategic actions are intertwined with time and circumstances in ways that confound even the most judicious attempts to formalize underlying norms of human rationality.

19. One of the problems with Habermas's distinction between communicative and strategic action is that it tends to construe too narrowly the strategic type of action, and wrongly characterize it, as David Ingram (1993, 308) notes, as "manipulative, egoistic and atomistic, as opposed to the openness, impartiality, and consensuality of communicative rationality" (see also Ingram 1994).

20. Here, of course, I am paraphrasing Machiavelli's (1950, 56) famous line in chapter 15 of *The Prince*, "A man who wishes to make a profession of goodness in everything must necessarily come to grief among so many who are not good." The message concludes with this consummately strategic advice: "Therefore it is necessary for a prince, who wishes to maintain himself, to learn how not to be good, and to use this knowledge and not use it, according to the necessity of the case."

21. In any case, knowing exactly what it means to say that discourse ethics is the "practical activity" of redeeming validity claims is greatly impaired by the fact that Habermas and his commentators rarely offer very complex examples of the activity of discourse, and certainly none that are equal to the multilayered and multivocal dynamics of political speech. Indeed, most efforts to clarify what constitutes the redemption of validity claims or moral conversation rely either on abstract examples of communicative interaction between two individuals (Bernstein 1983, 186) or interacting parties (McCarthy 1981, 288–289), or on prosaic examples of communicative interaction between two individuals, such as Giddens's (1985, 128 f.) example of the traveler and the ticket clerk at a railway station, or Benhabib's (1990, 358 f.) example of the admonition of a parent to a child. Chambers's (1996, 95 f.) example of the giving and taking of commands, although political, hardly begins to capture the complex dynamics of "breakdown" in irreducibly particular speech situations where authority is challenged. Of course, to expect that it *could* do so is to demand far too much of a political theory—and perhaps too little of the politician or the citizen.

22. In returning to Timothy Garton Ash's observation that politicians work (rather than live) in half-truth, I am mindful of Charles Taylor's (1988, 227) observation that "the affirmation of ordinary life" is one of the "great revolutionary forces of modern culture." Under "ordinary life" Taylor includes "the belief that the central point of human existence and human fulfillment is to be found in the life of production and reproduction, or work and the fam-

ily, or labour and sexual love." Taylor does not include politics in his homage to ordinary life, nor (for different reasons) does Ash; nor does Machiavelli. Habermas presents a different, although inconclusive, case. Given both his frequent references to communicative action as "day-to-day" or "everyday" discourse, and the linkage he draws between communicative action and discursive democracy, it may be that Habermas absorbs politics into everyday life, thereby obliterating the difference that the Machiavellian maintains between two conflicting systems of value (see Berlin 1982, 58).

23. Failing to recognize this may lead those who partake in politics to grief. A contemporary example is found in Walter Mondale's sincerity and truth telling about the necessity of raising taxes, made in the course of what would be his disastrous presidential bid against Ronald Reagan in 1984. As Mondale allowed in speculating upon the reality of raising taxes and Reagan's response to this fact, "Ronald Reagan will raise your taxes, and so will I. He won't tell you, I just did." The way of a truly moral or honest politics, as Havel avers and Mondale discovered, is neither simple nor easy. From a partisan perspective it may also be self-defeating, if not disastrous, for the politician, and also for the body politic.

24. Thus, working in half-truth involves, in rhetorical form, the art of creating illusions or a "false world" that others will accept as real. As Wolin (1960, 213) notes, however: "Where the actors were all intent on creating false worlds, success depended not only on the ability to distinguish the true world from the false, but also in avoiding the trap of one's own deceptions."

25. Chambers (1996, 100, emphasis added) recognizes this when she allows that "It is not entirely correct to say that discourse does not contain any instrumental calculation. Discourse is goal-oriented in the sense that participants are looking for the best means of attaining the goal of mutual understanding. *Thus, it is not means/ends rationality that is excluded from discourse but only viewing one's dialogue partner as the means to attaining one's own ends.*" Similarly, Benhabib (1990, 354, emphasis added) attempts to soften what she calls "the stark opposition between political utopianism and political realism" that is introduced by the distinction communicative:strategic by formulating the relationship in this way: "Communicative ethics anticipates *nonviolent strategies of conflict resolution* as well as encouraging cooperative and associative methods of problem solving." Whether or not these qualifications align with Habermas's views, they certainly weaken the practical (if not the analytical) strength and coherence of the communicative:strategic distinction upon which Habermas's defense of the "priority" of communicative (that is, noninstrumental, non-means/ends, nonstrategic) action depends. In any case, once Chambers and Benhabib allow instrumental calculation, "means/ends rationality" and "nonviolent strategies" of action into communicative ethics, as they do in these respective passages, the game is up. In effect, what they both finally if indirectly articulate (despite their Habermasian leanings) is precisely what I have been

calling the "Machiavellian view" of the "intrinsic impurity of politics." This strategic calculation may be the aim of the political theorist who writes for those in power as well. For an interpretation along these lines that applies to Machiavelli himself, see Dietz (1986).

26. A considerable amount of commentary has also been directed to the apparent curiosity that Diodotus argues for saving the Mitylenians in the name of expediency, while Cleon urges their death in the name of justice. I think that this central element of the debate must also be understood in terms of the interrelation of communicative and strategic action and an analysis that, in effect, shifts attention from the "morality" of the interlocutors (that is: Is Cleon more moral because he argues from justice? Is Diodotus less principled because he argues from expediency?) and instead focuses on the rhetorical contingencies of politics. In this instance, Cleon successfully co-opts the language of justice, leaving Diodotus without much recourse to that vocabulary (and certainly without much time to undertake a theoretical reconceptualization of "justice" for the benefit of the demos). So it becomes expedient for Diodotus to rely upon the principle of "expediency" and thereby further the disintegration of the political vocabulary of justice in Athens. For one account of why such a choice proved disastrous, see White (1985); for an account that is more sympathetic to Diodotus, see Orwin (1994).

27. Ingram (1993, 320 n. 45) develops this thought significantly, as follows: "No set of political principles can assure against tyrannical outcomes. Democracy governed by the principles of discourse ethics is no exception, for the demand that all needs be validated through public discourse favors the political activist (and orator) over the domestic caretaker."

28. This is not to say that Machiavelli (1950, 85) posits some (much less one) other "end" of politics. In fact, *The Prince* countenances a heterogeneity of ends in politics, not the least of which is "the majesty of his dignity," in bearing and demeanor, of the prince himself.

29. Merleau-Ponty (1964, 223, emphasis added) is quite sure that Machiavelli is a humanist, but of a very particular kind. "If by humanism we mean a philosophy of the inner man," he writes, "Machiavelli is not a humanist. But if by humanism we mean a philosophy which *confronts* the relationship of *man to man* and the *constitution of a common situation* and a *common history* between men as a problem, then we have to say that Machiavelli formulated some of the conditions of any serious humanism." Also see Taylor (1988).

CHAPTER 8

1. Although I hope that I have made clear in chapter 7 that Habermas's theory of discourse ethics is not something that I support without reservation, I am most sympathetic to the democratic dimension of his political thought,

his sociological analysis of the transformation of the public sphere, and his expressly contemporary political writings (for example, 1997).

2. There are, of course, significant differerences between Arendt and Habermas. See Habermas (1977), as well as Benhabib (1992b); Bernstein (1983); Honneth (1982); and Villa (1992). Here I wish simply to underscore the distinctively modern commitments to action and an egalitarian politics of speech or communication (over and against work and strategic instrumentalism) that Arendt and Habermas share as theorists of the public realm. Of course, none of what follows implies that public realm theory has nothing to gain from numerous forms of contemporary critique, including Marxism, feminist theory, hermeneutics, genealogy, poststructuralism, various forms of democratic theory, and studies of discourse, ethics, and culture.

3. It is important to note, however, that various critics of public realm theory have lodged important objections to both Habermas's and Arendt's analyses of social labor and instrumental action. On Habermas, see Agger (1979); Eyerman and Shipway (1981); Giddens (1982); Honneth (1982); Keane (1975); McCarthy (1981); and Winfield (1975). On Arendt, see Pitkin (1998); Bakan (1979); Honneth (1982); Jay (1978); and Parekh (1979).

4. Assessing Habermas's conceptual strategy is a more difficult proposition that I cannot address here, but see chapter 7. His early distinction between work and interaction (later reformulated into the dichotomy strategic:communicative action) is more ambiguous than Arendt's. He allows, for instance, that work can be called praxis, yet he also insists upon the irreducibility of work and interaction, to *technē* and praxis (1973, 158 f.). Habermas (1977, 16; 1996a, 147–151) has criticized Arendt for screening all "strategic" elements out of politics. Yet at the same time he subsumes strategic action, along with instrumental action, within the sphere of "work," or purposive-rational action, and dissociates the latter (which is based on rational decision and the instrumentally efficient implementation of technical knowledge) from communicative action (based on complementarity, reciprocity, and mutual recognition). There is some evidence that Habermas has adjusted these views in his more recent work; but an extended journey into this Habermasian realm must be deferred. A helpful attempt to sort out, if not resolve, some of the ambiguities can be found in McCarthy (1981, 16–40); White (1988b, 44–47); Johnson (1991); and Ingram (1993).

5. I refer specifically to the Polish Solidarity movement, under the leadership of Adam Michnik, the great dissident and practical theorist who went on to become editor in chief of *Gazeta Wyborcza*, Poland's largest daily newspaper (personal conversation with Adam Michnik, University of Minnesota, Minneapolis, 1991). For Michnik's respectful view of Habermas, see Michnik and Habermas (1994).

6. Until recently, in fact, Weil's writings have been rather dimly lit in twentieth-century political thought, overshadowed by those of her more lumi-

nous French colleagues and perhaps by the oddity of her own remarkable life and intractable personality, which have received much attention. Fortunately, sustained studies of her political and social thought have now begun to appear. See, among others, Blum and Seidler (1989); Dietz (1989); Nevin (1991); McLellan (1990); and Winch (1989).

7. See Benhabib (1992b); d'Entreves (1989b); Honig (1992); Villa (1992); and Disch (1994). None of these commentators (although in some lively disagreements with each other about the "discursive," "communicative," "agonistic," "dramaturgical," or "narratival" status of the Arendtian public realm) contest the strategy that conceptually dichotomizes work:interaction or instrumental:communicative. As a result, they collectively promote an Arendtian perspective on politics that is (1) theoretically constrained, because it presumes the inapplicability of instrumental action to an action concept of politics, and (2) practically constrained, because it leans in the direction of an expressive (rather than a purposeful) orientation toward politics. Of course, Arendt's public realm theory is vulnerable to just this sort of speech-action interpretation and (mis)appropriation, and that is part of the problem.

8. Arendt (born in 1906) and Weil (born in 1909) both lived in Paris in the late 1930s. In the increasingly perilous atmosphere for European Jews, both emigrated to New York (residing, at different times, on Riverside Drive). Weil stayed in the United States for only seven months, leaving for London in 1941. Despite their intellectual affinities and a shared friendship with the philosopher Jean Wahl, Arendt and Weil traveled in different circles and apparently never met. There is no evidence to suggest that Weil, who died in 1943, knew anything of Arendt. Arendt (1958) was familiar with some of Weil's writings. (Arendt's close friend, Anne Mendelssohn Weil, was not related to Simone Weil.)

9. Without question, the threat of totalitarianism, obvious to Weil in the 1930s—and its unprecedented horrors, which were to become the pressure point of much of Arendt's subsequent political thought—also shaped their shared sense of "the process of world alienation" (Arendt 1958, 257). Yet it is also true that both of them understand totalitarianism within the context of technical progress, objectifying processes and dehumanizing institutions that distinguish late modern societies, rather than viewing these developments the other way around, as emanations of totalitarianism. Weil (1973, 119), for example, can write, "It is quite unfair to say . . . that fascism annihilates free thought; in reality it is the lack of free thought which makes it possible to impose by force official doctrines entirely devoid of meaning." A profoundly similar thesis informs Arendt's (1963) notion of the banality of evil in *Eichmann in Jerusalem*.

10. Weil's and Arendt's respective critiques of algebraic physics are matters of sufficient complexity to warrant study in their own right. Clearly, they share an implicit philosophy of psychology that is critical of attempts to reduce the mind to one or another aspect of a material world that can be fully described

by the facts of physics. What such descriptions leave out are phenomena that are *irreducible* to material explanations: thought and consciousness, perception, desires—in short, the intrinsically human world of the senses and appearances. Thus, a phenomenological (or at least perceptual) approach to reality informs both Weil's and Arendt's critiques of contemporary physics, and it is quite obviously carried through in their common admiration for geometry and the science of the Greeks, as well as their respective analyses of the history and social construction of science, the problem of objectivity (or the "Archimedean point"), and the violence that symbolic mathematics exerts upon "common sense" (see Arendt 1958, 1969; and Weil 1968). Thanks to one of her graduate students, Arendt was apparently familiar with Weil's essay "Reflections on Quantum Theory," which she acknowledges briefly in *The Human Condition* (1958, 287 n. 53).

11. Philosophers refer to this operation as following the "rules of syntax," according to which someone could be trained to do something automatically, using a set of rules, tables, and symbols, without understanding the meaning (or following the "rules of semantics") of the operation as a whole. Although the implications of such syntactical operations have spawned a great deal of philosophical debate in the computer age, Weil obviously anticipated them in 1933 and addressed them within the context of social and political life. Along these same lines, see Arendt's remarks (1958, 172) on the logical processes of "the newly invented electronic machines" and their "worldlessness," as well as Havel's discussion (1985, 32 f.) how "a formalized language deprived of semantic contact with reality" replaces reality with pseudoreality.

12. This is how Weil characterized "Reflections concerning the Causes of Liberty and Social Repression" (Weil 1973), the long essay she wrote in 1934, following a year of hard labor in various French factories located within the "Red belt" outside Paris.

13. Arendt (1958, 188; cf. 1969, 154) calls the theater "the political art *par excellence*" because it is "the only art whose sole subject is man in his relationship to others." The allusion to theater calls up the importance of dramatic display in Arendtian politics. It represents the notion of a space wherein human beings appear before each other—each as a uniquely distinct character—and enact a performance that ultimately becomes a part of "the storybook of mankind," a part of theater history (1958, 184). In the society of *animal laborans*, we might imagine not only mechanized petrification but also terribly dull theater.

14. With Weil's indebtedness to Greek philosophy in mind, I use the term *methodus* to convey the Greek *met hodos* (*meta*, after + *hodos*, way) and the *Oxford English Dictionary*'s (I.3) "a way of doing anything, especially according to a defined and regular plan; a mode of procedure." *Methodus* does not correspond to *OED* (II): "a systematic arrangement, order." The latter, as Wolin (1972) argues, is a usage that originated within the disciplines of logic and philosophy

in the sixteenth century, and places more emphasis on technique-oriented activity and scientific objectivity than I wish to convey.

15. Rather surprisingly, McLellan (1990, 72) contends that Weil "saw work as inherently servile, . . . as permitting not an embodiment, but a transcendence, of the human condition." This is quite at odds with the argument in "Reflections concerning the Causes of Liberty and Social Oppression" where Weil (1973) conceives of work as an activity through which the world is disclosed, not transcended. However, in essays and notebooks written later, especially in response to an intensifying mystical turn, Weil (1952b, 158) emphasizes "the spirituality of work." "Work makes us experience in the most exhausting manner the phenomenon of finality rebounding like a ball. . . . It is when man sees himself as a squirrel turning round and round in a circular cage that, if he does not lie to himself, he is close to salvation." Also see Dietz 1989, 122–125.

16. I am indebted to Winch's distinction (1989, 84 f.) between Weil's "thought-action account of freedom," in which "the point of the action lies in the character of the action itself," and a "desire-satisfaction account of freedom," where "the point of the action depends on its outcome." Arendt (1958, 154, 225) also pursues a thought-action account of freedom and criticizes utilitarianism for its "innate incapacity to understand the distinction between utility and meaningfulness." As we shall see, however, the dimensions of Arendt's account are significantly different from Weil's.

17. Weil recognizes that conceiving of a method and applying it are two different operations. Even in an emancipatory context, where the agent elaborates and executes the method or "plan of action" at issue, it may be "impossible to combine the examination of these difficulties with the accomplishment of the work" simultaneously (1973, 91 f.; Arendt 1958, 92, makes a similar point). But freedom is only in jeopardy when the elaboration of a method and its execution are decisively divided, and method transfers "its abode from the mind into the matter"—with which the subject works but over which he or she has no mental control (Weil 1973, 92).

18. Weil (1973, 92), for instance, admits that "in reality, there is nothing in common between the solution of a problem and the carrying out of an even perfectly methodical piece of work, between the sequence of ideas and the sequence of movements."

19. Beginning with the seafaring Athenians, sailing becomes a commonplace reference in the discourse and rhetoric of Western political thought. The focus, however, is almost always on a ship (not a boat), which serves as an analogue for the city, or the constitution of the state. As Nussbaum (1986, 59) notes, "The city-ship, in the tradition of the image, is something safely watertight, a barrier against imminent external dangers." In Weil's image (and in another I shall consider later), the focus is on the action context of sailing and hence upon the sheer complexity of a practical task—in which the boat is not a ship, a barrier against imminent dangers, or a locus of stability in wild waters

but rather the means through which dangers are encountered, with a greater or lesser measure of success.

20. In an age of electronic signals, automatic pilots, and computerized navigational instruments, this metaphor, too, loses its meaning. For an instructive parallel to a Weilian perspective on methodical thinking as a human form of navigation with mere "boards" at hand, see William Finnegan's fine essay (1992, 46) concerning the legendary surfer "Doc" Mark Renneker of San Francisco and the "ineffable skill" of "wave judgment" in surfboarding the pounding waters of Ocean Beach off Sloat Boulevard. Also see Aristotle, who calls upon the technique of sailing in his discussion of "hitting the mean" and moral virtue (1980, 46).

21. For an instructive discussion of Arendt's "interrogation and reappropriation" of Heidegger's *praxis/poiēsis* paradigm, see Villa 1996, 250-251.

22. Feminist critiques of Arendt's political thought have generally overlooked her gendering of the *vita activa*, where we find the oppositional alliance between *animal laborans* (gendered female) and *homo faber* (gendered male) set against the public realm and the condition of plurality. Under these terms, Arendtian politics may be interpreted as (1) an overcoming of the gendered alliance rooted in being and subjectivity through the actualization of doing and interaction, and (2) a destabilization of the symbolic order of feminine/masculine line through the proliferation of distinctive, individual speech-acts that are not *whats* (that is, representations of class, race, gender) but *whos* (uniquely distinct personalities). (See chapter 6.)

23. Arendt (1958, 157) seems to grasp this differentiation when she writes, "The issue at stake is, of course, not instrumentality, the use of means to achieve an end, . . . but rather the generalization of the fabrication experience [as] the ultimate standard[s] for life and the world of men." But she proceeds to characterize instrumentality as "the experience of ends and means, as it is present in fabrication." So although she initially differentiates instrumentality in work from instrumentality as a generalized phenomenon, she nevertheless reverts to a concept of instrumentality that is wholly informed by her (negative) concept of work.

24. Winch (1989, 99) does not overstate when he argues that Weil's theory of action views "the individual and his or her thinking in uncompromisingly individualistic terms." Weil (1973, 82) argues, for example, "Several human minds cannot become united in one collective mind, and the expressions 'collective soul,' 'collective thought,' so commonly employed nowadays, are altogether devoid of meaning." At a later stage in her work (1952a), when she turns more toward ethos, habituation, and the "need for roots" in order to formulate the content of free and ethical life, Weil's negative view of collectivities relaxes. But to say that she arrives at a concept of emancipatory dialogic interaction would be a gross exaggeration. For a discussion of Weil's antipolitics, see Dietz (1989); and Ignatieff (1990).

25. On a similar point, see Knauer (1985, 187) who also argues that "Arendt's account of the *vita activa* needs reformulation as a theory of democratic praxis." His useful reformulation of *praxis* posts a dialectical relation among *labor:work:interaction* that, he argues (90), Arendt herself recognized but did not adequately develop. Thus "the task is to illuminate the ways in which beings gathered in political community could choose to live their lives together as workers and laborers . . . so as to nurture political community." By infusing an action dimension into labor and work, Knauer humanizes Arendt's categories and translocates action (politics) as "political community." The problem with this approach, however, is that it collapses action into labor and work and then calcifies Arendt's concept of politics into a communitarian normative ideal. It thereby evades precisely what needs to be examined, namely, Arendt's concept of politics as a concrete, practical *activity*.

26. In his thoughtful essay, Lawrence Biskowski (1993, 880) argues that there is substantive purpose in Arendt's politics, which is "inherently connected to care for the world, not only for what the world thinks . . . but for what the world will be like in the wake of one's acting." Thus we find substantive ethical content for Arendtian politics in the doctrine of *amor mundi* (887). In speech and action, citizens keep alive the space of appearances itself. I agree with Biskowski's claim that the concept of "care for the world" that informs Arendt's understanding of politics carries substantive ethical content. What I am interested in here, however, is the substantive *cognitive* content of Arendtian politics. Since Arendt (1958, 170 f.) identifies cognition as "the pursuit of an aim which can be set by practical considerations" and aligns it with *homo faber*, fabrication, and scientific processes, I think we have to conclude that cognition plays a very small role in Arendtian politics. Despite its ethical purpose, then, I want to maintain that Arendt's politics is inadequate as a cognitive purposeful enterprise.

27. As Knauer (1985) and d'Entreves (1989b) correctly note in criticizing Jay (1978), Arendt does not exclude instrumentalism from politics. But my point is that instrumentality is always formulated negatively. What Arendt and her commentators seem to share is a congealed concept of instrumental action that cannot distinguish instrumentality as utilitarian objectification from instrumentality as purposeful performance. This is clear in Knauer's (1980, 733) rhetorical query, "Why should [Arendt] emphasize the instrumental aspect of all politics when her aim was to overcome its instrumentalization and trivialization?" Also see d'Entreves's (1989b, 333, 335) observations that action is *constrained and hampered* by instrumental concerns that can never be fully "eliminated" and that politics is emancipatory only when it is able to "transcend mere instrumental concerns" (emphasis added).

28. Along these lines, Wiggins (1978, 150) seeks to recover a dimension of deliberation over ends in Aristotelian practical reasoning. Aristotle, he argues, "has been incorrectly interpreted or translated . . . as saying that delib-

eration is not of ends. He is always prepared to describe practical reason . . . in its concern with the question what objectives a man *is* to form (in general, of here and now), and what particular concerns he is to put first, in the light of how the Good appears to him." With this argument in mind, we might understand Weilian methodical thinking (despite her odd dislike of Aristotle) as fully in keeping with some aspects of Aristotelian *phronésis*, although elaborating the linkages is beyond my scope here.

29. I hasten to add that although I find this metaphor for political activity appealing, I do not share Oakeshott's commitment to a "tradition of behavior" as the locus for political life. The notion rests uneasily with the technicization of modern life that has, with tragic consequences, forged a tradition of its own and supplanted precisely those traditions that Oakeshott wants to recover. For an insightful critique of Oakeshott's politics, see Pitkin (1974) and Gerenser (2000).

30. There is a wide array of views concerning the ethical dimension of Arendt's politics. Knauer (1980); Hinchman (1984b); Isaac (1989); and Biskowski (1993)—in various ways—make strong cases for locating an ethical commitment to human dignity, mutuality, and civility in Arendt's condition of plurality and concept of world. Kateb (1984); Jay (1978); and Villa (1992)—in various ways—make strong cases against it. I shall not attempt a consideration of this debate here. Nor is this the place to undertake the philosophical task of justifying the reconciliation of instrumental and strategic action with dialogic or communcative interaction, but see chapter 7 for a start.

31. These repetitious and relentless patterns are also the domain in which "questionnaires and motivation research" and other "gadgets in the arsenal of the social sciences" operate (Arendt 1958, 8). Arendt's phenomenological rescue of action must, therefore, be understood as a form of resistance against a world in which the theories of behaviorism "could actually become true" (1958, 322).

32. In a symposium on intellectuals and social change in Central and Eastern Europe, Doris Lessing (1992, 727) noted that "revolutionary politics, the house committees, the vigilante slogans, are intoxicating drugs." She also recalled one European commentator's remarks about "demonstrations that seem to have little point . . . from the point of view of actually achieving something. . . . The ends are not the point. The means are the point." These remarks serve to remind us that the politics of revolutionary, theatrical spontaneity are as potentially susceptible to meaninglessness and excess (including murderous excess) as the politics of "ends" and ideology that Arendt powerfully condemns. Indeed, these are often elements of the same complex of experience. Compare the violence of Bucharest's revolutionary politics in 1989, for example, to the "velvet" revolutionary politics of Prague, or even Berlin.

33. Actually, as Jon Pareles reports in his obituary of Milan Hlavsa (who died of cancer in January 2001, at the age of forty-nine), the Plastic People's

songs were generally "surreal and black-humored" but not particularly political. Their first album, *Egon Bondy's Happy Hearts Club Banned*, was released by Czech émigrés in France (Egon Bondy, a poet who had been banned since the Russian invasion, wrote the lyrics). As for the group's emergence as the band that galvanized a movement for human rights and democracy in Czechoslovakia, Hlavsa remarked, "We felt more like a guerrilla group than a rock 'n' roll band. We didn't play this role intentionally—it was forced upon us from outside" (Pareles 2001, A19).

CHAPTER 9

1. See, for example, Fackenheim (1978); Fein (1979); Pawelczynska (1979); Kren and Rappoport (1980); Friedlander and Milton (1980); Aries (1981); Bauer and Rotenstreich (1981); Dawidowicz (1981); Hilberg (1985); Gilbert (1985); Rosenberg and Myers (1988); Goldhagen (1996); and Hartman (1996).

2. See Bauman (1989) on how the presentation of the Holocaust "as something that happened to the Jews; as an event in *Jewish* history" belittles and misjudges this event by making it "comfortably uncharacteristic and sociologically inconsequential . . . the continuation of antisemitism through other means." In this way, the Holocaust can be "shunted into the familiar stream" of persecutions and oppressions that mark human history. Thereby, consideration of its unprecedented implications for humanity and modernity can be evaded.

3. See in particular, Arendt (1945, 1946a, 1950a, 1950b, 1950c, 1951, 1953a, and 1954); all republished in 1994.

4. By grouping *Origins* and *Eichmann* together, as responses to the first problem of comprehending totalitarianism and the Holocaust, I do not mean to imply that there are no significant differences between them as historical or political projects. Indeed, Arendt's own struggle to comprehend totalitarianism might fruitfully be understood, as Pitkin argues (1998, 208), as "a series of shifts within an ongoing ambivalence" revealed in one way in *Origins* and another in *Eichmann*, especially concerning the problem of evil and mythologizing the horrible. My rather more limited point is that, whatever else differentiates them, *Origins* and *Eichmann* might be cast as efforts to "come to terms with" the factual reality of the Holocaust, whereas *The Human Condition* needs to be understood in a different way, as a project directed toward the restorative surmounting of the "factual territory" (that is, German complicity and Jewish absolute hatred) that Auschwitz had left in its terrible wake.

5. See, for example, Schwartz (1989); Pitkin (1998, 112–114); Benhabib (1996b, 199–215); and Villa (1996). Villa also provides an instructive (critical) overview of the various neo-Aristotelian (republican), Nietzschean (agonistic),

and Habermasian (discursive) appropriations of Arendt's concept of political action in the secondary literature. (See also chapter 6.)

6. An important exception is Margaret Canovan (1992, 7) who explicitly seeks to explore the connections between Arendt's writings on totalitarianism and *The Human Condition*. Canovan asserts that "virtually the entire agenda of Arendt's political thought was set by her reflections on the political catastrophes of the mid-century." She interprets the central concepts of *The Human Condition* (especially "labor" and "society") as "moulded by [an] interpretation of totalitarianism," and in response to its "analogues": "the belief that everything is possible, and . . . that everything is determined within an inevitable process" (103). Similarly, Barnouw (*Visible Spaces*) argues that the need "to strain against necessity . . . fed by the experience of total war and holocaust" was the main source of Arendt's distinction between labor and work in *The Human Condition*. Both Canovan and Barnouw recognize Arendt's "middle work" not only as a project addressing mass technocracy in late modernity but also as an effort, in Barnouw's words (1990, 195), to articulate "a culturally secured quality of life which would defeat the senselessness of past mass destruction of human life." Richard Bernstein (1996) also observes (more briefly) that "most of the motifs of [Arendt's] understanding of politics" in *The Human Condition* "are worked out in her attempt to comprehend the events of twentieth-century totalitarianism." I wish to endorse all of these insights by way of taking them (and the meaning of "comprehension") in a rather different direction.

7. The capacity for "moving on" is a process for which English has no single word but German has two (lengthy) ones: *Geschichtsaufarbeitung* and *Vergangenheitsbewältigung*. Both capture the idea of "treating," "working through," "coming to terms with," or even "overcoming" the past, as Felman implies in the reference to "moving on." I do not wish to confuse this idea with the effort to find some way of distilling hope, or at least consolation, from the vast sea of despair and systematic extermination that was the Holocaust. If there is any element of "triumph of the spirit" to be found here, it is not within the Holocaust itself but rather in relation to its aftermath and the surmounting of its pernicious legacy of evil, guilt, hatred, and recrimination.

8. This moving image of reunification I draw from Jaspers's remark, quoted by Arendt ([1948] 1994, 216): "We live as if we stood knocking at gates that are still closed to us. Today something may perhaps be taking place in the pure personal realm that cannot yet found a world order because it is only given to individuals, but which will perhaps someday found such an order when these individuals have been brought together from their dispersion." Jaspers, in turn, may have adapted this language of "dispersion" and reconciliation from Augustine, who writes movingly in the *Confessions* of his own self-dispersion: "your right hand upholds me, my Lord, in your son, who rejoins dividedness in your oneness, that through him I may comprehend my comprehender that from days of prior dispersion I may collect myself into identity, putting the old

behind me, not yet tugged toward future temporal things . . ." (in Wills 1999a, 95). Perhaps here it is worth recalling that Arendt wrote her dissertation, *Der Liebesbegriffe be Augustin*, on Augustine's thought (Young-Bruehl 1982, 490–500).

9. This starting point is not as unusual as it may at first appear. Arendt often referred to Nietzsche and was certainly influenced by his thinking. A most provocative footnote in *The Human Condition* (1958, 245 n. 83) also provides a linkage between Arendt and Nietzsche on the meaning of memory and forgetting. Arendt refers to "unique" insights of Nietzsche's that mark off human from animal life and that are "frequently overlooked" by scholars. They are found in the first two aphorisms of the second treatise in *On the Genealogy of Morals* ([1887] 1969, 57–60). Although Arendt does not proceed to identify these insights, the curious reader will discover that in them Nietzsche addresses (1) "forgetting" as the "positive faculty of repression," and "active forgetfulness" as the "preserver of psychic order, repose, and etiquette; and (2) the origination of "responsibility" in the emancipated individual's "right" to make promises.

10. The term "imagistic symbol" comes from Harry Berger (1988, 460–461).

11. Nietzsche's German reads: *noch einmal wie eine verklarende Abendrothe aufleuchten,, bei der man den schlimmen Tag vergessen soll, der ihr vorangieng.* The German word *vergessen* can mean, in addition to "to forget," "to leave (behind)," "to overlook," "to omit," or "to neglect." Perhaps it is instructive that Nietzsche chose this word, for unlike other German expressions for forgetting (for example, *nicht denken an nicht bedenken: velernen) vergessen* does not seem to imply actively or intentionally blocking something out or choosing not to remember it, but rather suggests forgetting that simply happens or occurs. (I thank Dan Hope for clarifying the point for me.) The significance of memory, remembrance, nonforgetting, and memorialization is a central theme in Holocaust studies, which tend primarily (and variously) to focus the problem as one of "coming to terms with the past." See, for example, Friedlander (1979); Vidal-Nacquet ([1985], 1992); Delbo [1985] 1990); Langer (1991); Young (1993); and Hartman (1994).

12. Arendt's critics are by no means incorrect in emphasizing the significance she places upon the "prephilosophical Greek experience of action and speech," the Hellenic world of the Greek *polis*, and the glory of Periclean Athens, "which bestowed upon politics a dignity which even today has not altogether disappeared" (1958, 207, 205). What I wish to suggest, however, is that although accurate as descriptions, the critics' renderings of Arendt's recourse to Hellas as evidence of utopianism or an antiquated nostalgia for a forgotten past or a masculinist fixation with heroic glory (see chapter 6) prematurely and hastily convert description to (negative) evaluation, without adequately attending to Arendt's own disparagement of nostalgic yearnings or, more important, without considering the complicated way in which the

images of the Greek *polis* may be operating in *The Human Condition* as part of an interplay with the aftermath of the Holocaust.

13. Harry Berger's work (1988) on conspicuous exclusion in the art of Johannes Vermeer is appropriated by Lawrence Weschler in his (1995) essay on the Yugoslav War Crimes Tribunal in The Hague. Weschler suggests that when Vermeer was painting those images, otherwise the very emblem of peacefulness and serenity, "*all Europe was Bosnia*" (57). Thus war is present-as-missing, a felt absence, in Vermeer's art. Viewed within this political context, Vermeer "can be seen . . . to have been asserting or *inventing* the very idea of peace," Weschler suggests, in response to the "horrors of his age," which are ever present as "felt absence" in his art (59).

14. Jaspers's remark about the lightness and transparency that mark what is simultaneously the "great seriousness" of *The Human Condition* echoes another intriguing hermeneutic theme that Berger (1988, 458–459) develops under the terms "heterocosmic thought and the second world" and finds in certain works of Renaissance art, especially Vermeer's. Heterocosmic thought "withdraws from the given world to alternate frames of reference," Berger suggests, and presents an alternate "imaginary world" in "an attitude of serious playing; *serio ludere* means playing seriously with full knowledge; however seriously you play, you are only playing." The attitude of reflexive awareness embedded in playing seriously makes the imaginary world "secure for the systole of withdrawal but not secure enough to discourage or prohibit the diastole of return." I want to build upon both Jaspers's comment and Berger's notion to suggest that Arendt's image of the "space of appearance" may be appreciated as precisely such a form of withdrawal and return, as heterocosmic theorizing.

15. If we take into consideration Joanne Jacobson's (1996, 31) remark that "the most profound legacy of the Holocaust may be silence; language's promise of order and beauty seems insulting," then the conspicuous exclusion—the palpable but unspoken presence—of this trauma in *The Human Condition* becomes an even more poignant and powerful aspect of Arendt's writing. The most compelling Holocaust texts, as Geoffrey Hartman observes and Jacobson reports (31), "are those whose authors have intentionally let the difficulties of representation drift close to the surface . . . their art makes us feel there is something that cannot be presented." In this sense, Jacobson is correct to insist that no matter how compelling they may be, trauma on the scale of the Holocaust remains at odds, or at least in a terribly uneasy relation, with explicit narrative and symbol and image.

16. Arendt (1958, 80) notes that "The German *Arbeit* applied originally only to farm labor executed by serfs and not to the work of the craftsman, which was called *Werk*." (See also chapter 5.)

17. Of course, I have offered similar interpretations of Arendt's action concept of politics in chapters 2 and 5 (and to a lesser degree in chapter 8). To

the extent to which this chapter moves away from interpreting Arendt's concept of action in terms of a participatory democratic politics, it is itself a "turning operation" on what has come before (but by no means a repudiation of my previous interpretations).

18. See, for example, Benhabib (1996b, chap. 6); d'Entreves (1994, chap. 4); Dossa (1989); Hansen (1993); Knauer (1985); and Parekh (1981). I am not suggesting that there is a uniform line on the meaning of Arendtian politics or that Arendt's commentators are not fully appreciative of what Canovan (1992, 131) calls "the very considerable complexities" in Arendt's concept of action.

19. See Arendt (1958, 181–186, 194, 198–199, 208, 211).

20. "No doubt this concept of action is highly individualistic, as we would say today. It stresses the urge toward self-disclosure at the expense of all other factors and therefore remains relatively untouched by the predicament of unpredictability" (Arendt 1958, 194).

21. Here I think it is important to reassert that I am not suggesting that we interpret the healing illusion of the space of appearance as an effort on Arendt's part to draw some positive lesson from the Holocaust. I tend to share Young's (1998, 696) view that "Neither art nor narrative redeems the Holocaust with meaning—didactic, moral, or otherwise"; nor do I think that Arendt's space of appearance fulfills this function in any way.

Bibliography

Acklesberg, Martha. 1983. "Sisters or Comrades? The Politics of Friends and Families." In *Families, Politics, and Public Policy: A Feminist Dialogue on Women and the State*, ed. Irene Diamond. New York: Longman.

Adams, Parveen, and Jeff Minson. 1990. "The 'Subject' of Feminism." In *The Woman in Question*, ed. Parveen Adams and Elizabeth Cowie. Cambridge: MIT Press.

Agger, Ben. 1979. "Work and Authority in Marcuse and Habermas." *Human Studies* 2:191–208.

Alcoff, Linda. 1988. "Cultural Feminism versus Post-Structuralism: The Identity Crisis in Feminist Theory." *Signs: Journal of Women in Culture and Society* 13:405–436.

Alford, Fred. 1985. "Is Jürgen Habermas's Reconstructive Science Really a Science?" *Theory and Society* 14:321–340.

Althusser, Louis. 1999. *Machiavelli and Us*, ed. F. Matheron, trans. G. Elliott. London: Verso.

Annas, Julia. 1977. "Mill and the Subjection of Women." *Philosophy* 52:179–194.

Arendt, Hannah. [1945] 1994. "Organized Guilt and Universal Responsibility." In *Essays in Understanding, 1930–1954*, ed. Jerome Kohn. New York: Harcourt Brace.

———.[1946a] 1994. "The Image of Hell." In *Essays in Understanding, 1930–1954*, ed. Jerome Kohn. New York: Harcourt Brace.

———. [1946b] 1994. "What Is Existential Philosophy?" In *Essays in Understanding, 1930–1954*, ed. Jerome Kohn. New York: Harcourt Brace.

———. [1948] 1994. Dedication to Karl Jaspers. In *Essays in Understanding, 1930–1954*, ed. Jerome Kohn. New York: Harcourt Brace.

———. [1950a] 1994. "Social Science Techniques and the Study of Concentration Camps." In *Essays in Understanding, 1930–1954*, ed. Jerome Kohn. New York: Harcourt Brace.

———. [1950b] 1994. "The Aftermath of Nazi Rule: Report from Germany." In *Essays in Understanding, 1930–1954*, ed. Jerome Kohn. New York: Harcourt Brace.

———. [1950c] 1994. "The Eggs Speak Up." In *Essays in Understanding, 1930–1954*, ed. Jerome Kohn. New York: Harcourt Brace.

———. 1951. *The Origins of Totalitarianism.* New York: Harcourt Brace.

———. [1951] 1994. "At Table with Hitler." In *Essays In Understanding, 1930–1954*, ed. Jerome Kohn. New York: Harcourt Brace.

———. [1953a] 1994. "Mankind and Terror." In *Essays in Understanding, 1930–1954*, ed. Jerome Kohn. New York: Harcourt Brace.

———. [1953b] 1994. "A Reply to Eric Voegelin." In *Essays in Understanding, 1930–1954*, ed. Jerome Kohn. New York: Harcourt Brace.

———. [1953c] 1994. "The Ex-Communists." In *Essays in Understanding, 1930–1954*, ed. Jerome Kohn. New York: Harcourt Brace.

———. [1954] 1994. "Understanding and Politics." In *Essays in Understanding, 1930–1954*, ed. Jerome Kohn. New York: Harcourt Brace.

———. 1958. *The Human Condition.* Chicago: University of Chicago Press.

———. 1963. *Eichmann in Jerusalem: A Report on the Banality of Evil.* New York: Penguin.

———. 1965. *On Revolution.* New York: Viking.

———. 1968. *Men in Dark Times.* New York: Harcourt, Brace and World.

———. 1969. *Between Past and Future: Eight Exercises in Political Thought.* New York: Viking.

———. 1974. *Rahel Varnhagen: The Life of a Jewish Woman.* New York: Harcourt Brace Jovanovich.

———. 1978. *The Jew as Pariah: Jewish Identity and Politics in the Modern Age*, ed. Ron Feldman. New York: Grove.

———. 1994. *Essays in Understanding, 1930–1954*, ed. Jerome Kohn. New York: Harcourt Brace.

Arendt, Hannah, and Karl Jaspers. 1992. *Hannah Arendt–Karl Jaspers: Correspondence, 1926–1969*, ed. L. Kohler and H. Saner. New York: Harcourt Brace Jovanovich.

Ariès, Philippe. 1962. *Centuries of Childhood: A Social History of Family Life*, trans. Robert Baldick. New York: Vintage.

————. 1981. *The Hour of Our Death*, trans. Helen Weaver. New York: Knopf.

Aristotle. 1962. *The Politics of Aristotle*, ed. and trans. Ernest Barker. Oxford: Oxford University Press.

————. 1980. *Nicomachean Ethics*. Trans. David Ross. Oxford: Oxford University Press.

Ascher, Carol. 1987. "Simone de Beauvoir—Mother of Us All." *Social Text* 17:107–109.

Ash, Timothy Garton. 1990. *The Magic Lantern*. New York: Random House.

————. 1995. "Prague: Intellectuals and Politicians." *New York Review of Books*, 12 January, 34–41.

Atwood, Margaret. 1986. *The Handmaid's Tale*. New York: Simon and Schuster.

Augustine. 1960. *The Confessions of St. Augustine*, trans. John K. Ryan. New York: Image/Doubleday and Co.

Bair, Deirdre. 1990. *Simone de Beauvoir: A Biography*. New York: Summit Books.

Bakan, Mildred. 1979. "Hannah Arendt's Concepts of Labor and Work." In *Hannah Arendt: Recovery of the Public World*, ed. Melvyn A. Hill. New York: St. Martin's.

Barber, Benjamin R. 1996. "Foundationalism and Democracy." In *Democracy and Difference: Contesting the Boundaries of the Political*, ed. Seyla Benhabib. Princeton: Princeton University Press.

Barber, Benjamin. 1984. *Strong Democracy: Participatory Politics for a New Age*. Berkeley: University of California Press.

Barnouw, Dagmar. 1990. *Visible Spaces: Hannah Arendt and the German-Jewish Experience*. Baltimore: Johns Hopkins University Press.

Barrett, Michèle. 1980. *Women's Oppression Today: Problems in Marxist Feminist Analysis*. London: Verso.

Bauer, Yehuda, and Nathan Rotenstreich. 1981. *The Holocaust as Historical Experience*. New York: Holmes and Meier.

Bauman, Zygmunt. 1989. *Modernity and the Holocaust*. Ithaca, N.Y.: Cornell University Press.

————. 1999. *In Search of Politics*. Stanford: Stanford University Press.

Beauvoir, Simone de. [1947] 1952. *America Day by Day*, trans. Patrick Dudley. London: Duckworth.

————. [1948] 1991. *The Ethics of Ambiguity*, trans. Bernard Frechtman. New York: Citadel.

————. [1949] 1974. *The Second Sex*, ed. and trans. H. M. Parshley. New York: Vintage.

Beiner, Ronald. 1989. "Do We Need a Philosophical Ethics? Theory, Prudence, and the Primacy of *Ethos*." *The Philosophical Forum* 20:234–243.

————, ed. 1995. *Theorizing Citizenship*. Albany: State University of New York Press.

Benhabib, Seyla. 1990. "Communicative Ethics and Current Controversies in
    Practical Philosophy." In *The Communicative Ethics Controversy*, ed.
    Seyla Benhabib and Fred Dallmayr. Cambridge: MIT Press.
———. 1992a. *Situating the Self: Gender, Community, and Postmodernism in
    Contemporary Ethics.* New York: Routledge.
———. 1992b. "Models of Public Space: Hannah Arendt, the Liberal
    Tradition, and Jürgen Habermas." In *Habermas and the Public Sphere*,
    ed. Craig Calhoun. Cambridge: MIT Press.
———. 1993. "Feminist Theory and Hannah Arendt's Concept of Public
    Space." *History of the Human Sciences* 6:98–114.
———, ed. 1996a. *Democracy and Difference: Contesting the Boundaries of the
    Political.* Princeton: Princeton University Press.
———. 1996b. *The Reluctant Modernism of Hannah Arendt.* Thousand Oaks,
    Calif: Sage.
Berger, Harry. 1988. "Conspicuous Exclusion in Vermeer: An Essay in
    Renaissance Pastoral." In *Second World and Green World: Studies in
    Renaissance Fiction-Making.* Berkeley: University of California Press.
Berlin, Isaiah. 1969. *Four Essays on Liberty.* Oxford: Oxford University Press.
———. 1982. "The Originality of Machiavelli." In *Against the Current: Essays
    in the History of Ideas.* New York: Viking.
Berman, Marshall. 1983. "Feminism, Community, Freedom." *Dissent*
    30:247–249.
Bernstein, Richard. 1983. *Beyond Objectivism and Relativism: Science,
    Hermeneutics, and Praxis.* Philadelphia: University of Pennsylvania
    Press.
———. 1996. *Hannah Arendt and the Jewish Question.* Cambridge: MIT Press.
Bickford, Susan. 1996. *The Dissonance of Democracy: Listening, Conflict, and
    Citizenship.* Ithaca, N.Y.: Cornell University Press.
Biskowski, Lawrence J. 1993. "Practical Foundations for Political Judgment:
    Arendt on Action and World." *Journal of Politics* 55:867–887.
Blum, Lawrence. 1982. "Kant and Hegel's Moral Paternalism: A Feminist
    Response." *Canadian Journal of Philosophy* 12:287–302.
Blum, Lawrence, and Victor Seidler. 1989. *A Truer Liberty: Simone Weil and
    Marxism.* London: Routledge and Kegan Paul.
Boling, Patricia. 1996. *Privacy and the Politics of Intimate Life.* Ithaca, N.Y.:
    Cornell University Press.
Botwinick, Aryeh. 1993. *Postmodernism and Democratic Theory.* Philadelphia:
    Temple University Press.
Bourdieu, Pierre. 2001. *Masculine Domination*, trans. Richard Nice. Stanford:
    Stanford University Press.
Braidotti, Rosi. 1991. *Patterns of Dissonance: A Study of Women in Contemporary
    Philosophy*, trans. Elizabeth Guild. New York: Routledge.

Brennan, Teresa, and Carole Pateman. 1979. "'Mere Auxiliaries to the Commonwealth': Women and the Origins of Liberalism." *Political Studies* 27:183–200.

Bridges, Thomas. 1994. *The Culture of Citizenship Inventing Postmodern Civic Culture*. Albany: State University of New York Press.

Brightman, Carol. 1992. *Writing Dangerously: Mary McCarthy and Her World*. New York: Clarkson Potter.

Brown, Wendy. 1988. *Manhood and Politics*. Totowa, N.J.: Rowman and Littlefield.

———. 1995. *States of Injury: Power and Freedom in Late Modernity*. Princeton: Princeton University Press.

———. 1998. "The Impossibility of Women's Studies." In *differences: A Journal of Feminist Cultural Studies*. 9:79–101.

Butler, Judith. 1986. "Sex and Gender in Simone de Beauvoir's *Second Sex*." In "Simone de Beauvoir: Witness to a Century," ed. Hélène Vivienne Wenzel, special issue of *Yale French Studies* 72:35–49.

———. 1987. "Variations on Sex and Gender: Beauvoir, Wittig and Foucault." In *Feminism as Critique*, ed. Seyla Benhabib and Drucilla Cornell. Minneapolis: University of Minnesota Press.

———. 1991. "Contingent Foundations: Feminism and the Question of 'Postmodernism.'" *Praxis International* 11:150–165.

———. 2000. *Antigone's Claim: Kinship between Life and Death*. New York: Columbia University Press.

Butler, Melissa A. 1978. "Early Liberal Roots of Feminism: John Locke and the Attack on Patriarchy." *American Political Science Review* 72:135–150.

Canovan, Margaret. 1992. *Hannah Arendt: A Reinterpretation of Her Political Thought*. Cambridge: Cambridge University Press.

Card, Claudia. 1990. "Lesbian Attitudes and *The Second Sex*." In *Hypatia Reborn: Essays in Feminist Philosophy*, ed. Azizah Y. Al-Hibri and Margaret A. Simons. Bloomington: Indiana University Press.

Castoriadis, Cornelius. 1992. "Individual, Society, Rationality, History." In *Between Totalitarianism and Postmodernity*, ed. Peter Beilharz, Gillian Robinson, and John Rundell. Cambridge: MIT Press.

Chambers, Simone. 1996. *Reasonable Democracy: Jurgen Habermas and the Politics of Discourse*. Ithaca, N.Y.: Cornell University Press.

Chodorow, Nancy. 1978. *The Reproduction of Mothering: Psychoanalysis and the Sociology of Gender*. Berkeley: University of California Press.

Clark, Lorenne M. G. 1979. "Women and Locke: Who Owns the Apples in the Garden of Eden?" In *The Sexism of Social and Political Theory*, ed. Lorenne M. G. Clark and Lynda Lange. Toronto: University of Toronto Press.

Cocks, Joan. 1984. "Wordless Emotions: Some Critical Reflections on Radical Feminism." *Politics and Society* 13:27–57.

Cogan, Marc. 1981. *The Human Thing: The Speeches and Principles of Thucydides's History*. Chicago: University of Chicago Press.

Cohen, Joshua, and Joel Rogers. 1983. *On Democracy: Toward a Transformation of American Society*. New York: Penguin.

Crittenden, Ann. 2001. *The Price of Motherhood: Why the Most Important Job in the World Is Still the Least Valued*. New York: Metropolitan Books.

Culler, Jonathan. 1985. "Communicative Competence and Normative Force." *New German Critique* 35:133–144.

Cutting-Gray, Joanne. 1993. "Hannah Arendt, Feminism, and the Politics of Alterity: 'What Will We Lose If We Win'?" *Hypatia* 8:35–54.

Dalla Costa, Maria, and Selma James. 1972. *The Power of Women and the Subversion of Community*. Bristol, England: Falling Wall Press.

Dallery, Arleen B. 1990. "Sexual Embodiment: Beauvoir and French Feminism." In *Hypatia Reborn: Essays in Feminist Philosophy*, ed. Azizah Y. Al-Hibri and Margaret A. Simons. Bloomington: Indiana University Press.

Daly, Mary. 1978. *Gyn/Ecology: The Metaethics of Radical Feminism*. Boston: Beacon.

Dawidowicz, Lucy S. 1981. *The Holocaust and the Historians*. Cambridge: Harvard University Press.

Delbo, Charlotte. [1985] 1990. *Days and Memory*, trans. Rosette C. Lamont. Marlboro, Vt.: Marlboro Press.

d'Entreves, Maurizio Passerin. 1989a. "Agency, Identity, and Culture: Hannah Arendt's Conception of Citizenship." *Praxis International* 9:1–24.

———. 1989b. "Freedom, Plurality, Solidarity: Hannah Arendt's Theory of Action." *Philosophy and Social Criticism* 15:319–350.

———. 1994. *The Political Philosophy of Hannah Arendt*. London: Routledge.

Dewey, John. [1929] 1960. *The Quest for Certainty*. New York: Capricorn Books.

———. [1939] 1993. "Democratic Ends Need Democratic Methods for Their Realization." Reprinted in *John Dewey: The Political Writings*, ed. Ian Shapiro and Debra Morris. Indianapolis: Hackett.

Diamond, Irene, ed. 1983. *Families, Politics, and Public Policy: A Feminist Dialogue on Women and the State*. New York: Longman.

Dietz, Mary G. 1985. "Citizenship with a Feminist Face: The Problem with Maternal Thinking." *Political Theory* 13:19–38.

———. 1986. "Trapping the Prince: Machiavelli and the Politics of Deception." *American Political Science Review* 80:777–799.

———. 1987. "Context Is All: Feminism and Theories of Citizenship." *Daedalus* 116:1–24.

———. 1989. *Between the Human and the Divine: The Political Thought of Simone Weil*. Totowa, N.J.: Rowman and Littlefield.

———. 1990. "Hannah Arendt and Feminist Politics." In *Feminist Interpretations and Political Theory*, ed. Mary Lyndon Shanley and Carole Pateman. Cambridge, Mass.: Polity Press.

Dijkstra, Sandra. 1980. "Simone de Beauvoir and Betty Friedan: The Politics of Omission." *Feminist Studies* 6:290–303.

Dinnerstein, Dorothy. 1977. *The Mermaid and the Minotaur*. New York: Harper Colophon.

Disch, Lisa Jane. 1994. *Hannah Arendt and the Limits of Philosophy*. Ithaca, N.Y.: Cornell University Press.

———. 1995. "On Friendship in 'Dark Times.'" In *Feminist Interpretations of Hannah Arendt*, ed. Bonnie Honig. University Park: Pennsylvania State University Press.

Di Stefano, Christine. 1991. *Configurations of Masculinity: A Feminist Perspective on Modern Political Theory*. Ithaca, N.Y.: Cornell University Press.

Dossa, Shiraz. 1989. *The Public Realm and the Public Self: The Political Theory of Hannah Arendt*. Waterloo, Ont.: Wilfred Laurier University Press.

Echols, Alice. 1989. *Daring to Be Bad: Radical Feminism in America, 1967–1975*. Minneapolis: University of Minnesota Press.

Edmond, Wendy, and Suzi Fleming, eds. 1975. *All Work and No Pay: Women, Housework and the Wages Due*. Bristol, England: Falling Wall Press.

Ehrenreich, Barbara. 1983. "On Feminism, Family, and Community." *Dissent* 30:103–106.

Eisenstein, Zillah, ed. 1979a. *Capitalist Patriarchy and the Case for Socialist Feminism*. New York: Monthly Review Press.

———. 1979b. "Developing a Theory of Capitalist Patriarchy and Socialist Feminism." In *Capitalist Patriarchy and the Case for Socialist Feminism*, ed. Zillah Eisenstein. New York: Monthly Review Press.

———. 1981. *The Radical Future of Liberal Feminism*. New York: Longman.

Elshtain, Jean Bethke. 1979. "Feminists against the Family." *The Nation*, 17 November, 497–500.

———. 1981. *Public Man, Private Woman*. Princeton: Princeton University Press.

———. 1982a. "Antigone's Daughters." *Democracy* 2:46–59.

———. 1982b. "Feminism, Family and Community." *Dissent* 29:442–449.

———. 1982c. "Feminist Discourse and Its Discontents: Language, Power, and Meaning." *Signs: Journal of Women in Culture and Society* 3:603–621.

———. 1982d. "On Beautiful Souls, Just Warriors, and Feminist Consciousness." *Women's Studies International Forum* 5:341–348.

———. 1983a. "On 'the Family Crisis.'" *Democracy* 3:137–139.

———. 1983b. "On Feminism, Family and Community: A Response to Ehrenreich." *Dissent* 30:106–109.

———. 1986. *Meditations on Modern Political Thought: Masculine/Feminine Themes from Luther to Arendt*. New York: Praeger.

———. 1989. "Antigone's Daughters Reconsidered: Continuing Reflections on Women, Politics, and Power." In *Life-World and Politics: Between Modernity and Postmodernity*, ed. Stephen K. White. Notre Dame, Ind.: University of Notre Dame Press.

Elster, Jon. 1983. *Sour Grapes: Studies in the Subversion of Rationality*. Cambridge: Cambridge University Press.

Euben, Peter. 1990. *The Tragedy of Political Theory: The Road Not Taken*. Princeton: Princeton University Press.

———. 1997. "Antigone and the Languages of Politics." In *Corrupting Youth: Political Education, Democratic Culture, and Political Theory*. Princeton: Princeton University Press.

Evans, Martha Noel. 1986. "Murdering L'Invitée: Gender and Fictional Narrative." *Yale French Studies* 72:67–86.

Evans, Sara. 1980. *Personal Politics: The Roots of Women's Liberation in the Civil Rights Movement and the New Left*. New York: Vintage.

———. 1989. *Born for Liberty: A History of Women in America*. New York: Free Press.

Evans, Sara, and Harry C. Boyte. 1982. "Schools for Action." *Democracy* 2:55–65.

———. 1986. *Free Spaces: The Sources of Democratic Change in America*. New York: Harper and Row.

Eyerman, Ron, and David Shipway. 1981. "Habermas on Work and Culture." *Theory and Society* 10:547–566.

Fackenheim, Emil. 1978. *The Jewish Return into History: Reflections in the Age of Auschwitz*. New York: Schocken.

Fairchild, B. H. 1998. *The Art of the Lathe*. Farmington, Me.: Alice James Books.

Fein, Helen. 1979. *Accounting for Genocide: National Responses and Jewish Victimization during the Holocaust*. New York: Free Press.

Felman, Shoshana. 1995. "Education and Crisis, or the Vicissitudes of Teaching." In *Trauma: Explorations in Memory*, ed. Cathy Caruth. Baltimore: Johns Hopkins University Press.

Finley, Moses I. 1983. *Politics in the Ancient World*. Cambridge: Cambridge University Press.

Finnegan, William. 1992. "The Sporting Scene: Surfing." *The New Yorker*, 31 August, 39–58.

Firestone, Shulamith. 1970. *The Dialectic of Sex: The Case for Feminist Revolution*. New York: Bantam.

Folbre, Nancy. 2001. *The Invisible Heart: Economics and Family Values*. New York: New Press.

Foucault, Michel. 1982. "The Subject and Power." In *Michel Foucault: Beyond Structuralism and Hermeneutics*, ed. Hubert Dreyfus and Paul Rabinow. Chicago: University of Chicago Press.

———. 1984a. "What Is Enlightenment?" In *The Foucault Reader*, ed. Paul Rabinow. New York: Pantheon.

———. 1984b. "Polemics, Politics and Problemizations: An Interview." In *The Foucault Reader*, ed. Paul Rabinow. New York: Pantheon.

———. 1984c. "Politics and Ethics: An Interview." In *The Foucault Reader*, ed. Paul Rabinow. New York: Pantheon Press.

———. 1986. *The Care of the Self: The History of Sexuality*, vol. 3, trans. Robert Hurley. New York: Random House.

Fraser, Nancy. 1986. "Toward a Discourse Ethic of Solidarity." *Praxis International* 5:425–429.

———. 1989a. *Unruly Practices: Power, Discourse and Gender in Contemporary Social Theory*. Minneapolis: University of Minnesota Press.

———. 1989b. Introduction to Special Issue on French Feminist Philosophy. *Hypatia* 3:1–10.

———. 1992a. "Introduction." In *Revaluing French Feminism: Critical Essays on Difference, Agency and Culture*, ed. Nancy Fraser and Sandra Lee Bartky. Bloomington: Indiana University Press.

———. 1992b. "Rethinking the Public Sphere: A Contribution to the Critique of Actually Existing Democracy." In *Habermas and the Public Sphere*, ed. Craig Calhoun. Cambridge: MIT Press.

Friedan, Betty. 1963. *The Feminine Mystique*. New York: Dell.

Friedlander, Henry, and Sybil Milton. 1980. *The Holocaust: Ideology, Bureaucracy, and Genocide*. Millwood, N.Y.: Kraus International.

Friedlander, Saul. 1979. *When Memory Comes*. New York: Farrar, Straus and Giroux.

Gerencser, Steven Anthony. 2000. *The Skeptic's Oakeshott*. New York: St. Martin's Press.

Giddens, Anthony. 1982. "Labour and Interaction." In *Habermas: Critical Debates*, ed. John B. Thompson and David Held. Cambridge: MIT Press.

———. 1985. "Jurgen Habermas." In *The Return of Grand Theory in the Human Sciences*, ed. Quentin Skinner. Cambridge: Cambridge University Press.

Gilbert, Martin. 1985. *The Holocaust: The Jewish Tragedy*. New York: Holt, Rinehart and Winston.

Gilligan, Carol. 1982. *In a Different Voice: Psychological Theory and Women's Development*. Cambridge: Harvard University Press.

Goldhagen, Daniel Jonah. 1996. *Hitler's Willing Executioners: Ordinary Germans and the Holocaust*. New York: Vintage Press.

Goodwyn, Lawrence. 1976. *Democratic Promise: The Populist Movement in America*. New York: Oxford University Press.

Gordon, Linda. 1979. "The Struggle for Reproductive Freedom: Three Stages of Feminism." In *Capitalist Patriarchy and the Case for Socialist Feminism*, ed. Zillah Eisenstein. New York: Monthly Review Press.

Green, T. H. [1880] 1964. "Liberal Legislation and Freedom of Contract." In *The Political Theory of T. H. Green*, ed. J. Rodman. New York: Crofts.

Habermas, Jürgen. 1973. *Theory and Practice*, trans. John Viertel. Boston: Beacon Press.

———. 1977. "Hannah Arendt's Communications Concept of Power." *Social Research* 44:3–24.

———. 1987. *The Philosophical Discourse of Modernity: Twelve Lectures*, trans. Frederick G. Lawrence. Cambridge: MIT Press.

———. 1990. *Moral Consciousness and Communicative Action*, trans. Christian Lenhardt and Sherry Weber Nicholsen. Cambridge: MIT Press.

———. 1993. *Justification and Application: Remarks on Discourse Ethics*, trans. Ciaran Cronin. Cambridge: MIT Press.

———. 1996. "Three Normative Models of Democracy." In *Democracy and Difference: Contesting the Boundaries of the Political*, ed. Seyla Benhabib. Princeton: Princeton University Press.

———. 1997. *A Berlin Republic: Writings on Germany*, trans. Steven Rendall. Lincoln: University of Nebraska Press.

Hansen, Karen. 1987. "Feminist Conceptions of Public and Private: A Critical Analysis." *Berkeley Journal of Sociology* 32:105–128.

Hansen, Phillip. 1993. *Hannah Arendt: Politics, History and Citizenship*. Stanford: Stanford University Press.

Hanson, Russell L. 1985. *The Democratic Imagination in America: Conversations with Our Past*. Princeton: Princeton University Press.

Harding, Sandra. 1986. "The Instability of the Analytical Categories of Feminist Theory." *Signs: Journal of Women in Culture and Society* 11:645–664.

Hardwick, Elizabeth. 1953. "The Subjection of Women." *Partisan Review* 20:321–331.

Hartman, Geoffrey H., ed. 1994. *Holocaust Remembrance: The Shapes of Memory*. Oxford: Blackwell.

———. 1996. *The Longest Shadow: In the Aftermath of the Holocaust*. Bloomington: Indiana University Press.

Hartmann, Heidi. 1981. "The Unhappy Marriage of Marxism and Feminism: Toward a More Progressive Union." In *Women and Revolution: A Discussion of the Unhappy Marriage of Marxism and Feminism*, ed. Lydia Sargent. Boston: South End Press.

Hartouni, Valerie. 1986. "Antigone's Dilemmas: A Problem of Political Membership." *Hypatia* 1:3–20.

Hartsock, Nancy C. M. 1983. *Money, Sex, and Power: Toward a Feminist Historical Materialism*. New York: Longman.

Havel, Václav. 1985. "The Power of the Powerless." In *The Power of the Powerless: Citizens against the State in Central-Eastern Europe*, ed. John Keane. Armonk, N.Y.: Sharpe.

———. 1990. *Disturbing the Peace*, trans. Paul Wilson. New York: Knopf.

Hawkesworth, Mary. 1989. "Knowers, Knowing, Known: Feminist Theory and Claims of Truth." *Signs: Journal of Women in Culture and Society* 14:533–557.

Hegel, G. W. F. 1967. *The Phenomenology of Mind*, trans. J. B. Baillie. New York: Harper and Row.

Heidegger, Martin. 1977. *The Question concerning Technology*, trans. William Lovitt. New York: Harper Colophon.

Hekman, Susan. 1991. "Reconstituting the Subject: Feminism, Modernism, and Postmodernism." *Hypatia* 6:44–63.

Held, Virginia. 1990. "Birth and Death." In *Feminism and Political Theory*, ed. Cass R. Sunstein. Chicago: University of Chicago Press

Hilberg, Raul. 1985. *The Destruction of the European Jews*, rev. ed., 3 vols. New York: Holmes and Meier.

Hinchman, Sandra K. 1984a. "Common Sense and Political Barbarism in the Theory of Hannah Arendt." *Polity* 17:317–339.

———. 1984b. "In Heidegger's Shadow: Hannah Arendt's Phenomenological Humanism." *Review of Politics* 46:183–211.

Hobbes, Thomas. [1839] 1966. *The English Works of Thomas Hobbes*, ed. William Molesworth. London: Longman.

Honig, Bonnie, ed. 1995. *Feminist Interpretations of Hannah Arendt*. University Park: Pennsylvania State University Press.

———. 1992. "Toward an Agonistic Feminism: Hannah Arendt and the Politics of Identity." In *Feminists Theorize the Political*, ed. Judith Butler and Joan W. Scott. New York: Routledge.

Honneth, Axel. 1982. "Work and Instrumental Action." *New German Critique* 26:31–54.

hooks, bell. 1984. *Feminist Theory from Margin to Center*. Boston: South End Press.

Ignatieff, Michael. 1990. "The Limits of Sainthood." *The New Republic*, 18 June, 40–46.

Ingram, David. 1993. "The Limits and Possibilities of Communicative Ethics for Democratic Theory" *Political Theory* 21:294–321.

———. 1994. "Foucault and Habermas on the Subject of Reason." In *The Cambridge Companion to Foucault*, ed. Gary Gutting. New York: Cambridge University Press.

Isaac, Jeffrey C. 1989. "Arendt, Camus, and Postmodern Politics." *Praxis International* 9:48–71.

———. 1995. "The Strange Silence of Political Theory." *Political Theory* 23:636–688.

Jacobson, Joanne. 1996. "Speech after Long Silence." *The Nation*, 11 November, 30–32.

Jaggar, Allison M. 1983. *Feminist Politics and Human Nature*. New York: Rowman and Allenheld.

Jardine, Alice. 1979. "Interview with Simone de Beauvoir." *Signs: Journal of Women in Culture and Society* 5:224–236.

Jay, Martin. 1978. "Hannah Arendt: Opposing Views." *Partisan Review* 45:348–367.

Johnson, James. 1991. "Habermas on Strategic and Communicative Action." *Political Theory* 19:181–201.

Jonas, Hans. 1976. "Hannah Arendt, 1906–1975." *Social Research* 43:3–5.

Jones, Ann Rosalind. 1984. "Julia Kristeva on Femininity: The Limits of a Semiotic Politics." *Feminist Review* 18:56–73.

Jones, Kathleen. 1993. *Compassionate Authority: Democracy and the Representation of Women.* New York: Routledge.

Kaplan, Morris. 1995. "Refiguring the Jewish Question: Arendt, Proust, and the Politics of Sexuality." In *Feminist Interpretations of Hannah Arendt,* ed. Bonnie Honig. University Park: Pennsylvania State University Press.

Kaplan, Temma. 1981. "Female Consciousness and Collective Action: The Case of Barcelona, 1910–1915." In *Feminist Theory: A Critique of Ideology,* ed. Nannerl O. Keohane, Michelle Z. Rosaldo, and Barbara C. Gelpi. Chicago: University of Chicago Press.

Kateb, George. 1984. *Hannah Arendt: Politics, Conscience, Evil.* Totowa, N.J.: Rowman and Littlefield.

Katzenstein, Mary Fainsod. 1998. *Faithful and Fearless: Moving Feminist Protest inside the Church and Military.* Princeton: Princeton University Press.

Kaufmann, Dorothy. 1986. "Simone de Beauvoir: Questions of Difference and Generation." *Yale French Studies* 72:121–131.

Kautz, Steven. 1995. *Liberalism and Community.* Ithaca, N.Y.: Cornell University Press.

Keane, John. 1975. "On Tools and Language: Habermas on Work and Interaction." *New German Critique* 6:82–100.

Kerber, Linda K. 1980. *Women of the Republic: Intellect and Ideology in Revolutionary America.* Chapel Hill: University of North Carolina Press.

Knauer, James T. 1980. "Motive and Goal in Hannah Arendt's Concept of Political Action." *American Political Science Review* 74:721–33.

———. 1985. "Re-thinking Arendt's 'Vita Activa': Towards a Theory of Democratic Praxis." *Praxis International* 5:185–194.

Kren, George M., and Leon Rappoport. 1980. *The Holocaust and the Crisis of Human Behavior.* New York: Holmes and Meier.

Kristeva, Julia. 1981. "Women's Time." In *Feminist Theory: A Critique of Ideology,* ed. Nannerl O. Keohane, Michelle Z. Rosaldo, and Barbara C. Gelpi. Chicago: University of Chicago Press.

———. 2000. *The Crisis of the European Subject,* trans. Susan Fairfield. New York: Other Press.

————. 2001. *Hannah Arendt*, trans. Ross Guberman. New York: Columbia University Press.

Krouse, Richard W. 1982. "Patriarchal Liberalism and Beyond: From John Stuart Mill to Harriet Taylor." In *The Family in Political Thought*, ed. Jean Bethke Elshtain. Amherst: University of Massachusetts Press.

Kruks, Sonia. 1992. "Gender and Subjectivity: Simone de Beauvoir and Contemporary Feminism." *Signs: Journal of Women in Culture and Society* 18:89–110.

————. 2000. *Retrieving Experience: Subjectivity and Recognition in Feminist Politics*. Ithaca, N.Y.: Cornell University Press.

Laclau, Ernesto, and Chantal Mouffe. 1985. *Hegemony and Socialist Strategy: Towards a Radical Democratic Politics*. London: Verso.

Landes, Joan. 1988. *Women and the Public Sphere in the Age of the French Revolution*. Ithaca, N.Y.: Cornell University Press.

————. 1992. "Jürgen Habermas, *The Structural Transformation of the Public Sphere:* A Feminist Inquiry." *Praxis International* 12:106–127.

Lane, Ann M. 1983. "The Feminism of Hannah Arendt." *Democracy* 3:101–117.

Langer, Lawrence L. 1991. *Holocaust Testimonies: The Ruins of Memory*. New Haven: Yale University Press.

————. 1995. *Admitting the Holocaust: Collected Essays*. Oxford: Oxford University Press.

Le Doeuff, Michele. 1980. "Simone de Beauvoir and Existentialism." *Feminist Studies* 6:277–289.

Lessing, Doris. 1992. "The Humanities and Culture Heroes." *Partisan Review* 4:722–751.

Levi, Primo. 1961. *Survival in Auschwitz: The Nazi Assault on Humanity*, trans. S. Woolf. New York: Collier Books.

Lloyd, Genevieve. 1984. *Man of Reason*. Minneapolis: University of Minnesota Press.

Lummis, C. Douglas. 1982. "The Radicalization of Democracy." *Democracy* 2:9–16.

Lyotard, Jean–François. 1984. *The Postmodern Condition: A Report on Knowledge*. Minneapolis: University of Minnesota Press.

Machiavelli, Niccolò. 1950. *The Prince and the Discourses*, trans. E.R.P. Vincent. New York: Modern Library.

————. 1957. *Mandragola*, trans. Anne Paolucci and Henry Paolucci. New York: Bobbs-Merrill.

MacKinnon, Catherine. 1981. "Feminism, Marxism, Method and the State: An Agenda for Theory." In *Feminist Theory: A Critique of Ideology*, eds. Nannerl O. Keohane, Michelle Z. Rosaldo, and Barbara C. Gelpi. Chicago: University of Chicago Press.

Macpherson, C. B. 1962. *The Political Theory of Possessive Individualism*. Oxford: Oxford University Press.

————. 1977. *The Life and Times of Liberal Democracy*. Oxford: Oxford University Press.

Mansbridge, Jane. 1980. *Beyond Adversary Democracy*. Chicago: University of Chicago Press.

————. 1984. "Feminism and the Forms of Freedom." In *Critical Studies in Organization and Bureaucracy*, ed. Frank Fischer and Carmen Siriani. Philadelphia: Temple University Press.

Marks, Elaine. 1986. "Transgressing the (In)cont(in)ent Boundaries: The Body in Decline." *Yale French Studies* 72:181–200.

Markus, Maria. 1987. "The 'Anti-Feminism' of Hannah Arendt." *Thesis Eleven* 17:76–87.

Marx, Karl. [1845] 1978. *The German Ideology*. In *The Marx-Engels Reader*, ed. Robert Tucker. New York: Norton.

McCarthy, Mary. 1976. "Saying Good-by to Hannah." *New York Review of Books*, 22 January, 5.

McCarthy, Thomas. 1981. *The Critical Theory of Jürgen Habermas*. Cambridge: MIT Press.

————. 1991. *Ideals and Illusions: On Reconstruction and Deconstruction in Contemporary Critical Theory*. Cambridge: MIT Press.

————. 1994. "Kantian Constructivism and Reconstructivism: Rawls and Habermas in Dialogue." *Ethics* 105:44–63.

McClure, Kirstie. 1992. "On the Subject of Rights: Pluralism, Plurality and Political Identity." In *Dimensions of Radical Democracy: Pluralism, Citizenship and Community*, ed. Chantal Mouffe. London: Verso.

McLellan, David. 1990. *Utopian Pessimist: The Life and Thought of Simone Weil*. New York: Poseidon.

Merleau-Ponty, Maurice. 1964. "A Note on Machiavelli." In *Signs*, trans. Richard C. McCleary. Evanston, Ill.: Northwestern University Press.

Meron, Theodor. 1993. *Henry's Wars and Shakespeare's Laws: Perspectives on the Law of War in the Later Middle Ages*. Oxford: Oxford University Press.

Michnik, Adam, and Jürgen Habermas. 1994. "More Humanity, Fewer Illusions—A Talk between Adam Michnik and Jürgen Habermas." *New York Review of Books* 41:24–29.

Mill, John Stuart. [1854] 1961. *On Liberty*. In *The Essential Works of John Stuart Mill*, ed. Max Lerner. New York: Bantam.

Millett, Kate. 1969. *Sexual Politics*. New York: Avon Books.

Mitchell, Juliet. 1971. *Woman's Estate*. New York: Vintage.

————. 1975. *Psychoanalysis and Feminism: Freud, Reich, Laing, and Women*. New York: Vintage.

Moruzzi, Norma. 1990. "Re-Placing the Margin: (Non)Representations of Colonialism in Hannah Arendt's *The Origins of Totalitarianism*." *Tulsa Studies in Women's Literature* 10:109–120.

Mouffe, Chantal. 1993. *The Return of the Political*. London: Verso.

Mueller, Jan. 2000. "Preparing for the Political: German Intellectuals Confront the 'Berlin Republic.'" In *Political Thought and German Reunification: The New German Ideology?* eds. H. Williams, C. Wright, and N. Kapferer. New York: St. Martin's.

Narayan, Uma. 1997. "Towards a Feminist Vision of Citizenship: Rethinking the Implications of Dignity, Political Participation, and Nationality." In *Reconstructing Political Theory: Feminist Perspectives*, ed. Mary Lyndon Shanley and Uma Narayan. University Park: Pennsylvania State University Press.

Nevin, Thomas R. 1991. *Simone Weil: Portrait of a Self-Exiled Jew.* Chapel Hill: University of North Carolina Press.

Nicholson, Linda. J. 1986. *Gender and History.* New York: Columbia University Press.

Nicholson, Linda J., ed. 1990. *Feminism/Postmodernism.* New York: Routledge.

Nietzsche, Friedrich. [1878] 1996. *Human, All Too Human: A Book for Free Spirits*, trans. R. J. Hollingdale. Cambridge: Cambridge University Press.

———. [1887] 1969. *On the Genealogy of Morals*, trans. Walter Kaufmann and R. J. Hollingdale. New York: Random House.

———. 1968. *Twilight of the Idols* and *The Anti-Christ*, trans. R. J. Hollingdale. New York: Penguin.

Nussbaum, Martha C. 1986. *The Fragility of Goodness: Luck and Ethics in Greek Tragedy and Philosophy.* Cambridge: Cambridge University Press.

Oakeshott, Michael. 1962. *Rationalism in Politics.* New York: Methuen.

O'Brien, Mary. 1981. *The Politics of Reproduction.* Boston: Routledge and Kegan Paul.

Okin, Susan Moller. 1979. *Women in Western Political Thought.* Princeton: Princeton University Press.

———. 1990a. "Reason and Feeling in Thinking about Justice." In *Feminism and Political Theory*, ed. Cass R. Sunstein. Chicago: University of Chicago Press.

———. 1990b. "John Rawls: Justice as Fairness for Whom?" In *Feminist Interpretations and Political Theory*, ed. Mary Lyndon Shanley and Carole Pateman. Cambridge: Polity Press.

———. 1998. "Gender, the Public and the Private." In *Feminism and Politics*, ed. Anne Phillips. Oxford: Oxford University Press.

Orwin, Clifford. 1994. *The Humanity of Thucydides.* Princeton: Princeton University Press.

Parekh, Bikhu. 1979. "Hannah Arendt's Critique of Marx." In *Hannah Arendt: The Recovery of the Public World*, ed. Melvyn A. Hill. New York: St. Martin's.

———. 1981. *Hannah Arendt and the Search for a New Political Philosophy.* London: Macmillan.

Pareles, Jon. 2001. "Milan Hlavsa, Rock Star of a Revolution." *New York Times*, 8 January, A19.

Pateman, Carole. 1970. *Participation and Democratic Theory*. Cambridge: Cambridge University Press.

———. 1975. "Sublimation and Reification: Locke, Wolin, and the Liberal Democratic Conception of the Political." *Politics and Society* 5:441–467.

———. 1980. "Women and Consent." *Political Theory* 8:149–168.

———. 1983. "Feminist Critiques of the Public/Private Dichotomy." In *Public and Private in Social Life*, ed. S. I. Benn and G. F. Gaus. London: Croom Helm.

———. 1988. *The Sexual Contract*. Stanford: Stanford University Press.

Pawelczynska, Anna. 1979. *Values and Violence in Auschwitz: A Sociological Analysis*. Berkeley: University of California Press.

Phillips, Anne. 1991. *Engendering Democracy*. University Park: Pennsylvania State University Press.

———. 1993. *Democracy and Difference*. University Park: Pennsylvania State University Press.

Pitkin, Hanna Fenichel. 1974. "Michael Oakeshott and the Roots of Conservatism." In *The New Conservatives: A Critique from the Left*, ed. Lewis A. Coser and Irving Howe. New York: Quadrangle.

———. 1981. "Justice: On Relating Private and Public." *Political Theory* 9:303–326.

———. 1984. "Food and Freedom in *The Flounder*." *Political Theory* 12:467–490.

———. 1998. *The Attack of the Blob: Hannah Arendt's Concept of the Social*. Chicago: University of Chicago Press.

Pocock, J. G. A. 1975. *The Machiavellian Moment: Florentine Political Thought and the Atlantic Republican Tradition*. Princeton: Princeton University Press.

Pollitt, Katha. 2001a. *Subject to Debate: Sense and Dissents on Women, Politics and Culture*. New York: Modern Library.

———. 2001b. "Happy Mother's Day." *The Nation*, 28 May, 10.

Rabinow, Paul, ed. 1984. *The Foucault Reader*. New York: Pantheon.

Rasmussen, David M. 1990. *Reading Habermas*. Cambridge, England: Basil Blackwell.

Rawls, John. 1971. *A Theory of Justice*. Cambridge: Harvard University Press.

———. 1985. "Justice as Fairness: Political Not Metaphysical." *Philosophy and Public Affairs* 14:223–251.

———. 1993. *Political Liberalism*. New York: Columbia University Press.

Rich, Adrienne. 1979. *On Lies, Secrets, and Silence: Selected Prose, 1966–1978*. New York: W. W. Norton.

Ring, Jennifer. 1985. "Mill's *Subjection of Women*: The Methodological Limits of Liberal Feminism." *Review of Politics* 47:27–44.

————. 1991. "The Pariah as Hero: Hannah Arendt's Political Actor." *Political Theory* 19:433–452.

————. 1997. *The Political Consequences of Thinking: Gender and Judaism in the Works of Hannah Arendt.* Albany: State University of New York Press.

Rosenberg, Alan and Gerald Myers, eds. 1988. *Echoes from the Holocaust: Philosophical Reflections on a Dark Time.* Philadelphia: Temple University Press.

Rowbotham, Sheila. 1972. *Women, Resistance and Revolution: A History of Women and Revolution in the Modern World.* New York: Random House.

————. 1973. *Woman's Consciousness, Man's World.* New York: Penguin.

Ruddick, Sara. 1980. "Maternal Thinking." *Feminist Studies* 6:342–367.

————. 1983a. "Pacifying the Forces: Drafting Women in the Interests of Peace." *Signs: Journal of Women in Culture and Society* 8:471–489.

————. 1983b. "Preservative Love and Military Destruction: Reflections on Mothering and Peace." In *Mothering: Essays on Feminist Theory*, ed. Joyce Trebilcot. Totowa, N.J.: Littlefield Adams.

————. 1989. *Maternal Thinking: Toward a Politics of Peace.* Boston: Beacon Press.

Ryan, Mary P. 1990. *Women in Public: Between Banners and Ballots, 1825–1880.* Baltimore: Johns Hopkins University Press.

Sandel, Michael J. 1982. *Liberalism and the Limits of Justice.* Cambridge: Cambridge University Press.

————. 1984. "The Procedural Republic and the Unencumbered Self." *Political Theory* 12:81–96.

Sargent, Lydia. 1981. *Women and Revolution.* Boston: South End Press.

Schwartz, Joseph M. 1989. "Arendt's Politics: The Elusive Search for Substance." *Praxis International* 9:25–47:

Schwarzer, Alice. 1984. *Simone de Beauvoir Today: Conversations, 1972–1982*, trans. Marianne Howarth. London: Chatto & Windus.

Scott, Joan W. 1986. "Gender: A Useful Category of Historical Analysis." *American Historical Review* 91:1053–1075.

Seigfried, Charlene Haddock. 1990. Second Sex: Second Thoughts. In *Hypatia Reborn: Essays in Feminist Philosophy*, ed. Azizah Y. Al-Hibri and Margaret A. Simons. Bloomington: Indiana University Press.

Shanley, Mary Lyndon. 1979. "Marriage Contract and Social Contract in Seventeenth Century English Political Thought." *Western Political Quarterly* 32:79–91.

————. 1983. "Afterword: Feminism and Families in a Liberal Polity." In *Families, Politics and Public Policy: A Feminist Dialogue on Women and the State*, ed. Irene Diamond. New York: Longman.

Shapiro, Ian. 1994. "Three Ways to Be a Democrat." *Political Theory* 22:124–151.

Simons, Margaret A. 1983. "The Silencing of Simone de Beauvoir: Guess What's Missing from *The Second Sex?*" *Women's Studies International Forum* 6:559–564.

———. 1986. "Beauvoir and Sartre: The Philosophical Relationship." *Yale French Studies* 72:165–179.

———. 1989. "Two Interviews with Simone de Beauvoir." *Hypatia* 3:12–27.

———. 1992. "Lesbian Connections: Simone de Beauvoir and Feminism." *Signs: Journal of Women in Culture and Society* 18:136–161.

———. 1998. "Beauvoir and the Roots of Radical Feminism." In *Reinterpreting the Political: Continental Philosophy and Political Theory*, ed. Lenore Langsdorf and Stephen H. Watson with Karen A. Smith. Albany: State University of New York Press.

Singer, Linda. 1990. "Interpretation and Retrieval: Rereading Beauvoir." In *Hypatia Reborn: Essays in Feminist Philosophy*, ed. Azizah Y. Al-Hibri and Margaret A. Simons. Bloomington: Indiana University Press.

Sophocles. 1991. "Antigone." In *Sophocles I: Oedipus the King, Oedipus at Colonus, Antigone*, trans. David Grene. Chicago and London: University of Chicago Press.

Spelman, Elizabeth V. 1988. *Inessential Woman: Problems of Exclusion in Feminist Thought*. Boston: Beacon Press.

Steiner, George. 1982. *Antigones*. New York: Oxford University Press.

Taylor, Charles. 1988. "The Hermeneutics of Conflict." In *Meaning and Context: Quentin Skinner and His Critics*, ed. James Tully. Princeton: Princeton University Press.

———. 1989. "Cross-Purposes: The Liberal-Communitarian Debate." In *Liberalism and the Moral Life*, ed. Nancy Rosenblum. Cambridge: Harvard University Press.

Thucydides. 1982. *The Peloponnesian War*, trans. Richard Crawley. New York: Modern Library.

Tilly, Louise. 1981. "Paths of Proletarianization: Organization of Production, Sexual Division of Labor, and Women's Collective Action." *Signs: Journal of Women in Culture and Society* 7:400–417.

Tronto, Joan. 1987. Women's Morality: Beyond Gender Difference to a Theory of Care. *Signs: Journal of Women in Culture and Society* 12:644–663.

———. 1993. *Moral Boundaries: A Political Argument for an Ethic of Care*. New York: Routledge.

Udovicki, Jasminka. 1983. "The Uses of Freedom and the Human Condition." *Praxis International* 3:54–61.

Vidal-Nacquet, Pierre. [1985] 1992. *The Assassins of Memory: Essays on the Denial of the Holocaust*. New York: Columbia University Press.

Villa, Dana. 1992. "Postmodernism and the Public Sphere." *American Political Science Review* 86:712–721.

———. 1996. *Arendt and Heidegger: The Fate of the Political*. Princeton: Princeton University Press.

Walzer, Michael. 1980. *Radical Principles*. New York: Basic Books.

———. 1988. "Simone de Beauvoir and the Assimilated Woman." In *The Company of Critics: Social Criticism and Political Commitment in the Twentieth Century*. New York: Basic Books.

Weber, Max. 1946. *From Max Weber*, ed. Hans H. Gerth and C. Wright Mills. New York: Oxford University Press.

———. 1958. *The Protestant Ethic and the Spirit of Capitalism*, trans. Talcott Parsons. New York: Charles Scribners and Sons.

Weeks, Kathi. 1998. *Constituting Feminist Subjects*. Ithaca, N.Y.: Cornell University Press.

Weil, Simone. 1952a. *The Need for Roots*, trans. Arthur Wills. Boston: Beacon Press.

———. 1952b. *The Notebooks of Simone Weil*, 2 vols., trans. Arthur Wills. London: Routledge and Kegan Paul.

———. 1968. *On Science, Necessity, and the Love of God*, ed. and trans. Richard Rees. London: Oxford University Press.

———. 1973. *Oppression and Liberty*, trans. Arthur Wills and John Petrie. Amherst: University of Massachusetts Press.

———. 1977. "Factory Work." In *The Simone Weil Reader*, ed. George Panichas. New York: McKay.

Wenzel, Hélène. 1986. "Interview with Simone de Beauvoir." *Yale French Studies* 72:5–32.

Weschler, Lawrence. 1995. "Inventing Peace: What Do Vermeer's Beautiful, Serene Paintings Teach Us about War in Bosnia?" *The New Yorker*, 20 November, 56–64.

———. 1996. "Take No Prisoners." *The New Yorker*, 17 June, 50–59.

———. 1999. *Calamities of Exile: Three Nonfiction Novellas*. Chicago: University of Chicago Press.

White, James Boyd. 1985. *When Words Lose Their Meaning: Constitutions and Reconstitutions of Language, Character, and Community*. Chicago: University of Chicago Press.

White, Stephen K. 1988a. "Poststructuralism and Political Reflection." *Political Theory* 16:186–208.

———. 1988b. *The Recent Work of Jürgen Habermas: Reason, Justice, and Modernity*. Cambridge: Cambridge University Press.

Wiggins, David. 1978. "Deliberation and Practical Reason." In *Practical Reasoning*, ed. Joseph Raz. Oxford: Oxford University Press.

Williams, Bernard. 1993. *Shame and Necessity*. Berkeley: University of California Press.

Wills, Garry. 1999a. *Saint Augustine*. New York: Penguin.

———. 1999b. "Augustine's Magical Decade." *New York Review of Books*, 6 May, 30–32.

Winant, Terry. 1987. "The Feminist Standpoint: A Matter of Language." *Hypatia* 2:123–148.

Winch, Peter. 1989. *Simone Weil: The Just Balance*. Cambridge: Cambridge University Press.

Winfield, Richard. 1975. "The Dilemma of Labor." *Telos* 24:115–128.

Wolin, Sheldon. 1960. *Politics and Vision: Continuity and Innovation in Western Political Thought*. Boston: Little, Brown.

———. 1972. "Political Theory as a Vocation." In *Machiavelli and the Nature of Political Thought*, ed. Martin Fleisher. New York: Atheneum.

———. 1981. "The Peoples' Two Bodies." *Democracy* 1:9–24.

———. 1982. "Revolutionary Action Today." *Democracy* 2:17–28.

———. 1996a. "Fugitive Democracy." In *Democracy and Difference: Contesting the Boundaries of the Political*, ed. Seyla Benhabib. Princeton: Princeton University Press.

———. 1996b. "Democracy and Counterrevolution." *The Nation*, 22 April, 22–24.

———. 2000. "Political Theory: From Vocation to Invocation." In *Vocations of Political Theory*, eds. Jason A. Frank and John Tambornino. Minneapolis: University of Minnesota Press.

Yack, Bernard. 1993. *The Problems of a Political Animal: Community, Justice and Conflict in Aristotelian Political Thought*. Berkeley: University of California Press.

Yaeger, Patricia. 1988. *Honey-Mad Women: Emancipatory Strategies in Women's Writing*. New York: Columbia University Press.

Young, Iris Marion. 1986a. Impartiality and the Civic Public: Some Implications of Feminist Critiques of Moral and Political Theory. *Praxis International* 5:381–401.

———. 1986b. The Ideal of Community and the Politics of Difference. *Social Theory and Practice* 12:1–26.

———. 1987. "Impartiality and the Civic Public: Some Implications of Feminist Critiques of Moral and Political Theory." In *Feminism as Critique*, eds. Seyla Benhabib and Drucilla Cornell. Minneapolis: University of Minnesota Press.

———. 1989. "Polity and Group Difference: A Critique of the Ideal of Universal Citizenship." *Ethics* 99:250–274.

———. 1990. *Justice and the Politics of Difference*. Princeton: Princeton University Press.

———. 1997. *Intersecting Voices: Dilemmas of Gender, Political Philosophy and Policy*. Princeton: Princeton University Press.

Young, James. 1993. *The Texture of Memory: Holocaust Memorials and Meaning in Europe, Israel, and America*. New Haven: Yale University Press.

————. 1998. "The Holocaust as Vicarious Past: Art Spiegelman's *Maus* and the Afterimages of History." *Critical Inquiry* 24:667–699.

Young-Bruehl, Elisabeth. 1982. *Hannah Arendt: For Love of the World*. New Haven: Yale University Press.

Zerilli, Linda M. G. 1991. "Machiavelli's Sisters: Women and 'the Conversation' of Political Theory." *Political Theory* 19:252–276.

————. 1992. "A Process without a Subject: Simone de Beauvoir and Julia Kristeva on Maternity." *Signs: Journal of Women in Culture and Society* 18:111–135.

————. 1995. "The Arendtian Body." In *Feminist Interpretations of Hannah Arendt*, ed. Bonnie Honig. University Park: Pennsylvania State University Press.

————. 2000. "Feminism's Flight from the Ordinary." In *Vocations of Political Theory*, ed. Jason A. Frank and John Tambornino. Minneapolis: University of Minnesota Press.

Zolo, Danilo. 1992. *Democracy and Complexity: A Realistic Approach*. University Park: Pennsylvania State University Press.

Index